LAW AND WAR

LAW AND WAR

INTERNATIONAL LAW & AMERICAN HISTORY

[REVISED EDITION]

PETER MAGUIRE

COLUMBIA UNIVERSITY PRESS *New York*

COLUMBIA UNIVERSITY PRESS

PUBLISHERS SINCE 1893

NEW YORK   CHICHESTER, WEST SUSSEX

This is a revised edition of *Law and War: An American Story.*

Library of Congress Cataloging-in-Publication Data

Maguire, Peter (Peter H.)

Law and war : international law and American history / Peter Maguire. — Rev. ed.

p.   cm.

"This is a revised edition of Law and War : an American Story."

Includes bibliographical references and index.

ISBN 978-0-231-14646-3 (cloth : alk. paper) — ISBN 978-0-231-14647-0 (pbk. : alk. paper) —

ISBN 978-0-231-51819-2 (electronic)

1. War crimes. 2. War (International law) 3. Nuremberg War Crime Trials, Nuremberg,

Germany, 1946–1949. 4. United States—Foreign relations—20th century. I. Title.

K5301.M34   2010

341.6′9—dc22

2009018411

This book was printed on paper with recycled content.

Printed in the United States of America

c 10 9 8 7 6 5 4 3 2 1

p 10 9 8 7 6 5 4 3 2 1

References to Internet Web sites (URLs) were accurate at the time of writing. Neither the author nor Columbia University Press is responsible for URLs that may have expired or changed since the manuscript was prepared.

CONTENTS

PREFACE

"Think of the new era that is being born. The world has learned its lesson at last, at last. The closing chapter to ten thousand years of madness and greed is being written here and now—in Nuremberg. Books will be written about it. Movies will be made about it. It's the most important turning point in history." I believed it.

"Walter," she said, "sometimes I think you are only eight years old."

"It is the only age to be," I said, "when a new era is being born." . . .

"Well," said Ruth, "when you eight-year-olds kill Evil here in Nuremberg, be sure to bury it at a crossroads and drive a stake through its heart—or you just might see it again at the next full mooooooooooooooooooooooooooon."

KURT VONNEGUT, *Jailbird*

"'NUREMBERG' IS BOTH WHAT ACTUALLY HAPPENED AND WHAT people think happened," wrote Nuremberg prosecutor Telford Taylor, before adding a prophetic afterthought: "the second is more important than the first."[1] When *Law and War* was released in the spring of 2001, "the legacy of Nuremberg" was in the process of being selectively appropriated by activist journalists and human rights advocates to justify a new generation of diverse war crimes trials and an International Criminal Court empowered with "universal jurisdiction." It was thought that universal jurisdiction would compensate for the fundamental weakness of international law since the time of Grotius: enforcement. Pulitzer Prize–winning journalist Tina Rosenberg offered this application of the theory: "If the Spanish government had discovered Lt. William Calley vacationing in Barcelona and America had refused to put him on trial, Spain would have been within its legal rights to have held him and brought him to justice for the My Lai massacre in Vietnam."[2]

Many made extremely broad and unsubstantiated claims about the therapeutic benefits of war crimes trials—not only would they punish the guilty and exonerate the innocent, they would also provide "truth," "reconciliation," "healing," and "closure" because, these advocates claimed, that is what Nuremberg had done for the Germans. According to this most recent

myth of Nuremberg, the landmark trials did not simply determine legal innocence and guilt, they brought about a West German national catharsis
during the 1950s.[3] Groundbreaking books by professional historians were
largely ignored, while popular pedestrian works were treated as if they had
broken new scholarly ground. Compared to the careful Nuremberg scholarship of the 1970s and 1980s, much of the 1990s scholarship was both naive
and inadequate. One leading Nuremberg scholar characterized much of the
1990s literature as "Over argued, under researched, nit-picky but mistaken
about Nuremberg and uncritical about the current tribunals, factually inaccurate, and worst of all, stubbornly uncurious."[4]

More troubling than the war crimes trial triumphalism was the fact that
few of the assumptions stood up to analysis. Not only were important parts
of the "legacy of Nuremberg" left out, criticism beyond the ritualistic complaints about ex post facto law and victor's justice was considered to be in
bad taste in anything but far left and far right academic circles. As a result,
analysis of the trials rarely went deeper than American prosecutor Robert
Jackson's opening address.[5] While selective case studies were offered to but-
tress claims about the benefits of therapeutic legalism, conspicuously absent were references to the British, French, and American war crimes clemencies of the 1950s, not to mention the West German rejection of the legal
validity of all the Allied postwar trials. This revised version of Law and War
is intended to reemphasize and update my central thesis concerning America's opportunistic relationship to international law and to argue that it is
the task of historians to distinguish carefully the actual legacies of Nuremberg and their true impact on realpolitik from what we would like these to
have been.

LAW AND WAR

INTRODUCTION

W HEN I WAS TWELVE, THE OREGON BAR ASSOCIATION HELD
a special memorial session in the chambers of the U.S. District Court of Oregon to honor my recently deceased great-grandfather, Robert Maguire. I
had never been to a funeral or a trial, and the stark wood-paneled chambers
and the somber demeanor of the old men in their black robes filled me with
equal parts fascination and fear. After gaveling the court into session, the
judge announced "the presence in the courtroom of the following members
of Mr. Maguire's family." I grew increasingly nervous as he ran down the
list: "Mrs. Robert F. Maguire; Robert F. Maguire Jr."—I winced, waiting
for my name—"Peter Maguire, a great-grandson; Robert F. Maguire III,
grandson. . . ." Just as my breath began to return, the door of the judge's
chambers opened slowly and a young woman entered, pushing a wheelchair in which sat a very haunting old man.[1]

For a brief moment my young mind began to reel. Was this the corpse
of my great-grandfather? My father, recognizing the ten-thousand-yard
stare, reassured me that the man in the wheelchair was former Supreme
Court Justice William O. Douglas, not my great-grandfather. He added that
the two men had agreed on very little, but today was a day when past differences were set aside. The only time I had ever met Robert Maguire was
at my grandfather's house in Ventura, California. I was very young, but I

remember his stately demeanor contrasting starkly with the southern Californian environs. One by one the children were taken to his knee and introduced with a solemn handshake. Though the judge was very old, his mind was razor sharp and he was very stylish in a three-piece, gray pinstripe suit.

At first glance, Robert Maguire appeared to be a typical conservative Republican. However, he was the son of two very atypical Americans. His mother, Kate or Kitty, was the daughter of L. H. Harlan, one of Ohio's leading intellectuals. She was described in her obituary as "a pioneer social worker in the United States." Robert's high school thesis, "John Mitchell and the Miners," reflected his upbringing: "The United States will see the greatest conflict of the world. Where capital is strongest there will be the fight, conservatism against progress. . . . Future generations will call upon John Mitchell as the man who gave the death blow to . . . industrial slavery."[2]

During high school Robert Maguire taught himself shorthand. In 1905 he received a civil service clerkship in Washington, D.C.; during the day he worked as a court reporter and at night he attended Georgetown University Law School. After receiving his L.L.B. in 1909, Maguire took a job with the U.S. Land Service and was sent to Oregon to work as a border marker. The slight twenty-one-year-old was issued a horse, a gun, and a badge and thrown headlong into the rough-and-tumble disputes of eastern Oregon. In 1910, Robert Maguire married Ruth Kimbell of Massachusetts and moved to Portland, Oregon, where he had just been named Assistant U.S. Attorney. For several years, Maguire honed his skills as a trial lawyer, and in 1915, he entered private practice with Edwin Littlefield. The majority of the firm's work involved representing large insurance companies.

Robert Maguire led two legal lives. Although he had become what today would be described as a corporate lawyer, he remained a public-spirited jurist. In 1917, he was appointed Standing Master in Chancery of the Federal Court of Oregon, a position he would hold for the next thirty-three years.[3] Throughout the 1920s, Maguire worked on behalf of the infant Oregon Bar Association; he was named its first president in 1929. His professional rise continued throughout the 1930s, and he seemed destined for a seat on the Oregon Supreme Court. Clients such as Union Pacific allowed him to earn a large salary, while his post as Master in Chancery and bar association prominence gave his voice more resonance than a corporate lawyer could normally expect. When the clouds of war gathered over Europe in the late '30s, Maguire echoed the sentiments of his favorite statesman, Winston Churchill, arguing that Hitler's incursions needed to be met with force.

When the war ended, he supported the idea of a European recovery program, but had no idea that he would actively participate in it.

As the memorial continued, Robert Maguire was described by his colleagues as "one of the finest if not the finest trial lawyer in the Pacific Northwest," a man of "rocklike integrity." What piqued my curiosity was a one-sentence biographical detail: "In 1948 he served as a Judge of the U.S. Military Tribunal for the War Crimes Trials in Nuremberg, Germany."[4] That was the first time I had heard of the Nuremberg trials. After the ceremony, we were led through the crowd and into the judge's chambers. From there, we were taken to an even deeper recess, steered to the foot of the wheelchair, and introduced to Justice Douglas. He took my hand and did not release it immediately. When he looked into my eyes, I was reminded of that first encounter with Robert Maguire.

I proudly regaled my fifth-grade classmates with my great-grandfather's historical significance. But my pronouncements were met with the same dull response someone receives for bragging that their forefathers sailed aboard the *Mayflower*. A few years later, when my ninth-grade history class staged a trial of Napoleon Bonaparte, I jumped at the opportunity to play the French leader. It was with a great sense of purpose that I cynically argued that sovereign leaders are immune from prosecution.

My first serious attempt to obtain more information about the Nuremberg trials was in junior high school. Although there were books on the subject, Robert Maguire could not be found in the group photos or the indexes. When I pressed my father and grandfather for details, they could only respond that "he was a judge at Nuremberg" and point to a faded black-and-white photograph on the wall of three black-robed men sitting in front of a large American flag. Over the years my curiosity about the trials grew. In college I reluctantly told a political science professor about the family's claims. He informed me that after the international tribunal, there had been a series of American trials at Nuremberg. When I asked German history professor John Fout if he knew anything about those American trials, he took me to the library, where we found fifteen formidable-looking green books. We took them down and began to search.

Each volume had a picture of a three-man tribunal and their biographical information. As I scanned the tomes, my heart began to sink—we had checked nine of twelve cases and still no Robert Maguire. Then suddenly my professor said, "Yes, he does sort of look like you," and handed me one of the volumes. I looked down and there was Robert F. Maguire staring at me once again. It was the same picture that hung in my grandfather's hallway. His case was number 11, *United States Government v. Ernst von Weizsaecker,* also known as the Ministries case.

My subsequent research efforts yielded an undergraduate thesis and raised many more questions than I could possibly answer. The most puzzling discovery was a 1953 U.S. High Commission Report on Germany. Buried deep in the report was a chart of charges, pleas, and sentences. The chart seemed suspiciously overcomplicated. However, there was one column that was straightforward, headed: "In custody as of February 30, 1952." When I looked at the Ministries case, I noticed that, despite a number of lengthy sentences, none of the defendants remained in prison after 1952. Even stranger was the number of death sentences that had been reduced to prison terms.

William Manchester's *Arms of Krupp* gave me a first, rather sensational account of the war criminal amnesty of the early 1950s. In an attempt to solve this and other mysteries, I contacted former Nuremberg chief counsel Telford Taylor. Our first meeting was in his Morningside Heights office in 1987; he was seventy-nine, I was twenty-two. When I produced the chart, Taylor put on his glasses and carefully studied it. He agreed that the sentences had been reduced way beyond the controversial McCloy decisions. However, he could offer no explanation why.[5]

Law and War is an attempt to transcend the simple oppositions of realism and idealism, positivism and natural law, liberalism and conservatism, might and right. During the 1990s, war crimes very much returned to center stage. If Nuremberg provides the legal and symbolic framework for defining and dealing with war criminals, its lessons remain unclear. In part, this is because what that name represents is really a series of contradictory trials that lead to no single, simple conclusion. It is my contention that over the course of the twentieth century, the United States attempted to broaden the laws of war to include acts that had previously been considered beyond the realm of objective judgment. During the early twentieth century, American leaders argued that law would replace blind vengeance as a means of conflict resolution. The apogee of this movement came at Nuremberg in 1946. In order to understand the context for America's radical post–World War II war crimes policy, it is necessary to know how the U.S. conception of international law differed from its European predecessor.

Generally speaking, after the Thirty Years War (1618–48), the era of the modern nation-state began.[6] European leaders viewed international politics as a never-ending and ever-changing struggle in which sovereignty and the national interest were the highest political ideals.[7] Americans tended to view war more like a contest in which total victory was the ultimate objective. The notion that enemies and their policies could be criminalized was not uniquely American; however, American lawyer-statesmen gave this idea its greatest impetus. After I examined the larger history of conflict resolution, it became obvious that the *U.S.–Dakota War Trials*, the trial of Captain Henry Wirz, the Dachau trials, and the Yamashita case were examples of traditional postwar political justice and that the Nuremberg trials were the anomaly. Under the traditional rules, the victor has no historical obligation to extend a wide latitude of civil rights to the vanquished. After reading Hans Delbrück, Michael Howard, Charles Royster, David Kaiser, John Keegan, and the more extreme views of J.F.C. Fuller on the history of war and conflict resolution, I began to see the American Civil War and the two World Wars as exceptional events that had raised the stakes of international conflict. After reading German military political and legal theorists like Carl von Clausewitz, Heinrich von Treitschke, and Friedrich Meinecke on international politics, and Carl Schmitt on the concept of "neutrality," I began to realize how radical and threatening America's punitive occupation policies, outlined in Joint Chiefs of Staff Directive 1067, must have appeared to post–World War II Germans.[8] Impressions, as my former professor Robert Jervis pointed out, are often more important than empirical facts, because they can be shaped to conform to the observers' preconceptions and expectations.

However, it was the foreign policy of my own country that made me question the sincerity of America's commitment to the new principles of international conduct that we had so aggressively advocated during the first half of the twentieth century. Although the second half of this book will focus very sharply on the Nuremberg trials, first I will take a step backward in order to examine America's unique historical relationships with law and war. The episodic histories in the first three chapters help to establish a much larger historical, legal, and political context from which the Nuremberg trials stand out as the legal, political, and historical revolution that they were intended to be. This three-dimensional, multidisciplinary approach is absolutely necessary if one is to enter the storm where war, law, and politics swirl and oscillate in a constant state of flux. As Otto Kirchheimer argued so eloquently, political justice is not illegitimate by its very nature; however, he warned that this is a high-risk arena where the line between "blasphemy and promise" is a very fine one.[9]

AMERICA'S POLITICAL IDEOLOGY POSED UNIQUE PROBLEMS for U.S. foreign policy. It became increasingly difficult to justify an expansive, essentially imperialistic foreign policy within the framework of an egalitarian political ideology. As America grew into a regional and later a global power, this simple hypocrisy evolved into a more profound duality. More than the obvious gap between words and deeds, from the beginning, there was a tension between America's much-vaunted ethical and legal principles and its practical policy interests as an emerging world power. In his book *American Slavery, American Freedom,* Edmund Morgan argues that the simultaneous rise of personal liberty and slavery on the North American continent was the great paradox of the first two centuries of American history.

What also became clear, long before the United States even gained independence, was that the "others," in this case the slave population and North America's native inhabitants, would pay the greatest price for American freedom. Whether it was the Algonquin and the Pequot in the northeast, the Sioux in the Dakotas, or the Chumash in California, U.S. expansion cost American Indians their civilization. Initially colonial leaders deemed both slaves and Indians "barbarians" and "savages" and refused to grant them their natural rights. They would, however, grant them financial credit; as much as the West was won with blood and iron, it was won with whiskey, dependence, and debt. However, from the point of view of American leaders, these dualities were neither problematic nor paradoxical until well into the twentieth century. So what emerges quite naturally, even organically, are two sets of rules for war. When U.S. soldiers faced British and other European armies, they fought according to the customary European rules, with few exceptions. However, when American settlers and soldiers squared off against foes they deemed "savage" or "barbarian," they fought with the same lack of restraint as their adversaries.

The "barbarian" distinction allowed early U.S. leaders to offer messianic justifications for the forcible seizure of the American West and the brutal suppression of those unwilling to give in to the ever-increasing demands of a land-hungry American population. Although they did not hesitate to use force, early American leaders were careful to legalize their actions in the form of treaty law. After reading Dee Brown's sad and moving account of the fall of traditional North American Indian civilization, *Bury My Heart at Wounded Knee,* I was shocked not so much by the flagrant use of force as by the U.S. government's inability to honor either its treaties or its word. Carol Chomsky's excellent article on the Minnesota Indian War of 1862 and the trials and executions that followed, and Sven Lindqvist's provocative study of the role of colonial warfare in European history, *Exterminate All the Brutes,* were extremely helpful.

In 1862, for a brief moment, the United States simultaneously fought Sioux Indians in Minnesota and Confederate troops in the South. Although the Confederacy would not be crushed until 1865, comparing the U.S. government's treatment of the two groups of vanquished foes is very telling and again points to the fact that America fought according to different sets of rules depending on its adversaries. However, this was consistent with the military practices of the European powers, who fought formal restrained wars against one another and operated with a freer hand in their colonial wars. After 1860, the Indian Wars entered a more brutal, final stage in which American Indians were settled onto reservations. Those who refused were deemed hostile and hunted down by specially trained cavalry units like the one led by Colonel Chivington at Sand Creek in 1864. This policy successfully cleared the American frontier for settlement and reached a sad and inevitable apogee at Wounded Knee in 1890.

All of this was justified with a home-grown American doctrine of innate superiority that matured into the political ideology of Manifest Destiny by the late nineteenth century. However, by 1898, American foreign policy was crossing into a new and uncharted territory. It was one thing to justify domestic atrocities on the ground of innate inferiority; similar justifications would not work on the global stage. After the United States soundly defeated Spain in Cuba, the new imperial power faced one in what would become a series of moments of truth—an either/or situation: either the United States would free Spain's former colonies in the Caribbean and the Philippines, or it would reimpose colonialism in its own name. When American leaders attempted to justify their absorption of the former Spanish colonies with the doctrine of Manifest Destiny, the argument was unconvincing both at home and abroad. American statesmen would require new and more sophisticated justifications in the coming years, and where ideology had failed them, law would serve them.

The American duality was embodied in Secretary of War Elihu Root, whose appointment in 1899 marked an important moment in the history of U.S. foreign policy. He was an outspoken advocate of the new codes of international law like the Hague Agreements of 1899 and even an international court, but he had no qualms about using Manifest Destiny to justify a brutal colonial war in the Philippines. Richard Drinnon's *Facing West* outlines the similarities between America's conduct in the Indian Wars and the Philippine War. American President Theodore Roosevelt dismissed the

Philippines' calls for independence by claiming that granting it would be like granting independence to an "Apache chief."

However, much of the American public was unconvinced by their leaders' official explanations. In order to contain the public dissent and the outcry over American conduct in this brutal war, Root ordered a number of war crimes trials for American officers like Major Littleton Waller and General Jacob Smith in Manila in 1902, after the war had been largely won. Although the court went through all the proper motions, the charges were hazy and in the end, the sentences were extremely light. Secretary of War Root used law strategically in order to quell a public relations problem that threatened to undermine American foreign policy. He also employed what would become the favorite device of the strategic legalists—using post-trial, nonjudicial means to further reduce already lenient sentences. In other words, once the public had been served its "justice," the sentences were quietly reduced behind the scenes. Earlier in his career, as a Wall Street lawyer, Root had learned how to use the law to further his clients' interests irrespective of facts. In the case of the Philippines, everyone from his biographer and noted international lawyer Phillip Jessup to biographer Godfrey Hodgson to journalist Jacob Heilbrunn pointed to Root's use of his considerable legal skills to deny charges that were basically true. In fact, one of the major arguments of this book is that the American lawyers who came to shape and dominate twentieth-century U.S. foreign policy employed and interpreted international law in an extremely cynical manner. I call this "strategic legalism," meaning the use of laws or legal arguments to further larger policy objectives, irrespective of facts or moral considerations. As Root pointed out: "It is not the function of law to enforce the rules of morality."

Throughout the early twentieth century, a long line of Wall Street–trained American lawyer-statesmen took the lead in pushing for radical new codes of international conduct that threatened by implication to undermine many of the traditional European rules of statecraft. The Europeans resisted these efforts, and no country more vehemently than Germany. Their representatives at the 1899 and 1907 Hague conferences made clear that they wanted no part of the new international laws and courts. Above all, the Germans viewed war, not law, as the value-free means of dispute resolution. They rejected the "neutrality" of international law and any international court. To the leaders of the Second Reich, in the arena of international affairs there were only friends and enemies, and the only sacred international political principle was sovereignty. As a result of these views,

American lawyer-statesmen like Elihu Root deemed Germany "the great disturber of world peace."

World War I was a very different kind of war, in both scale and aims. With the American entry in 1917, it was fully transformed into a crusade against German tyranny, or as Root described it, "A battle between Odin and Christ." The emergence of democracy and total war in the late nineteenth century began to erode Europe's customary rules of warfare. The popular support required for total war also included a vilification of the enemy, and by the twentieth century, amnesties for wartime atrocities were being replaced by more punitive approaches. With the defeat of Germany came a window of opportunity for U.S. leaders to transform international relations. Germany was not only labeled with war guilt but also fined with reparations. Most dramatic of all, by indicting Kaiser Wilhelm and attempting to put him on trial, the world powers crossed a threshold, challenging the sanctity of sovereignty.

The American duality was alive and well at the Paris Peace Conference and even in the fine print of the Treaty of Versailles. This time American President Woodrow Wilson and his Secretary of State, Robert Lansing, personified it. While President Wilson was attempting to overturn many of the traditional European rules of statecraft, Lansing and colleague James Brown Scott stood unequivocally against the trial of the Kaiser, the punishment of the "Young Turks" for their genocide of over one million Armenians, and more generally, the expansion of international law. Like Elihu Root, both men were extremely successful Wall Street lawyers who argued that the prosecution of individuals for war crimes would imperil America's postwar strategic interests. In this case, Lansing was concerned that a breakdown of the old German social and political order could lead to a Bolshevik takeover. Another facet of the American duality was buried in a single, very significant amendment to the Treaty of Versailles. Although the League of Nations proposed outlawing colonialism and extending natural rights on a global basis, the United States was allowed to preserve its right to hemispheric intervention under the terms of the Monroe Doctrine.

The Leipzig trials, held in the German *Reichsgericht* in 1921, provide yet another example of that new form of twentieth-century political justice, strategic legalism. Unlike the General Jacob Smith case, where the U.S. government acted voluntarily, in the Leipzig trials the Germans were forced to prosecute their soldiers under the terms of the Versailles Treaty. But as in the Smith case, the Germans were no strangers to strategic legalism. They coupled stern and solemn judgments with very light sentences that also were subject to post-trial, nonjudicial modification. German authorities simply allowed convicts to "escape" after their trials.

The interwar period saw a flurry of American-inspired international legal efforts, the most radical of which was the Kellogg-Briand Pact of 1928. Elihu Root was near the end of his life by then and had passed the torch to his apprentice, Henry Stimson, who had begun his career in Root's Wall Street law firm. Stimson was a forceful advocate of revolutionary new treaties like the Kellogg-Briand Pact. After the Japanese seized Manchuria in 1931, he declared, in what would come to be known as the Stimson Doctrine, that the United States reserved the right of "non-recognition" for governments that did not come to power through what it considered to be "legitimate means."

The rise of National Socialism in Germany came at a time when European leaders were both war weary and unprepared to confront an aggressive regime willing to couple bad-faith diplomacy with military force. The Rhineland, Austria, and Czechoslovakia were taken over with minimum force, maximum bluff, and all the diplomatic trappings. Moreover, Hitler forced occupied nations like Czechoslovakia to accept the Munich Agreement or face destruction. In between more naked acts of aggression, Hitler's diplomats employed their own form of strategic legalism by providing careful legal justifications for each takeover.

So by the late 1930s, Hitler had, for all intents and purposes, rendered the Treaty of Versailles null and void. Certainly one of the overlooked tragedies of World War II is the fate of Poland. Not only were Polish civilians of all religions killed, but Allied leaders failed to keep their word both during and after the war. The Poles suffered the horror of both Nazi and Soviet occupations. Once Hitler had attained the goals he outlined in *Mein Kampf,* Poland became the site of Nazi Germany's unique contribution to the twentieth century—the death camp. However, unlike the residents of Indian reservations of the American West or the U.S. *reconcentrado* camps in the Philippines, the inmates of these camps were "less than slaves." If they could not be worked to death, they were killed with cold precision.

It would become very clear after the war that the Nazis fought according to different sets of rules, depending on their theater of operations. As Sven Lindqvist observes, "In the war against the western powers, the Germans observed the laws of war. Only 3.5 percent of English and American prisoners of war died in captivity, though 57 percent of Soviet prisoners of war died." In the East, the Third Reich waged a war of annihilation. The records left behind by the *Einsatzgruppen* and other sadistic execution squads like the *Dirlewanger* Regiment provide ample evidence that the Nazis spared few during Operation Barbarossa. However, on the Western Front, with a few famous exceptions, American POWs were treated far better by the Germans than by the Japanese in the Pacific Theater. Roughly 27 percent of the American POWs in Japanese captivity died, compared to only 3 to 5 percent in German and Italian captivity. Japanese contempt for the weak, defeated, and defenseless led to carnivals of atrocity that lasted for weeks in Asian cities like Nanking and Manila, where tens of thousands of women were raped and hundreds of thousands of civilians slaughtered. Books by Iris Chang, Sheldon Harris, Yuki Tanaka, John Dower, and Hal Gold helped me to better understand the contempt that the Japanese military forces displayed toward the weak and the vanquished.

However, it was the Third Reich's systematic aggression and the killing of millions of European Jews that motivated American lawyer-statesmen like Root's protégé Henry Stimson to find a way to try German leaders. Because the Nazis had so carefully bureaucratized and legalized not just their invasions but even their killings, this posed new and insurmountable challenges for the traditional laws of war. Germany's Jews were German nationals; the atrocities committed against them, no matter how horrific, were outside the jurisdiction of the laws of war. Punishment for the defendants was absolutely dependent on legal innovation, or as many would later argue, *ex post facto* law. Once the defeat of the Third Reich was imminent, the advocates of a punitive peace were led by Secretary of the Treasury Henry Morgenthau. The U.S. State Department objected to this plan, favoring German rehabilitation (for similar reasons to those employed by Robert Lansing after World War I) to prevent the expansion of the Soviet sphere of influence. It was left to a fragile coalition of second- and third-generation American lawyer-statesmen like Henry Stimson and John McCloy and liberal New Dealers like Telford Taylor and Robert Jackson to argue that German leaders should be tried under the interwar nonaggression treaties like the Kellogg-Briand Pact.

Once the protrial faction emerged victorious from the internecine domestic battle in Washington in 1945, it had to convert very skeptical European allies to the idea that the trials would do more than render justice; they would also serve to "reeducate" the German people. Although they were able to get the Allies to agree to charge German leaders under the radical new rules of statecraft that the United States had been pushing since at least 1907, ironically, they were unable to convert their scattered domestic critics on the right and the left. By 1945, the U.S. State Department was already resurrecting Nazi intelligence infrastructure and operations in order to get a jump on the Soviet Union's efforts along similar lines.

However, this posed unique problems for U.S. foreign policy because military defeat was not the sole objective of the American war effort. U.S. leaders committed themselves to radical and wide-ranging social reform policy called "denazification." Although this was unlike anything Europeans had ever seen, it was all too familiar to Americans south of the Mason-Dixon Line, who had undergone a similarly resented postwar reconstruction after the Civil War. The German reconstruction effort was founded upon the assumption that if only the Allies could somberly present evidence of Hitler's war guilt, Germans would recognize and acknowledge the criminality of their leadership. It turned out to be significantly more complicated than this.

While the Nuremberg trial is often referred to in the singular, there were actually three major trials, all different in scope and meaning. As American political scientist Quincy Wright pointed out in the 1950s, the Nuremberg trials provided a fresh setting for positivists and natural advocates to settle old scores. The leading American historian of the International Military Tribunal, Bradley F. Smith, concludes that although the trials were in many ways hypocritical, in the end their collective judgments were conservative and on the whole quite sound. Although British historians John and Ann Tusa take a harder view of U.S. prosecutor Robert Jackson and the Americans, they too have a favorable view of the trials. German historians Werner Maser and Jörg Friedrich point out important flaws in the trials and most important, how the Soviet inclusion tainted the proceedings in the eyes of many Germans.

Nuremberg's International Military Tribunal (IMT), the first trial, continues to be the most popular model for contemporary international criminal courts and the central object of inquiry for almost all books on the subject. Between November 20, 1945 and October 1, 1946, a 4-nation international court indicted 22 of Nazi Germany's highest ranking survivors under a radical indictment that included charges of aggression or crimes against peace, crimes against humanity, and conspiracy. The tribunal sentenced 12 men to death, 7 to prison terms, and acquitted 3. Initially the international court was planning to try more cases against German military and civilian leaders. Because of U.S.–Soviet tensions, however, President Truman was advised by the IMT's Chief Prosecutor, Robert Jackson, not to participate in another international trial. Instead, the President asked OSS Colonel and IMT prosecutor Telford Taylor to create and staff American courts in Nuremberg to try the remaining high-level war criminals. Armed with an indictment modeled on the IMT's, American lawyers and judges tried 185 men in 12 cases at Nuremberg's Palace of Justice between 1947 and 1949. What initially interested me in these trials was the conspicuous absence of secondary sources about them. These were the more interesting trials because the courts were forced to address the same vexing questions as the IMT had but in far less certain cases, long after the passions of war had cooled. As the Cold War intensified, a new American duality emerged as political concerns began to eclipse moral and legal ones.

In trying to obtain even the most basic information about the American Nuremberg trials, I found a glaring historiographic omission—the absence of a single English-language study. Although Telford Taylor's *Final Report to the Secretary of the Army on the Nuernberg War Crimes Trials*, books like Joseph Borkin's *The Crime and Punishment of I. G. Farben*; Josiah Dubois's *The Devil's Chemists*; William Manchester's *The Arms of Krupp*; more recently, Ian Buruma's *The Wages of Guilt*; and Richard von Weizsäcker's *From Weimar to the Wall* examine specific cases, none offers a comprehensive analysis of the subsequent proceedings and the war criminals' changes of fate during the 1950s. In German there is more literature, Jörg Friedrich's *Das Gesetz Des Krieges* being by far the most comprehensive account of any single American Nuremberg trial.

The American Nuremberg trials resembled the IMT in a number of ways. In addition to punishing the guilty, the American courts intended to create an irrefutable record of Hitler's Third Reich. Defendants were not simply charged with violations of the customary rules of war, they were subject to the same unprecedented standards of international conduct as the defendants at the IMT. Military leaders, politicians, lawyers, doctors, businessmen, and bankers faced charges of aggression, conspiracy, and crimes against humanity. Each case produced a voluminous historical record composed of documentary evidence and testimony. The transcripts of the final American Nuremberg trial alone ran to 28,000 pages. The defendants included industrialist Alfried Krupp, diplomat Ernst von Weizsäcker, *Einsatzkommando* Otto Ohlendorf, Field Marshal Wilhelm von List, Judge Rudolf Oeschey, and many other high-ranking Third Reich officials. Originally Telford Taylor had hoped to try as many as 300 individuals, but by 1949 it was clear that these punitive policies did not fit with the new American plan for West Germany.

Initially I was interested in the final American trial at Nuremberg because my great-grandfather had been a judge. I quickly learned that *United States v. Ernst von Weizsaecker* was an extremely complicated case that brought charges against twenty-one high-ranking Nazis from all sectors of the Third Reich. The Ministries case could best be described as a Cold War IMT. Its roster of defendants included Ernst von Weizsäcker, SS General Walter Schellenberg, banker Emil Puhl, industrialist Wilhelm Keppler, Chief of the Reich Chancellery Hans Lammers, Reich Minister of Public Enlightenment Otto Dietrich, SS General Gottlob Berger, and fourteen others.

The American Nuremberg trials and especially the Ministries case would serve as yet another test of America's commitment to the trials themselves and to their international legal legacy. The prosecution charged former State Secretary Ernst von Weizsäcker with the radical and recent crime of aggression (crimes against peace) for his role in the Nazi takeover of Czechoslovakia. His five-man defense team included his son Richard, who would later serve as the President of the Federal Republic of Germany and become one of the most eloquent spokesmen of his generation. This was the only American court to convict under the controversial aggression charge. However, the decision was not unanimous: Judge Leon Powers blasted the majority decision in his dissenting opinion.

Few historians have attempted to consider the Nuremberg trials within the context of America's larger post–World War II war crimes policy. The first thing that becomes apparent is that the Nuremberg trials compare very favorably to the trial programs run by the various branches of the American military. The most glaring victor's justices came in the Yamashita case and the Malmedy trials. These proceedings were held immediately after the war when passions had not yet cooled; the cry for vengeance outweighed considerations of due process. This was traditional postwar military justice, after all.

Aside from a single French trial in 1947 (Hermann Roechling), the only other court to employ a Nuremburg-like indictment was the International Military Tribunal Far East ("Tokyo Trial"). The eleven-man international tribunal arraigned twenty-eight of Japan's military and civilian leaders on May 3, 1946. Although Emperor Hirohito was not among the defendants, they did include Hideki Tojo and a number of other military and political officials. After two and a half strife-filled years, the court sentenced seven men to death and seventeen to life in prison on November 4, 1948. Three of the eleven judges filed dissenting opinions. Justice Radhabinod Pal of India issued a scathing dissenting opinion that found all of the accused not guilty on every count of the indictment. Fueled by anti-imperialism, Pal wrote, "It would be sufficient for my present purpose to say that if any indiscriminate destruction of civilian life and property is illegitimate in war-fare, then . . . this decision to use the atom bomb is the only near approach to the directives of . . . the Nazi leaders." In an effort to place the Nurem-berg trials within the context of post–World War II war crimes adjudica-tion, I have included summary analyses of the IMT, IMTFE (Tokyo Trial), and a few of the more significant military cases. The published secondary works of Bradley F. Smith, John and Ann Tusa, Robert Conot, Eugene Da-vidson, Drexel Sprecher, James Willis, Thomas Schwartz, Telford Taylor, Frank Lael, John Dower, James Weingartner, Frank Buscher, Phillip Pic-cigallo, James Bosch, Howard Levie, Michael Marrus, and John Pritchard were particularly helpful.

I then go on to examine the paroles of convicted war criminals in West Germany and Japan during the 1950s carried out by the U.S. Army (low level) and the State Department (high level). What interests me here is the clash between the geopolitical need for "reconciliation" with new and im-portant allies and the traditional U.S. commitment to principles of law and human rights. Many West Germans, their leaders included, found the Nuremberg manner of punishment and parole confusing, unprecedented, and ultimately legally illegitimate. In the end, the United States and the Fed-eral Republic found a face-saving way of resolving the war crimes question to West Germany's advantage. The ensuing story of how some of the worst war criminals of World War II were quietly paroled is worth telling. It is widely known that Rudolf Hess and the other IMT defendants were shown little mercy under quadripartite control in Berlin's Spandau Prison. How did the war criminals in the western prisons (Werl, Wittlich, and Lands-berg) fare?

After I read Frank Buscher's groundbreaking study, *The American War Crimes Program in Germany,* and spent some time at the National Archives reading the State Department legal advisor's war crimes files, my eyes were opened to a far more complex picture that consisted of many levels of activ-ity. In 1951, less than two years after the last Nuremberg sentence was handed down, U.S. High Commissioner John McCloy ordered the first large-scale sentence reductions; he has provided a convenient scapegoat for histori-ans ever since. Although McCloy's justifications for the sentence reductions were weak and often disingenuous, his actions were nowhere near as dra-matic as the releases that came after 1953.

With the exception of Buscher's study, most of the accounts of war crimes clemency focus too heavily on John McCloy and his motives. Buscher pow-erfully demonstrates that by 1953, American leaders viewed the war criminals as a political question they wanted to resolve as quickly and quietly as possible. For German views on the subject I relied on Jörg Friedrich, Norbert Frei, Anna and Richard Merrit, Thomas Schwartz, Jeffrey Herf, and Verene Botzenhart-Viehe. My real education on the German side of these questions began in the summer of 1995, when I was hired as a historical advisor for a Chronos Films documentary entitled *Nuremberg: A Courtroom Drama*, working with German historian Jörg Friedrich under the direction of Spiegel Television's Michael Kloft. Not only did we watch all the American and Soviet footage of the trials, Kloft also interviewed everyone from Telford Taylor to Markus Wolf to Louise Jodl. I was able to interview Nuremberg's most successful defense attorney, Otto Kranzbühler, in the summer of 1996. After representing Admiral Doenitz, Alfried Krupp, and many other prominent defendants at Nuremberg, Kranzbühler advised Chancellor Adenauer on the war crimes question throughout the 1950s. He proudly described how he had engineered both the early releases of Germany's most notorious war criminals and the official West German nonrecognition of the legal validity of the original sentences. Friedrich and I carefully examined the treaties restoring German sovereignty in the early 1950s and found the final and official German expression of Nuremberg's illegitimacy in paragraphs 6.11 and 7 of the Paris Treaty on the Termination of the Status of Occupation of 1952. Buried in the paragraph regarding war criminals, just as Kranzbühler had told us, is a confusing caveat. In it the West German government, in a roundabout way, refused to accept the legal validity of not just the Nuremberg trials but all of the Allied war crimes trials.

I returned to the National Archives in College Park, Maryland in 1997 and, thanks to the help of archivist Martin McCaan, found the secret correspondence between the State Department legal advisors and the American members of the various war crimes parole boards. This material demonstrates how American leaders caved in to official West German pressure to release war criminals and as a result cast a shadow of doubt over the legal legitimacy of those trials in Germany. Many argue that however misguided the war crimes clemencies were, they did not detract from "the lessons of Nuremberg." I reject this view. In 1958, a parole board composed of Germans and Americans released the final four war criminals. Three of the four men had been members of the *Einsatzgruppen*, sentenced to death by an American tribunal at Nuremberg in 1948.

American clemency board member Spencer Phenix wrote State Department Assistant Legal Advisor John Raymond a telling memo on the eve of the decision: "I can answer all your questions and between us we can reach substantial agreement on what can and should be done to get this bother-some problem quietly out of the way where it will no longer complicate international relations." Because the question of war crimes clemency was usually linked to German rearmament, it created the impression that the United States was trading war criminals for West German rearmament and allegiance.

Did America fail to punish convicted German war criminals due to a lack of resolve? Or were there more serious internal problems with the Nuremberg approach to war crimes adjudication? It is my contention that a number of international political factors combined to force American and Allied authorities to abandon their controversial war crimes policy. In the United States, many scholars continue to point to the Allied war crimes tri-als, especially Nuremberg's IMT, as the centerpiece of a successful reeduca-tion effort. But the American flight from the radical and punitive policies of the occupation period coincided with the release and social reinstitution of prominent war criminals like Alfried Krupp and Ernst von Weizsäcker. This sent a powerful message to the West German body politic. The ques-tion was further confused when President Eisenhower asked West Germany to rearm under the European Defense Community Treaty during the early 1950s. The abrupt and often contradictory shifts in American foreign policy reopened the question of Nuremberg's legitimacy in West Germany. Finally, we are left with two equally inaccurate Nuremberg myths: the American myth of the redemptive trial and the German myth of the victor's justice.

CHAPTER 1

THE END OF LIMITED WAR

TODAY, THERE IS A TENDENCY TO ROMANTICIZE BOTH THE
chivalric era and the early years of the European state system as more
humane times, when soldiers were governed by codes of honor and civilians
were not targeted for wanton destruction.[1] However, what is often overlooked is that the gentlemanly rules of war outlined by Christian scholars
applied only to warriors of the same race and class. When invasive "others"
like Norsemen and Muslims descended on early European states, the only
law of war was survival.[2] As military historian Michael Howard points
out, neither the laws of nations nor "warriors' honor" meant much "when
Norsemen were raging through the land like devouring flames." In wars
against pagans, no holds were barred, no prisoners were taken; this was in
keeping with the *guerre mortale* doctrine.[3]

Although America had no Norsemen or Magyars, it did have an indig-
enous population of at least five million scattered across the continent.[4]
The Seneca, Sioux, Iroquois, Cheyenne, Arapaho, Apache, Chippewa, Nez
Perce, and numerous others had lived free, according to their own rules,
for thousands of years. However, even in America there was freedom only
for some, and this was consistent with Thomas Jefferson's original vision.
According to nineteenth-century American historian Frederick Jackson
Turner, the first period of U.S. history was spent clearing and pacifying the

western frontier—no small feat, and one that required equal parts determination and brutality.[5]

What were the moral implications of forcibly uprooting America's native inhabitants to make way for the republic founded upon the principles of "liberty and justice for all"?[6] A previous generation of European leaders had been content to invoke the divine right of God or king to justify war and territorial acquisition, but American leaders outwardly scorned the European model of power politics. The United States was founded and built upon a contradiction; as Edmund Morgan observes in *American Slavery, American Freedom*, the simultaneous development of both slavery and freedom on the American continent is the "central paradox" of early American history.[7] As with the slaves, if American leaders denied the Indians their humanity, they could deny them their natural rights. Before there were "war criminals," there were "barbarians," "heathens," and "savages" who did not qualify as equals in the arena of "civilized warfare." From the beginning, America's founding fathers considered the American Indians barbarians.[8] "Humanity," or in this case, a lack thereof, allowed European and U.S. armies to justify occupying territory and exploiting it unhindered by the restraints of the traditional European rules of statecraft. The early American settlers granted their continent's native inhabitants no natural rights. "To think of raising these hideous creatures into our holy religion!" wrote Puritan leader Reverend Cotton Mather. "All was diabolical among them."[9]

The American frontier and especially the northern plains were inhabited by fierce and seasoned Indian warriors whom military historian John Keegan counts "among the most remarkable of all the world's warrior peoples." By the end of the eighteenth century they possessed horses and guns and "combined their use into terrifyingly effective military practice."[10] Many of the American tribes lived in "hard primitive" societies in which war played an important role. Keegan argues that of all the eighteenth- and nineteenth-century colonial armies, the U.S. Army had the most difficult job, in the American plains. The enemies of the British, French, and Spanish, "cunning, tough, and brave though they were—did not approach the Plains Indians in qualities of harsh individual warriordom."[11]

American settlers faced fearsome foes who shared none of their ethical assumptions about life and death, much less war. Because the customary laws of war forbade guerrilla warfare, the taking of hostages, and the massacre of civilians, the early colonists and the U.S. government never recognized the legitimacy of the American Indian resistance. Historian William Fowell remarks on the differing perceptions of war: to the American mind, the so-called Indian raids "amounted simply to massacre, an atrocious and utterly unjustifiable butchery of unoffending citizens." But for the Sioux, it was a war for national survival: "The Indian, however, saw himself engaged in war, the most honorable of all pursuits, against men who, as he believed, had robbed him of his country and his freedom."[12]

Colonial leaders had no qualms about slaughtering those tribes that resisted their "civilizing" influence. As early as 1675, colonists nearly wiped out the Algonquin Indians for attacking and destroying colonial settlements in what would come to be known as King Philip's War.[13] In the end, King Philip, the Algonquin Indian leader, was captured and killed. His wife and children were sold as slaves in the West Indies, and his head was exhibited in Plymouth for the next twenty years.[14] Reprisal would become the key word in America's emerging Indian policy. Tribes that resisted and refused American demands were subjected to harsh punitive measures.

America's first President, George Washington, ordered Major General John Sullivan to "chastize" hostile Iroquois in a May 31, 1779 letter. Washington wanted the Indian villages "not merely overrun but destroyed. But you will not by any means, listen to any overture of peace before the total ruin of their settlements is effected." He wanted to establish a precedent of terror: "Our future security will be in their inability to injure us . . . and in the terror with which the severity of the chastizement they receive will inspire them."[15] Major General Sullivan shared his commander-in-chief's view that "the Indians shall see that there is malice enough in our hearts to destroy everything that contributes to their support."[16]

When George Hammond, the first British ambassador to the United States, asked Thomas Jefferson in 1792 what he "understood as the right of the United States in Indian soil," Jefferson responded, "We consider it as established by the usage of different nations into a kind of jus gentium (Law of Nations) for America," arguing that while the United States would treat the invasion of Indian territory by "any other white nation" as an act of war, America assumed "no right of soil against the native possessors." Hammond was unconvinced and told Jefferson that the British believed the United States planned "to exterminate the Indians and take their lands." "On the contrary, our system was to protect them, even against our own citizens," Jefferson replied defensively. "We wish to get lines established with all of them, and have no views even of purchasing any more land of them for a long time."[17] The U.S. government's actions, however, would speak louder than their words.

When Thomas Jefferson became President in 1801, the duality of American frontier policy became clear for all to see. Contradicting the arguments he had made to the British diplomat in 1792, the United States underwent a massive territorial expansion during his presidency. The precedent for America's nineteenth-century Indian policy can be found in an 1803 letter from Jefferson to Indiana Territory Governor William Henry Harrison. The plans were a passive-aggressive and uniquely American form of conquest— credit and debt: "To promote this disposition to exchange lands, which they have to spare and we want, we shall push our trading uses, and be glad to see the good and influential individuals among them run in debt, because we observe that when these debts get beyond what individuals can pay, they become willing to lop them off by a cessation of lands."[18] The President noted the importance of appearances and encouraged Governor Harrison to soothe the Indians "by liberalities and sincere assurances of friendship." Jefferson's objective was to "finally consolidate our whole country to one nation only."[19] By 1812, the United States had acquired 109,884,000 acres of former Indian territory, and the American slave population had grown to more than 1.2 million.[20] As Alexis de Toqueville observed in the 1830s, "The Americans are already able to make their flag respected; in a few years, they will make it feared."[21]

James Madison seemed to recognize the American paradox in an 1826 letter: "Next to the case of the black race within our bosom, that of the red on our borders is the problem most baffling to the policy of our country."[22] Even as late as 1831, the legal status of the American Indians was unclear. Supreme Court Chief Justice Marshall called the various tribes "domestic dependent nations" in *Cherokee Nation v. Georgia* (1831):

The Indians are acknowledged to have unquestionable and heretofore an unquestioned right to the lands they occupy until that right shall be extinguished by a voluntary cessation to the Government. It may well be doubted whether those tribes which reside within the acknowledged boundaries of the United States can with strict accuracy be denominated domestic dependent nations. They occupy territory to which we assert a title, independent of their will, which must take effect in point of possession when their right of possession ceases; meanwhile they are in a state of pupilage. The relations with the United States resemble that of a ward to his guardian. They look to our Government for protection; rely upon its kindness and its power; appeal to it for relief to their wants, and address the President as their great father.[23]

However, Indians' legal rights meant little if the federal government was unwilling to uphold the court's decisions. "Andrew Jackson's refusal to enforce Marshall's decision gave mute testimony that, if the tribes had legal rights affirmed by the highest court in the land, their political status made it easy to void such rights."[24]

After a successful war against Mexico, the United States took possession of Texas and California. With the discovery of gold in California in 1848, wagon trains filled with hopeful settlers streamed west onto "the permanent Indian frontier." What the U.S. government did not take by treaty, the settlers simply occupied. The American Indians would soon learn that under the white man's law, possession by squatting could be translated into ownership. Not surprisingly, many tribes were unwilling to give up their land without a fight. By the time Minnesota became a state in 1860, the various bands of Sioux had sold more than 24,000,000 acres of their territory to the U.S. government.[25] Two treaties signed by Sioux leaders in 1837 and 1851 relieved them of 90 percent of their property in exchange for annuity payments from the American government. The 1851 treaty promised a lump-sum payment that the Sioux had still not received by 1862.[26]

The tension in Minnesota was exacerbated during the 1850s by more than 150,000 settlers who moved into the state and, in many cases, pushed onto land reserved for the Sioux as "permanent Indian frontier."[27] Often the government's annuity payments went straight to frontier traders for supplies already purchased on credit. When the Sioux chiefs demanded to be paid directly, the traders refused to extend them further credit. The situation reached a point of crisis during the summer of 1862.

Due to crop failure and drastically reduced hunting grounds, many Santee Sioux were going hungry and turned to their chief Little Crow for help. Although he was the son and grandson of Santee chiefs, Little Crow decided that resisting the white expansion would be futile. After a tour of American cities, he returned to Minnesota, joined the Episcopal church, built a house, and even started to farm. Little Crow not only signed the two treaties surrendering Sioux territory but had even visited Washington and met "the Great Father," President Buchanan.[28]

Although Little Crow had become a "model Indian" in the eyes of the white men, as the summer of 1862 dragged on and no payments arrived, even he began to lose faith in the American government. In July, he led several thousand Santee to Upper Agency to collect their government annuity payments and to purchase food and other supplies. When the payments did not arrive, a rumor began to circulate that the U.S. government had spent all their gold in the Civil War.[29] Little Crow approached the U.S. Indian Agent, Thomas Galbraith, and asked why his people could not be issued food instead of gold if the storehouses were full and they were starving. Galbraith refused the request and called in one hundred U.S. soldiers to guard the storehouses. More than five hundred Santee surrounded them in Upper Agency on August 4; outnumbered, the soldiers watched as the Indians took flour and other basic supplies. Little Crow was still not satisfied and demanded on August 13 that Galbraith distribute more supplies in the neighboring settlement, Lower Agency.[30] Two days later, Little Crow and several hundred of his followers arrived in Lower Agency. However, this time the Indian Agent refused to distribute goods.[31] When Little Crow tried to reason with Galbraith, the agent said nothing, but storekeeper Andrew Myrick responded derisively, "So far as I am concerned, if they are hungry let them eat grass or their own dung."[32] This public insult, coupled with Little Crow's failure to obtain food, cost the Santee leader the trust of his own people.

Four Sioux braves attacked and killed a group of settlers near Acton, Minnesota on August 17, 1862.[33] Late that night, Little Crow was informed of the massacre. He immediately realized that "No Santee's life would be safe, not after these killings. . . . It was the white man's way to punish all Indians for the crimes of one or a few."[34] Little Crow did not want to go to war; he told his braves they were "full of the white man's devil water" and compared them to "dogs in the Hot Moon when they run mad and snap at their own shadows."[35] When the warriors began to question his bravery, Little Crow quieted them with a grim prophecy: "Braves, you are like little children— you are fools. You will die like rabbits when the hungry wolves hunt them in the Hard Moon of January."[36]

The war council continued through the night; although chiefs Little Crow and Big Eagle called for peace, they were shouted down by a firm majority set on vengeance. Finally, Little Crow reluctantly agreed to wage war, and sent word to neighboring tribes that there would be an early morning surprise attack on Lower Agency.[37] The next day at 6:00 a.m., Little Crow and other Santee gathered near the stores that would not extend them credit and waited for their signal. At 6:30, a young warrior named Wasu-ota ran toward Andrew Myrick's store, shouting, "Now, I will kill the dog who would not give me credit."[38] Myrick ran upstairs to the second floor. When the Indians set fire to the building, he jumped from a window. The shopkeeper's body was later found dead and scalped with a mouth full of grass.[39] Very quickly, Minnesota settlers were forced to realize that the Sioux did not recognize the most basic distinction between soldier and civilian.[40]

When settlers from the nearby Beaver Creek settlement loaded their wagons and fled, they had barely traveled a mile before they were surrounded by painted Santee warriors. After they surrendered their wagons and livestock, the Indians opened fire on them. Two settlers tried to surrender under a white flag; according to a witness, "it was not regarded, and Wedge was shot dead, and Henderson lost the fingers off one hand. The Indians then came up and pulling the bed with Mrs. Henderson on it to the ground, set fire to it. One of the infant children was beaten to death over the wagon wheel, and thrown in the fire, the other was cut to pieces and thrown in piecemeal."[41] Mary Schwandt was fourteen when the Sioux killed her family and took her prisoner: "They then took me out by force, to an unoccupied tepee . . . and perpetrated the most horrible and nameless outrages upon my person. These outrages were repeated, at different times during my captivity."[42] If the American Indians employed these methods against one another, why should the American settlers be exempt? Historian William Fowell observes, "He [Sioux] was making war on the white people in the same fashion in which he would have gone against the Chippewa or the Foxes."[43]

Forty-seven settlers managed to escape the slaughter at Lower Agency thanks to the heroic efforts of a ferryman named Herbert Millier.[44] The survivors traveled thirteen miles downstream toward the federal garrison at Fort Ridgely, where Company B of the Fifth Minnesota Voluntary Infantry Regiment was stationed. Captain John Marsh and forty-six mounted U.S. soldiers intercepted the fleeing settlers and rode for Acton. When the relief party was ambushed, Captain Marsh tried to escape by crossing a river, but he drowned.[45] Sergeant John Bishop managed to straggle back to Fort Ridgely with twenty-four survivors.[46]

The Sioux rampage in Minnesota came as an especially unwelcome distraction to President Abraham Lincoln, who was trying to rally the Union Army after poor initial outings against the Confederacy. A short front-page story in the August 22 edition of *The New York Times* reported that four companies of U.S. soldiers under the command of former Minnesota Governor Colonel Henry H. Sibley were on the way to assist the embattled Minnesota settlers.[47] Henry "Long Trader" Sibley had a long and troubled history with the Santee that went back to the governor's days as a trader on the Minnesota frontier. According to historian Dee Brown, "Of the $475,000 promised the Santee in their first treaty, Long Trader Sibley claimed $145,000 for his American Fur Company as money due for overpayments to the San- tees." At the time, Santee leaders argued that the company had underpaid them, but when they complained to their Indian Agent, Alexander Ramsey, he sided with Sibley.[48] By 1862, Ramsey was the Governor of Minnesota, and "Long Trader" Sibley was in charge of the Sixth Minnesota Regiment.

Nearly 600 painted Santee warriors descended on the settlement of New Ulm on August 23. During the next 30 hours, 34 settlers died and 60 were wounded in the valiant defense of their town.[49] Although the Sioux suc- ceeded in burning 190 buildings, they were unable to capture or destroy the settlement. The next day, the 2,000 settlers set out in a convoy of 153 wag- ons for Manakato, nearly 30 miles away.[50] The August 24, 1862 *New York Times* described the conflict: THE INDIAN MASSACRES—Terrible Scenes of Death and Misery in Minnesota—Five Hundred Whites Supposed to Be Murdered—The Sioux Bands United Against the Whites.[51]

The Minnesota Indian War would be headed by Army Major General John Pope, who had suffered an embarrassing defeat at the second Battle of Bull Run on August 6. President Lincoln ordered him to the northwest territories to put down the uprising.[52] General Pope was outraged by the Santee attacks on civilians, particularly the raping and killing of women and children. Pope informed Colonel Sibley that the Sioux needed to be "badly punished." Reprisals would be carried out before any surrender was accepted or any settlement made.[53] Pope was very explicit: "It is my pur- pose to utterly exterminate the Sioux if I have the power to do so and even if it requires a campaign lasting the whole of next year. Destroy everything belonging to them and force them out to the plains, unless, as I suggest, you can capture them." He considered the Indians outside the circle of humanity; they would be "treated as maniacs or wild beasts, and by no means as people with whom treaties of compromises can be made."[54]

Once advance troops from the Sixth Minnesota Regiment began to ar- rive, the Santee retreated up the Minnesota Valley with more than 100 pris- oners and set up a camp 40 miles north of Upper Agency.[55] With 1,450 men and two cannons, Colonel Sibley set out for Little Crow's camp on Sep- tember 19. The wagon train was ambushed near the Yellow Medicine River, and although Little Crow succeeded in drawing the soldiers into his trap, he was unable to overrun Sibley's forces. When the U.S. troops opened fire with their cannon, a direct hit killed six Santee instantly and wounded 15 others.[56] Overwhelmed by the American soldiers' firepower, the Indians retreated into the forest. Colonel Sibley was horrified when he found his soldiers scalping dead Santee warriors and issued an immediate order that the dead, "even of a savage enemy, shall not be subjected to indignities by civilized and Christian men."[57]

After Sibley's victory on the battlefield, he began surrender negotiations with Sioux leaders, including Little Crow.[58] Although many Santee would surrender in the coming months, Little Crow would not be among them. He wanted to keep the prisoners and to continue the war because he had "no confidence that the whites will stand by any agreement they make if we give them up."[59] The Indian chief pointed to the Santee's sad history of relations with the U.S. government and the American settlers. "Ever since we treated with them, their agents and traders have robbed and cheated us. Some of our people have been shot, some hung; others placed upon floating ice and drowned."[60] By early September, Little Crow realized that events had gained too much momentum and was resigned to his fate. "We may regret what has happened, but the matter has gone too far to be remedied. We have got to die. Let us, then, kill as many of the whites as possible, and let the prisoners die with us."[61]

By the end of September 1862, hundreds of Santee had surrendered to Colonel Sibley, who in turn promised that he only sought to punish those who had committed atrocities against civilians.[62] Once 1,200 Sioux were in government custody, Sibley established a five-man Court of Inquiry to "try summarily the Mulatto, and Indians, or mixed bloods, now prisoners . . . and pass judgment upon them, if found guilty of murders or other outrages upon Whites, during the present State of hostilities of the Indians." The Sioux were not charged with violations of the customary laws of war because the U.S. government did not consider them lawful combatants. To grant them that status would have been to recognize their sovereignty and their inherent right to wage war. The colonel planned to execute the guilty immediately to create a spectacle of vengeance that would serve as a deterrent against future attacks: "An example is . . . imperatively necessary and I trust you [the court] will approve the act, should it happen that some real criminals have been seized and promptly disposed of."[63]

The chairman of the Court of Inquiry was a missionary named Stephen Riggs who had worked with the Sioux since 1837.[64] The court offered a plea bargain to a mulatto named Godfrey who was married to a Sioux woman and had fought with the Indians, earning the sobriquet "he who kills many." Godfrey would testify in fifty-five cases, and even though he was known to have killed many settlers at Upper Agency, his sentence was commuted in exchange for his testimony.[65] These "trials" were so summary that on the first day, the count sentenced ten to death and acquitted six. The Court of Inquiry would try as many as forty-two Santee in a single day.[66]

General Pope approved of the speedy trials and warned that he now had sufficient troops at his disposal to "exterminate them all, if they furnish the least occasion for it."[67] Because some of the Sioux had not yet given themselves up, Colonel Sibley postponed the executions so as not to discourage their surrender.[68] General Pope wrote General Henry Halleck to find out if he needed further authorization before proceeding, while Minnesota Governor Ramsey wrote to President Lincoln on October 10 requesting "nothing less than the removal of the whole body of Indians to remote districts, far beyond our borders."[69] Colonel Sibley received a response from the President on October 17 stating in no uncertain terms that no executions would take place until he personally reviewed the death sentences. Lincoln was facing problems commonly found when war, law, and politics converge. His most immediate concern was the need for an immediate postwar show of vengeance in order to prevent vigilante retribution on a much larger scale.[70] In the end, the Court of Inquiry tried 394 Santee; 303 were found guilty and sentenced to death.

It appeared that nothing short of a mass execution would satisfy the citizens of Minnesota. DEATH TO BARBARIANS IS THE SENTIMENT OF OUR PEOPLE read the headline of the *Minnesota Messenger* on November 11. Minnesota Senator Morton Wilkinson wrote President Lincoln and warned that "the Outraged people of Minnesota will dispose of these wretches without law. These two people cannot live together. We do not want to see mob law inaugurated in Minnesota."[71] A few weeks later, when a wagon train of prisoners was attacked by a group of settlers, it took an army bayonet charge to disperse the crowd, but not before a Santee baby was torn from the arms of his mother and killed by the mob.[72] Late on the night of December 4, several hundred settlers threatened to attack the prison camp but were quickly surrounded and disarmed by soldiers.[73]

President Lincoln was in a very difficult position. He was clearly torn between the need to maintain the most minimal standards of justice and the demands of contemporary politics. Would he be able to satisfy all of his constituencies? If the Indians were not punished, what message would that send the settlers? If the U.S. government were to execute all 303 Santee, what message would that send the rest of America's Indian population? After the U.S. Commissioner of Indian Affairs, William Dole, visited Minnesota, he characterized the sentences as "more of the character of revenge than of punishment."[74] The interrogator, Reverend Riggs, urged the

President to draw a distinction between those braves who were involved in combat and those who murdered and tortured civilians.[75] In the end, President Lincoln ordered the execution of only the Santee "proved guilty of violating females" and singled out those "who were proven to have participated in massacres as distinguished from participation in battles." The number of death sentences was reduced from 303 to 38.[76]

According to the *St. Paul Daily Press,* the captive Santee did not react to the news of their impending executions with surprise: "Several Indians smoked their pipes composedly during the reading, and we observed one in particular who, when the time of the execution was designated, quietly knocked the ashes from his pipe and filled it afresh with his favorite Kinnekinnick."[77] When one reporter spoke with the Indians, he found them a rather stoic bunch. "When the condemned are talked to on that subject they say, 'Kill me, kill me. I would kill you if I had you.'" The reporter recognized that to the Sioux brave, war was a calling, a *raison d'etre*: "He would prefer death by the slow, lingering torture, such as none but an Indian can devise and execute, to a death on the gallows."[78] On the day before the executions the condemned sang, danced, and met with male relatives.[79]

A crowd of settlers began to gather as a small army of carpenters worked around the clock constructing a giant, four-sided scaffold, custom designed to hang all 38 men at once. This was a late example of the old style of corporal punishment. Under the traditional model, as French philosopher Michel Foucault points out so graphically in *Discipline and Punishment,* "public torture and execution must be spectacular, it must be seen by all as its triumph."[80] The sale of all intoxicants was banned for 48 hours and martial law was imposed in Minnesota on December 25, 1862. Early the next morning, the condemned Santee began their haunting death chants as 1,400 soldiers kept the crowd of 3,000 spectators at bay.[81] At 10:00 a.m., the convicts were hooded, unshackled, and led up the stairs of the hanging platform. Some continued to sing death hymns and held hands with their neighbors. The army drummer signaled the moment of execution with three beats and William Duley, a man whose family had been killed by the Sioux, cut the rope. At that moment a cheer came from both soldiers and settlers.[82] More than nine years later, it was admitted that two of the men hanged were not on President Lincoln's list. However, this mattered little: by 1863 the State of Minnesota was offering a $25 bounty for the scalp of any Sioux. Although Little Crow escaped the hangman's noose, he was shot and mortally wounded on July 3, 1863 by two settlers out hunting deer.[83] His killers were given a $500 bounty for the Santee chief's remains and his skull and scalp were put on display in St. Paul.[84]

This early attempt to apply law to war (even though the U.S. government did not consider the ongoing battles with the Indians a war) produced a primitive form of political justice; guilty convictions were based on rumor and hearsay and individuals were singled out for punishment in order to quench the domestic population's thirst for vengeance. Although he presided over the largest mass execution in American history, Abraham Lincoln probably averted a larger bloodbath. This was by far the simplest form of political justice because there was no presumption of fairness or impartiality. A few especially odious and well-deserving felons were publicly prosecuted and punished, after which the rest were given formal or informal amnesties for wartime atrocities. The outcome was largely known before the trial began, so the "legal" proceedings became part of the display—hence the term "show trial." German legal theorist Otto Kirchheimer describes cases like the *U.S.–Dakota War Trials* as "a spectacle with prearranged results." However, Kirchheimer makes a subtle and often overlooked point, warning that any trial "presupposes an element of irreducible risk for those involved" and "even in the administration of injustice there are gradations." Above all, he warns that "justice in political matters is more tenuous than in any other field of jurisprudence, because it can so easily become a mere farce."[85] The questions in the *U.S.–Dakota* trials were less about guilt and innocence than the manner of punishment and the drama of public execution.

At the same time as the Indian wars, the U.S. Army was engaged in another war against another foe, fought according to a different, significantly more formal set of rules. As Geoffrey Best observes, "What could be got away with in wars against 'Red Indians' and Mexicans would not wash in a contest with Southern gentlemen."[86] During the time of the 1862 Indian War in Minnesota, Union General Henry Halleck read excerpts from a lecture on the laws of war by Francis Lieber, a professor of history, political science, and law at Columbia College. It was ironic that the United States, at the beginning of one of the world's first modern wars, was turning to an old Prussian soldier for advice. A veteran of the Battle of Waterloo, the Battle of Namur, and the Greek War of Independence, Lieber was well schooled in the traditional rules of war.[87] How would these apply to a form of combat that was fast erasing the distinction between soldier and civilian? General Halleck wrote the professor, requesting a definition of guerrilla war; Lieber replied with two essays, one on guerrilla warfare and another that would form the basis for the Lieber Code.

When the War Department decided to revise and update the rules of land warfare, they appointed Lieber to prepare a draft. The Lieber Code, known as General Order No. 100, was approved by President Lincoln on April 24, 1863. Lieber's 159 articles covered very traditional and practical subjects like guerrilla warfare, captured enemy property, and the treatment of prisoners.[88] The code was significant because it marked the first time in Western history that the government of a sovereign nation established formal guidelines for the conduct of its army in the field. However, the rules were really a codification of long-standing Western military customs.[89]

Most significantly, the Lieber Code drew a sharp line between civilian and soldier. Article 22 states: "Nevertheless, as civilization has advanced during the last centuries, so has likewise steadily advanced, especially in war on land, the distinction between the private individual belonging to a hostile country and the hostile country itself."[90] However, like all warrior's codes, the Lieber Code contained significant loopholes, and Lieber's experience as a soldier informed his decision to define "military necessity" very broadly. For example, a commander was not obliged to give quarter to enemy soldiers if the lives of his men were in danger. Article 27 left a key gray area that granted broad and vague powers under the doctrine of retaliation: "The law of war can no more wholly dispense with retaliation than can the law of nations, of which it is a branch. Yet civilized nations acknowledge retaliation as the sternest feature of war."[91] Article 24 distinguished between "barbaric" and "civilized" military practices: "The almost universal rule in remote times was, and continues to be with barbarous armies, that the private individual of the hostile country is destined to suffer every privation of liberty and protection and every disruption of family ties. Protection was, and still is with uncivilized people, the exception."[92]

Because the federal government refused to recognize the sovereignty of the Confederacy, it did not consider the rebel army lawful combatants. However, given their early battlefield successes, the Union had no choice but to grant them *de facto* recognition by observing the laws of war on the battlefield. Even though the United States considered the Confederates "rebels," they were not considered barbaric "others," a distinction reserved for racial and cultural opponents who flouted the military customs of the West.

Although the Lieber Code was a clear outline of European norms, it already appeared outdated, given contemporary military practices. Ironically, this effort to limit the ravages of war came at a time when armed conflict was growing increasingly destructive and unlimited. The Civil War was nothing less than a preview of the bloody "total" wars of the coming century. None of the prudent restraint of the old European warlords was shown by American generals at Shiloh, Antietam, Gettysburg, and dozens of other battles that left more than 600,000 Americans dead.[93]

Above all, what the Civil War demonstrated was that the military was no longer the praetorian guard of the political elite. It was now an instrument of democracy, and democratic political leaders could not be content to win a limited military victory and strike an advantageous diplomatic solution. Instead, President Lincoln sought an unconditional surrender and to overthrow the preexisting Southern political and social structure.[94] The losers were not simply defeated on the battlefield; their entire social structure was overturned.

General William Tecumseh Sherman was among the first of his generation to realize that modern war could not be waged without the support of the domestic population, who needed to be beaten and demoralized before their army would collapse. His "war is hell" dictum was a harbinger of things to come, as controversial British military historian J. F. C. Fuller pointed out: "Terror was the basic factor in Sherman's policy, he openly says so."[95] As George Nichols, Sherman's aide-de-camp, noted, "the only possible way to end this unhappy and dreadful conflict . . . is to make it terrible beyond endurance."[96] General Sherman, on the eve of his invasion of South Carolina, mentioned the Union Army's desire to settle the score. "The whole army is burning," he wrote, "with an insatiable desire to wreak vengeance upon South Carolina. I almost tremble at her fate, but feel that she deserves all that seems in store for her."[97] As Charleston went up in flames, Sherman remarked: "They have brought it on themselves." When Confederate General John Bell Hood warned his adversary of the implications of his actions, Sherman informed him that "war is cruelty and you cannot refine it. Those who brought war into our country deserve all the curses and maledictions a people can pour out."[98] He asserted, "we are not only fighting hostile armies, but a hostile people, and must make old and young, rich and poor, feel the hard hand of war."[99]

The defeat of the Confederacy was followed by a costly and hugely ambitious social engineering plan known as Reconstruction. Northern troops did more than defeat the Confederate Army on the battlefield; they toppled the government and social institutions that lay at the root of the entire Southern belief system as well.[100] Punishment for wartime atrocities was swift and sure and, like the *U.S.–Dakota War Trials,* provides an excellent example of primitive political justice.

When the war ended and photographs of skeletal-looking Union POWs appeared in Northern newspapers, there was a resounding cry for vengeance. The Union Military Commission charged the Confederate commandant of Andersonville Prison in Georgia, Henry Wirz, under a thirteen-count indictment on August 23, 1865.[101] Wirz was a Swiss immigrant who had married a woman from Kentucky and fought for the Confederacy. Severely wounded in the Battle of Seven Pines, promoted to captain for "bravery on the field of battle," Wirz served as a diplomatic emissary for Jefferson Davis and traveled to Berlin and Paris in 1862. When he returned to the United States in 1864, he was ordered to serve as commandant of the prison.[102]

Designed to hold a maximum of 10,000 men, by August 1864, Andersonville had a population of 33,000, swelled by captives from Sherman's army and the Eastern Theater. An average inmate's daily rations were down to a few tablespoons of salt, beans, and a half pint of unsifted cornmeal.[103] The only source of water was a brackish stream fouled by human excrement and corpses. "If the Yankees should ever come," wrote one Southern woman who surveyed the camp from an observation tower, "and go to Anderson and see the graves there, God have mercy on the land."[104] By the summer of 1864, Union soldiers in Confederate camps were dying by the thousands of gangrene, scurvy, dysentery, and starvation. When intelligence reports filtered back to the North about the conditions in the camps, Secretary of War Stanton charged the Confederacy with instituting "a deliberate system of savage and barbarous treatment."[105]

The majority of the counts in *The Trial of Captain Henry Wirz* charged the camp commandant with personally murdering or abusing inmates. The most far-reaching count of the indictment accused Wirz of having been part of a conspiracy led by Confederate President Jefferson Davis that sought

> to impair and injure the health and to destroy the lives, by subjecting to great torture, and suffering, by confining in unhealthy and unwholesome quarters, by exposing to the inclemency of winter and to the dews and burning sun of summer, by compelling the use of impure water, and by furnishing insufficient and unwholesome food, of a large number of federal prisoners . . . to the end, that the armies of the United States might be weakened and impaired.[106]

Due to lack of evidence, the conspiracy charge was not easily proven. Although the government presented 160 witnesses, none of the alleged victims was named.[107]

Like the *U.S.–Dakota* trials, *The Trial of Captain Henry Wirz* provided a dramatic spectacle of vengeance. Traditionally there had never been a presumption of fairness or impartiality in such events, only a very public display of retribution followed by an amnesty for wartime acts. American leaders would attempt to give legitimacy to this type of proceeding by adding legal trappings to something that had formerly only been about revenge. Unlike the Indian braves who taunted death, Henry Wirz proved a pathetic sight in the courtroom. Due to gangrenous wounds, he was unable to sit in a chair and viewed the proceedings from a couch.[108]

The witnesses painted a Hieronymus Bosch–like portrait of a squalid, overcrowded, and lawless camp. Dr. John C. Bates, a surgeon at Andersonville, described "20,000 or 25,000 prisoners crowded together; some had made holes and burrows in the earth." The strain of gangrene at the camp was so potent that "if a person should perchance stump a toe or scratch the hand, the next report to me was gangrene."[109] Bates "saw men lying partially naked, dirty and lousy in the sand; others were crowded together in small tents. . . . Clothing we had none; the living were supplied with the clothing of those who had died. Of vermin and lice there was a prolific crop." The prisoners lived in a Hobbesian state of nature and did little to help one another: "There was much stealing among them. All lived for himself."[110] Another surgeon at Andersonville described the prisoners as "the most horrible specimens of humanity I ever saw."[111] Prison guard Nazareth Allen and Captain John Heath testified to Wirz's use of stocks, the deadline, and whippings.[112] Union prisoner Abner Kellog described a inmate standing at the Andersonville gate with a "sore on him as large as the crown of my hat, filled with maggots, fly-blown; the sergeant asked Capt. Wirz to have the man carried to the hospital; No, said Wirz; let him stay there and die. The man was afterward carried as a corpse."[113]

Henry Wirz attacked the government's murder charges on the grounds that "In no instances were the name, date, regiment, or circumstances stated in the specifications, and in the whole mass of testimony."[114] His second defense strategy would be employed by Germans nearly a century later: Wirz argued that he was only following orders. "I now bear the odium, and men who were prisoners there seem disposed to wreak their vengeance upon me for what they have suffered, who was only the medium, or I may better say, the tool in the hands of my superiors."[115] Henry Wirz pleaded not guilty to all charges because he had merely followed the orders of General John Winder: "I think I may also claim as a self-evident proposition that if I, a subaltern officer, merely obeyed the legal orders of my superiors in the discharge of my official duties, I cannot be held responsible for the motives that dictated such orders."[116] The prosecution countered that "superior orders" was no defense and in no way mitigated his guilt: "General Winder could no more command the prisoners to violate the laws of war than could the prisoners do so without orders. The conclusion is plain, that where such orders exist both are guilty."[117]

The court found Captain Henry Wirz guilty of "conspiring . . . against the United States, against the laws of war, to impair and injure the health, and to destroy large numbers of Federal prisoners" and sentenced him to death. The sentence was confirmed by President Andrew Johnson on November 3, 1865.[118] Once again an especially odious individual was singled out for summary "justice" and the victors were able to vent their wartime passions in a powerful public spectacle.

The *U.S.–Dakota War Trials* (1862) and the *Trial of Captain Henry Wirz* (1865) provide excellent examples of traditional, limited, and punitive political settlements. Both cases were tried by victor regimes with monopolies on political and military power. The expression *vae victis* or "woe to the conquered" best describes this type of primitive political justice. The drama was completed on November 11, 1865 when Henry Wirz walked to gallows constructed just outside Washington's Old Capital Prison as Union soldiers formed a human corridor and chanted, "Wirz, remember Andersonville!"[119] Although Wirz was portrayed in Southern accounts as a hero and a martyr, the mortality rate at Andersonville was 29 percent, while the mortality rate at the Union prison at Johnson's Island was 2 percent.[120]

More important than the trial of Captain Henry Wirz was the fact that the Lieber Code was fast providing the foundation for a body of treaty law that codified the customary rules of war.[121] Lieber's prediction that his General Order No. 100 would "be adopted as a basis for similar works for the English, French, and Germans" soon came true.[122] Although it was heartening that Prussia adopted the Lieber Code in 1870 to govern its forces in the Franco-Prussian War, the American Civil War had shown a new, horrible face of conflict—industrial total war that blurred the line between soldier and civilian. It was ironic that the new international humanitarian laws were being formulated at a time when America's Indian wars were entering their most brutal phase.

About six hundred Cheyenne and Arapaho Indians established a winter camp at an elbow-shaped bend at Sand Creek, Colorado in November 1864. The Indians had enjoyed good relations with the American army commander, Wyn Koop, at the nearby fort, and he had granted them permission to camp at the creek.[123] In late November, Koop was replaced by Major Anthony, who immediately ordered the Indians to surrender all of their weapons and told the chiefs that they would be safe as long as they flew the American flag.[124] Anthony also informed the Indian leaders that their rations would be cut in half and gave them permission to leave the area to hunt buffalo. Many of the braves departed for the hunting grounds and some of the Arapaho headed south, as they did not trust "the red-eyed soldier."[125] Reinforcements arrived from the Third Colorado Regiment under the command of a Methodist minister named Colonel J. M. Chivington. This six-hundred-man cavalry force had been formed specifically to fight Indians.[126]

Colonel Chivington had barely gotten off his horse before he informed Major Scott Anthony that the time for "wading in the gore" had come.[127] Although Chivington wanted to attack the Indian camp at Sand Creek, there was some dissent to the brash newcomer's bloodlust. Captain Silas Soule, Captain Joseph Cramer, and Lieutenant James Conner reminded their commanders of their promises made to the Indians and argued that an attack on the Sand Creek camp "would be murder in every sense of the word."[128] Colonel Chivington damned "any man who sympathizes with Indians" and announced that he had "come to kill Indians, and believe it is right and honorable to use any means under God's heavens to kill Indians."[129]

The next day seven hundred mounted American soldiers moved out in four columns. Colonel Chivington was reported to have ordered his men "to kill and scalp all, big and little; nits make lice."[130] Chivington grew impatient with his Indian guide and rousted a rancher named Robert Bent from his bed to lead them to the Indian camp. Bent was married to a Cheyenne woman, and his three sons were with their Indian relatives at Sand Creek.[131] Of the six hundred or so Indians at the camp, two thirds were women and children; most of the warriors were away hunting buffalo.[132]

The Cheyenne and Arapaho felt and heard the hoofbeats before they saw the mounted U.S. soldiers approaching at a full gallop. The Indians all began to run to the American flag and the white flag that were flying prominently on a lodgepole in front of Chief Black Kettle's encampment. The rancher noted the presence of the flags, "in so conspicuous a position that they must have been seen."[133] The rancher heard the chief "call to his people not to be afraid, that the soldiers would not hurt them; then troops opened fire from two sides of the camp."[134]

This was a full-scale massacre in which no quarter was given and no prisoners were taken. When twenty or thirty women were found hiding in a hole, they sent out a young girl with a white flag on a stick; "she had not proceeded ten steps when she was shot and killed. All the squaws in that hole were afterwards killed."[135] Not content with simply killing the Indians, many soldiers dismounted and set about mutilating the bodies in what would become one of the darkest episodes in the annals of American military history.[136] One soldier bragged that he planned to make a tobacco pouch out of the penis and testicles of one Indian leader. Another recalled, "I saw one squaw cut open with an unborn child, as I thought, lying by her side. . . . I heard one man say that he had cut out a woman's private parts and had them for exhibit on a stick."[137] Colonel Chivington would later claim that his forces had killed 400 to 500 Indian warriors at Sand Creek. In truth the Third Colorado Regiment killed only 28 men; the other 105 dead were women and children.[138] No matter, the former Methodist minister returned to Denver a hero, and the 100 Indian scalps collected by Chivington's forces were put on display in a Denver theater.

After the Sand Creek Massacre, the Cheyenne, Arapaho, and Sioux tribes called for a war of revenge on the white men. This would speed the destruction of traditional American Indian life because attacks on frontier outposts were followed by increasingly brutal reprisals by the U.S. Army. One of Geronimo's U.S. Army captors put it best: "His crimes were retail, ours wholesale."[139] British historian Hugh Brogan makes a telling observation about nineteenth-century U.S.–Indian relations: "The records of the American past re-echo with denunciations of the fiendishness of the savages, just as the Negroes were accused of insatiable lust, bloodlust and criminal propensities of all kinds . . . but the Christians themselves raped, scalped, looted, murdered, burned, and tortured, the very deeds by which they justified their contempt and loathing for the Indian."[140]

The Sioux got some revenge in 1866, when they lured an entire regiment of American soldiers into a canyon and killed and scalped all eighty members of the Twenty-Seventh Infantry.[141] When the news reached Washington, General Sherman outlined the final phase of America's Indian policy in a letter to his trusted comrade in arms, General Ulysses S. Grant. Sherman wanted to take his total war strategy a step further: "We must act with vindictive earnestness against the Sioux, even to their extermination, men, women, and children. Nothing else will reach the root of this case."[142] After

General Custer's defeat at Little Big Horn in 1876, General Sherman received presidential authority to assume control of the Sioux reservations and treat the inhabitants as prisoners of war.[143]

The U.S. government maintained that the Sioux had violated the treaty of 1868, which had granted them reservations in the Black Hills of South Dakota and on the Powder River. A new Indian Commission led by Newton Edwards, Bishop Henry Whipple, and Reverend Samuel Hinman traveled to the reservation to meet with Indian leaders. The commission wanted them to sign over their rights to the Black Hills in exchange for a piece of arid land on the Missouri River. Chief Red Dog reminded the Americans that "it is only six years since we came to live on this stream where we are living now and nothing that has been promised us has been done."[144] Another chief pointed out that he had been moved by the Great Father in Washington five times, and each time he had been promised that he would never be moved again: "I think that you had better put the Indians on wheels and you can run them about whenever you wish."[145] According to the terms of the 1868 treaty, any changes in Sioux reservation boundaries required the signatures of three quarters of the tribe's males. This would be impossible to obtain because more than half of the warriors were off the reservation with the more militant leaders, Sitting Bull and Crazy Horse.[146]

The commission gave the chiefs a week to discuss their proposal and deemed all Indians off the reservation "hostile." Now, "only friendly Indians were covered by the treaty."[147] When the Sioux refused to sign over the Black Hills and their hunting grounds on the Powder River, the American delegation threatened to cut all their government rations. Faced with the starvation of their women and children, chiefs Red Cloud and Spotted Tail signed the additions to the 1868 treaty.[148]

Historian Hermann Hagedorn, author of *Roosevelt in the Badlands*, described the Indian wars of the 1880s as "peculiarly atrocious warfare. Many white men shot whatever Indians they came upon like coyotes, on sight; others captured them, when they could, and, stripping them of their clothes, whipped them till they bled."[149] Future American President Theodore Roosevelt had a less forgiving perspective. In 1886, he wrote: "I suppose I should be ashamed to say that I take the Western view of the Indian. I don't go so far as to think that the only good Indians are dead Indians, but I believe nine out of ten are, and I shouldn't like to inquire too closely in the case of the tenth."[150]

The Indian wars reached their sad and inevitable apogee on December 29, 1890 when Colonel James Forsythe, leading the late George Armstrong

Custer's Seventh Cavalry Regiment, opened fire with rifles and four Hotch-kiss guns on the four hundred Sioux camped at Wounded Knee Creek.[151] When the smoke had cleared and a three-day blizzard passed, at least three hundred Sioux were dead from wounds and exposure. Black Elk summarized the significance of the Wounded Knee Massacre: "I can see that something else died there in the bloody mud, and was buried in the blizzard. A people's dream died there."[152] Twenty Congressional Medals of Honor were awarded to members of the reconstituted Seventh Cavalry for their actions at Wounded Knee.[153]

CHAPTER 2

THE CHANGING RULES OF WAR AND PEACE

IN FITTINGLY PARADOXICAL FASHION, THE UNITED STATES, while driving the American Indians to the brink of extinction, was simultaneously advocating stringent new standards of military conduct for the rest of the world. Though the major legal efforts of the late nineteenth and early twentieth centuries differed in tone, they evolved logically from the Lieber Code.[1] By the late nineteenth century, the efforts to limit war with law grew more intellectually adventurous. Russia's Czar Nicholas II called for a conference on the limitation of armaments in 1898[2] and representatives of twenty-six states met at The Hague that year.[3] Like the Lieber Code, most of the Hague Conventions were practical measures designed to mitigate excessive suffering in war. Rules were laid down relating to the treatment of prisoners, casualties, and spies; flags of truce; capitulation; armistice; and neutrality.[4] Three of the conference's declarations addressed technological developments that fell outside the previously accepted rules of war; bombing from balloons was prohibited for a period of five years and the use of poison gas was banned.

American statesmen were not content to codify customary military law; they wanted to reform statecraft itself by creating a permanent international court.[5] Signatories to the Hague Conventions would resort to the court to settle differences "which could not be adjusted by diplomatic negotiations, and were not of a character compelling or justifying war."[6] The Americans argued that arbitration would eventually replace war as the most common means of conflict resolution, a view based on the assumption that delinquent or aggressive states could be treated under international law the same way that criminals were handled under domestic law.[7] However, this was a difficult proposition: was there a "community" of nations, and if so, would they punish grave human rights violations without a monopoly on state power? The Americans would have to dislodge the keystone of the European state system—sovereignty—to implement their radical new plan. If they could not revoke the principle of sovereign immunity, their plan had no chance.

German leaders were incensed by the implications of the American plan; they were not about to cede at the bargaining table what they had won on the battlefield. Outnumbered and surrounded by hostile neighbors, Germany had no choice but to develop a practical relationship with war. The leadership of the Second Reich believed that treaties to limit arms and provide for "neutral" arbitration of disputes negated their most important strategic advantage: the ability to mobilize and strike more quickly and effectively than any other nation. The Germans also rejected the concept of neutrality, arguing that in international politics there were only friends and enemies. At one point during the Hague Conference, a German representative voiced opposition to a permanent court of arbitration on the ground that such an idea was too radical for his government to accept. The German delegation refused to sign the relevant convention until they had hamstrung the proposed court with limitations. The most significant omission in the final draft was of the phrase "obligatory arbitration." Although the spirit of the convention remained unchanged, it was no longer binding.[8]

Colonel von Schwarzhoff, the military member of the German delegation, rejected mandatory disarmament and instead advocated preparedness and self-reliance: "As for compulsory military service, which is intimately associated with these questions, the German does not regard it as a heavy burden but a sacred patriotic duty, to the performance of which he owes his existence, his prosperity, his future."[9] As historian John Keegan wrote, "The truth of Europe's situation at the turn of the century lay rather with the German than the American."[10]

The 1898 Hague Conference saw the beginning of an American effort to broaden the laws of war to include acts that had previously been considered beyond the realm of objective judgment. Francis Lieber was a soldier; he accepted war as a constant in human affairs and had hoped only that his code would help to mitigate its ill effects. What occurred at The Hague was the tentative first attempt to go beyond laws regulating war to laws governing the conduct of international relations. At the vanguard of this movement were American lawyer-statesmen like Elihu Root and Joseph Choate, who had come of age far from the Byzantine power struggles and diplomatic double-crossing that characterized European international relations. Choate, the American representative at The Hague, claimed war was "an anachronism, like dueling or slavery, something that international society had simply outgrown."[11] However, there was still a duality inherent in the American position.

By 1893, historian Frederick Jackson Turner had deemed the American frontier closed; to him this marked the end of "the first period of American history."[12] John Fiske, an early advocate of Charles Darwin's theory of evolution, coined the term "Manifest Destiny" in an 1880 speech. Fiske believed that the American Anglo-Saxon was "one of the dominant races of the world" and freely admitted the American duality, or as he put it, "the seeming paradoxes" in U.S. policy and argued that "peace can be guaranteed only through war." Many Manifest Destiny advocates were drawing explicitly or implicitly on Darwin's recent work to justify American expansion. In *The Descent of Man* (1871), Darwin had predicted that "at some future period, not very distant as measured by centuries, the civilised races will almost certainly exterminate, and replace, the savage races throughout the world."[13]

To secular advocates of Manifest Destiny like Fiske, it was self-evident that non-Anglo-Saxons like the American Indians must either accept America's civilizing influence or face extinction: "So far as relations of civilization with barbarism are concerned to-day, the only serious question is by what process of modification the barbarous races are to maintain their foothold upon the earth at all."[14] In his book *The Beginnings of New England,* Fiske argued that in wars against "savages," Western armies could fight with significantly less restraint: "the annihilation of the Pequots can be condemned only by those who read history so incorrectly as to suppose that savages, whose business is to torture and slay, can always be dealt with according to methods in use between civilized peoples." Finally, Fiske justified any military action taken against savages and barbarians on the ground of racial superiority: "The world is so made that it is only in that way that the higher races have been able to preserve themselves and carry on their progressive work."[15]

By 1898, Admiral Alfred Thayer Mahan's plan for the U.S. expansion, outlined in his widely read 1890 book, *The Influence of Sea Power Upon History,* was unfolding nicely as the United States was rapidly acquiring overseas territories in both the Pacific (Hawaii and Samoa) and the Caribbean. After crushing the Spanish in Cuba, American leaders had to decide what to do with Spain's other colonial war prize, the Philippine Islands. San Juan Hill veteran Theodore Roosevelt remarked to Senator Henry Cabot Lodge in a June 24, 1898 letter, "Mahan and I talked the Philippines . . . for two hours"; all agreed that the United States "could not escape our destiny there."[16]

The most vexing questions revolved around the Spanish possession of the islands. Twenty-nine-year-old revolutionary leader Emilio Aguinaldo believed that if, with U.S. assistance, he ousted the Spanish from the archipelago, it would become an independent republic. But once the Spanish were defeated in Cuba, President McKinley refused to grant independence to the Philippines.[17] Aguinaldo and a group of prominent Filipinos refused to accept the American assumption of power and declared the Philippines an independent republic on June 18, 1898, holding up the American republic as their model: "Filipino citizens! We are not a savage people; let us follow the example of the Europeans and American nations. . . . Let us march under the flag of Revolution whose watchwords are Liberty, Equality, and Fraternity!"[18]

McKinley's decision to send a 59,000-man expeditionary force to crush the movement for Philippine independence raised a number of difficult questions: how could the champion of liberty and self-determination fight to thwart independence and reimpose colonialism? American leaders justified this action with the language of Manifest Destiny: this was not colonialism; the United States was rescuing the natives from their own barbarism.[19] It was clear that the new laws of war did not apply universally. Britain's Lord Salsbury was very frank about this in a speech at Albert Hall: "One can roughly divide the nations of the world into the living and the dying . . . the living nations will fraudulently encroach on the territory of the dying."[20] At roughly the same time, British forces under the command of General Horatio Herbert Kitchener mowed down approximately 11,000 Sudanese warriors and lost fewer than 100 soldiers in the Battle of Omdurman in 1898. Whether it was the U.S. Army fighting the Sioux on the American plains or European armies fighting in Africa, Western armies had few restraints in nineteenth-century colonial wars.

When President McKinley appointed New York corporate lawyer Elihu Root Secretary of War in 1899, it marked the beginning of a new strategic legalist era in American foreign policy. Political scientist Judith Shklar has defined "legalism" as "the ethical attitude that holds moral conduct to be a matter of rule following, and moral relationships to consist of duties and rights determined by rules."[21] More often than not, the United States would define and redefine these rules according to the needs of policy.

The choice of a Wall Street lawyer to conduct a colonial war says a great deal about the convergence of law and war in twentieth-century American foreign policy. As America's global aspirations grew, so did the need for justifications more sophisticated than Manifest Destiny. The American leaders who wielded law as a political tool most effectively had learned their trade on Wall Street, where what could be justified legally did not have to be justified morally.[22] They would try to apply the same tactics to foreign policy and their "strategic legalism" would become America's dominant "nonideological" ideology.[23]

Elihu Root articulated the American lawyer-statesmens' view in an 1899 letter: "It is not a function of law to enforce the rules of morality."[24] As the United States became a global power, a two-sided relationship with international law developed, and what began as the simple hypocrisy of the age grew into a more profound and lasting tension between the ethical and legal principles and the actual conduct of American foreign policy. At moments of crisis and contradiction, U.S. leaders attempted to rephrase complex moral questions into apolitical disputes that required only the application of law to a set of facts. Was it that simple? American leaders were no longer content to use law for primitive forms of political justice; they were growing more ambitious, and now had the power to back their words with force.

In his first public speech as Secretary of War on October 7, 1899, Elihu Root flatly rejected the calls for Filipino independence and argued that there were no Philippine people, only tribes of barbarians scattered throughout the archipelago. As with America's Indians, if he could deny their civility, he could deny them both natural rights and their territory. The new Secretary of War asked, "Well, whom are we fighting? Are we fighting the Philippine nation? No! . . . There is none."[25] Root saw the American acquisition as a legal question of contracts and titles, not people and sovereignty: "Gentlemen, the title of the America to the island of Luzon is better than the title we had to Louisiana."[26] He declared that the Jeffersonian principle that a government derives its just powers from the consent of the governed did not apply to the Filipinos because they were unfit for self-government: "Nothing can be more misleading than a principle misapplied. . . . Government does not depend on consent. The immutable laws of justice and humanity require that people shall have government, that the weak shall be protected, that cruelty and lust shall be restrained, whether there be consent or not."[27]

According to nineteenth-century German nationalist scholar Heinrich von Treitschke, the laws of war only applied to wars between European nations: "International law becomes phrases if its standards are also applied to barbaric people. To punish a Negro tribe, villages must be burned, and without setting examples of that kind, nothing can be achieved." To apply international law to the indigenous others "would not be humanity or justice but shameful weakness."[28] Root tried to cast the new American soldier less as a warrior than as an ambassador of democracy and Christianity—a social worker with a Springfield rifle: "I claim for him the higher honor that while he is as stern a foe as ever a man saw on the battlefield, he brings the schoolbook, the plow, and the Bible. While he leads the forlorn hope of war, he is the advance guard of liberty and justice, of law and order, and peace and happiness."[29] The task of restraining the "cruelty and lust" of the Philippine insurgents fell to the U.S. military.

The leaders of America's expeditionary force had a more sober opinion of their foes. General Henry Lawton, veteran of twenty-six Civil War battles, recipient of the Congressional Medal of Honor, best known for capturing Geronimo in 1886, called his adversaries in the Philippines "the bravest men I have ever seen."[30] Before he was killed by a sniper's bullet in San Mateo on December 18, 1899, Lawton contradicted Secretary Root's glib assessment of the situation: "Such men have a right to be heard. All they want is a little justice."[31]

Winning this undeclared war was not as easy as American political leaders had imagined. The insurgent forces, despite their inferior weaponry, proved to be fierce and terrifying adversaries. The Filipinos had a great deal of experience fighting invading armies. When the Spanish tried to disarm them, they simply replaced their bolo knives with rattan sticks and the martial art of escrima was born. Although they used firearms whenever possible, the guerrillas' favorite method of attack was with a bolo or machete-type knife in each hand. Because the Filipinos responded to the American invasion with guerrilla warfare, the distinction between soldier and civilian began to disappear. There were a number of instances where the insurgents used the Americans' self-restraint to their strategic advantage, for example, raising a white flag and then opening fire on the approaching troops.[32]

Some of Aguinaldo's orders (captured by the Americans) described a different style of war, far removed from the gentlemanly rules of engagement outlined by Francis Lieber: "The Chief of those who go on to attack the barracks should send in first four men with a good present for the American commander. They should not, prior to the attack, look at the Americans in a threatening manner. To the contrary . . . the attack should be a complete surprise with decision and courage."[33] Three men and a man dressed as a woman would enter the camp and attack only with their bolos: "The Sandatahan should not attempt to secure rifles from their dead enemies, but shall pursue slashing right and left until the Americans surrender."[34] Men on nearby rooftops would drop furniture, boiling oil, molasses, and red-hot iron on retreating American troops passing below.[35]

Although there is no formal record of a policy of not taking prisoners, the U.S. government's own casualty list raises a troubling question: was the army refusing to grant quarter to the Philippine guerrillas? Brigadier General Lloyd Wheaton left Manila and traveled down the bank of the Pasig River in March 1899. One week later, when he reached Laguna de Bay Lake, according to the U.S. Army, his expedition had killed 2,500 Filipinos and lost only 36 men.[36] "In the path of the Washington regiment and Battery D of the Sixth Artillery there were 1,008 dead niggers and a great many wounded," one soldier wrote. "We burned all their houses. I don't know how many men, women and children the Tennessee boys did kill." One infantryman recalled, "They would not take any prisoners."[37] Army Private Barnes's letter to his brother provides strong evidence that the distinction between soldier and civilian had disappeared in the Philippines: "I am probably growing hard-hearted, for I am in my glory when I can sight my gun on some dark skin and pull the trigger. Should a call for volunteers be made for this place do not be so patriotic as to come here."[38]

During the bloodiest battles of the American Civil War, the ratio of dead to wounded soldiers was never higher than 1:5. At Gettysburg, for example, 2,834 were killed and 13,709 wounded. Even in Great Britain's brutal Boer War, the dead-to-wounded ratio was 1:4. In the Philippines the ratio of dead to wounded guerrillas was an astounding 5:1, five dead for every wounded man.[39] As early as 1899, soldiers like Captain Edwin Boltwood wrote that "On more than one battlefield they were treated like Indians. At Caloocan I saw natives shot down that could have been prisoners, and the whole country around Manila set ablaze with apparently no other object than to teach the natives submission by showing them that with the Americans war was hell."[40]

Secretary of War Elihu Root announced in December 1900 that the United States would adopt the "methods which have proved successful in our Indian camps in the West" to defeat the insurgents.[41] General Arthur MacArthur placed Philippine civilians under martial law, and the U.S. military resettled much of the population into concentration camps throughout the island chain. Not unlike the methods employed by the Spanish in Cuba and the British in South Africa, anyone found outside of the resettlement camps was considered hostile and shot on sight. Soldiers relied on a favorite Spanish torture technique called "the water cure" to get information from prisoners. Gallons of water mixed with salt were funneled down the throat and nose of the victim, coupled with a few blows to the stomach; this made even the hardest guerrillas talk.[42] When reporters tried to file stories about the harsh nature of this war, they were censored. The journalists became so enraged by the U.S. government's attempts to silence them that in February 1900, eleven reporters denounced the censorship in a letter sent by regular mail (to avoid army censors) to Hong Kong.[43] By this time, prominent citizens were lining up against the American annexation of the Philippines. The anti-imperialist outcry was led by Andrew Carnegie, Samuel Gompers, William Jennings Bryan, Mark Twain, and others who wondered how the brutal suppression of an indigenous independence movement served American interests.

When President McKinley was assassinated in 1901, Vice President Theodore Roosevelt assumed the Presidency. A veteran of the Spanish-American War, Roosevelt had no moral qualms about annexing the Philippines. Like Senators Henry Cabot Lodge and Albert Beveridge, he was a confident exponent of Manifest Destiny.[44] Senator Beveridge argued, "God has been preparing the English-speaking and Teutonic peoples for a thousand years for nothing but vain and idle self-admiration? No! He has made us the master organizers of the world where chaos reigns."[45] President Roosevelt considered the war against Spain "a great anti-imperialist stride."[46] Like Secretary Root, he compared the Filipinos to American Indians: "Of course the presence of our troops in the Philippines . . . has no more to do with military imperialism than their presence in the Dakotas, Minnesota and Wyoming during the many years which elapsed before the final outbreaks of the Sioux were definitely put down." To Roosevelt, granting independence to Aguinaldo and his followers "would be like granting self-government to an Apache reservation under some local chief."[47] After Emilio Aguinaldo was captured in an elaborate ruse on March 23, 1901, the war entered its most brutal phase. By that time, the last insurgent strongholds were the island of Samar and southern Luzon. American generals like Lloyd Wheaton recommended that the United States emulate the colonial methods that the Europeans "found necessary . . . through centuries of experience in dealing with Asiatics."[48]

September 26, 1901, was an exciting day for the seventy-four American soldiers stationed at the small garrison at Balangiga on the island of Samar. They were about to receive their first mail in four months. The American commander, a "puritanical Irish Catholic" captain named Thomas Connell, was in the process of "cleaning and civilizing" the town. The Filipino mayor asked Connell if men could "work off back taxes" by laboring for the Americans. When Connell agreed, the mayor contacted rebel leader Vicente Lukban, who transferred one hundred of his best soldiers to masquerade as laborers.[49] The guerrillas worked peacefully for two weeks before they struck.[50] When the American mail boat arrived in the evening of September 26 it delivered the news of President McKinley's assassination. Captain Connell ordered his men to make preparations for a memorial service in honor of the fallen president the next day.[51] The following morning, after a 6:30 reveille, the troops began to eat in an outdoor dining area, their rifles were stacked outside their barracks. When the church bell rang, a conch shell blew and hundreds of Filipinos descended on the camp, swinging bolos and hatchets. Most of the officers were killed in their quarters; many in the dining area were butchered in their chairs. A cook armed with a cleaver threw cans and pots of boiling water to stave off a blur of slashing bolomen. After Captain Connell was hacked to death, Sergeant Breton took command of the American survivors. They gathered in a British square infantry formation and killed approximately 250 Filipinos (in the end, 59 Americans were killed at Balangiga, 23 were wounded, and only six came away unscathed).

When the survivors of the Balangiga massacre arrived at the American garrison at Basey, the American commander, Captain Bookmiller, planned a reprisal mission. He led fifty-five of his men and the six uninjured survivors back to Balangiga on the gunboat *Pittsburgh*. When the Americans returned to the scene of the massacre, they found Captain Connell's corpse decapitated and a fire smouldering in his nearby head. Also missing was the finger on which he wore his West Point ring. The American troops stumbled upon a mass funeral for the Filipinos killed at Balangiga and immediately captured twenty men; the soldiers ordered them to remove the Filipino dead from their mass grave and to replace them with the American dead. The soldiers built a giant fire and began to burn the exhumed Filipinos. According to historian Stuart Creighton Miller, as the pyre's flames leaped in the background and the bodies burned, Captain Bookmiller read from the Bible: "They have sown the wind and they shall reap the whirlwind."

Bookmiller then handed the twenty prisoners over to the survivors from Company C, and as they were being executed, the Americans set the town ablaze. Captain Bookmiller reported back to Manila, "Buried dead, burned town, returned Basey."[52]

General "Hell Roaring" Jacob Smith was sent to Samar to put down the insurgents. Another old Indian fighter who had participated in the Wounded Knee Massacre in 1890, Smith told one group of reporters that fighting Philippine rebels was "worse than fighting Indians." According to Miller, "he had already adopted the appropriate tactics that he had learnt fighting 'savages' in the American West, without waiting for orders to do so from General Otis." Smith had made a name for himself as an aggressive leader. Traveling to Balangiga with him were Marine Major Littleton Waller and three hundred U.S. Marines.[53] When the relief party finally arrived, they saw a man hanging out of a window. His face was hard to make out because it was covered with swarming ants. Upon closer inspection, they could see that his eyes were gouged out, his face was cut from nose to throat, and the wound was filled with jam. They were horrified to find that hogs had dug up and partly eaten the American bodies that Captain Bookmiller and his men had carefully buried.[54] When a Major Combe entered the town, he found more atrocities: "a deep wound across the face of Lieutenant Bumpus had been filled with jam"; another man had "his abdomen cut open and codfish and flour had been put in the wound."[55]

According to Major Combe, the guerrillas had consistently and flagrantly violated the laws of war: "No prisoners of war were taken. Noncombatants were put to death. Poison was used. Flags of truce were not respected and persons traveling under their protection were killed."[56] After General Smith examined the carnage, he issued the following orders to Major Waller: "I want no prisoners. I wish you to kill and burn. The more you kill and burn, the better you will please me. The interior of Samar must be a howling wilderness." Even a seasoned veteran like Waller was shocked by Smith's order, and when he passed it on to Captain David Porter, he tempered it: "Porter, I've had instructions to kill everyone over ten years old. But we are not making war upon women and children, only on men capable of bearing arms. Keep that in mind no matter what other orders you receive."[57] Captain Porter, also present when Smith issued his order, would later claim that the general's command was a reprisal for the Balangiga Massacre and that this was clearly allowed by Article 24 of the Lieber Code: "After describing the situation General Smith spoke of the 'need to adopt a policy that will create in the minds of the people a burning desire for the war to cease.'"[58] Smith was voicing what had been American policy for most of the war. The *Manila Times* gave this account of General Smith's first ten days on Samar: "He already ordered all natives to present themselves in certain of the coastal towns saying that *those who were found outside would be shot and no questions asked.* The time limit had expired ... and General Smith was as good as his word."[59] Major Waller reported from Basey, "in accordance with my orders, destroyed all villages and houses, burning in all 165." Smith recommended a decoration for Waller, who was "an officer of exceptional merit and carries out my wishes and instructions loyally and gallantly."[60]

When news of General Smith's orders reached the United States, however, there was an uproar that threatened to derail Roosevelt's Philippine policy. An American officer who served in the war wrote in a letter to the *Philadelphia Ledger* on November 11, "Our men have been relentless, have killed to exterminate men, women, and children, prisoners, and captives, active insurgents and suspected people, from lads of ten up, an idea prevailing that the Filipino was little better than a dog."[61]

In early January 1902, Major Waller launched an ill-fated land campaign in which his troops got lost and ran out of supplies. When Waller and the remnants of his forces returned from the field, he charged eleven of his Philippine porters with "treachery" and had them shot by a firing squad. He informed his superiors that he had had "to expend eleven prisoners" just as a Senate investigation into the Philippine War was getting under way in Washington.[62]

Subsequently Secretary of War Root cabled General Adna Chaffee and ordered a number of the participants to Manila:

> The President intends to back up the army in the heartiest fashion in every lawful and legitimate method of doing its work, he also intends to see that the most rigorous care is exercised to detect and prevent any cruelty or brutality, and that men guilty thereof are punished. Great as the provocation has been in dealing with foes who habitually resort to treachery, murder, and torture against our men, nothing can justify or will be held to justify, the use of torture or inhuman conduct of any kind on the part of the American Army.[63]

Major Littleton Waller was brought before military court in Manila in March 1902. The anti-imperialist press in the United States called him "the butcher of Samar" and compared his actions to Lord Kitchener's in the Boer War. Major Waller was tried by a five-man court-martial presided over by Major General William Bisbee on March 7. Although Waller admitted to ordering executions, he claimed that they were justified by both General Smith's orders and the laws of war. The Marine officer described similar executions he had witnessed in Egypt in 1892 and China in 1900 and used the Lieber Code to justify his actions as reprisals, "the sternest feature of war." When Major General Jacob Smith appeared in court as a witness for the prosecution and tried to claim that the Marine had acted on his own by executing the prisoners, a shocked Major Waller produced both General Smith's written orders and witnesses who convincingly refuted Smith.[64] Although he was found not guilty of murder and sentenced only to a loss of pay, Waller had implicated Smith, whose order to kill and burn was condemned in the strongest terms by the anti-imperialist press in the United States. The headline of the April 8, 1902 *New York Journal* read, "KILL ALL: Major Waller Ordered to Massacre the Filipinos." The media focused their enmity on Jacob Smith, now known as "Howling Jake," or more simply, "The Monster." The United States would have to investigate him to extinguish this controversy. Like Waller, Smith argued that his action was totally justified by the Lieber Code. When President Roosevelt signed the indictment of Jacob Smith on April 21, 1902, the general was not charged with murder or war crimes; instead, he faced the far more benign charge of "conduct to the prejudice of good order and military discipline."[65]

The Jacob Smith case, very different from the primitive political justice exercised in the Sioux and the Wirz cases, was an early example of American strategic legalism. The Roosevelt administration needed to close the gap between words and deeds in its Philippine policy, so Secretary Root attempted to use judicial machinery to resolve a controversial political problem that threatened to undermine the larger American foreign policy objectives. When the trial began, most of the witnesses were very friendly to General Smith and attempted to establish the savage and irregular nature of their foes. Lieutenant Baines testified: "All the natives that I have seen in the interior of Samar, outside of the towns, were what I consider savages; they were very low intelligence, treacherous, cruel; seemed to have no feeling, either for their families or for anybody else."[66] Lieutenant Hoover stated that the fighting ability of twelve-year-old guerrillas was sufficient that they should be considered both "legitimate and fearsome, maniacal adversaries."[67] Lieutenant Ayer testified: "When one gets to the interior among the tribes who live there, religious fanaticism, stolid indifference, and great personal bravery are conspicuously in evidence."[68] Major Waller testified that under the laws of war he was not obliged to give quarter and again cited the Lieber Code. "General Orders, No. 100, covers it. For instance, if in actual experience we find that certain bands give us no quarter, or surrender and then become treacherous immediately afterwards—and we had that experience several times—we had a perfect right under the laws of war to shoot anybody belonging to that band."[69] Waller said that he tempered General Smith's order: "Always when prisoners came in and gave themselves up they were saved, they were not killed—not slaughtered, at that time. But in the field, whenever they opposed us we fought until there was nothing else to fight."[70] His testimony demonstrated how blurry the line between soldier and civilian was in the war in the Philippines.

> Q: What do you mean by insurrectos in the island of Samar?
> WALLER: I mean those people actually bearing arms against us or who were openly aiding or abetting the insurrection.
> Q: Whether they had arms or not?
> WALLER: They all had arms. Even the women carried arms.[71]

The court ruled that General Smith "did not mean everything that his unexplained language implied." After hearing the court's decision, one paper reported that an unrepentant Jacob Smith turned to the press in the courtroom and declared "he meant every word and that burning and shooting 'the treacherous savages' was the only way to win the war." Although he had been found guilty of the vague crime of "prejudicing officers," Smith was not sentenced and boarded a steamship bound for the United States on August 1, 1902. In a letter, President Roosevelt recalled a conversation with Inspector General Breckinridge about Smith. Breckinridge told the President, "he met him [Smith] and asked him what he was doing, he responded, 'Shooting niggers.' Breckinridge thought this a joke. I did not."[72] The proceedings of the general court-martial were submitted to Roosevelt, who made the final ruling. The President qualified his decision:

> I am well aware of the danger and difficulty of the task our Army has had in the Philippine Islands and of the . . . intolerable provocations it has received from the cruelty treachery, and total disregard of the rules and customs of civilized warfare on the part of its foes. I also heartily approve of the employment of the sternest measures necessary to put a stop to such atrocities, and to bring this war to a close.[73]

Roosevelt was careful to distinguish the American atrocities as exceptional events and praised the army's "wonderful kindness and forbearance in dealing with their foes." Smith's order was considered an "isolated incident," not a matter of policy. "Loose and violent talk by an officer of high rank is always likely to excite to wrongdoing . . . [those] among his subordinates whose will are weak or whose passions are strong," Roosevelt wrote. General Smith's offense was mitigated by "a long career distinguished for gallantry and on the whole for good conduct." Finally, the President ordered General Smith "retired from the active list."[74]

Shortly after the trials, antiwar activists Moorefield Storey and Julian Cadman wrote a 119-page pamphlet analyzing Elihu Root's handling of the atrocities and concluded that the trials had been a farce. Storey wrote that Root "was silent in the face of certain knowledge and by his silence he made himself responsible for all that was done in his acquiescence. . . . Mr. Root, then is the real defendant in this case. The responsibility for what has disgraced the American name lies at his door."[75]

The War Department telegraphed a summary of the attack to Secretary of War Root. In response, Root argued that the guerrillas had waged war "with the barbarous cruelty common among uncivilized races, and with the general disregard for the laws of civilized warfare."[76] Although he defended the American military's "scrupulous regard for the rules of civilized warfare," when pressed, he offered a more complex defense, pointing to the "history and the conditions of the warfare with cruel and treacherous savages who inhabited the island" and offering two "precedents of the highest authority."[77] The first was George Washington's 1779 order to General John Sullivan to carry out reprisals against hostile Iroquois Indians; the second was General William T. Sherman's reprisal order after the Fort Kearney Massacre in 1866. Historian Richard Drinnon attaches great importance to these selections: "Now, in the process of ransacking the War Department records for authorizations of terror, Root had unwittingly disclosed . . . important and related truths. The first was that the national past contained authorizations of terror and could easily be made to share the guilt of current killings, hurtings and burnings."[78]

In the Jacob Smith case, strategic legalism came in the form of a vague indictment, a sympathetic court, and a narrow reading of the laws of war that in the end produced little more than a symbolic chastisement. This action allowed the U.S. government to admonish a scapegoat and to deem the atrocities isolated incidents, the work of a "few bad apples." An important element of strategic legalism was and remains the public-private split.

Once the public has been served its symbolic "justice," post-trial, nonjudicial legal "devices," like pardon, clemency, and parole, are used to mitigate the original sentence. The case of American Lieutenant Preston Brown provides a good example. Tried in Manila and found guilty of killing a prisoner of war, Brown was originally sentenced to five years of hard labor. However, after the trial, Secretary of War Root quietly reduced his sentence to the loss of half his pay for nine months and a demotion in the army promotions list.[79]

By the time the United States prevailed in the Philippines, approximately 200,000 Filipinos and 5,000 Americans were dead.[80] The duality in America's relationship with international law was personified by Elihu Root. With no sense of hypocrisy or contradiction, he defended America's brutal colonial acquisition on the narrowest positive legal grounds, while simultaneously advocating a radical expansion of international law. As historian Godfrey Hodgson points out, "It is hard to avoid the judgment that Root did know that things had gone badly wrong in the Philippines, and that he used his lawyer's skill with words to deny charges that were in substance true."[81] To men like Roosevelt and Root there was nothing odd about this duplicity—they believed that equity only existed among equals. Again, there were clearly two sets of rules and American leaders were very candid about this until the twentieth century.

Many of the Americans who were beginning to dominate the field of international law were high-level corporate lawyers from New York City. The late New York Senator Daniel Patrick Moynihan noted, "This indeed gave a legalist cast to American foreign relations that was distinctive among nations."[82] Under the strategic Monroe Doctrine, American leaders could create and enforce stern new rules for the rest of the world to follow while keeping a free hand in the Western Hemisphere. Addressing a group in New York in December 1904, Elihu Root declared, "Today the United States is practically sovereign on this continent, and its fiat is law upon the subjects to which it confines its interposition."[83]

President Theodore Roosevelt negotiated an end to the Russo-Japanese War at the Lotos Club on Fifth Avenue in New York City in 1905. Encouraged by the success of this effort, he called for a second conference at The Hague. The American delegation was led by Joseph Choate, General G. B. Davis, Admiral Charles Sperry, David Hill, General Horace Porter, and Dr. James B. Scott. The group was given special marching orders from (now) Secretary of State Root, who urged them to take the most "progressive" view and to "always keep in mind the promotion of this continuous

process through which the progressive development of international justice and peace may be carried on."[84] Forty-four nations convened in The
Hague in June 1907. Because the first conference had more or less codified
the practical rules of war, the second could address more radical issues like
international arbitration.

When the American delegation pressed for an international court with
compulsory jurisdiction, the Germans again refused to relinquish their
national interests to a court. Foreign Minister Bernard von Bülow ordered
the German delegation to omit all references to obligatory jurisdiction.[85] In
the end, the second Hague Conference succeeded in further defining the
rules of war and committing more nations to observing them, but again,
America's more ambitious plans were foiled by German conservatism. It
was obvious that the Germans were not comfortable with the American assumption that war could be judged legitimate or illegitimate. To them, it
was an instrument of policy bound by its own set of rules.[86]

Undaunted, Secretary of War Root said that the second conference provided concrete evidence that the world "had entered upon a more orderly
process."[87] Joseph Choate went one step further, describing the accom-
plishments of the conference in the grandest terms: "And so at last, after
three centuries, will be realized the dream of Grotius, the founder of international law, that all civilized nations of the earth will submit to its dictates,
whether in war or peace."[88] Choate's celebration of the "completion of a
century of unbroken peace between ourselves and all of the other great nations of the earth" begs another question: did the skirmishes with Indians,
Mexicans, and Filipinos simply not count? The movement at the second
Hague conference was for equity among established powers.

Because the German contingent was unwilling to consent to America's
new conception of international order, they were branded "troublemakers"
by U.S. leaders. Elihu Root called Germany "the great disturber of peace
in the world." In a 1909 letter to Andrew Carnegie, Root declared that "the
obstacle to the establishment of arbitration agreements, to the prevention
of war, to disarmament, to the limitation of armaments, to all attempts to
lessen the suspicions and alarm of nations toward each other, is Germany,
who stands, and has persistently stood since I have been familiar with foreign affairs, against that kind of progress."[89] The United States prepared for
a third Hague Conference, scheduled for 1914, but it never convened, as
hopes for international peace were dashed by a bullet in Sarajevo.

Although the American Civil War had provided a preview of twentieth-
century military conflict, it had been only a dress rehearsal for the "war to

end all wars." The colonial conflicts of the nineteenth century did not prepare European armies for the trench battles of the Western Front, where combat was no longer a matter of killing natives armed with rattan sticks and bolo knives.[90] Modern democracy profoundly changed the nature and objectives of warfare. "Speaking for their peoples, governments demanded extraordinary rewards for unprecedented national sacrifices," wrote Major-General J. F. C. Fuller. "Specifically, they sought either the total defeat and subjugation of the enemy, or a reorganization of the European and world community that would make war impossible—two goals which they proved unable to achieve."[91]

The outbreak of World War I in 1914 demonstrated how vulnerable international law was to the aggressive policies of a nation ready, willing, and able to employ military force. Once national survival was at stake, international law fell victim to German military necessity or "*Kriegsraison*." When it appeared to the Kaiser and the General Staff that war was inevitable, they launched their much-vaunted Schlieffen Plan.[92] Germany planned to encircle France and attack quickly in the west before engaging Russia in the east.[93] The problem with the plan was that it required a massive violation of Belgian neutrality (which had been guaranteed by a treaty in 1911 and reassured in 1913).[94] German Chancellor Bethman Hollweg candidly acknowledged this in an address to the Reichstag: "Gentlemen, we are now in a state of necessity and necessity knows no law. Our troops have already entered Belgian territory. Gentlemen, that is a breach of international law."[95]

The Schlieffen Plan failed to produce a quick victory. The Belgian army counterattacked and forced their foes back to Louvain. Over the next two days, the Germans killed more than two hundred civilians and burned parts of the old medieval city. They did not treat captured civilian combatants as prisoners of war but as "*franc-tireurs*," unlawful combatants not protected by the laws of war. The British press told horrendous tales of "Hunish atrocities"; however, these "war crimes" were not as clear cut as the British and American press made them out to be. The German government correctly argued that in order to be protected by the laws of war, armed opponents needed to be members of an identifiable and organized military force. Civilians could not offer armed resistance at one moment and claim immunity on the ground that they were civilians the next.[96] Five American newspaper correspondents attached to the German army in Belgium cabled the Associated Press: "In the spirit of fairness we unite in declaring German atrocities groundless."[97] When stories of "Hunish" illegal warfare filtered back to Great Britain, learned legal arguments fell on deaf ears. British

Prime Minister Herbert Asquith described the German action as "a shameless holocaust . . . lit up by blind barbarian vengeance."[98]

The failure of the Germans to secure a quick victory in Belgium gave England time to send troops to reinforce the French. The Russians also mobilized more quickly than anticipated and when they attacked Germany from the east, von Moltke recalled reinforcements meant for his end run through Belgium. Although the Russians were repelled, by the fall of 1914 the Germans were bogged down in France. As the Western Front settled down to trench warfare, battalion after battalion manned the ladders and threw themselves "over the top," but infantry charges proved no match for the machine gun.[99] In five months—July 1 to November 18, 1916—the British lost 419,654 and the French nearly 200,000.[100]

The term "war crimes" was first widely used during and after World War I. More often than not, war crimes accusations were propaganda designed to fuel the moral outrage necessary for modern war. Neither side was quick to prosecute those charged during wartime because they feared reprisals.[101] A number of people in Britain and France began a movement that aimed to try the German Kaiser for "war crimes" after World War I. The German government feared such prosecutions for a different reason. The ever-practical General Staff believed that if common soldiers were encouraged to examine orders as international legal questions, military discipline would disintegrate.[102]

The German leaders would soon find out that morality has a prudential role in any foreign policy.[103] Flagrant violations of the law of nations and insensitivity to the subsequent international outcry doomed the Reich in the now important court of public opinion.[104] This lack of prudence was demonstrated in 1915 when German authorities captured Edith Cavell, the head of a nursing school in Brussels, and charged her with helping 600 British prisoners to escape. Under German military law, aiding and abetting the escape of the enemy was punishable by death.[105] Hours after Cavell confessed and was found guilty by a military court, she was shot by a firing squad.[106] As historian James Willis notes, Cavell's execution was a typical German miscalculation, "an example of a lack of sensitivity to world public opinion. . . . Even those sympathetic described the German action as one characterized by 'incredible stupidity.'"[107]

Technological advances posed even more vexing questions about the laws of war. If the small German fleet had observed existing regulations, the sailors would have signed their own death warrants. Maritime law required submarines to surface, warn the targeted ship of its imminent destruction, and allow the crew to lower the lifeboats before sinking the vessel. Although this sounded sporting enough, the early submarines were slow and frail, and the British were not passive victims of submarine aggression. The British Admiralty had issued standing orders for merchant vessels to ram German submarines.[108] Armed British merchantmen "used decoy ships to lure U-boats into traps, flew neutral flags, and rammed whenever possible any submarines that complied with international law by surfacing to warn British merchant vessels of imminent destruction."[109] Once the merchant vessels were armed they technically became warships. The situation was further complicated when the Associated Powers invoked the legal doctrines of retaliation and contraband without officially declaring a blockade.[110]

The most famous British war crime occurred in 1915 when a merchant ship, H.M.S *Barlong*, sank German submarine *U-27* and shot the surviving crew members.[111] The German reprisal was swift and draconic. After a U-boat captured the British steamship *Brussels* on July 27, 1916, German POW authorities determined that British captain Charles Fryatt had attempted to ram a German U-boat a year earlier. A German navy court-martial tried Fryatt, declared him a *franc-tireur* who had committed a "crime against armed German sea forces," sentenced him to death, and executed him all on the same day.[112]

The British steamship *Llandovery Castle* was returning to England after having delivered wounded and sick Canadian soldiers to Halifax, Nova Scotia in June 1916. The ship left Halifax for England with 258 crew members aboard. On the night of June 27, it was intercepted by German submarine *U-86*, captained by First Lieutenant Helmutt Patzig. Although the steamer was clearly marked with Red Cross flags and lights according to the Tenth Hague Convention of 1907, *U-86* fired a torpedo that hit the *Llandovery Castle* squarely, and the ship sank in only 10 minutes, in the middle of the deep, black Atlantic, 116 miles southwest of Fastnet, Ireland.[113]

Of the five lifeboats lowered by Second Officer Chapman, only three managed to escape being pulled under by the sinking ship. The boat that contained Chapman was rescuing survivors when *U-86* surfaced and called for the lifeboats to pull alongside. When they didn't comply, a pistol was fired as a warning and the lifeboats went up to the submarine. Captain Sylvester was taken aboard and accused of having eight American airmen on the *Llandovery Castle*. Two Canadian medical corpsmen were also taken aboard the sub and questioned, but all three men denied that they were pilots and were released. *U-86* submerged, only to reappear and demand that two of the ship's officers come aboard for an interrogation. They were asked to explain why the ship had exploded so violently if it was not carrying munitions. The officers were released and the submarine disappeared for a second time. The third time, *U-86* surfaced like a great white shark, headed for Captain Sylvester's lifeboat, then veered slightly at the last moment and avoided the boat. The submarine circled, made another close pass, and vanished into the inky depths. The survivors in the captain's lifeboat were rigging a small sail when they heard firing, and two shells sailed over their boat. Thirty-six hours later, one lifeboat was picked up by the British destroyer *Lysander*. Captain Sylvester and the 23 men in it were the only survivors of the *Llandovery Castle*.[114] The day after the sinking of the hospital ship, First Lieutenant Patzig of *U-86* held a meeting and made his crew swear an oath of silence about the previous night's activities.

When Germany accused the Associated Powers of using hospital ships to ferry troops and munitions in 1917, British officials claimed that the munitions were defensive.[115] The German government announced that due to what they considered to be a double standard—their enemies could transport men and arms clandestinely while their submarines were required to surface before attacking—they would wage unrestricted submarine warfare; all ships would be sunk without warning. American President Woodrow Wilson claimed that the use of submarines violated the "law and principles of humanity," and this would not be tolerated by the "civilized world."[116] It is interesting to note that Wilson did not invoke the laws of war but the laws of "humanity." As a result of the German resumption of unrestricted submarine warfare, the United States entered World War I on April 6, 1917.

The American entry transformed the conflict into a contest between civilizations. At the time, Secretary of State Elihu Root announced: "To be safe, democracy must kill its enemy when it can and where it can. The world cannot be half democratic and half autocratic. It must be all democratic or all Prussian. There can be no compromise. If it is all Prussian, there can be no real international peace."[117] Root advocated a muscular brand of American legalism that was prepared to use force to uphold treaties. He believed that if Germany's flagrantly illegal invasion of Belgium and conduct during the war were tolerated, the Hague rules and other advances in international law would be reduced to "mere scraps of paper." According to Root, democracy could only survive by "destroying the type of government which has shown itself incapable of maintaining respect for law and justice and resisting the temptation of ambition."[118] By 1918, he described World War I as nothing less than a battle between "Odin and Christ."[119]

There was much less clamor over massive atrocities committed outside of Europe. This pointed to a duality not only in American foreign policy but also in international law. Rather than expel or resettle Turkey's minority Armenian population, Turkish leaders chose simply to kill them. When Turkey's Ittihad allied with Germany, its "Young Turk" leaders enslaved the Armenians and forced them to build public works projects. By 1915, according to David Kaiser,

> the Young Turks decided . . . to solve the problem of the Armenian minority by exterminating the Armenians. . . . But the deportation was only a pretext: the Turks shot Armenian men and marched the Armenian women and children into the mountains and the desert, where they starved to death. Between 1 and 1.5 million Armenians perished.[120]

The U.S. government was divided over its official response. Although the U.S. Ambassador to Turkey, Henry Morgenthau, spoke out against the massacres, the State Department took a different view. In 1915, the governments of France, Great Britain, and Russia declared the Turkish atrocities "crimes against humanity and civilization" and threatened to hold the ringleaders "personally responsible."[121] However, American leaders neither supported nor took actions against the perpetrators.

The German government agreed to an armistice on November 11, 1918. When President Woodrow Wilson unveiled his revolutionary peace plan, war crimes were a minor detail. His outline for a new international political system was by far the most radical American attempt to dislodge the cornerstone of the old European state system—sovereignty. Wilson's "Fourteen Points" set out to model international relations after a modern constitutional democracy, complete with "consent of the governed, equality of rights, and freedom from aggression." Points 1 through 5 proposed the creation of an international system characterized by "open covenants, openly arrived at, freedom of navigation on the seas, equal trade opportunities and the removal of tariffs, general disarmament and an end to colonialism." Points 6 through 13 intended to spread "democracy" by advocating the self-determination of national minorities in Europe. Topping the call to end colonialism and to disarm, point 14 called for the construction of an international government, the League of Nations, to guarantee "political independence and territorial integrity to great and small nations."[122] The league's covenant applied a variation of constitutional democracy to international conflict. Rather than fight, nations would enter into arbitration and settle differences diplomatically with nonmilitary sanctions. In the event of war, the league was to coerce the parties into arbitration. The terms "just" and "unjust" were changed to the more up-to-date "lawful" and "unlawful."[123] The traditional rules of the European state system were further challenged by the introduction of the concept of "war guilt."

When the Paris Peace Conference opened in January 1919, a "Commission on Responsibility of the Authors of War and the Enforcement of Penalties" was assigned to examine the war crimes question. A group of fifteen international law experts was chaired by American Secretary of State Robert Lansing. Although the American President and his Secretary of State had very dissimilar views on international relations, in this instance they were in agreement because Wilson did not want his peace plan tainted by the demands of vengeance. As James Willis points out, Lansing "opposed international punishment of war crimes, believing observance of the laws of war should be left to the military authorities of each state."[124] President Wilson's advisor Edward House wrote tellingly of the Secretary of State's international legal mindset: "He believes that almost any form of atrocity is permissible provided a nation's safety is involved."[125] Lansing used his skills as America's most successful international lawyer to frustrate the European efforts to try the Kaiser and in the process to broaden the laws of war.

After two months of private meetings, the commission issued its report on March 29, 1919. They boldly rejected the doctrine of sovereign immunity and proclaimed the Kaiser accountable for: "(a.) Acts which provoked the world war and accompanied its inception. (b.) Violations of the laws of customs of war and the laws of humanity."[126] American representatives Robert Lansing and James Brown Scott issued an extremely conservative dissenting opinion in the form of the American and Japanese "Reservations to the Majority Report." Their critique of the proposed expansion of international criminal law would serve as one of the touchstones for positivist war crimes trial critics throughout the coming century. Ironically, the Americans echoed the arguments made by German representatives at the 1899 and 1907 Hague Conferences. It was one thing to try Germans for violations of the laws of war, "a standard certain, to be found in books of authority and the practice of nations," but "the laws of humanity" were a different and entirely unprecedented matter because they "vary with the individual, which, if for no other reason, should exclude them for consideration in a court of justice, especially one charged with the administration of criminal law."[127]

The American "Reservations" upheld the principle of sovereign immunity with no reservations or qualifications: "the Commission erred in seeking to subject Heads of State to trial and punishment by a tribunal to whose jurisdiction they were not subject when the alleged offenses were committed." According to the Americans, "war was and is by its very nature inhuman, but acts consistent with the laws and customs of war, although these acts are inhuman, are nevertheless not the object of punishment by a court of justice." Most important, Secretary of State Lansing concluded that "The essence of sovereignty was the absence of responsibility. When the people confided it to a monarch or other head of State, it was legally speaking to them only that he was responsible, although there might be a moral obligation to mankind. Legally, however, there was no super-sovereignty."[128] Lansing believed the League of Nations was a military alliance like any other, and its success or failure would depend on its ability to project force: "Justice is secondary. Might is primary."[129] He objected to a trial, writing that "the practical standard of conduct is not moral or humane ideas but the necessity of the act in protecting the national existence or in bringing the war to successful conclusion."[130] Lansing read the laws of war with one eye to the East: "We have seen the hideous consequences of Bolshevik rule in Russia, and we know that the doctrine is spreading westward. . . . We must look to the future, even though we forget the immediate demands of justice."[131] With logic and language that foreshadow the post–World War II period, the Secretary of State warned that a punitive policy might also lead to a breakdown of authority that would "hinder the resistance to Bolshevism." He added that President Wilson "approved entirely of my attitude only he is more radically opposed than I am to this folly."[132]

The disparity in the public positions of President Wilson and his Secretary of State says a great deal about the duality of twentieth-century American foreign policy. While Wilson was attempting to rewrite the rules of statecraft, Lansing was unequivocally invoking the rules that the President sought to overturn. The paradox was captured in an amendment to the League of Nations Charter obtained by the United States that legitimized the Monroe Doctrine. While the European powers were restrained by new rules ending colonialism and supporting national self-determination, the United States retained a free hand in North America.[133]

After much procrastination, the American delegation agreed to a retributive peace and signed the Treaty of Versailles' infamous "war guilt clause," which held Germany responsible for all of the war's damages.[134] Article 231 of the treaty provided a very specific legal basis for financial reparations: "The Allied and Associated Governments affirm and Germany accepts the responsibility of Germany and her Allies for causing all the loss and damage to which the Allied and Associated Governments and their nationals have been subjected as a consequence of a war imposed upon them by the aggression of Germany and her Allies."[135] Originally President Wilson resisted the effort to brand Germany with war guilt, but French and British leaders forced him to compromise. Naming Germany an "aggressor" introduced the concept into positive international law. This article and another indicting the Kaiser marked the formal end of the traditional European rules of statecraft and the beginning of a shift toward more discriminatory and subjective codes of international law.[136] Under the old European state system, war was considered an instrument of policy whose ill effects should be limited by the self-restraint of the soldiers on the battlefield. Did the American leaders really believe that war was a social wrong that should—or could—one day be outlawed? According to legal theorists Paul Piccone and G. L. Ulmen, "The turn to a discriminatory concept of war and the criminalization of the enemy . . . certainly contributed to the concept of total war."[137]

Germans of all political persuasions were enraged and urged their leaders to reject the *schmachparagraphen* or "shame paragraphs." Conflict over the treaty caused the downfall of one German cabinet and civil unrest. German President Fredrich Ebert signed the treaty only after determining military resistance was not an option.[138] Under Article 227, the Kaiser was threatened with a trial by an international court. He was charged not with specific war crimes but with "a supreme offense against international morality and the sanctity of treaties."[139] Articles 228–230 called for trials for traditional war crimes. Unlike the conflict resolutions of old, the victors did not execute a handful of deserving felons and issue an amnesty for acts committed during wartime. Instead, they attempted to broaden the scope of international criminal law to hold individuals personally accountable for acts of nations.[140]

However, once again judicial resolution gave way to political considerations that prevented a trial for the Kaiser.[141] European leaders realized that due to weak domestic support, the German government might not be able to endure the humiliation of such a procedure. Even British Prime Minister Lloyd George faced the opposition of his king and began to think in terms of compromise. The Kaiser scoffed at the idea from the relative safety of the Netherlands: "A court which is impartial does not at present exist in Europe. Against a single person . . . such a proceeding cannot be initiated.

It must be directed against all sovereigns and statesmen who partook in the war. . . . The procedure would mean a dishonoring of the principle of monarchy. . . . I do not have any guilt and do not recognize any court having jurisdiction over me."[142] The Dutch government officially refused to extradite the Kaiser because of family ties on January 22, 1920.[143]

The victors called on the German government to live up to Article 228 of the Treaty of Versailles and to hand over 854 men accused of war crimes, among them were some of Germany's most venerated military leaders: Ludendorff, von Moltke, von Tirpitz, and von Hindenburg.[144] The German government refused and stated firmly, "the extradition of those blacklisted for a trial by an Entente court is a physical and moral impossibility."[145] However, they did agree to try a limited number of men before the German Supreme Court (Reichsgericht) in Leipzig. The Associated Powers presented a revised list of 45 defendants.[146] The British carefully chose three submarine and three prison camp cases where the violations of the laws of war were flagrant and documented.The Leipzig trials opened on May 23, 1921 in the Reichsgericht with Dr. Schmidt, the presiding judge, and his six colleagues, cloaked in crimson robes and berets, sitting around a horseshoe-shaped table.[147] Immediately following the war, First Lieutenant Helmutt Patzig of *U-86*, the submarine that sank the hospital ship *Llandovery Castle*, returned home to Danzig and vanished, leaving his subordinates to take the fall.[148] When Ludwig Dithmar and John Boldt, the subordinate officers aboard the U-boat, were brought before the court, they refused to testify on the ground that they had taken an oath of silence concerning the events. Even the German court looked sternly upon their unwillingness to cooperate: "If the firing could be explained in any other way it cannot be imagined that the agreement of the accused to maintain silence could prevent them from denying firing on the boats, without entering into other matters."[149] The testimony of other crew members made it clear that their commander, Patzig, attempted to cover up his action by altering the submarine's logs and changing the ship's course on the charts.[150]

Based on the testimony of Chapman and the other survivors, the court determined, "the lifeboats of the *Llandovery Castle* were fired on in order to sink them." The court ruled sternly: "The firing on the boats was an offense against the law of nations. In war the killing of unarmed enemies is not allowed."[151] It determined that neither of the accused had actually shot at the lifeboats and thus the "principal guilt rests with Commander Patzig, under whose orders the accused acted." With some qualifications, the court accepted the defense of superior orders: "They should certainly have refused to obey the order. This would have required a specially high degree of resolution. . . . This justifies the recognition of mitigating circumstances in determining the punishment."[152] The defendants were sentenced to four years' imprisonment.

The decisions in the British cases against Karl Heynen and Emil Müller were equally schizophrenic. Heynen was accused of beating British POWs working in a Westphalian coal mine. Müller, a German prison camp commandant, was similarly charged with nine instances of personal cruelty. They were sentenced to ten and six months respectively, and while the court sternly condemned beating prisoners as "unworthy of a human being," they concluded, "It must be emphasized that the accused has not acted dishonorably, that is to say, his honour both as a citizen and as an officer remains untarnished."[153]

The most uncomfortable moment of the Leipzig trials came when the court heard charges against Franz Stenger, a decorated German officer who had lost a leg to a French artillery shell.[154] Accused of issuing a no quarter order and ordering his men to shoot prisoners in August 1914, another German officer, Major Benno Cruscius, testified that he had received the order from Stenger, carried it out, and passed it on. However, Stenger argued that his troops were fighting illegitimate combatants who did not observe the laws of war: "At mid-day, numerous reports had come in of the French method of fighting, feigning to be dead or wounded, or appearing offering to surrender and from the rear shooting with rifles and machine guns at troops that passed by."[155] In his final statement before the court, the defendant declared: "I did nothing in the war except my duty and obligation to the leaders of the German fatherland, to my Kaiser, the Supreme War Lord, and in the interest of the lives of my fighting German soldiers."[156] The speech was met with wild applause and an acquittal.[157] His accuser was not so fortunate—Major Crucius was sentenced to two years for "killing through negligence." The French prosecutors were heckled and spat upon by unruly German spectators. After the defendants in three of their cases were acquitted, the French withdrew from the trials. In the six British cases, five of the defendants were convicted; the French obtained only one conviction in their five cases.[158] In the Belgians' case, they charged Max Ramdohr, the head of the German secret police in Belgium, with torturing young boys. The court acquitted him and maintained that the stories were the products of overactive adolescent imaginations.[159] After Ramdohr's acquittal, the Belgians also withdrew from the trials.

Like the sentences in another trial conducted by a friendly regime, the Jacob Smith case of 1902, the sentences in the *Llandovery Castle* case did not match the tone of the judgments. While the two defendants were sentenced to four years, they were "accompanied to prison by a cheering crowd."[160] As in the Jacob Smith case, the sentences were subject to a crude form of strategic legalism—post-trial, nonjudicial modification. Both Boldt and Dithmar "escaped" from prison with the help of their captors (in November 1921 and January 1922 respectively).[161] The Associated Powers repudiated the compromise arrangement for the trials in 1922 and reserved all formal rights under Articles 228–230 of the Treaty of Versailles.[162] Germany's failure to meet the terms of the treaty moved French leader Raymond Poincaré to occupy the Ruhr Valley with French and Belgian troops.

The traditional European rules of statecraft had been declining steadily since the late nineteenth century, and the Treaty of Versailles marked their end.[163] With the indictment of the former Kaiser and the war guilt clause came the return of a discriminatory conception of war. During the years following World War I, governments redoubled their efforts not merely to limit war but to outlaw it.[164] The effort to criminalize aggression was a secular reinterpretation of the just and unjust war doctrine.[165] Professor Quincy Wright, one of America's leading international legal scholars at the time, considered the Peace of Paris revolutionary because of its juridical view of war. According to Wright, man had passed through the "Grotian phase" in which war was considered a right, through the "Vattellian phase" in which war was a fact, and into a new phase in which war was a crime.[166]

The interwar period brought a flurry of legal efforts to restrict and even ban war.[167] During the 1920s there were several attempts to criminalize aggression. The Assembly of the League of Nations declared in 1927 "That all wars of aggression are, and shall always be, illegal." A year later, the Sixth Pan-American Conference declared war "an international crime against the human species."[168] However, by far the best-known piece of antiwar legislation was the Kellogg-Briand Pact or the Pact of Paris, signed by sixty-three nations on August 27, 1928. Article I stated: "The High Contracting Parties solemnly declare in the names of their respective peoples that they condemn recourse to war for the solution of international controversies, and renounce it as an instrument of national policy."[169] Yet this pronouncement contained neither contractual obligations nor a criterion for aggression.[170] With no enforcement mechanism in place and an international unwillingness to back tough words with force, the Kellogg-Briand Pact was violated with impunity throughout the 1930s: by Japan in China, the Soviet Union in Finland, Italy in Ethiopia and Spain, and Germany in Czechoslovakia. Some of the signatories were condemned, but none was punished.[171]

Nonetheless, America's lawyer-statesmen continued to push for a new set of international norms that aimed to one day outlaw war. The most important step on this path was the criminalization of an American definition of "aggression." Henry Stimson, Elihu Root's heir apparent, was a second-generation American lawyer-statesman. Given that Stimson's career had begun in Root's Wall Street law firm, it is safe to assume that he shared his predecessor's desire to broaden the rules of statecraft.[172] Like Elihu Root, he believed that the new standards of international law needed to be upheld with force if necessary. Stimson unequivocally declared: "This country was one of the authors of one of the greatest changes in International Law that has ever taken place . . . the 'Pact of Paris' or the Kellogg-Briand Pact."[173]

Stimson considered the Treaty of Versailles' war guilt clause a turning point in the history of international relations. In his mind, the traditional rules of the European state system had been buried once and for all: "Henceforth when two nations engage in armed conflict . . . we no longer draw a circle around them and treat them with the punctilio of the dueler's code. We denounce [the wrongdoers] as lawbreakers."[174]

Under Henry Stimson, a new passive-aggressive principle was added to the strategic legalists' arsenal. Now the United States reserved the right to recognize only nations that came to power through means it judged "legitimate." Stimson attempted to force the Japanese to withdraw from Manchuria by issuing an ultimatum in 1932 that came to be known as the Stimson Doctrine. It was an American announcement of nonrecognition of "any situation, treaty or agreement which may be brought about by means contrary to the Pact of Paris." According to historian Godfrey Hodgson, American statesmen now reserved the right to judge the parties in the conflict and to define "legitimate means."[175] Again, the new standards of international conduct were, to borrow a term from contemporary art, "site specific." To German legal theorist Carl Schmitt, this redefinition of "recognition" was interventionist by its very nature: "It meant that the United States could effectively control every governmental and constitutional change in every country in the Western Hemisphere."[176] Paul Piccone and G. L. Ulmen wrote, "According to the Tobar Doctrine of 1907, only those governments should be recognized which are 'legal' in the sense of a 'democratic' constitution. In practice, what was meant concretely by 'legal' and 'democratic' was decided by the U.S., which defined, interpreted, and reinterpreted." For the United States during the twentieth century, "the source of its power, the secret of its historical actuality—aracanum—lies in international law."[177]

Although the Germans signed many of the radical treaties like the Kellogg-Briand Pact, their commitment to the new rules was questionable, given the lack of respect the Schlieffen Plan had shown for the nonaggression treaty with Belgium. From the German point of view, after World War I there was little left to lose, and they benefited greatly from the world's unwillingness to confront an aggressive nation.[178] Adolf Hitler took advantage of the uncertain state of European politics and combined mendacious diplomacy with overwhelming force. What he could not browbeat out of world leaders, he took by storm. The Nazi effort was extremely sophisticated and used a number of modern political devices: propaganda, fifth columnists, legalism, military force, and the murder of civilians. In many ways, Nazi Germany became the "criminal nation" or "rogue state" by which all others would be judged. From 1939 to 1941, the *Wehrmacht's blitzkrieg* campaign conquered central and Western Europe with a speed, precision, and "frightfulness" that would have pleased their Prussian forefathers. By the end of 1941, Germany controlled most of the European continent. Early in the Second World War, Allied leaders accused the Germans and the Japanese of atrocities and treaty violations. Initially the charges looked similar to those leveled against the Kaiser during World War I—propaganda intended to rally domestic support. Because the Third Reich's future seemed so promising in the early 1940s, war crimes were not an issue because only victors prosecute war crimes cases. It was not until the Japanese attack on Pearl Harbor on December 7, 1941, that the United States entered World War II and the possible outcomes of the conflict changed.

Representatives of nine Nazi-occupied nations met in London in January 1942 and announced their intention to punish Germans who committed crimes against civilians. The St. James Declaration was the first call for something other than traditional vengeance: "international solidarity is necessary to avoid the repression of these acts of violence simply by acts of vengeance on the part of the general public."[179] This declaration was also the first mention of trials. In addition to the occupied nations, the United States, Great Britain, and the USSR signed. The Allies established the United Nations War Crimes Commission to collect war crimes evidence on October 7, 1942. Based in London, the commission faced the logistical problem of investigating atrocities in occupied nations. Like the threats of World War I, these early pronouncements raised more questions than they answered.[180] In January 1943, at the Casablanca Conference, Roosevelt and Churchill called for the unconditional surrender of the Axis powers. The United States argued that the vanquished should be tried in legitimate courts of law under the antiaggression treaties signed after World War I.[181]

The first specific commitment to a war crimes trial came when the foreign secretaries of the United States, the Soviet Union, and Great Britain met in Moscow for a week in late October 1943. The resulting Moscow Declaration threatened "those German officers and men and members of the Nazi party who have been responsible for atrocities, massacres, and executions" with being "sent back to the countries in which their abominable deeds were done in order that they may be judged and punished according to the laws of these liberated countries." There was even a clause for the Axis leaders: "The above declaration is without prejudice to the case of the major war criminals whose offenses have no particular geographic localization and who will be punished by a joint decision of the governments of the Allies."[182]

As the ring tightened around Germany in the summer of 1944, American and British army officials drafted plans for the occupation. The American plan, "The Handbook of Military Government for Germany and the Interim Directive on Occupation Procedures," was not an outline of American policy but merely a loose set of guidelines designed to get the army through the invasion and early occupation.[183] Earlier that year, U.S. Secretary of the Treasury Henry Morgenthau Jr. read Dean Acheson's "Report on Reparation, Restitution, and Property Rights—Germany," and came away convinced that the State Department was "soft and coddling" toward Germany.[184] This was the beginning of a long-running dispute within the U.S. government between those who favored a punitive peace and those who favored enlisting Germany as an ally against the Soviet Union. Up to this point, American leaders had followed the British, who wanted the summary execution of German political and military leaders. Less interested in elaborate forms of punishment than in postwar strategy, very early on, the British and some within the U.S. State Department recognized the vital role that Germany would play in the postwar world.

Morgenthau was the most forceful advocate of a vindictive peace. He considered the German atrocities more significant than violations of the laws of war: in his mind, the Third Reich had broken more basic codes of human decency.[185] A political veteran whose father had battled the State Department over the U.S. response to Turkish atrocities, he understood the game and had an ally in the Oval Office. President Roosevelt had either read or been briefed on the army proposals; in a memo to Secretary of War Stimson, he described them as "pretty bad" and sided with Morgenthau. FDR believed that the Germans had to understand the magnitude of their crimes: "Too many people here and in England hold to the view that the German people as a whole are not responsible for what has taken place—that only a few Nazi leaders are responsible. This unfortunately is not fact." The President endorsed the concept of collective guilt. "The German people as a whole must have it driven home to them that the whole nation has engaged in a lawless conspiracy against the decencies of modern civilization."[186]

Secretary Morgenthau delivered a memo to the President with his plan for postwar Germany on September 5, 1944. Morgenthau recommended that "the cauldron of wars," Germany's industrial regions (Ruhr and Saar), be stripped of all mines, industry, and people. The Saar would go to France, while East Prussia and Silesia would be surrendered to Poland and Russia, respectively. Morgenthau hoped to transform Germany into a nation "primarily agricultural and pastoral in character."[187] He would not waste due process on Germany's "arch criminals" because their "obvious guilt has generally been recognized." Once the Nazi leaders were positively identified they should "be put to death forthwith by firing squad."[188] The military, however, had more traditional ideas about war crimes punishment. General Dwight David Eisenhower felt that a harsh peace was necessary and suggested executing the entire German General Staff.[189] Eisenhower was influenced by wartime passions, and these feelings grew as American forces liberated concentration camps and had a first-hand look at the effects of Nazi depravity.[190]

The leadership of the U.S. Army, the agency in charge of the European invasion and occupation, was worried by the Morgenthau Plan because dismantling Germany economically would create disorder and chaos that would hamper both the invasion and the occupation.[191] The initial approval with which the plan was greeted forced those who favored a trial to state their case more carefully. Many considered the Morgenthau Plan a bureaucratic coup that invaded provinces controlled by the military and State Department. Because Morgenthau was Jewish, some in the War Department, and especially the State Department, considered his plan a "Judaic act of revenge" committed in the name of the United States.[192] This debate was about much more than the fate of German leaders; it was about the shape of the postwar peace. The opponents of the plan were led in both mind and spirit by second-generation American lawyer-statesman Henry Stimson.[193]

Secretary of War Stimson called the Morgenthau Plan "a Childish folly!"and mockingly described it as "a Beautiful Nazi program! This is to laugh!" With world leadership came responsibility—a certain *noblesse oblige*. In a memo to the President, Stimson wrote that "enforced poverty is even worse, for it destroys the spirit not only of the victim but debases the victor."[194] Historian Bradley F. Smith has pointed to the social conflict behind the Stimson–Morgenthau clash: "The Secretary of War bore certain disdain for the marks of crude aggressiveness and new money that clung to Morgenthau. Stimson was a social anti-Semite, as were the vast majority of old family New York aristocrats in the 1940s."[195] Stimson worried that having a prominent Jew so involved in the planning for postwar Germany would provide "ammunition for those who would attribute all stringent controls on Germany to a mere 'Jewish' desire for revenge."[196] When President Roosevelt left for the Quebec Conference on September 11, 1944, Treasury Secretary Morgenthau was the only high-ranking American representative to accompany him.[197] The main purpose of this conference among American and British leaders was to discuss the terms of American economic aid to Great Britain. When the subject of war criminals came up, the delegates agreed that summary execution was the best solution. Churchill and Roosevelt initialed a draft of the Morgenthau Plan on September 15.

Although the British did not deny the existence of profound legal questions, they wanted to avoid the maelstrom where justice, politics, and public policy converged. The spokesman for the British position, Lord John Simon, offered a traditional plan more restrained than Morgenthau's. Unlike the Americans, the British candidly admitted that the treatment of the vanquished was and had always been a political question. The British labored under no fictions of due process and reeducation because they did not consider an international trial a practical possibility. Lord Simon argued that these questions were inherently political and subjective.[198] Although Morgenthau carried the day, this was only the first exchange in what Bradley F. Smith describes as "the Great German War on the Potomac."[199]

In meetings and memos, Secretary of War Stimson voiced disapproval of the "economic oppression" implicit in the Morgenthau Plan and argued that vindictive peace treaties "do not prevent war" but "tend to breed war."[200] Stimson felt that punishment should not be the sole objective of the occupation; treatment of the Nazi leaders should also serve an educational role. In a memo to Henry Morgenthau, he described the benefits of a more judicious approach:

> It is primarily by the thorough apprehension, investigation, and trial of all
> the Nazi leaders and instruments of the Nazi system of state terrorism such

as the Gestapo with punishment delivered as promptly, swiftly and severely as possible that we can demonstrate the abhorrence which the world has for such a system and bring home to the German people our determination to expiate it and all its fruits forever.[201]

President Roosevelt's views on the question of Nazi Germany's "arch-criminals" tended to reflect the ebb and flow of public opinion rather than a deep commitment to any one approach.

Six weeks prior to the 1944 presidential election, a draft of the Morgenthau Plan was leaked to the press. Nazi Minister of Propaganda Joseph Goebbels declared himself the "number one war criminal" and urged his countrymen to fight to the death rather than face vindictive conquerors.[202] After the uproar, President Roosevelt began to distance himself from the Morgenthau Plan. Although Stimson's most immediate threat was now gone, there was another fire to put out: Roosevelt had casually agreed with Churchill that Nazi leaders should be identified and executed.[203] When the Secretary of War learned of this vague promise, he devised an alternative and from this bureaucratic struggle, concrete plans for a trial emerged.

Henry Stimson felt that America held a unique position in human history, and that a transition to peace without vengeance would provide a stable foundation for the postwar world.[204] Simple revenge would only give rise to a new version of the "stab in the back" myth. After World War I, German nationalists claimed their political leadership had stabbed the military leadership in the back by negotiating a peace. Stimson did not want to "create Nazi martyrs and an opportunity for revisionists and isolationists to claim once more that charges against the German enemy were fabrications."[205] This warning proved very prescient given the final outcome of American war crimes policy.

The Secretary of War wanted to force Germans to face an irrefutable record of Nazi atrocities.[206] To deal with the Nazi leaders, "we should participate in an international tribunal constituted to try them."[207] Like Civil War reconstruction, America's postwar occupation of Germany and Japan would try to meld social work with military policy. However, the war was not over as long as the Wehrmacht could mount offensives in the West; the treatment of the losers was a premature question.

Although the Nazi crimes were known long before 1944, some recalled the tales of marauding Huns bayoneting babies during World War I and suspected that the stories of current atrocities were similar exaggerations; others questioned reports from Jewish sources.[208] It was clear to Secretary of War Stimson that the Germans had committed singularly horrible acts and that they should be tried publicly. This would present the American lawyer-statesmen with their best opportunity during the twentieth century to translate their ideas into practice.[209] These men had no qualms about pushing the army's Judge Advocate General aside, and most shared the belief that summary execution was only a topical solution. As Stimson later wrote, "we at last reach to the very core of international strife, and we set a penalty not merely for war crimes, but for the very act of war itself."[210]

Stimson gave his reasoning in a letter to President Roosevelt:

> The method of dealing with these and other criminals requires careful thought and a well-defined procedure. Such a procedure must embody, in my judgment, at least the rudimentary aspects of the Bill of Rights. . . . The very punishment of these men in a manner consistent with the advance of civilization, will have all the greater effect upon posterity. Furthermore, it will afford the most effective way of making a record of the Nazi system of terrorism and of the effort of the Allies to terminate the system and avoid its recurrence.[211]

These radical views were not shared by all his colleagues in Washington, but with patrons like FDR and salesmen like Assistant Secretary of War John McCloy, the lawyer-statesmen were able to outmaneuver those they could not convert. The task of planning the first war crimes trial was assigned to McCloy, who passed it to Murray Bernays in the War Department's Special Projects Division. Because Bernays did not consider the laws of war broad enough to cover the scope of the Nazi crimes, he stressed the need for legal innovation. and argued that "undoubtedly, the Nazis have been counting on the magnitude and ingenuity of their offenses, the number of offenses, the number of offenders, the law's complexity, and delay and war weariness as major defenses against effective prosecution. Trial on an individual basis, and by old modes and procedures would go far to realize the Nazi hopes in this respect."[212]

Bernays's greatest concern was that individuals could not be charged with the killing of German Jews, which was not by definition a war crime. Civil wars and atrocities committed against domestic populations fell outside the laws of war.[213] Not content to simply try individuals for recognized violations, Bernays proposed trying Nazi organizations for conspiring to commit aggressive war. He borrowed the thesis of Polish émigré and international legal expert Raphael Lemkin, who argued in *Axis Rule in Occupied Europe* that the SS, Gestapo, and other Nazi organizations were an international version of La Cosa Nostra, "a criminal organization of volunteer gangsters."[214] Legal theorist David Luban makes a similar observation: "The framers of Nuremberg were confronted with a new offense, the bureaucratic crime, and a novel political menace, the criminal state." Under Bernays's broad-reaching proposal, the central crime from which all others sprang was a conspiracy to dominate the world. This concept would close legal loopholes that might allow guilty men to escape punishment.[215] Bernays wrote: "This conspiracy, based on the Nazi doctrine of racism and totalitarianism, involved murder, terrorism, and the destruction of peaceful populations in violation of the laws of war."[216]

There was nothing basic about the "Basic Objectives" of the Bernays Plan; they were in fact revolutionary. The second-tier War Department lawyer's three-page memo challenged long-standing maxims of international relations. The first objective rejected the concept of sovereign immunity: "Alleged high interests of state are not acceptable as justification for national crimes of violence, terrorism and the destruction of peaceful populations."[217] Objectives two and three broadened the laws of war and issued a statement of collective German war guilt, "bringing home to the world the realities and menace of racism and totalitarianism; and . . . arousing the German people to a sense of their guilt, and to a realization of their responsibility for the crimes committed by their government."[218]

Again, social work would be wedded to jurisprudence: the War Department did not seek only to punish, but also to reform and reeducate: "If these objectives are not achieved, Germany will simply have lost another war. The German people will not know the barbarians they have supported, nor will they have any understanding of the criminal character of their conduct and the world's judgment upon it."[219] Under the conspiracy plan, law was tailored to fit the unique crimes. Although simple in theory, this effort was fraught with legal and political difficulties. Perhaps the greatest problem was that it was an unfamiliar concept in international and German constitutional law.[220] According to the Anglo-American definition, members and leaders of a group were responsible for the crimes of that group even if they did not actively participate. But even in American courts, where the concept was familiar, judges tended to narrow their interpretation. Bernays advocated just the opposite.[221]

Criminal accessory, the Continental system's closest approximation to conspiracy, was defined far more narrowly.[222] The conspiracy charge allowed the Allies to move up the chain of command, past triggermen who personally violated the rules of war. Theoretically, this would open the way for a blanket conviction of hundreds of thousands of members of the SS and other Nazi organizations without trials. Although the severity of the penalty depended on the individual's crimes and the body of evidence against him, many were troubled that voluntary membership in one of the "criminal" organizations would provide sufficient evidence for a guilty verdict. It looked to the naked eye as if a massive charge of collective guilt was being prepared in the name of the United States. Although the Allies warned Axis leaders of war crimes prosecutions, there was no mention of a criminal conspiracy.

On November 11, the Secretaries of State, War, and the Navy signed and delivered a memo to President Roosevelt that affirmed the conspiracy plan and suggested establishing a court by international treaty. Stimson viewed the trial as an educational device:

> Not only will the guilty of this generation be brought to justice according to due process of law, but in addition, the conduct of the Axis will have been solemnly condemned by an international adjudication of guilt that cannot fail to impress generations to come. The Germans will not again be able to claim, as they have been claiming with regards to the Versailles Treaty, that an admission of war guilt was exacted under duress.[223]

The most significant criticism of the War Department plan came from President Roosevelt's trusted advisor, Assistant Attorney General Herbert Weschler. In two memos (December 29, 1944 and January 5, 1945), he recommended more conventional proceedings based on traditional war crimes charges and criticized the conspiracy charge, doubting that "conspiracy is criminal under international law" and declaring that its inclusion "would entail hopeless confusion."[224] Attorney General Francis Biddle shared Weschler's view that the traditional war crimes case was sound; why risk turning the trials into a forum in which to debate vanguard issues of international law?[225] These points became moot after a military event forced Franklin Roosevelt's position on war crimes policy and once again demonstrated the incalculable role that domestic politics played in the development of American war crimes policy.

Germany's Sixth Panzer Army mounted a final offensive in the predawn hours of December 16, 1944. The spearhead was led by Sepp Dietrich and Joachim Peiper. Not only the battlefield component of the *Waffen* SS, these forces were Hitler's former SS bodyguards—Nazi Germany's black knights, "red in tooth and claw."[226] The German forces traversed the Ardennes mountains and tried to advance to the Meuse River to split Allied forces. After two days of sporadic combat, the commander of one of Peiper's battle groups informed him of a "mix-up" near Ligneauville. A tank gunner had "spontaneously" opened fire on a group of prisoners.[227] The same day, a message was received by the U.S. First Army: "SS troops vicinity L8199 captured U.S. soldier, traffic M.P. with about two hundred other U.S. soldiers. American soldiers searched. When finished, Germans lined up Americans and shot them with machine pistols and machine guns. Wounded informant who escaped and more details to follow later."[228]

The U.S. Army eventually recovered seventy-two bullet-riddled bodies from a frozen field. Compared to atrocities committed against Russians, Poles, and Jews, the shooting of captive soldiers in the heat of battle does not seem as horrendous.[229] But these victims of the SS were American, and as historian James Weingartner notes, this event, dubbed the "Malmedy Massacre," "had entered the consciousness of the American people as an example of Axis barbarity alongside the bombing of Pearl Harbor and the Bataan 'death march.'"[230] The Malmedy Massacre convinced high-ranking American officials that the Nazis were involved in a "conspiracy to achieve domination of other nations."[231] By January 1945, the tide had turned once and for all in favor of the War Department. President Roosevelt informed Secretary of State Cordell Hull that the coming trial of Nazi war criminals should include a charge for "waging aggressive warfare, in violation of the Kellogg-Briand Pact. Perhaps these and other charges might be joined in a conspiracy indictment."[232]

The Secretaries of State and War and the Attorney General signed a memo proposing a war crimes plan that included the Bernays "Basic Objectives" on January 22, 1945. When Secretary of War Stimson and President Roosevelt discussed the fate of the Axis leaders a few days later, Stimson held firm to his belief that the proceedings should do more than simply render justice: they should make an example of the Nazi leaders.[233] Roosevelt hedged throughout the discussions of war crimes policy. Stimson's inability to get a straight answer is apparent in his January 19 diary entry: "He [FDR] assented to what I said, but in the hurry of the situation I am not sure whether it registered." With the end of the war in sight, Stimson now had to sell the War Department plan to the Allies. The Americans had a strong bargaining position, and as long as reconstruction aid was forthcoming, France and England would surely indulge them.[234]

An American delegation led by Judge Samuel Rosenman traveled to London on April 4, 1945 to confer with the British about war crimes policy.

Lord Simon, the British foreign secretary, attempted to force the Americans to accept a more traditional arraignment plan with summary trials and executions for Hitler and his cohorts. The two delegations failed to agree, so the British submitted a plan to their War Cabinet and the United States submitted another to the President. On April 15, the War Cabinet issued a scathing response to Simon's proposal, claiming that it was not conservative enough and insisting on executions.

After Roosevelt's death on April 12, Henry Stimson met with President Harry Truman. Among other things (the atom bomb), they discussed war crimes policy. With none of the guile of his predecessor, the President told the Secretary of War that he approved of Stimson's plans for a trial.[235] Buoyed by this unequivocal support, another American delegation (McCloy, Weschler, Ami Cutter, and John Weir) returned to London in late April. Assistant Secretary of War McCloy brushed the British resistance aside and called it "retrogressive," urging them to seize the opportunity "to move forward" as part of a larger effort to bring "international law into action against the whole vicious broad Nazi enterprise."[236] McCloy felt that "Hitler and his gang had offended against the laws of humanity," and the time had arrived to make an example of them.[237] According to British historians John and Ann Tusa, "McCloy's certainty and energy was hard to resist."[238]

By the end of April, the Assistant Secretary had gained the support of French Premier Charles de Gaulle and Soviet Premier Josef Stalin. Faced with this *fait accompli,* the British gracefully conceded, announcing that "the United States has gone a long way to answer cabinet objections and [we have] signed on to the international trial."[239] Although the protrial faction had outgunned their opponents, they had not gone very far in addressing their substantive criticisms.

President Harry Truman appointed U.S. Supreme Court Justice Robert Jackson to head the prosecution team.[240] British war crimes prosecutor Sir David Maxwell Fyfe described Jackson as "a romantic of the law" who embraced "the traditions of natural justice, reason and human rights."[241] Although he was a New Yorker, Jackson came from a different background than the American lawyer-statesmen. He looked toward an era governed by an American redefinition of international law and not only rejected the doctrine of sovereign immunity and *raison d'etat* but also took the criminalization of aggression to its ultimate conclusion: "A system of international law which can impose no penalty on a law breaker and also forbids other states to aid the victim would be self-defeating and would not help . . . to realize man's hope for eternal peace."[242]

Robert Jackson was a fitting leader for the Americans and would passionately advocate their revolutionary plan. Like Henry Stimson, he was intent on reforming international relations by criminalizing aggression and believed that a grand trial would set the tone for the postwar period and give greater meaning to the war.[243] The vanquished would not be wantonly slaughtered. The fate of the Germans was contained in a telling euphemism that was part America and part Orwell: the Germans were to be "reeducated."[244]

CHAPTER 3

THE AMERICAN WAR CRIMES PROGRAM

The American plan for an international trial based on radical and untested international legal principles raised a number of difficult questions. Was accounting for atrocities in the aftermath of a total war a moral act or a political act, or a bit of both? Did the rules apply to the victors as well as the vanquished? Would the inclusion of Stalinist judges cost the international tribunal its credibility?

In Japan, America's city-bombing campaign would not reach its atomic climax for many months. In the meantime, General Curtis LeMay had taken over XXI Bomber Command in 1944 and ushered in a new era of civilian death and destruction. British officer and military historian B. H. Liddell Hart was so appalled by city bombing that he described it as "the most uncivilized method of warfare the world has known since the Mongol devastations."[1] On a single night in March 1945, American planes dropped incendiary bombs that turned Tokyo into an inferno, burning out 16 square miles of the city and killing between 90,000 and 100,000 civilians. General LeMay had no qualms about targeting civilians: "Nothing new about death, nothing new about death caused militarily. We scorched and boiled and baked to death more people in Tokyo on the night of 9–10 March than went up in vapor at Hiroshima and Nagasaki combined."[2] How would the new court rule on city bombing? Would Great Britain's Arthur "Bomber" Harris and American Curtis LeMay remain above the law?

Although the United States waged total war against the Axis powers, the extermination of entire ethnic, racial, religious, and economic groups was never among its wartime goals. However, similar claims could not be made for the Soviets. Stalinist participation in any trial left the Allies open to charges of employing a double standard, also known as *tu quoque*.[3] For this reason alone, it was shortsighted of the Secretary of War to adopt a tone and legal procedure that did not reflect post–World War II geopolitical realities. The belief that war crimes proceedings were not political was at best naïve and at worst disingenuous—but certainly consistent with America's two-faced relationship with international law.

With the memory of Stalin's unique contribution to political justice, the 1936–1938 Moscow Trials, fresh in their minds, many American and British foreign policy professionals shuddered at the thought of sharing a bench with Soviet judges. John Troutbeck of the British Foreign Office wrote a scathing memo about the proposed international trial: "Surely to have a Russian sitting in a case of this kind will be regarded as almost a high point of international hypocrisy." Troutbeck tried to wake his superiors from the moral amnesia that total war and an alliance with Stalin had required. He argued that Russian aggression, atrocities, and persecutions rivaled those of the Nazis, and moreover, the Soviet conquests had just begun: "Is not the Soviet Government employed today in that very same thing in Poland, the Baltic States, Turkey and Persia? There have been two criminal enterprises this century—by Germans and Russians."[4]

The fate of Poland was one of the many tragedies of World War II. During the glory days of the Hitler-Stalin Pact (the Molotov-Ribbentrop Pact stipulated nonagression between Germany and the Soviet Union and divided Eastern Europe into spheres of influence), both nations sank their talons into the geographically unfortunate country. Eastern Poland was seen as the strong point of Russia's *cordon sanitaire,* which extended from the Black Sea to Finland. Like the Jews, the Polish were subjected to "industrialized extermination, mass deportations, and police state terror."[5] While the *Wehrmacht* was cutting a swath through central and Western Europe, the Molotov-Ribbentrop agreement was in effect, and the Soviets had shared in the spoils of the German conquest.[6] Only in 1941, after the Nazis launched Operation Barbarossa, was Stalin forced to cast his lot with the Western Alliance.

The most politically damaging Soviet war crime was uncovered in the winter of 1943. A group of Russian laborers working for the Wehrmacht in the Katyn forest near Smolensk, Poland came across fresh human bones that had been dug up by wolves. The Germans exhumed 4,143 neatly stacked corpses buried in eight mass graves.[7] Small birch trees had been planted on top of the graves in an effort to render the site indistinguishable from the other scenic vistas overlooking the Dnieper River. Nazi Propaganda Minister Josef Goebbels announced in April 1943: "A report has reached us from Smolensk to the effect that the local inhabitants have mentioned to the German authorities the existence of a place where mass executions had been carried out by the Bolsheviks and where 10,000 Polish officers had been murdered by the BPU. . . . They were fully dressed, some were bound, and all had pistol shots to the back of the head."[8]

It was not so easy to dismiss this as yet another missive from Goebbel's Ministry of Propaganda; all evidence pointed to the Soviet Union. The bodies were found on territory the Soviets had previously occupied and the men had disappeared in 1940 while in Soviet custody. But the telltale clue was the manner of execution—one quick shot to the back of the head at close range. The Soviets responded defensively to the accusations, but their denials were unconvincing, particularly to the Polish government in exile. However, Poland had other problems by 1945. The nation was in the process of being absorbed into the Soviet Union's sphere of influence. Would its British and American "friends" shirk the lofty principles of the Atlantic Charter and look the other way?[9]

The Allies faced a moral dilemma: should they act according to conscience and reveal the massacre as Stalin's, or turn a blind eye in order to maintain strategic trim? The question highlights the flexibility of morality in twentieth-century international politics. The odious task of informing the Polish leaders that they were about to be sold down the river in the name of strategy fell to Sir Owen O'Malley, British ambassador to the Polish government in exile. In a confidential memo to the British War Cabinet, O'Malley wrote, "We have in fact perforce used the good name of England like the murderers used the little conifers to cover up a massacre."[10] The need to placate a key strategic ally forced Churchill and Roosevelt to aid Stalin in suppressing evidence and to thwart Polish efforts to expose the truth about the fate of their military elite.[11] This would not have posed such a problem had the Allies not already transformed the war into a crusade against evil. If the new war crimes standards were applied across the board, none of the Allied nations would be exempt from prosecution.

By April 1945, Allied atrocities were overshadowed by the grisly discoveries made by American soldiers as they swept into formerly Nazi-held territory and liberated several concentration camps. Soldiers from Patton's Third Army accidentally discovered the Ohrdürf concentration camp on April 4 and 5 when they found a large pit filled with charred, half-burned bodies on the camp's outskirts. American generals Dwight Eisenhower, George Patton, and Omar Bradley toured Ohrdürf on April 11. More than the lice-ridden dead, it was the systematic dehumanization that shocked them. Eisenhower cabled Washington, "We are constantly finding German camps in which they have placed political prisoners where unspeakable conditions exist. From my own personal observation, I can state unequivocally that all written statements up to now do not paint the full horrors." He wanted American troops to visit the camp: "We are told that the American soldier does not know what he is fighting for. Now, at least, he will know what he is fighting against."[12] These were not even the worst concentration camps; the Nazi leaders had been careful to construct their archipelago of death camps in Poland.

As the liberation of the camps continued, captured German guards and officials were subjected to spontaneous reprisals. U.S. Army Rabbi Max Eichhorn was among the first to enter Buchenwald, and he described his feelings at the time: "We cried not merely tears of sorrow. We cried tears of hate. Then we stood aside and watched while the inmates of the camp hunted down their former guards, many of whom were trying to hide in various parts of the camp." American veteran Fred Maercer watched a German soldier attempt to surrender to American forces. However, he was intercepted by an inmate with a large wooden club: "He just stood there and beat him to death. He had to—of course, we did not bother him."[13] After American soldiers allowed the former inmates to kill German prisoners at Buchenwald, Heinrich Himmler issued this April 14, 1945 Order: "No prisoners shall be allowed to fall into the hands of the enemy alive. Prisoners have behaved barbarously to the civilian population at Buchenwald."[14]

After a prolonged attack on Munich, U.S. soldiers discovered the Dachau concentration camp on April 29. As the Americans approached the camp gate, they were fired on by a last line of SS defenders. Near the train depot that abutted the camp, the soldiers were confronted by forty open freight cars filled with dead bodies in striped uniforms. Some of the soldiers retched from the sight and smell; others openly wept.[15] When the American soldiers stormed Dachau's interior, they were greeted by inmates who had survived the horror. Again, American soldiers watched and even encouraged concentration camp victims to hunt down and kill their former captors. American veteran Jack Hallett recalled, "Control was gone after the sights we saw, and the men were deliberately wounding guards that were available and then turning them over to the prisoners and allowing them to take their revenge." Hallett saw an American soldier give his bayonet to an inmate "and watched him behead the man. It was a pretty gory mess."[16] Several haunting photographs survive of the Dachau liberation; in one, two inmates tower over a collapsed guard. The German is not yet dead, and by the looks on their faces, the inmates are savoring their revenge. In the background lies a mound of crumpled bodies—not dead camp victims but recently executed German soldiers. According to historian Robert Abzug, an American squad guarding 122 German prisoners spontaneously opened fire and killed them all.[17]

Writer Paul Fussell served as an American infantry soldier in France until he was wounded by German artillery and concluded that modern war was "the very quintessence of amoral activity with its mass murders of the innocents" Quite simply, war is "not an appropriate context for invoking moral criteria."[18] After Fussell's F Company found a dozen German soldiers trapped in a bomb crater in the forest, the enemy attempted to surrender, but the American soldiers simultaneously opened fire. "Laughing and howling, hoo-ha-ing and cowboy and good-old-boy yelling, our men exultantly shot into the crater until every man down there was dead."[19] Fussell felt no remorse—quite the contrary: "The result was deep satisfaction, and the event was translated into an amusing narrative, told and retold over campfires all that winter."[20]

Meanwhile, far from the hostilities and the realities of the battlefield, Allied leaders were finalizing their plans for the trial of the German leaders in a conference room in London. An American delegation led by Robert Jackson and former OSS chief William Donovan left for London to hammer out the details of the international trial on May 28, 1945, and had to convert the British, French, and Russians to their radical trial proposal.[21] The London Conference opened in early June. Many of the initial sessions were spent wrangling over fundamental differences between the Anglo-American and Continental legal systems.[22] The British and American systems were adversarial by design: the prosecution filed a brief indictment in open court that contained no evidence and the judge knew only the general nature of the case. French delegate and Sorbonne professor of international law André Gros was shocked by the implications of this.[23] The French objected to the presentation of evidence in open court "by the lawyers, who examine and cross-examine the witnesses and who may exploit and must confront the element of surprise." Under the Continental legal system, evidence was assembled by a court magistrate. If a sufficient basis for a trial was established, the dossier and the indictment were given to the court and the defendant. Judges, prosecutors, and defense attorneys worked together to arrive at the truth and reach a just decision.[24]

The Soviet insistence on a full presentation of evidence provided the first opportunity for American prosecutor Robert Jackson to make his distrust of the Russians publicly known. When Jackson informed his colleagues that this would not sit well with the American public, the French delegate retorted that their system ensured a fair trial and was "not designed to satisfy an ill-informed American public."[25] U.S.–Soviet differences came to an ugly head on July 1, when Soviet representative I. T. Nikitchenko issued a statement that overshadowed all procedural squabbles and seemed to justify the worst assumptions about the Soviet conception of justice. Nikitchenko announced that the defendants had already been convicted by political decree: "The fact that the Nazi leaders are criminals has already been established. The task of the Tribunal is only to determine the measure of guilt of each particular person and mete out the necessary punishment—the sentences."[26] As if this declaration of collective guilt were not enough, he spoke scornfully of the presumed "fairness" and "impartiality" of the Anglo-American system: "The case for the prosecution is undoubtedly known to the judge before the trial starts and there is therefore no necessity to create a sort of fiction that the judge is a disinterested person. If such a procedure is adopted that the judge is supposed to be impartial, it would only lead to unnecessary delays."[27] Nikitchenko's statements were a breaking point for Jackson, who had harbored deep reservations about the Soviets from the start and now hoped that they would withdraw from the trial.[28]

Robert Jackson and William Donovan traveled to Frankfurt to discuss the trial site with American General Lucius Clay and his political advisor, Robert Murphy, on July 7. General Clay suggested Nuremberg, for the practical reason that part of a courthouse and a jail were still standing. Although the city had otherwise been leveled by Allied bombs, the surrounding suburbs were intact and could house members of the court staff. There were also symbolic reasons for the choice: it was the site of the infamous Nuremberg Rallies and had lent its name to the laws that marked the beginning of the Nazi persecution of German Jews.[29] Justice Jackson returned to London more antagonistic toward the Soviets than ever before. Although this was partly the result of his own anti-Soviet feelings, the American negotiating position was strong: of the twenty-two "major war criminals," the United States held ten, the British five; three more were in joint custody.[30] The British were in no position to resist, as their government was in the midst of a transfer of power to the Labor Party.

When the delegations considered the crimes that would be charged, it quickly became obvious that the Americans would have to recapture old ground. French representative Gros objected to the aggression charge, contending that any such legislation would be *ex post facto* law. He offered American Secretary of State Robert Lansing's arguments from the Paris Peace Conference to support his claim. This, according to the Frenchman, undermined "any legal basis for imposing . . . criminal responsibility on individuals who launch aggressive wars."[31] Gros neatly summarized the disagreement by observing that "the Americans want to win the trial on the ground that the Nazi war was illegal, and the French people and other people of the occupied countries just want to show that the Nazis were bandits."[32]

Jackson dismissed the French and Russian reservations and the Lansing precedent: "I must say that sentiment in the United States and better world opinion have greatly changed since Mr. James Brown Scott and Secretary Lansing announced their views as to criminal responsibility for the first World War."[33] Jackson argued that punishing Germans was not the sole objective of the American proposal and seemed to imply that the same rules would apply to American soldiers and statesmen: "If certain acts of violation of treaties are crimes, they are crimes, whether the United States does them or whether Germany does them, and we must be prepared to lay down the rule of criminal conduct against others which we would not be willing to have invoked against us."[34] The debate raged for five sessions of the conference.[35]

The British considered the Americans quarrelsome and felt that Robert Jackson was trying to disrupt the conference. Patrick Dean of the Foreign Office described the American judge as "afraid of the Russians, particularly their method of trial."[36] British Treasury official R. S. Clyde agreed and stated that that "The Russians . . . have begun to question . . . whether he [Jackson] is seeking to codify international law for their discomforture."[37] Jackson cabled Assistant Secretary of War John McCloy on July 24 and described the discussions in London in very bleak terms: "Our conference is in serious disagreement today over definition war crimes. All European powers would qualify criminality of aggressive war and not go along on view in my report to President."[38] Jackson met with Secretary of State James Byrnes, who told him that a four-power trial was preferable but that the final decision was Jackson's alone. At the Potsdam Conference, the Big Three discussed the war crimes negotiations in London. Stalin proposed naming the defendants, but President Truman refused to commit until he had discussed the issue with Jackson. Though the two never spoke directly, a message was relayed via Truman's close advisor, Judge Samuel Rosenman. On August 1, the Big Three agreed to try the major Nazi war criminals before an international tribunal. Article VII of the Potsdam Agreement officially committed them to "bring those criminals to swift and sure justice."[39]

However, the conferees had not yet formulated the charges. When the American plan was tabled, the French and the Soviets launched into a now familiar series of critiques. They did not want the court to declare the innocence or guilt of the defendants. The Soviet representative, Nikitchenko, argued heatedly against "trying an organization to reach all of its members."[40] In the drafting session the charge was diluted to an accusation of "planning" or "organizing" specific crimes.

After a month of contentious meetings, representatives of the four powers signed the London Agreement. The actual "agreement" was little more than a restatement of the Moscow Declaration, announcing quadripartite support for "a trial of war criminals whose offenses have no particular geographic location, whether they be accused individually or in their capacity as members of organizations or groups or in both capacities."[41] The London Agreement Charter contained the charges, defined the rights of the accused, and outlined many of the procedural issues. Count 1 charged the defendants with "The Common Plan or Conspiracy." Count 2, however, charged them with the crime of aggression; the Soviet representative, Professor Trainin, had renamed it "Crimes Against Peace." Ironically, with this count, the delegates were reestablishing a traditional view of statecraft that upheld the sanctity and centrality of sovereignty. According to legal theorist David Luban, "by criminalizing aggression, the Charter erected a wall around state sovereignty and committed itself to an old European model of unbreachable nation states."[42] In Luban's view, the Nuremberg planners came to the brink of challenging the traditional rules of statecraft but backed off in the end.[43] German leaders were charged with both aggression and "participation in the formulation or execution of a common plan or conspiracy to commit any of the foregoing crimes."[44] Count 3, "War Crimes," charged traditional violations of the laws of war, while under Count 4, "Crimes Against Humanity," the definition of war crimes was broadened so that the Germans could be charged with crimes against Jews and other German nationals.[45]

The Americans hoped that a "free and fair" trial would do more than simply render justice; it would also reeducate the German people after a decade of dictatorship. Traditionally, America's reform efforts had been aimed at non-European nations like the Philippines. While the Germans could accept total military defeat and occupation, "reeducation" at the knee of the United States was another matter. However, by 1945, the German population was resigned to having their cities bombed, their POWs executed, and their territory plundered by a marauding Red Army. "None of this was justified by international law, nor by justice, nor by humanity. It was brute revenge," explained German historian Jörg Friedrich. "The Germans understood this perfectly. Reprisals had been their customary method of occupation."[46] However, many Germans did not understand the American social and political reform policies. According to Friedrich, "Nazi propaganda chief Josef Goebbels had announced that the Allied forces, if successful, would destroy the vanquished. So the public regarded the International Military Tribunal as the Allies' way of eliminating an enemy, just as trials had been used in the Third Reich."[47] For the first time since Napoleon, German soil was occupied by foreign armies. World War II had cost millions of German lives (not including Jews and other persecuted minorities), and most of the nation's cities had been reduced to rubble by Allied bombing.

For those in the eastern provinces, Stalin's retribution had only just begun.[48] The ominous presence of Soviet purge trial prosecutor Andrei Vyshinsky in Nuremberg confirmed German suspicions that the international trial would be a theatrical prelude to the inevitable executions. This idea was not without merit, given Vyshinsky's view on the rule of law, outlined in his Stalin Prize–winning book, *Court Evidence in Soviet Law*. To Vyshinsky, the presumption of innocence was a bourgeois pretension. Under the Stalinist model of political justice, defendants were tortured until they were willing to "confess" to their crimes in open court.[49] When the Soviet delegation showed a group of Americans, including Judge Francis Biddle, a film of a Soviet "war crimes trial" conducted in Kharkov in 1943, the American delegation sat in stunned silence as starved German officers were hanged in front of a roaring crowd of 40,000. Biddle was appalled.[50]

The Soviet delegation was overseen by Vyshinsky and the "Supervisory Committee for the Nuremberg Trials," which included the USSR's chief prosecutor, K. P. Gorschenin, and Minister of Justice, I. T. Golyakov. The American trial participants believed that the Soviet delegation had to clear all their decisions with Moscow. The record of a discussion between Andrei Vyshinsky and B. Z. Kobulov illustrates the vigilance over potentially embarrassing evidence. When Kobulov expressed concern about "anti-Soviet diatribes," Vyshinsky instructed the chief prosecutor to interrupt a defendant "where necessary and deny him the opportunity of making any anti-Soviet attacks."[51] By the time the trial was ready to begin, the Soviet delegation at Nuremberg had been provided with a "list of questions provided by Comrade Vyshinsky which are to be regarded as not permissible for discussion before the Tribunal." The topics included the Hitler-Stalin Pact and Poland.[52]

Although the International Military Tribunal was now saddled with a revolutionary indictment, there was never a consensus on American war crimes policy, and the alliance between Republicans and Democrats would prove frail once the Cold War began.[53] The treatment of the vanquished would be heavily influenced by both domestic and international politics. The International Military Tribunal at Nuremberg, the International Military Tribunal for the Far East, and the subsequent Nuremberg trials (the highest-level war crimes courts) were all loosely modeled after the London Agreement and Charter. Although the three indictments on which the trials were based—the London Agreement, the Tokyo Charter, and Control Council Law No. 10—differed in small ways, they all contained traditional war crimes charges in addition to the novel aggression, conspiracy, and crimes against humanity counts. Each court would have to rule independently on these parts of the indictment.[54]

The international trial at Nuremberg, the symbolic flagship for American and Allied war crimes policy, produced a list of defendants on September 30, 1945 that included some of the highest-ranking Nazi survivors: Hermann Goering, Walther Funk, Wilhelm Frick, Alfred Speer, Julius Streicher, Martin Bormann, Alfred Rosenberg, Joachim von Ribbentrop, Rudolf Hess, Constantin von Neurath, Franz von Papen, Hjalmar Schacht, Baldur von Schirach, Ernst von Kaltenbrunner, Wilhelm Keitel, Alfred Jodl, Eric Raeder, Karl Doenitz, Artur Seyss-Inquart, Fritz Sauckel, and Hans Fritzsche. The defendants represented a good cross-section of both the military and the political leadership of the Third Reich.

In the days leading up to the trial, all the German defense lawyers signed a petition challenging the International Military Tribunal's legal validity. The petition argued that any state, "by virtue of its sovereignty, has the right to wage war at any time and for any purpose." While acknowledging the prosecution's challenge to the idea that "the decision to wage war is beyond good and evil," defense lawyers accused the Allies of trying to reestablish their own conception of just and unjust war. "More than that, it is demanded that not only should the guilty State be condemned and its liability be established, but that furthermore those men who are responsible for unleashing the unjust war be tried and sentenced by an International Tribunal."[55] The petition went on to make more familiar *ex post facto* and *nulla poena sine lege* arguments and asked "That the Tribunal direct that an opinion be submitted by internationally recognized authorities on international law on the legal element of this Trial under the Charter of the Tribunal."[56] Defense attorney Otto Kranzbühler held a view shared by many Germans in 1945: the Nuremberg trial was the "continuation of war by other means."[57] Rather than address this criticism, the IMT simply invoked Article 3 of the London Agreement Charter, which disallowed any direct challenges to the tribunal's legal jurisdiction or a reopening of the debate over the legal validity of the proceedings. German attorneys would not forget this slight, and an influential segment of the German population rejected Nuremberg's legal validity from day one. Legal positivism was a German science, and it would provide the Americans with a worthy foe.

The courtroom of Nuremberg's Palace of Justice was filled to capacity on November 6, 1945 as twenty-one Nazi leaders sat in the stagelike defendants' dock. The American prosecutors began by presenting Count 1 of the indictment. Robert Jackson opened the case for the United States on November 21. The first three sentences of his address would for many come to symbolize "Nuremberg":

> The privilege of opening the first trial in history for crimes against the peace of the world imposes a grave responsibility. The wrongs which we seek to condemn and punish have been so calculated, so malignant and so devastating, that civilization cannot tolerate their being ignored because it cannot survive their being repeated. That four great nations, flushed with victory and stung with injury, stay the hand of vengeance and voluntarily submit their captive enemies to the judgment of the law is one of the most significant tributes that Power ever has paid to Reason.[58]

The American prosecutor described "aggressive war" as "the greatest menace of our times."[59] He conceded that it was unfortunate that the victors were judging the vanquished; however, "The world-wide scope of the aggressions carried out by these men has left but a few real neutrals."[60] Jackson believed that the victors' conduct in this trial would also be sternly judged: "We must never forget that the record on which we judge these defendants today is the record on which history will judge us tomorrow. To pass these defendants the poison chalice is to put it to our own lips as well."[61] Although the defendants were "the first war leaders of a defeated nation to be prosecuted in the name of law," he added, "they are also the first to be given a chance to plead for their lives in the name of law."[62] While the Americans basked in the warm glow of Jackson's rhetoric, German defense attorneys like Otto Kranzbühler bristled: "He was a good speaker without a doubt. Rhetorically good, but totally unrestrained in exploiting emotions."[63]

From the beginning it was clear that the Americans planned to take the broadest view of the Nazi conspiracy. In order to establish the widest range of Nazi criminality, the American prosecutor introduced a diverse array of evidence. In addition to the 485 tons of diplomatic documents the Allies discovered in a castle near Marburg, there was even more graphic evidence.[64] In a very dramatic move, on November 29, the prosecution introduced Document 2430-PS. This one-hour documentary film on Nazi concentration camps showed the Allied liberation of Dachau, Buchenwald, and Bergen-Belsen. The defendants' dock remained lit as images of dead, emaciated bodies stacked in ditches flickered on the courtroom wall. Some defendants, like Ribbentrop, Funk, and Frank, were visibly shaken; others, like Hjalmar Schacht and Hans Fritsche, turned their backs to the screen.[65]

Great Britain's Attorney General, Sir Hartley Shawcross, opened the British case on December 4. Shawcross maintained that sovereignty no longer provided blanket immunity for national leaders and that the right to wage war "was no longer the essence of sovereignty."[66] He argued that "practically the whole civilized world abolished war as a legally permissible means of enforcing the law" and attached great importance to prewar legislation like the Kellogg-Briand Pact. The British prosecutor anticipated and dismissed many of the defense arguments out of hand. "Political loyalty, military obedience are excellent things, but they neither require nor do they justify the commission of patently wicked acts."[67] One of the prosecution's key pieces of evidence in their aggressive war case was the notes of Adjunct Colonel Friedrich Hossbach from a November 5, 1937 conference at the Reich Chancellery. According to the prosecution, it was there that Hitler introduced the concept of *Lebensraum* and offered various military scenarios that included taking Austria and Czechoslovakia.

The defendants had a pleasant day on December 11, when the prosecution introduced Document 3054-PS, a film entitled *The Nazi Plan*. This four-part film included scenes from Leni Riefenstahl's *Triumph of the Will*. Some of the defendants, Ribbentrop and Goering in particular, beamed. Goering joked that the film was so inspiring he was sure that Justice Jackson would now want to join the party.[68] The defendants' courtroom levity ended when the court reconvened in early January 1946 and *Einsatzgruppen* leader Otto Ohlendorf took the witness stand. Each of the four Einsatzgruppen (A–D) had been attached to a German army unit and followed them into the Soviet Union with the specific intent of killing Jews and Communist Party officials.

The U.S. Army had found the Einsatzgruppens' daily "Morning Reports" from June 23, 1941 through April 24, 1942. According to their own careful records, the Einsatzgruppen killed more than one million people during this period. When asked how many his men killed, Ohlendorf answered matter-of-factly, "In the year between June 1941 and June 1942 the *Einsatzcommandos* reported 90,000 people liquidated." Ohlendorf confirmed that this included women and children.[69] American prosecutor Telford Taylor remembers being amazed by Ohlendorf's casual ruthlessness: "He said it just that way, as if there was nothing remarkable about it. The whole audience was shocked."[70] Ohlendorf's explanation why he preferred his soldiers to shoot their victims reveals much about how guilt is diffused in a modern, bureaucratic state: "The aim was that the individual leaders and men should be able to carry out the executions in a military manner acting on orders. They should not have to make a decision on their own."[71]

Telford Taylor cross-examined SS General Erich von dem Bach-Zelewski on January 7. The witness had been in charge of SS antipartisan units and killing squads like the Einsatzgruppen and reported directly to Heinrich Himmler. Bach-Zelewski was best known for overseeing the brutal repression of the Warsaw ghetto uprising in 1944. Taylor attempted to establish that the Wehrmacht, contrary to their leaders' vigorous denials, had played an integral role in brutal "antipartisan" campaigns in the Soviet Union and that the execution squads' activities were coordinated by the German army. The American prosecutor asked Bach-Zelewski simple, direct questions and carefully built his case fact by fact. "In the course of your duties, did you confer with the commanders of army groups and armies on the Eastern Front?" The SS general's answer implicated the army leaders: "With the commanders of the army groups, not of the armies, and with the district commanders of the Wehrmacht." Taylor bore down: "Did the highest military authorities issue instructions that anti-partisan operations were to be conducted with severity?" "Yes," Bach-Zelewski replied. He claimed that because the German high command had not drafted detailed antipartisan orders, policy descended into "a wild state of anarchy in all anti-partisan operations." Taylor asked if the leaders of the German army were aware of this. "The state of affairs was generally known. There was no necessity to make a special report about it, since every operation had immediately to be reported in all detail, and was known to every responsible leader," Bach-Zelewski replied. Taylor was fast emerging as one of the legal stars of the IMT; many took notice of his skill as a cross-examiner.[72]

Soviet prosecutor Yuri Pokrovsky next took up the questioning. He tried to prove that the havoc wrought by the Wehrmacht during the invasion of the Soviet Union was the result of a specific plan. However, Bach-Zelewski stuck to his story that the mayhem had happened for the opposite reason—the lack of a clear policy directive. According to the witness, it was nearly impossible to punish a soldier for atrocities committed in the Soviet Union: "orders emanating from the highest authorities definitely stated that if excesses were committed against the civilian population in the partisan areas, no disciplinary or judicial measures could be taken." He confirmed that the Germans had waged an unrestricted war of annihilation in the USSR. "I believe that these methods would definitely have resulted in the extermination of 30 million if they had been continued, and if developments of that time had not completely changed the situation."[73] American prosecutors introduced a homemade, leather-bound book entitled *The Warsaw Ghetto Is No More* as evidence. Its author, SS Major General Jürgen Stroop, gleefully recounted the annihilation of more than 50,000 Polish Jews: "The resistance put up by the Jews and bandits could be broken only by the relentless and energetic use of our shock-troops by day and night." Stroop concluded his account with a tally of the dead: "Only through the continuous and untiring work of all involved did we succeed in catching a total of 56,065 Jews whose extermination can be proved. To this should be added the number of Jews who lost their lives in explosions or fires but whose numbers could not be ascertained."[74] Further evidence about the Final Solution came when Adolf Eichman's former assistant, Dieter Wisliceny, testified that European Jews were "all taken to Auschwitz and there to the Final Solution." Hermann Goering bristled in the defendants' dock, "What does the swine expect to gain by it? He'll hang anyway!"[75]

Although French prosecutor François de Menthon had been a member of his nation's resistance, many of his countrymen had collaborated with the Nazi-imposed Vichy government. De Menthon opened the war crimes case for the French on January 17. He argued that the Nazis had reintroduced "the most primitive ideas of the savage tribe. All the values of civilization accumulated in the course of centuries are rejected, all traditional ideas of morality justice, and law give way to the primacy of race, its instincts, its needs and interests."[76]

Soviet Major General Roman A. Rudenko was the last Allied chief prosecutor to give an opening address, on February 8, 1946. Rudenko anticipated the German defense claim that Operation Barbarossa was a "preventive" war—"Much as the fascist wolf might disguise himself in sheep's skin, he cannot hide his teeth!"[77]—and pointed to a June 17, 1941 order signed by Heinrich Himmler's deputy Reinhard Heydrich: "the systematic extermination of Soviet people in fascist concentration camps in the territories of U.S.S.R. and other countries occupied by the fascist aggressors was carried out under the form of 'filtration,' 'cleaning measures,' 'purges,' 'extraordinary measures,' 'special treatment,' 'liquidation,' 'execution,' and so on."[78] Rudenko offered this shocking (and probably exaggerated) inventory of the destruction wrought in the Soviet Union by marauding Nazi armies: "The German fascist invaders completely or partially destroyed or burned 1,710 cities and more than 70,000 villages and hamlets . . . or destroyed six million buildings."[79] According to the Soviet prosecutor, the German invasion left more than 25 million homeless and destroyed 40,000 hospitals and 65,000 of Russia's 122,000 kilometers of railroad tracks. In addition, Rudenko claimed that the German invaders killed 7 million horses, 17 million head of cattle, 20 million pigs, and 110 million chickens and put the cost of the German destruction at 679,000 million rubles.[80]

Rudenko next catalogued the human cost of the invasion. The wanton slaughter of civilians by the Wehrmacht, SS, and special killing squads like the Einsatzgruppen were clear violations of the traditional laws of war: the 1907 Hague Convention expressly forbade such blatant mistreatment of noncombatants and war prisoners. While the Germans had fought a cleaner war on the Western Front, on the Eastern Front they waged a war of annihilation that summoned memories of Count Wallenstein's ten-year rampage during the Thirty Years War.

Abram Suzkever, a Soviet Jew from Vilna, took the stand at Nuremberg on February 27 and described what happened when the Nazi *Sonderkammandos* came to his town. Under questioning from the Soviet prosecutor, the survivor painted a chilling portrait. The "man-hunters" broke into the Jewish houses day or night. The larger objectives of Nazi policy were not lost on their victims: "I have to say that the Germans declared that they were exterminating the Jewish race as though legally."[81] Suzkever's pregnant wife violated a Nazi order that required all pregnant Jewish women to abort and all Jewish babies to be killed. Sympathetic doctors delivered the baby and hid him in one of the hospital rooms. When the witness approached the hospital, he saw the Sonderkommandos dragging sick and old people outside. Suzkever felt a cold rush of terror but had to wait until the soldiers left before he could go in. When he found his wife, she was sobbing. "I saw that my baby was dead. He was still warm," he testified.[82] Of Vilna's original population of 80,000 Jews, Suzkever estimated that only about 600 survived.[83]

When German Field Marshal Wilhelm Keitel took the stand, he attempted to shift the blame for Nazi atrocities to the SS. Although he appeared genuinely shocked and horrified by the concentration camp films, he was unequivocal in his condemnation of the perpetrators: "It is terrible. When I see such things, I'm ashamed of being German!—It was those dirty SS swine!—If I had known I would have told my son, 'I'd rather shoot you than let you join the SS.' But I did not know.—I'll never be able to look people in the face again."[84]

Soviet prosecutors were unconvinced by Keitel's contrition and forced him to admit that Operation Barbarossa was a war of extermination. Under cross-examination on March 6 and 7, Rudenko produced a directive signed by Keitel a month after the beginning of the German invasion: "one must bear in mind that in the countries affected human life has absolutely no value and that a deterrent effect can be achieved only through the application of extraordinarily harsh measures."[85] Rudenko asked Keitel if he recalled the order; he replied affirmatively. Rudenko asked the Field Marshal to explain what the phrase "human life has absolutely no value" meant, and Keitel admitted that their army fought in the east according to a different set of rules: "It does not contain these words; but I knew from years of experience that in the Southeastern territories and in certain parts of Soviet territory, human life was not respected in the same degree."[86]

When Hermann Goering finally took the stand on March 13, 1946, he basked in the spotlight. After months in captivity, he had slimmed down from 264 to 186 pounds, and rid himself of a nasty Percodan-and-champagne habit.[87] It was clear from the moment that Goering was asked for his plea of guilty or not guilty that he would not play the game of Nuremberg. Unlike many of the other defendants, the former *Reichsmarshall* seemed proud of his role in Germany's National Socialist revival. Above all, Goering rejected the international legal presumptions of Nuremberg. Under the friendly questioning of defense attorney Otto Stahmer, Goering described why he considered the 1907 Hague Conventions outdated by modern warfare and the rapid expansion of technology.[88] Goering compared World War II to the Boer War and the Russo-Japanese War to show how the very nature of military conflict had changed. Legitimate targets now included food supplies, infrastructure, and civilians. According to the Reichsmarshall, nothing had done more to undermine the laws of war than city bombing: "A war at that time between one army and another, in which the population was more or less not involved, cannot be compared with today's total war, in which everyone, even the child, is drawn into the experience of war through the introduction of air warfare."[89] He dismissed the atrocities and similar acts as part of the war of propaganda.

Goering was especially incensed by the idea that soldiers should examine orders as international legal questions: "How does one imagine a state can be led if, during a war, or before a war, which the political leaders had decided upon, whether wrongly or rightly, the individual general could vote whether he was going to fight or not, whether his Army corps was going to stay at home or not, or could say, 'I must first ask my division.' Perhaps one of them would go along, and the others stay at home!" The Reichsmarshall simply rejected the idea that law had any place in international politics: "In the struggle for life and death there is in the end no legality."[90]

Goering's testimony began to lose momentum on March 14, when he was questioned about Nazi policy toward the Jews. "After Germany's collapse in 1918 Jewry became very powerful in Germany in all spheres of life, especially political, general intellectual and cultural, and, most particularly, the economic spheres," Goering stated. Prominent German Jews "did not show necessary restraint and . . . stood out more and more in public life." He and the early National Socialists were especially incensed by modernist "degenerate art": "I likewise call attention to the distortion which was practiced in the field of art in this direction, to plays which dragged the fighting at the front through the mud and befouled the ideal of the brave soldier."[91] When Goering began to discuss the Nuremberg Laws, he tried to portray himself as a moderating influence on Hitler when it came to the treatment of Germany's Jews. "I suggested to him that, as a generous act, he should do away with the concept of persons of mixed blood and place such people on the same footing as German citizens." The defendant claimed that although Hitler "took up the idea with great interest and was all for adopting my point of view," before the idea could be implemented "came more troubled times as far as foreign policy was concerned."[92] Although Goering claimed that the Final Solution had not been planned in advance, he was

significantly less gregarious when confronted with a July 31, 1941 communi-
qué to Reinhard Heydrich describing "a total solution to the Jewish question within the area of Jewish influence in Europe."[93]

After the friendly questioning of his defense counsel Otto Stahmer,
his cross-examination began on March 18, 1946. Goering's cynical candor
seemed to disarm Justice Jackson. The American prosecutor asked, "After
you came to power, you regarded it as necessary, in order to maintain power,
to suppress all opposition parties?" The former Reichsmarshall responded
affirmatively. "We found it necessary not to permit any more opposition,
yes."[94] Jackson's frustration grew as quickly as Goering's confidence. When
asked about Germany's secret plans to occupy the Rhineland, the defendant answered snidely, "I do not think I can recall reading beforehand the
publication of the mobilization preparations of the United States."[95] Finally,
Robert Jackson appealed to the bench, "We can strike these things out. I
do not want to spend time doing that, but this witness, it seems to me, is
adopting, and has adopted, in the witness box and in the dock, an arrogant
and contemptuous attitude towards the Tribunal which is giving him the
trial which he never gave a living soul, nor dead ones either."[96]

With that exchange, Justice Lawrence adjourned the proceedings for the
day. The next morning, Jackson again appealed to the bench to control the
defendant: "The difficulty arises from this, Your Honor, that if the witness
is permitted to volunteer statements in cross-examination there is no opportunity to make objection until they are placed on the record." Jackson
argued that under Article 18 of the London Agreement Charter, the tribunal could "rule out irrelevant issues and statements of any kind whatsoever." Lawrence asked Jackson, "What exactly is the motion you are making? Are you asking the Tribunal to strike the answer out of the record?"
The chief American prosecutor replied that the defendant's answers should
be limited to the issues in question: "Well, no; in a Trial of this kind, where
propaganda is one of the purposes of the defendant, striking out does no
good after the answer is made, and Goering knows that as well as I." Lawrence gently overruled him: "As to this particular observation of the defendant, the defendant ought not to have referred to the United States, but it is
a matter which I think you might well ignore."[97]

The professional military was watching the case of Admiral Karl Doenitz very closely. Although Doenitz was a devoted Nazi who had been hand-
picked by Hitler to serve as his successor, he made an unlikely war crimes
trial defendant because the submarine war had been relatively clean. Despite British objections, the Americans insisted on trying him. As in World

War I, it was impossible for submarine commanders to warn armed merchant ships of their imminent destruction and then rescue the survivors. Even so, Germany had lost 650 submarines and 25,000 of its 40,000-man U-boat force.[98]

Former German naval judge Otto Kranzbühler had been personally selected by Admiral Doenitz to defend him. At the time, Kranzbühler "felt myself obligated, on the German side, to cooperate as much as possible."[99] Although Doenitz was an unrepentant Nazi who, like Julius Streicher, continued to admire Adolf Hitler, had he committed war crimes? Kranzbühler was able to point to the gap between the victors' professed standards and contemporary naval practices. The admiral would contend that the "merchant vessels" attacked by German submarines not only were armed but also attacked German submarines, and could not be considered neutral. This was very similar to the situation that arose during World War I.

Although *tu quoque* arguments were banned by Article 3 of the London Agreement Charter, Kranzbühler found a way around this technicality and submitted interrogatory questionnaires to Admiral Chester Nimitz, the commander of America's Pacific fleet, and to the British Admiralty about Allied naval practices during World War II. Kranzbühler was trying to establish the fact that refusing to rescue survivors was not the same as ordering their killing. Both Nimitz and the British Admiralty admitted that they too waged unrestricted submarine warfare and considered it legal. Admiral Nimitz appeared to side with his former adversary:

[QUESTION]: Was it customary for submarines to attack merchant men without warning?

[NIMITZ]: Yes, with the exception of hospital ships and other vessels under safe conduct voyages for humanitarian purposes. . . . On general principles, U.S. submarines did not rescue enemy survivors if undue additional hazard to the submarine resulted, or the submarine would be prevented from accomplishing its further mission. Therefore, it was unsafe to pick up many survivors.[100]

Admiral Doenitz also challenged the prosecutor's claim that he had ordered survivors killed and grew especially irate when the prosecution raised the 1942 *Laconia* affair. After a German U-boat sank the British passenger ship *Laconia*, the commander realized his mistake and radioed Doenitz, who immediately ordered the submarines to rescue the survivors and take them to the nearest port under a Red Cross flag. When the German submarines surfaced, collected the survivors, and began to tow them to safety, two American B-24s attacked the flotilla, sank one submarine, and killed a number of survivors. It was after this event that Doenitz ordered his submarines not to pick up survivors. "I saved, saved, and saved! I didn't see any help from you!" declared the exasperated admiral. "It was quite clear to me that the time had passed where I was able to be on the surface and do things like that. You had a very powerful air force against me."[101]

Rudolf Hoess, who had been Auschwitz commandant from 1940 to 1943, took the witness stand on April 15, 1946. Located in Poland, Auschwitz held as many as 140,000 inmates while Hoess was in charge. The site was chosen because it was isolated and approachable by rail only. Although the town of Auschwitz was only three kilometers away, the death camp, deep in the woods, was in a "prohibited area and even members of the SS who did not have a special pass could not enter it." When the trains arrived, the prisoners were first examined by doctors, and according to one witness, "The internees capable of work at once marched to Auschwitz or to the camp at Birkenau and those incapable of work were at first taken to the provisional installations, then to the newly constructed crematoria."[102]

Defense attorney Kurt Kauffmann tried to push the majority of the blame onto SS-*Obersturmbannführer* Adolf Eichmann. Hoess claimed that he had no exact idea how many inmates had been killed because only Eichmann was allowed to keep records about the numbers exterminated. "Is it furthermore true that Eichmann stated to you that in Auschwitz a total sum of more than 2 million Jews had been destroyed?" asked Kaufmann. "Yes," replied Hoess. The Auschwitz commandant had been summoned to a meeting in Berlin in the summer of 1941 and received personal orders from SS Chief Heinrich Himmler. "He told me something to the effect—I do not remember the exact words—that the Führer had given the order for the Final Solution of the Jewish question. We, the SS, must carry out that order. If it is not carried out now then the Jews will later on destroy the German people."[103]

The low point in the IMT came when the Soviet prosecutor, over Western objections, acting on orders from Moscow, charged Nazi Germany with the murders of Polish officers at Katyn. Rudenko announced, "One of the most important criminal acts for which the major war criminals are responsible was the mass execution of Polish prisoners of war shot in the Katyn forest near Smolensk by the German fascist invaders."[104] Even in 1946, most suspected that the Soviets had committed the massacre, because all evidence pointed toward their guilt. None of the documents found on the victims was dated later than May 6, 1940 (when the USSR controlled the area), and the victims were dressed in winter clothes, hands tied with cord manufactured in the Soviet Union.[105] According to German historian Jörg Friedrich, nothing did more to discredit Nuremberg in the eyes of those they were trying to reeducate than the bogus Katyn charges. "The fact that the Soviet Union, an aggressive and genocidal state, was participating in a legal proceeding strengthened this belief. The masters of the gulag would convict the masters of Auschwitz for crimes against humanity."[106]

Much to the dismay of the Soviet delegation, defense attorney Alfred Seidl questioned former Nazi Foreign Secretary Joachim von Ribbentrop about the Hitler-Stalin (Molotov-Ribbentrop) Pact on April 1. The Foreign Secretary went out of his way to implicate the Soviet Union: "In keeping with this understanding, the eastern territories were occupied by Soviet troops and the western territories by German troops after the victory. There is no doubt that Stalin can never accuse Germany of an aggression or of an aggressive war for her action in Poland. If it is considered an aggression, then both sides are guilty of it."[107] Von Ribbentrop outlined the Soviet demands—Finland, the Balkans, Bulgaria, and the naval outlets in the Dardanelles and the Baltic Sea. If this was not sufficiently embarrassing, on May 21, while questioning former German State Secretary Ernst von Weizsäcker, Seidl claimed to have a copy of the Hitler-Stalin Pact's secret protocol and that "Ambassador [Friedrich] Gaus [Ribbentrop's senior legal advisor] harbors no doubt at all that the agreements in question are correctly set out in the text."[108]

Justice Lawrence interrupted the defense lawyer and reminded him that the document had been ruled out of evidence because of its unknown origin. However, Seidl had an affadavit from Gaus stating that he had witnessed the document's signing in Moscow. "Your Honors!" Soviet prosecutor Rudenko exploded, "I would like to protest against these questions for two reasons. First of all, we are examining the matter of crimes of the major German war criminals. We are not investigating the foreign polices of other states." He claimed that the document was a forgery and had no evidentiary value. However, Lawrence allowed Seidl to ask the witness, von Weizsäcker, "what his recollection is of the treaty without putting the document to him." The witness deftly summarized the salient details of the secret protocol from memory: "It is about a very incisive, a very far-reaching secret addendum to the nonaggression pact concluded at the time. The scope of this document was very extensive since it concerned the partition of spheres of influence and drew a demarcation line between areas which, under given conditions, belonged to the sphere of Soviet Russia and those which would fall in the German sphere of interest." The agreement included "a complete redirection of Poland's destiny." Although the court did not allow the introduction of the Hitler-Stalin Pact into evidence, on May 23, the *St. Louis Post-Dispatch* published the document.[109] Later that day, General N. D. Zorya, the Soviet official in Nuremberg responsible for the slip-up that allowed Seidl to introduce the Molotov-Ribbentrop Pact, was found dead from a single gunshot to the head. The Soviets regretfully informed Zorya's international colleagues that he had committed suicide at the Soviet residence in Nuremberg.[110]

The case of Minister of Armaments and War Production Albert Speer was growing increasingly complicated. Speer admitted his guilt, cooperated with the prosecution, and labored to save his life both in and out of the courtroom. However, he had clearly violated the Geneva conventions by demanding and utilizing concentration camp inmates and POWs as slave laborers on various armament-related projects. He had visited the underground factories that produced the engines for the V-2 rockets and the jet engines for the Messerschmitt 262 airplanes.[111] Not only had he taken 30,000 concentration camp inmates from Heinrich Himmler, Speer had also instituted a program under which factory "slackers" were sent to the camps.[112] If this blatant misuse of slave labor were not enough, between October 18 and November 2, 1941, he had helped Adolf Eichmann with the forced evictions of 50,000 German Jews from Berlin under the Reich's "Slum Clearance" project. "There was no comprehensive authority in my hands," Speer claimed on the stand. "But I, as the man responsible for production, had no responsibility in these matters. However, when I heard complaints from factory heads or from my deputies, I did everything to remove the cause of the complaints."[113] Most incriminating was the armament minister's presence at Posen during Himmler's famous October 6, 1943 speech on the "Final Solution," where Himmler personally addressed him as "party comrade Speer."[114]

Although Albert Speer pled weakly that he had considered assassinating Hitler in the final days of the war, his guilt was more certain than his innocence. On the stand, he claimed to have had little knowledge of his friend's intentions and never to have read *Mein Kampf*.[115] Under Soviet cross-examination, Speer was forced to admit that he'd been in close contact with Hitler and "heard his personal views."[116] Compared to the "Statement of Remorse" read by former Minister for Economic Affairs Walter Funk on May 6, 1946, many found his testimony unconvincing. "I nearly died of shame," Goering quipped after Speer's attorney had shown his client's hand by asking Otto Ohlendorf under cross-examination if his old friend, Albert Speer, had ever mentioned his plans to assassinate Adolf Hitler. Goering vividly expressed his disgust at the idea that Ohlendorf would have betrayed a comrade: "To think that a German could be so rotten, just to prolong his wretched life—to put it crudely, to piss in front and crap behind a little longer." As far as Goering was concerned, they would all surely be executed; however, there was "such a thing as honour."[117]

Contrasting most sharply with Speer's upper-middle-class propriety was the dark presence of Julius Streicher. Journalist Rebecca West described Streicher during the trial as "the sort who gives trouble in parks."[118] An unlikely choice as a defendant in a major war crimes trial, Streicher had been the publisher of the racist and borderline pornographic Nazi periodical *Der Strumer*. However, he had not been involved in either policy making or military decision making, and the prosecution would need to establish the fact that the periodicals he produced helped to create a climate conducive to carrying out the Final Solution. Of the defendants at Nuremberg, the former comic book publisher had scored the lowest on the I.Q. test given to all the prisoners.[119] Although Streicher expressed odious personal views, had he committed war crimes?

When the time came to rule, the IMT proved very conservative in applying the hotly debated conspiracy and aggression charges.[120] While the judges found eight guilty of crimes against peace (Goering, Hess, Ribbentrop, Keitel, Rosenberg, Jodl, Seyss-Inquart, Neurath, and Raeder), they acquitted four (Fritzsche, Speer, Schacht, and Papen) and offered no expansive definition of aggression, only vague references to "aggressive acts."[121] The cautious precedent did not establish a definitive standard for aggression, and as David Luban puts it, was "resting on the shakiest of grounds."[122] When it came to the Nazi organizations, the IMT carefully distinguished between the organs of state terror like the SS and the professional soldiers. While the court criminalized the *Schutzstaffel, Sicherheitsdienst*, Gestapo, and Leadership Corps of the Nazi Party, they acquitted the General Staff, High Command, Reich Cabinet, and *Sturmabteilung*.[123]

Otto Kranzbühler remembered the day of the sentencing as "full of gloomy tension. We knew that we would reckon with a large number of death sentences."[124] The IMT sentenced twelve men to death on October 1, 1946 (Goering, Ribbentrop, Keitel, Kaltenbrunner, Rosenberg, Frank, Frick, Streicher, Sauckel, Jodl, Bormann, and Seyss-Inquart). The biggest surprises were the acquittals of Schacht, Papen, and Fritzsche. Speer's repentance and his guilty plea got him twenty years in prison, Doenitz received a ten-year sentence, and Rudolf Hess was sentenced to life in Spandau Prison. Because of this and other examples of what they considered leniency, the Soviet judges issued a dissenting opinion on the acquittals; the majority's decision not to criminalize the Reich Cabinet, the General Staff, and the High Command; and finally the Hess sentence.[125] The IMT sentenced Hermann Goering to hang, but he had other plans. Goering had befriended an American guard named "Tex" Wheelis and plied him with expensive gifts like a Bulova watch and a Mont Blanc pen. Because Wheelis had access to the prisoners' baggage room, he could find and deliver Goering's hidden cyanide capsules. Hours before his scheduled hanging, the former Reichsmarshall was found dead in his cell from cyanide poisoning. "This grand finale is typical of the abysmal depths plumbed by the court and prosecution. Pure theater, from start to finish! All rotten comedy!" Goering wrote in his final letter. "I would have let you shoot me without further ado! But it is not possible to hang the German Reichsmarshall."[126]

The other convicts were hanged by Master Sergeant John Woods of the U.S. Army on October 16, 1946. Historian Jörg Friedrich describes how some of the German public reacted to the Nuremberg verdicts:

> The Germans learned from posters on the street that their former leaders had been hanged at Nuremberg. In the last three months of the war, more than 700,000 German soldiers and civilians had lost their lives. Now people crowded around the pillars on which the posters hung, reading in silence that ministers, field marshals and police chiefs had also died. There were no signs of remorse. In Wuppertal, schoolgirls dressed in black on the morning of the execution; in Hamburg, people whispered that the British leaders responsible for the bombing of the city also deserved to hang.[127]

In terms of providing fallen foes with a legitimate forum, the IMT was unprecedented in modern history. The accused were informed of the charges filed against them and given access to the evidence, legal representation, and an opportunity to state their cases in open court. The court simply refused to rule in the case of the Katyn Massacre, and any mention of it was conspicuously absent from the final judgment. The acquittals and even the Soviet dissents bolstered the court's credibility. Above and beyond all else, Nuremberg provided a unique international legal inquiry. Due to the acrimony surrounding the London Agreement Charter, the court began and ended divided, and an accidental result of this division were carefully considered judgments and dissenting opinions. One of the most significant challenges the judges faced was reconciling a number of interpretations of international law (Continental, Anglo, and American) and preventing the differences among them from undermining the trials.[128] This tribunal contrasts sharply with the forms of political justice exercised by both the Soviets and the Nazis against their respective enemies. Compared to Stalin and Vyshinsky's 1930s Moscow purge trials or Hitler's 1944 trial of the "Bomb plotters," Nuremberg stands up quite nicely. Ironically, the quadripartite disagreements over war crimes policy prevented the kinds of strategic legalist nonjudicial sentence reductions that would become all too familiar in Germany and Japan during the 1950s. Moreover, the Soviets failed to turn Nuremberg into "a continuation of political warfare in judicial robes."[129] The IMT proved that trials conducted by the victors of a conflict were not farcical by their very nature. The Allies not only managed to punish the guilty but also created a strong documentary record of the German dictatorship.

However, in terms of reeducation, reform, and overall social engineering, the trials were less successful.[130] The lessons of Nuremberg were lost on war-weary Germans, many of whom had grown cynical and apathetic and considered the process a form of ritual or political theater. The assumption that trials could reeducate an entire nation proved naïve and erroneous.[131] Instead of embracing national guilt after World War II, many Germans chose to become "blind in one eye": "German critics ignored—and continue to ignore—some distinctive characteristics of Nuremberg, such as due process of law. They glossed over the sober presentation of abundant evidence of German atrocities. Instead, they insisted that Nuremberg was legally flawed, with the reservation that the major Nazis got what they deserved," observes Friedrich.[132]

The IMT stands in stark contrast to the International Military Tribunal for the Far East (IMTFE) or the "Tokyo trial." The IMTFE arraigned twenty-eight of Japan's military and civilian leaders under a fifty-five-count indictment that included charges of crimes against peace and crimes against humanity on April 29, 1946. Although Emperor Hirohito was not among the defendants, they did include Hideki Tojo and a number of other high-ranking officials.[133] The decision not to try the emperor was made unilaterally by General Douglas MacArthur, who argued that if he were tried like a common criminal, the United States would need a million additional troops to restore order.

At lower levels, the Americans under the Supreme Commander Asia Pacific (SCAP) occupation government would attempt to purge the Japanese government of wartime functionaries, as had been done in Germany.[134] Japan was undergoing a similar social reconstruction, and they hoped that the trial of the high-ranking Japanese would, like Nuremberg's IMT, serve as the centerpiece of the American reeducation effort.

Unlike the IMT, whose indictment (the London Agreement and Charter) was an international agreement, the IMTFE was established by a proclamation issued by Allied Supreme Commander General Douglas MacArthur. The tribunal was composed of eleven judges from Australia, Canada, China, France, the Philippines, the Netherlands, New Zealand, the Soviet Union, Great Britain, the United States, and India. Dutch judge B.V.A. Röling later described the Tokyo trial as "very much an American performance. . . . I didn't see it at the time, and I didn't see that there were more 'Hollywood-esque' things around than there should have been."[135] The chief counsel for the United States was a former criminal lawyer and New Dealer named Joe Keenan who overzealously pushed the Americans' broadened conception of international criminality and claimed that the trial "served as a cockpit for a death struggle between two completely irreconcilable and opposed types of legal thinking" (natural law and positivism).[136]

The presiding judge in the Tokyo trial was William Webb of Australia. Unlike Justice Lawrence, the presiding judge in the IMT, who was elected by his peers, Webb was appointed by MacArthur. Years later, Judge Röling described Webb as "completely unsure of his position"; this manifested itself in "dictatorial behavior toward his colleagues as well as toward the prosecutors and defense counsel."[137] Legal historian John Appleman writes, "After examining the proceedings of the International Military Tribunal at Nuremberg . . . the proceedings before the International Military Tribunal for the Far East seem strangely autocratic."[138]

The case for German aggression was easily made; the mountains of captured German documents provided enough proof to make the crimes against peace charges arguable. The same charges were far less certain in the case of the Japanese because the prosecution lacked such documentary evidence. And because Nuremberg's IMT had not defined standards of aggression, the IMTFE had to render independent judgment.[139] The indictment in the Tokyo trial was significantly more complicated than the IMT's London

Agreement Charter. Crimes against peace were covered by Counts 1–36, murder by 37–52, and war crimes and crimes against humanity by 53–55. This indictment was legally problematic in a number of respects.[140] Some of the defendants were charged with not having prevented war crimes—in other words, negative criminality. The fifty-fourth count accused the defendants of having "deliberately and recklessly disregarded their legal duty to take adequate steps to secure the observance and prevent breaches" of the laws of war.[141] In other words, they were charged with what they didn't do. Due to the size of the court and the number of defendants, the prosecution case would take seven months to present and the trial would last more than two and half years.

U.S. Army defense lawyer Major General Ben Bruce Blakney challenged the court's jurisdiction on May 6, arguing that "war is not a crime."[142] Unlike the defense lawyers in the first Nuremberg trial, those in Tokyo were not forbidden to attack the court's international legal legitimacy. During the first week, the defense filed more motions challenging the trial's legal basis. Japanese defense counsel Kenzo Takayanagi questioned the criminality of aggression under international law on the grounds that the Kellogg-Briand Pact had a provision for self-defense and that the Japanese war effort had been an act of self-defense.[143] He also cited Robert Lansing's now well-worn rejection of aggression charges from the Paris Peace Conference.[144] Prime Minister Tojo accepted full responsibility for Japan's actions. In a 50,000-word statement, he argued that the attacks on Pearl Harbor, China, and Indonesia, and other so-called acts of "aggression," were responses to an Allied policy that intended to strangle the island nation with economic and military blockades. According to the defendant, the fact that the Japanese had fired the first shot was inconsequential in the larger context of U.S.–Japanese relations during the 1930s and early 1940s.[145]

Only the Axis leaders faced the War Department's aggression, conspiracy, and crimes against humanity charges and as a result, Allied war crimes policy was uneven in a number of ways. Because of the logistical requirements of two occupations, the policy had a strong ad hoc character; theater officials were often forced to interpret vague orders. Historian Kurt Tauber has offered this explanation for the confusion that resulted: "Without a clear unambiguous decision at the highest level in favor of one or the other course, there was uncertainty at the lower echelons, where policy is actually executed. The ambiguity was never entirely removed."[146] The end result was the emergence of a hydra-headed American war crimes policy. High-ranking Axis leaders were given elaborate trials and judged according to new standards of international law, while the overwhelming majority of war crimes cases were tried by the Allied military under military law. Of the 1,672 tried by the U.S. Army at the Dachau concentration camp, approximately two thirds of the defendants had been guards or personnel at the Buchenwald, Flossenburg, Mauthausen, Nordhausen, Hadamar, and Mühldorf concentration camps; another large group (1,000) was charged with lynching Allied pilots; and a small number were tried for the Malmedy Massacre.[147] In the Pacific theater, U.S. military courts tried 215 in Manila, 966 in Yokohama, and 116 at the Kwajalein Atoll and Guam for traditional war crimes.[148] The proceedings conducted by the U.S. Army in both Asia and Europe were not up to the lofty standards of the international courts, though they did provide traditional, punitive political justice. But because the Americans had loudly and conspicuously committed themselves to higher standards for the IMT and the IMTFE, all of their trials would be judged by those standards.

The most famous victor's justice occurred in the Philippines in 1945, where General Douglas MacArthur evened the score with his former Japanese adversaries Tomoyuki Yamashita and Masaharu Homma. General Yamashita had earned fame and glory in 1943 when with only 30,000 men he overwhelmed 100,000 British troops at Malaya.[149] Yamashita returned to Manila as Japanese Supreme Commander in the Philippines in October 20, 1944 and declared it open in January 1945 because the flat, spread-out city with its highly flammable buildings would be difficult to defend.[150] Yamashita retreated to Baguio, and beginning on February 3, 20,000 Japanese sailors and marines spilled into Manila and began to ransack the city and slaughter its inhabitants. When the general heard about the atrocities nine days later, he radioed the now dead Admiral Iwabuchia (the commander of the navy) and ordered him to withdraw.[151] General Yamashita would later claim that he was unable to command the troops due to a breakdown in communications caused by the onslaught of the U.S. forces. Two days before the trial began, defense attorney Frank Reel learned that the prosecution had added fifty-nine new charges to the indictment. Although Reel petitioned for more time to address the new charges, his request was denied.[152]

A reception hall in the High Commissioner's residence in Manila was transformed into a courtroom, and Yamashita was arraigned by a five-man military commission on October 8, 1945. General MacArthur charged that Yamashita "unlawfully disregarded and failed to discharge his duty as commander to control the ops of the members of his command." MacArthur divided the crimes into three categories: starvation, executions, and massa-cres; torture, rape, murder, and mass executions; and burning and demo-lition without military necessity.[153] Nuremberg this was not, and MacAr-thur offered no apologies or excuses. The "American Caesar" did not feel compelled to observe any law but his own. The trial of his former adversar-ies was a throwback to traditional, punitive political justice. Not only did MacArthur select the judges and draft the trial procedure, he commanded all of the generals on the five-man legal commission, and none of them was a lawyer. Moreover, the tribunal was not "bound by technical rules of evi-dence."[154] One prosecution witness testified that the Japanese soldiers had bayoneted her, and lifted her shirt to display twenty-six bayonet-wound scars. Another testified that Japanese soldiers had killed her young child in front of her; she began to shake her fist at the general and scream, "*Tandaan mo!* [Remember it!] Yamashita!"[155]

The prosecution did great damage to the trial's reputation when they in-troduced a pseudodocumentary movie as the "evidence which will con-vict." The film showed an American soldier removing a piece of paper from the pocket of a dead Japanese soldier; it read (in English), "Orders from Tokyo." The narrator broke in: "We have discovered the secret or-ders to destroy Manila."[156] After the prosecution rested on November 20, the defense called Australian Norman Sparnom, the Allied chief translator in charge of captured Japanese documents. The defense attorney asked, "A film was shown before this committee in which a statement was made that the United States of America had captured an order from Tokyo for the de-struction of Manila. Have you ever seen such an order among the captured documents?" "No, I have not," Sparnom replied.[157]

Yamashita's attorney, Frank Reel, did not challenge the evidence pre-sented by the prosecution. Instead, he attempted to distance the general from the atrocities committed in Manila, claiming that the general had been thrown into a desperate situation in the Philippines. After the Japanese en-tered Manila, Yamashita declared it indefensible and retreated to Baguio. Throughout his trial, he maintained that the defendant did not hear of the atrocities until more than a week after they had occurred:[158]

> I absolutely did not order [any atrocities] nor did I receive the order to do
> this from any superior authority, nor did I ever permit such a thing . . . and
> will swear to heaven and earth concerning these points. . . . The facts are that
> I was constantly under attack by large American forces, and I had been under

pressure day and night. . . . I believe that under the foregoing conditions I did the best possible job I could have done. However, due to the above circumstances, my plans and my strength were not sufficient to the situation, and if these things happened, they were absolutely unavoidable. They were beyond anything I would have expected.[159]

On December 7, 1945, the fourth anniversary of the Japanese attack on Pearl Harbor, MacArthur's military commission handed down their decisions. Robert Shaplen of *Newsweek* wrote, "In the opinion of probably every correspondent covering the trial the military commission came into the courtroom the first day with the decision already in its collective pocket."[160] They found that the atrocities were "not sporadic in nature but in many cases were methodically supervised by the Japanese officers and noncommissioned officers."[161] The second part of the opinion announced the most significant precedent to come out of the Yamashita case—"command responsibility," the idea that a commanding officer could be held accountable for the actions of his troops.[162]

General MacArthur's treatment of his former foe, although abhorrent when measured by the new standards of the U.S. War Department, was consistent with history.[163] In the Yamashita case, like the *U.S.–Dakota War Trials* and the trial of Captain Henry Wirz, the conquered had no choice but to submit to the judicial fiat of the victors. A soldier from an earlier era, MacArthur had few legal pretensions and considered professional military men bound by "warrior's honor." In the final opinion, he wrote: "The soldier, be he friend or foe, is charged with the protection of the weak and unarmed. It is the very essence and reason for his being. When he violates his sacred trust, he not only profanes the entire cult but threatens the very fabric of international society."[164] Major General Russell Reynolds, Major General Clarence Sturdevant, Major General James Lester, Brigadier General William Walker, and Brigadier General Egbert Bullens sentenced Tomoyuki Yamashita to death by hanging. Yamashita maintained his innocence until the end: "I wish to state that I stand here today with the same clear conscience as on the first day of my arraignment, and I swear to my Creator and everything that is sacred to me that I am innocent of all charges made against me."[165]

America's highest court had been conspicuously silent on the question of war crimes until Frank Reel, Yamashita's attorney, appealed to the U.S. Supreme Court for a writ of *habeas corpus*.[166] Although the court upheld

Yamashita's death sentence by a clear six-to-two margin in February 1946, the majority based their ruling on the 1942 decision in *Ex parte Quirin,* which authorized congressional passage of the articles of war and sanctioned the use of military tribunals during wartime.[167] The majority avoided the substantive legal questions of the Yamashita case, and Chief Justice Harlan Stone applied a narrow reading of the Constitution, concluding that it was not the court's responsibility to reexamine the case: "We do not here appraise the evidence on which petitioner was convicted.... These are questions within the peculiar competence of the military officers composing the commission and were for it to decide."[168]

Not all of Stone's Supreme Court brethren were willing to take such an easy way out: Justices Murphy and Rutledge issued strong dissenting opinions that did lasting damage to the reputation of the Yamashita case. Justice Murphy described the trial as "a practice reminiscent of that pursued in certain less respected nations in recent years" and went on to attack the logic of the army tribunal.[169] "We will judge the discharge of your duties," wrote Murphy,

> by the disorganization which we ourselves created in large part. Our standards of judgment are whatever we wish to make them. Nothing in all history or in international law, at least as far as I am aware, justifies such a charge against a fallen commander of a defeated force. To use the very inefficiency and disorganization created by the victorious forces as the primary basis for condemning officers of defeated armies bears no resemblance to justice or to military reality.[170]

Once General MacArthur received word that the U.S. Supreme Court had upheld the death sentence, he ordered Yamashita stripped of his uniform and decorations and hanged.

MacArthur's Manila tribunal arraigned Masaharu Homma on December 19, 1945; he too was charged with failure to control his troops. When American General Edward King surrendered to Homma's forces on Bataan on April 9, 1942, he was assured that his troops would be treated humanely. Between 80,000 and 100,000 American and Philippine soldiers began the 80-mile walk to Bataan; 7,000 died and 10,000 were killed by Japanese soldiers along the way. General Homma had few doubts about his fate: "Win and you are the official army, lose and you are the rebels." He argued very simply that "there is no such thing as justice in international relations in this universe." Unlike Yamashita, Homma was sentenced to death by firing squad. Again, the Supreme Court rejected Homma's lawyer's writ of *habeas corpus* by a six-to-two majority, with Rutledge and Murphy again issuing dissenting opinions.[171]

While it is important to note the legal irregularities in the Yamashita case, it is also important to keep in mind that legal guilt and moral guilt are two entirely different things. Japanese soldiers treated American POWs significantly worse than the Germans did. Of the approximately 235,000 American and British POWs taken by Germany and Italy, approximately 4 percent died in captivity, whereas of 132,000 British and American prisoners in Japanese captivity, 27 percent died. Australian POWs suffered most: of the 21,726 captured, 7,412 or 34 percent died. While the Manila trials contained some glaring procedural flaws, Yamashita and Homma were the leaders of a losing army that wantonly and brutally slaughtered civilians throughout Asia. Japanese soldiers tended to view POWs with contempt for surrendering. And while the motives will never be known, it is clear beyond a reasonable doubt that in Nanking, Manila, Canton, and many other parts of Asia, civilians were killed almost for sport. In six weeks in Nanking in 1937 and '38, Japanese soldiers killed approximately 300,000 civilians and raped 20,000 women. Two soldiers even engaged in a contest to see who would be first to behead 100 POWs, and the competition was closely monitored by a Japanese newspaper.[172]

With the surrender of Japan came the discovery of the Japanese special warfare Units 731, 100, and 112. In a laboratory in Manchuria the doctors conducted medical experiments on Chinese, Korean, and Russian POWs. Prisoners were frozen alive, infected with syphilis, given transfusions of horse blood, subjected to vivisection with no anaesthesia, and given numerous x-rays to test the effects of radiation. Although the Soviets captured the laboratories in Manchuria, most of the 3,600 doctors and technicians escaped and made their way back to Japan. The head of Unit 731, Lieutenant General Shiro Ishi, traded his research results to American authorities in exchange for immunity from prosecution, according to historian John Dower: "Americans who controlled the prosecution chose to grant blanket secret immunity to . . . the officers and scientific researchers in Unit 731 in Manchuria. . . . The data gained from human experimentation once again became ammunition: this time in the bargaining room, rather than on the battlefield."[173] As in Germany, war crimes prosecutions in Japan were extremely uneven.

The various and diverse post–World War II war crimes trials explored pro-found questions about the laws of war in the twentieth century. Was the ob-jective of modern total war to defeat the enemy's army on the battlefield, or to attack and demoralize their civilian population? If civilians had become legitimate targets, were the laws of war outdated by the expansion of mili-tary conflict? These questions were especially relevant in Germany, where many considered the destruction of their nation's cities and infrastructure punishment enough. Even William T. Sherman had advocated a merciful peace after total war. However, for the perpetrators of the Malmedy Massa-cre, initially it appeared that there would be no mercy.

Due to the symbolic importance of the slaughter of surrendered Amer-ican soldiers, the United States was under a great deal of pressure to iden-tify and prosecute their killers. American investigators were certain that *Kampfegruppe* Peiper, under the command of Sepp Dietrich and Joachim Peiper, had committed the Malmedy Massacre. Both were transferred to a century-old prison near Ludwigsberg called Schwabisch Hall and inter-rogated by army investigators who became frustrated by the stonewalling of the hardened Nazis. A suspiciously large number of men claimed that a dead SS Commander named Walter Pringel had ordered the killings.[174] The questioner, Lieutenant William Perl, was an Austrian lawyer who had been forced out of Vienna in 1938 because he was Jewish. Perl was trained by U.S. Military Intelligence, and sent back to Europe as a U.S. Army interrogator.

The interrogation of twenty-two-year-old Paul Zwiggart was described by his attorney in an obviously biased but telling account years later. Af-ter six weeks of solitary confinement in Schwabisch Hall, a guard entered his cell and put a hood over Zwiggart's head.[175] He and the other prison-ers were taken through long corridors and down a flight of stairs; "suddenly heavy iron chains had been trailed near the prisoners which rattle must pro-duce a corresponding psychological effect." According to the defense attor-ney, the men were forced to face the wall with their arms raised. "During about twenty minutes, he received in that position kicks without any inter-ruption." Finally Lieutenant Perl pulled the hood off Zwiggart's head and took him to a small room with a table on which sat a crucifix and two burn-ing candles. Behind the table sat an American officer, "who was indicated as being the judge. On the left stood Mr. THON who was presented as attor-ney-general and on the right of the prisoner First Lieutenant PEARL had taken place and told Zwiggart that he was his defense attorney and that this event was an 'American summary court.'" Because Zwiggart refused to con-fess, he was "sentenced" to death. According to the prisoner, the day after the fictitious trial, an execution was solemnly staged: "A cord was bound around the neck of the young Zwiggart—he still had the capuche over his head—and then he heard the voice of First Lieutenant PEARL who said that he had only one chance to save himself by pleading guilty for himselves and his comrades." Zwiggart finally signed a "statement" dictated by his interrogators.[176] Another of the accused, Arvid Freimuth, hanged himself after Lieutenant Perl threatened to hand him over to the Belgians.[177]

By December 1945, the Americans' interrogation techniques had generated a number of confessions.[178] The confession of Joachim Peiper provided the prosecution with a major break in their case. Like Yamashita, Peiper made no effort to challenge the facts of the case and candidly stated his orders: "considering the desperate situation of the German people, a wave of terror and fright should precede our troops."[179] Symbolically, Peiper was an important figure: to the Americans he was an unrepentant Nazi, to the Germans he was a decorated officer and war hero.

Seventy-four Waffen SS veterans were charged with various violations of the laws of war on May 16, 1946 in a makeshift courtroom in the Dachau concentration camp. As in the Yamashita case, the defense team was at a huge disadvantage because the army argued that the defendants were not prisoners of war, but "civilian internees" not protected by the Geneva Convention of 1929.[180] Therefore the tribunal had the power to create and employ any evidentiary standard it desired.[181] When the first reports of forced confessions had come in the spring of 1945, Theatre Judge Advocate Major Claude Mickelwaite investigated and determined that some of the prisoners had been punched or slapped by guards, but there was no evidence of systematic torture, only "psychological duress."[182] Even chief prosecutor Burton Ellis admitted that "all the legitimate tricks, ruses, and stratagems known to investigators were employed."[183]

Although the eight-man General Military Government Court was the highest level of military justice, it labored under none of the presumptions of the Nuremberg trial. When the defense argued that since the confessions had been obtained before the defendants' status had been changed, they were inadmissible, the tribunal dismissed these motions.[184] The prosecution was headed by Colonel Burton Ellis and the defense by Wallace Everett Jr. The defense was at a major disadvantage: not only did Everett have no prior courtroom experience, he had to defend seventy-four men.[185] The court was presided over by Brigadier General Josiah Dalbey.

The indictment stated that the defendants, "at the vicinity of Malmedy Honsfeld, Büllingen, Stavelot, Wanne and Lutrebois, all in Belgium, at sundry times between 16 December 1944 and 13 January 1945, willfully, deliberately and wrongfully permit, encourage, aid, abet and participate in the killing, shooting, ill-treatment, abuse and torture of members of the Armed Forces of the United States of America, then at war with the then Third Reich."[186]

Peiper fought in the courtroom with the same tenacity that had earned him the Iron Cross with the oak-leaf cluster. To the Nazi war hero, morality and restraint had no place in the final days of a total war; he did not need to tell his men to shoot prisoners of war "because those present were all experienced officers to whom this was obvious."[187]

Peiper attacked the prosecution for the way in which they obtained his confession.[188] He testified that after five weeks of solitary confinement, he was told by interrogators that his troops killed the sons of prominent American politicians and businessmen and that the cry for his head had grown so loud that not even the President of the United States could save him. However, if he cooperated with investigators and signed the confession of guilt prepared by Lieutenant Perl, the army would spare his men.[189] As for actual violations of the laws of war, Peiper believed that those laws had been rendered obsolete by the realities of total war: "During combat there are desperate situations, the answer to which is given out very fast to main reactions and which do not have anything to do with education and teaching."[190]

Joachim Peiper and Admiral Karl Doenitz became two of Germany's most important post–World War II martyrs. However, it was not only German nationalists who claimed that their military had been unjustifiably persecuted; a large portion of the world's professional soldiers were beginning to close ranks on the subject of war crimes. Although Peiper was tried by the U.S. Army under military law, such distinctions were lost on German nationalists, who considered all of the Allied war crimes trials part of a "victor's justice" with no legal legitimacy.[191]

Like the Yamashita case, the Malmedy trial dispensed traditional, punitive political justice. Although the format had to be updated to fit the twentieth century, the message remained the same. After a five-week trial, Peiper, Dietrich, and forty-two of their men were sentenced to death; twenty-two others were sentenced to life imprisonment. Defense counsel John Everett followed the example of Yamashita's attorney, Frank Reel, and petitioned the U.S. Supreme Court for a writ of *habeas corpus* because their confessions were obtained under torture.[192] Although the court rejected this argument, the fate of Kampfgruppe Peiper was by no means sealed. By the time the Malmedy trials and the international Nuremberg trial concluded, in late 1946, the geopolitical landscape was changing rapidly. German war crimes were now overshadowed by the perceived threat of the Soviet Union, and American policy toward Germany began to reflect this change.

CHAPTER 4

A SHIFT IN PRIORITIES

Joint Chiefs of Staff Directive 1067, approved by President Roosevelt on September 29, 1944, would govern the initial phase of the U.S. occupation of Germany. This huge task fell to the U.S. Military Government and Military Governor General Lucius Clay. Although the Americans were the most conspicuous advocates of reeducation, they were not alone. Prior to the defeat of the Third Reich, prominent European intellectuals like Thomas Mann and German historian Friedrich Meinecke called for some type of reform.[1] So there was a consensus that Germany needed to be transformed, but there was no agreement about how to do this. Americans like Justice Robert Jackson hoped that trials would aid the American reeducation effort by establishing an empirical record of Nazi crimes. Legitimate trials would prove to the German people that under an American-inspired system of justice, due process of law was extended to even the guiltiest.[2] Although the Morgenthau Plan had been rejected, JCS 1067 retained some of its punitive aspects.[3] Initially, the United States aimed to demilitarize, denazify, and deindustrialize the vanquished nation, removing the German threat by approaching it as a social problem. But because the German army had been crushed, demilitarization was never an issue.

Although the Nuremberg trials were the highest-profile legal proceeding, the vast majority of cases were tried by Allied denazification courts. German states in the American zone of occupation enacted the De-Nazification Law, which established four levels of offenses by members of the recently criminalized Nazi organizations, on March 5, 1946.[4] The implications of this vague commitment were both radical and enormous: a large percentage of the German population would have to be processed judicially.[5] More than 13 million Germans registered with denazification boards; 945,000 were tried by denazification courts, and 130,000 were found guilty under some category of law. However, penalties were not very severe; sentences ranged from ineligibility to hold public office to restricted employment, fines, and at worst, forced labor.[6] Many Germans considered the American questionnaire, or *Fragebogen*, an intrusively detailed accounting of individual wartime activities.[7]

The year 1946 was a transitional one in American foreign policy; Cold War historians agree that Secretary of State James Byrnes's Stuttgart speech on September 6 "renounced the more retributive elements of JCS 1067 and began to relax the external controls of the occupation in an effort to move Germany down the road to self-government."[8] From the beginning, the State Department had taken a dim view of war crimes trials and denazification, and felt that high-placed Jews within the Roosevelt administration had tainted the American occupation with "blind vengeance." According to Peter Grose's book *Operation Rollback*, "By the summer of 1946, Washington's top military intelligence officers had abandoned the fervor of de-Nazification and were arranging for ex-Nazis with 'special' qualifications, such as expertise in rocket science and other high technology, to be excused from the indignities of prisoner-of-war status and join the service of the United States for the demands of the postwar era."[9]

Denazification underwent a significant shift in March 1946, when the U.S. military turned the program over to the German zonal government. Many considered this an abandonment of the reeducation program, but General Clay argued that the best way for Germans to learn democracy was to live it.[10] Although denazification proceedings continued until 1949, they often appeared farcical under German administration. Former Assistant U.S. High Commissioner Benjamin Buttenweiser recalled that "some of the denazification trials were absolutely shocking mockeries . . . they were by no test a complete success."[11] The results were predictable. Like Reconstruction after the American Civil War, the grand social engineering project known as "reeducation" was quickly and quietly winding down. An important element of the American reeducation effort was to create a record of Nazi atrocities that would withstand the test of time, and this task remained unfinished.

The Allied war crimes effort provided one of the first rallying points for Germany's post–World War II nationalists. Their relationship with the trials was beginning to resemble that of a previous generation of German nationalists with the Treaty of Versailles. The theme remained the same: the expansion of Bolshevism was "divine retribution" for the "unjust" treatment of Germany.[12]

Robert Jackson probably never doubted that the United States should conduct subsequent proceedings under the laws created for the IMT. In a letter to President Truman on December 4, 1945, Jackson suggested that the United States hold another series of high-level trials and that Colonel Telford Taylor be put in charge of the preparations.[13] In a report to the President, Jackson offered practical reasons the United States should proceed alone: "A four-power, four-language, International trial, was inevitably the slowest and most costly method of procedure. The purposes of this extraordinary and difficult method of trial had been accomplished."[14] Jackson had distrusted the Soviets from the start and suggested holding a series of trials modeled after the IMT, under the auspices of General Lucius Clay's U.S. Military Government. Joint Chiefs of Staff directive 1023/10, issued in the summer of 1946, ordered the American Theatre Commander to identify, investigate, and apprehend all persons suspected of war crimes. The most important decree was Control Council Law No. 10, which was a mandate to take up where the IMT had left off and to "give effect to the terms of the Moscow Declaration of 30 October 1943 and the London Agreement of 8 August 1945, and the Charter issued pursuant thereto in order to establish a uniform legal basis in Germany for the prosecution of war criminals." Military Ordinance No. 7 established three-man tribunals to preside over the American trials.

U.S. Military Governor Lucius Clay was responsible for overseeing the American trials. A number of participants from the IMT joined the prosecution and defense staffs. Clay believed that the trials were an important part of the reconstruction and reeducation effort and argued that no new legal system could be established in Germany until all vestiges of the previous one had been swept away.[15] Since the trials were under military law, all verdicts were subject to the Military Government's review and confirmation. Clay's commitment to the proceedings would soon be tested; by 1947, high-level war crimes policy was the greatest anomaly in American foreign policy.[16]

The man directly in charge of the trials was Justice Jackson's deputy at the IMT, Brigadier General Telford Taylor. After the new chief prosecutor graduated from Harvard Law School in 1932, he advanced through a number of legal positions within the New Deal administration. Appointed a Special Assistant to Robert Jackson, then Attorney General, in 1939, Taylor attracted the attention of Henry Stimson during "the Great German War on the Potomac" when he argued that a major trial had the potential to do more than simply render justice: "it would give meaning to the war."[17] Justice Jackson felt that the trial's high aspirations would not be compromised under Taylor's leadership. Like those who had provided the impetus for the first trial, the prosecution staff included a disproportionate number of Harvard law school graduates, former New Dealers, and liberal Democrats.[18]

The most famous and, to some Germans, infamous prosecutor was neither a Harvard graduate nor a New Dealer—he was a German Jew named Robert Kempner. During the early 1930s, Kempner worked in the legal division of the Prussian police department until his opposition to National Socialism led to his expulsion from Germany. For Kempner, the trials were personal; he was settling old scores. "This trial started in 1930 in Berlin when I was Chief Legal Advisor of the Prussian Police. At the time I had my first fights with Hitler and his consorts. The people in Prussia tried to suppress the Nazi Party and to send Hitler, as a kind of enemy alien, back to Austria."[19] After he was forced to immigrate to the United States in 1940, Kempner began to collect war crimes evidence on behalf of the Department of Justice. His firsthand knowledge of German law and government made him valuable to the IMT, where he served as both an interrogator and a prosecutor. When he was brought in to interrogate Hermann Goering, the man who had stripped him of his German citizenship, Goering was startled to see his old adversary. "First he didn't want to answer me, he said, 'You are biased against me.' So I said to him, 'Reichsmarshall, I am not biased against you, I am very happy, you threw me out on February 3, 1933,'" Kempner recalled. "'If you hadn't done it I would have been smoke through a chimney.'"[20] Many would become critical of Kempner's heavy-handed interrogation methods. In one well-documented incident, he threatened to turn Friedrich Gaus, the Nazi Foreign Minister's former legal advisor, over to the Soviet Union unless he was willing to cooperate.

KEMPNER: Well, things aren't as simple as that. The Russians are interested in you. Do you know that?

GAUS: The Russians?

KEMPNER: Yes, as a professional violator of treaties.

GAUS: No, that is not correct in the least. My God.

KEMPNER: Well, let's finish for today. I'll tell you something . . .

GAUS (interrupting): Don't extradite me to the Russians.[21]

Telford Taylor prepared to try two to four hundred high-ranking suspected war criminals in the summer of 1946. The defendants in this second series of trials were a diverse mix. Although the laws that ultimately composed the London Agreement Charter had been written with the leaders of the Reich in mind, they were also designed to "cast a wider net" of criminality so that additional bankers, industrialists, and diplomats could be charged with war crimes. The problem facing the post–Nuremberg proceedings was that if a court rejected the prosecution's expanded definition of international criminality, the heart of a number of cases would be removed.

In an effort to give the decisions the greatest amount of credibility, Justice Jackson suggested that civilian judges should preside over the courts, but was thwarted by the newly appointed Supreme Court Chief Justice, Fred Vinson.[22] Clay recalled, "Great difficulty was experienced in obtaining qualified jurists for the courts and our hope of substantial representation from the federal judiciary was dashed by Chief Justice Fred Vinson's decision that federal court judges could not be granted leave for the purpose. It took a considerable period of time to obtain qualified jurists from the state judiciary system to form six courts."[23]

Some of America's most prominent judges were beginning to turn against the war crimes trials. More important than their specific opinions was the emergence of a conservative position that flatly rejected the presumptions of the Nuremberg trials. Supreme Court Chief Justice Harlan Fiske Stone privately described the IMT as "a high-grade lynching party . . . a little too sanctimonious a fraud to meet my old-fashioned ideas," and he was especially incensed by his colleague Robert Jackson's "pretense that he is running a court or proceeding according to common law."[24] Senator Robert Taft had criticized the Nuremberg trials in 1946 on the ground that they "accepted the Russian idea of the purpose of trials," and he believed that "by clothing policy in the forms of legal procedure, we may discredit the whole idea of justice in Europe for years to come."[25]

By 1947, the tone of the Nuremberg criticism had changed. Conservative congressmen like John J. Rankin launched a broader and more conspiratorial, anti-Semitic attack on the Nuremberg trials from the floor of the U.S. House of Representatives. According to Rankin, "a racial minority, two and a half years after the war closed, are in Nuremberg not only hanging German soldiers but trying German businessmen in the name of the United States."[26] Many midwestern isolationists felt that prominent American Jews had a disproportionately large say in American policy toward Germany. Although the Morgenthau Plan was their favorite example, Nuremberg was a close second.

On the diplomatic front, certain quarters within the State Department had opposed war crimes trials from the very beginning. Author of the Long Telegram and the famous "Mr. X" article published in *Foreign Affairs* magazine in 1947, George Kennan was a bitter critic of American war crimes policy. He later characterized the Germans under the American occupation as "sullen, bitter, unregenerate and pathologically attached to the old chimera of German unity."[27] To the architect of containment, the IMT was nothing more than a pretentious sham that created confusion and tarnished American foreign policy with hypocrisy: "The only implication this procedure could convey was . . . that such crimes were justifiable and forgivable when committed by the leaders of one government, under one set of circumstances, but unjustifiable and unforgivable, and to be punished by death when committed by another set of government leaders under another set of circumstances."[28] For the United States to turn a blind eye to the cruelties of the Russian Revolution, collectivization, purges of the 1930s, and Soviet wartime and postwar atrocities would "make a mockery of the only purposes the trials could conceivably serve, and to assume, by association, a share of the responsibility for these Stalinist crimes themselves."[29] Kennan favored traditional military justice:

> I personally considered that it would have been best if the Allied commanders had had standing instructions that if any of these men fell into the hands of Allied forces they should, once their identity had been established beyond doubt, be executed forthwith. But to hold these Nazi leaders for public trial was another matter. This procedure could not expiate or undo the crimes they had committed.[30]

Kennan viewed the Nuremberg trials with "horror." He and others in the State Department strongly objected to both the war crimes trial and the basic premises underlying the American reform and reeducation program. In a wartime memo to the European Advisory Commission in London, Kennan had written that "whether we like it or not, nine tenths of what is strong, able and respected in Germany has been poured into those very categories" slated for reform.[31]

Kennan did not consider the Nazi tactics unique; the Germans were Europeans, after all. He believed that Nazi atrocities in Eastern Europe and

Russia were consistent with the "customs of warfare which have prevailed generally in Eastern Europe and Asia for centuries in the past, they are not the peculiar property of the Germans."[32] However, he had certainly been wrong about the Nazis and their intentions in April 1941, when he was a State Department officer posted at the American embassy in Berlin and downplayed accounts of Nazi atrocities: "It cannot be said that German policy is motivated by any sadistic desire to see other people suffer under German rule."[33] The American policy maker also exhibited a strange unwillingness to consider whether or not the Nazi atrocities were *sui generis*. In a telling passage in his postwar memoirs, he wrote: "If others wish, in the face of this situation, to pursue the illumination of those sinister recesses in which the brutalities of war find their record, they may do so; the degree of relative guilt which such inquiries may bring to light is something of which I, as an American, prefer to remain ignorant."[34] But did Kennan really "remain ignorant" as OSS Chief Allen Dulles and General Edwin Siebert were enlisting former Nazis to aid America against the Soviets?

General Reinhard Gehlen, a former Nazi intelligence officer, provided the United States with exaggerated estimates of Soviet power and objectives in the years immediately following World War II. He had anticipated Hitler's defeat and a struggle between the United States and the Soviet Union. Gehlen and his senior officers microfilmed all the *Fremde Heere Ost* (military intelligence section of the General Staff) holdings on the Soviet Union, placed the data in steel drums, and buried them in the Austrian Alps in early March 1945. Once this task was complete, the officers surrendered to American counterintelligence agents.[35]

According to the Potsdam Agreements, the United States was obligated to send individuals involved in "Eastern" activities back to the Soviet Union. However, Generals Edwin Siebert and Walter Bedell Smith considered these intelligence assets too valuable to hand over.[36] According to Harry Rositzke, former CIA head of espionage in the Soviet Union, "in 1946 [U.S.] intelligence files on the Soviet Union were virtually empty."[37] As a result of this lack of basic information, Gehlen played a disproportionately large role in shaping American perceptions of Soviet military capabilities and intentions. According to historian Hugh Trevor Roper, Reinhard Gehlen "lived on the primacy of the Cold War and on the favor of those American and German governments which believed in the primacy of the Cold War."[38]

By 1947, General Clay was under pressure from the Department of the Army to finish the trials, and he set July 1, 1948 as the target date for completion.[39] Most of the American Nuremberg tribunals were presided over by retired state supreme court judges. "Some of them were very good," prosecution counsel Drexel Sprecher recalled. "On the other hand, there were some judges that weren't. The War Department didn't have any real means of checking them out."[40] The first indictment was filed on October 25, 1947.[41]

Case One, *United States v. Karl Brandt,* charged Nazi doctors with war crimes for conducting medical experiments on humans for the *Luftwaffe* at the Dachau concentration camp. Defendant Karl Brandt had been Hitler's personal physician before he was made an SS Major General and named Reich Commissioner of Health and Sanitation, the highest medical position in the Third Reich. Other defendants included the *Wehrmacht's* Chief of Medical Services, Lieutenant General Siegfried Handloser; the head Luftwaffe medical expert, Oskar Schroeder; Chief SS Surgeon Karl Gebhardt; and tropical medicine expert Gerhard Rose.[42] The doctors conducted experiments in which conditions of high altitude were simulated in low-pressure chambers. Inmates were immersed in extremely cold water for hours at a time, and doctors also infected concentration camp inmates with malaria, typhus, and other diseases in order to test tropical medicine vaccines.[43] In addition, some of the defendants were involved with the secret euthanasia programs that eliminated what they described as "useless eaters." Most victims were old, deformed, insane, or ill. Although the indictment included conspiracy and crimes against humanity charges, the Brandt case was fairly straightforward because the defendants' actions were clear violations of a number of the Hague and Geneva Convention articles.[44] Because the defendants could not dispute the facts of the case, some offered a superior orders defense, while others claimed to have been powerless to prevent the crimes. Karl Brandt and Wolfram Sievers had the most difficulty justifying their actions because the pair had carefully inspected hundreds of live concentration camp inmates before selecting 112 Jews for the skeleton collection at the Reich University at Strasbourg. The victims were measured and photographed alive, then killed and sent to Strasbourg for defleshing and preservation.[45]

The tribunal, headed by Judge Walter Beals of Washington state, handed down its decisions on August 19 and 20, 1947. The court rejected the defense of superior orders and the defendants' claims that they had been powerless to prevent the crimes. The unanimous opinion declared: "The protagonists of the practice of human experimentation justify their views on the basis that such experiments yield results for the good of society."[46] It included probably the most significant precedent to come out of the medical case: a ten-point list of scientific standards that required research on human subjects not only to be voluntary but also to lead to "fruitful results for the good of society."[47] This set of rules appears to have been one of the Nuremberg trials' most enduring legacies. The sentences served to bolster the stern tone of the tribunal opinion: seven defendants were sentenced to death, five to life, and three to prison terms, although seven were acquitted.[48]

Luftwaffe Field Marshal Erhard Milch was the only defendant in Case Two. He was charged under three counts—slave labor, war crimes, and crimes against humanity—for allocating slave labor and participating in the Luftwaffe's medical experiments at Dachau.[49] The head of Hitler's Central Planning Board, the agency established to govern wartime production, Milch conceded that many of the orders he had followed were violations of international law. His defense was a combination of denial, military necessity, and superior orders: "It was my duty toward my people to maintain my allegiance. I had sworn an oath to keep allegiance to Hitler, too."[50] His counsel, Dr. Bergold, contended that any protest would have effectively sentenced Milch to death.[51] The superior orders defense would be heard many times in the coming months as various defendants argued that under a dictatorship there was only one leader. When the tribunal handed down their decisions on April 17, 1947, Milch was found not guilty of the charges relating to the medical experiments and guilty of the slave labor charges, and was sentenced to life in a unanimous decision.[52]

Eighteen leading members of the Economic and Administrative Department of the SS were charged with crimes arising from their duties as administrators responsible for the allocation of labor for concentration camps, factories, and mines in *U.S. v. Oswald Pohl et al.* (the Pohl case).[53] Although the indictment contained crimes against humanity and conspiracy charges, as in the Brandt case, the prosecution had a solid, traditional war crimes case. The majority of the concentration camp administrators could not contest the mountains of documentary evidence and offered variations of the superior orders defense.[54] The tribunal ruled firmly and unequivocally—"It was a national Reich-approved plan for deliberate and premeditated murder on a large scale"—and pointed to the Nazis' careful accounting of personal property: "After the extermination, the victim's personal effects, including the gold in his teeth, were shipped back to the concentration camp and a report of 'death from natural causes' was made out."[55]

The judgment in the Pohl case came on November 3, 1947. The court was not swayed by the defense arguments; their opinion read: "Under the spell of National Socialism, these defendants today are only mildly conscious of any guilt in the kidnapping and enslavement of millions of civilians. The concept that slavery is criminal per se does not enter into their thinking."[56] Four were sentenced to death, three to life, and nine to various prison terms; only three were acquitted. The judgments in the first three cases followed the cautious precedent of the IMT: the convictions were for violations of the laws of war, not the more novel legal constructions of the War Department.[57] However, legally speaking, these were relatively simple cases compared to *U.S. v. Josef Altstoetter* (the Justice case); *U.S. v. Ernst von Weizsaecker et al.* (the Ministries case), *U.S. v. Alfried Krupp et al.* (the Krupp case), *U.S. v. Friedrich Flick et al.* (the Flick case), and *U.S. v. Carl Krauch et al.* (the Farben case).

The tribunal in the Justice case, with Oregon's James Brand presiding, handed down its judgments on December 3 and 4, 1947. Nazi judges, prosecutors, and ministerial officers were accused of "crimes committed in the name of law." Because the highest-ranking Nazi legal officials were dead (Minister of Justice Otto Thierack, President of the *Reichsgericht* Erwin Bumke, and People's Court President Roland Freisler), three Under-Secretaries of the Reich's Justice Ministry were indicted instead.[58] The defendants included Franz Schlegelberger, Curt Rothenberger, Herbert Klemm, Chief Public Prosecutor of the Reich Ernst Lautz, three Chief Justices from the "Special Courts," and judges from Hitler's infamous "People's Courts."[59]

This promised to be an important test case for the more radical charges of the indictment. The defendants were charged with conspiracy, war crimes, crimes against humanity, and membership in a criminal organization. The prosecution's opening statement accused them of "judicial murder and other atrocities, which they committed by destroying law and justice in Germany, and then utilizing the emptied forms of the legal process for persecution, enslavement, and extermination on a vast scale." Although they did not physically commit the crimes, the defendants were held accountable for them because they were committed pursuant to Nazi legal decrees. The prosecution introduced the *Nacht und Nebel* (Night and Fog) order and argued, "The dagger of the assassin was concealed beneath the robe of the jurist."[60]

Witness Herbert Lipps described defendant and former Nazi Judge Rudolf Oeschey's courtroom manner: "Defendants were . . . told by Oeschey right at the beginning of their session that they had forfeited their lives."[61] Defendant Curt Rothenberger described the relationship between politics and law in a wartime memo: "The independent judge is a sad remnant of a liberalistic epoch. Law must serve the political leadership." Defendant Schlegelberger's novel argument would be heard many times in the coming months. He claimed to have stayed in the Ministry of Justice in order to prevent the department from being absorbed by Himmler's SS.[62] Because the defendants could not deny the existence of the legislation they had written and enforced, they attacked the indictment on the ground that it applied retroactive law. This was a classic legal tactic that would serve the Germans well in the coming years—when the facts were against them, they argued the laws; when the laws were against them, they argued the facts; when both were against them, they attacked the other side.

When the tribunal handed down its decisions on December 4, 1947, it was clear that they would take the broadest reading of their mandate. The court unanimously rejected a traditional reading of international law and argued instead that "The force of circumstance, the grim fact of worldwide interdependence, and the moral pressure of public opinion have resulted in international recognition that certain crimes against humanity committed by Nazi authority against German nationals constitute violations not alone of statute but also of common international law."[63] The tribunal unanimously rejected the defense of necessity: "He feared that if he were to resign, a worse man would take his place. . . . Upon analysis this plausible claim of the defense squares neither with the truth, logic, or the circumstances."[64] The tribunal also addressed the *ex post facto* arguments put forward by the defense:

> It would be sheer absurdity to suggest that the ex post facto rule, as known to constitutional states, could be applied to a treaty, a custom, or a common law decision of an international tribunal, or to the international acquiescence which follows the event. To have attempted to apply the ex post facto principle to judicial decisions of common international law would have been to strangle the law at birth.[65]

The decision in the Justice case would be one of the high points for those who favored a broadened conception of international criminality at Nuremberg. The tribunal sentenced Franz Schlegelberger, Oswald Rothaug, Herbert Klemm, and Rudolf Oeschey to life, and six others to prison terms, and acquitted four.[66]

After presiding in the Justice case, Judge James Brand was asked to stay on for a second trial. He declined but recommended his colleague and friend from Oregon, Robert Maguire. The attorney was at an American Bar Association meeting in Cleveland when he received the invitation. Robert Maguire was "flattered and pleased" by the offer and assumed that it was "an opportunity which comes only once in a lifetime."[67] He returned to Portland and told his partners that he would need a six-month leave of absence. It was with great excitement and a sense of purpose that he boarded a converted navy frigate and set sail for Europe.[68]

In late November 1947, Robert Maguire arrived in Berlin, where he met with General Clay and was assigned to a tribunal. The other two judges, Leon Powers and William Christianson, were retired state supreme court justices (from Iowa and Minnesota, respectively). After the judges had been convened as a tribunal, the Supervisory Committee of Presiding Judges assigned them Case Eleven, *The United States Government v. Ernst von Weizsaecker*, which would come to be known as the Ministries or *Wilhelmstrasse* case. The indictment was filed on November 1, 1947 against Ernst von Weizsäcker, Gustav Adolf Steengracht von Moyland, Wilhelm Keppler, Ernst Wilhelm Bohle, Ernst Woermann, Karl Ritter, Otto von Erdmannsdorff, Edmund Veesenmayer, Hans Heinrich Lammers, Wilhelm Stuckart, Richard Walther Darré, Otto Meissner, Otto Dietrich, Gottlob Berger, Walter Schellenberg, Lutz Graf Schwerin von Krosigk, Emil Puhl, Karl Rasche, Paul Koerner, Paul Pleiger, and Hans Kehrl. Of all the American Nuremberg trials, the Ministries case most closely resembled the IMT in its importance.

Among other things, the Ministries case explored the culpability of bureaucratic leaders in a totalitarian state. As Robert Jackson had remarked in his opening statement before the IMT, "whatever else we may say of those who were the authors of this war, they did achieve a stupendous work in organization."[69] In many instances these were the "CEOs" of the Third Reich—the efficient bureaucrats who translated Hitler's words into deeds. But had they committed war crimes?[70] The answer to that question depended on the court's reading of their legal mandate. Case Eleven was the prosecution's last hope for a crimes against peace conviction because the diplomats were the best candidates for the aggression and conspiracy charges since the IMT. However, the prosecution faced a daunting task—convincing a conservative American court both that the aggression and conspiracy charges were valid and that the defendants had violated them.

When Telford Taylor opened the prosecution's case on January 7, 1948, the Chief Counsel derisively referred to the defendants as "the gentlemen of the *Wilhelmstrasse*." "We have indicted in this case the chief civil executives of the Third Reich," he told the tribunal. "Without their administration and implementation, and without the directives and orders which they prepared, no Hitler, no Goering, could have planned and waged aggressive wars."[71] He recognized that convictions for aggression in the Ministries case could bolster the IMT's aggression precedent. However, up to this point at Nuremberg, there had not yet been a single conviction for aggression among the thirty-five defendants charged in the pending Farben, Krupp, and the High Command cases.[72] The defense was fully aware of the prosecution's need for legal innovation.

During Hitler's early campaign of lightning wars (1939–41), the Foreign Office provided lists of alleged violations of neutrality that served as pretexts for the various Nazi invasions.[73] Eight of the Ministries case defendants were career diplomats who had risen through the ranks of the German Foreign Office. Former State Secretary Ernst von Weizsäcker entered the German Foreign Office in 1921 and served for seventeen years in Switzerland, Denmark, Norway, and Berlin. Although he would later claim to loathe the boorish Nazis, he was a German nationalist and they shared many goals: the repudiation of the Treaty of Versailles, a return to the status of a great power, and rearmament.[74]

After accepting the post of State Secretary in 1938, von Weizsäcker helped to orchestrate the Third Reich's absorption of her neighbors. Although he would present evidence that he had helped the German resistance, many questions remained. Most difficult to explain were two memos from Heinrich Himmler to von Weizsäcker that authorized the deportation of a total of 6,000 French Jews to Auschwitz. The defendant had been named Ambassador to the Vatican in 1943 and remained there until the end of the war. In addition to keeping the Pope silent about the Final Solution, Ernst von Weizsäcker had played a key role in the deportation of Rome's Jews. The German diplomat would present one of the most legally and morally complex defenses of the Nuremberg trials. The court would be forced to reexamine their definition of resistance in the unique circumstances of the Nazi dictatorship. The von Weizsäcker case would also highlight differences between legal and moral guilt.[75]

Defendant Wilhelm Keppler was not a Foreign Office aristocrat but a Nazi true believer. He joined the National Socialist Party in 1927 as an economic advisor and never left. In 1936, he was named Plenipotentiary for Austria, where he organized Nazi fifth columnists and delivered Hitler's ultimatum to Austrian President Wilhelm Milkas.[76] For his role in the *Anschluss*, SS Chief Heinrich Himmler thanked him, "I would like to express to you, Keppler, once more, in writing, how you have accomplished a very difficult task under very difficult conditions, so clearly and bravely for the Führer. I do not have to reassure you that it will be a joy for me to allow

SS men to work under your leadership in the future for these tasks."[77] When Germany invaded Poland, Hitler demanded the return of Danzig and the emancipation of "oppressed" German minorities.[78] Keppler played an important behind-the-scenes role: he and defendant Veesenmayer incited border incidents so that Germany would have a pretext for invasion.

The other two State Secretaries, Gustav Adolf Steengracht von Moyland and Ernst Bohle, were responsible for similar acts of "Germanism beyond the borders of the Reich."[79] From his position at the *Auslandsorganization,* Bohle directed fifth column activities. The other four members of the Foreign Office were lower in rank. Under-Secretary of State Ernst Woermann acted as von Weizsäcker's man in the field. In Czechoslovakia he provided military and financial assistance to the Sudeten German Party; in Poland he helped fabricate border incidents.[80]

The second group of defendants were Reich ministers involved in domestic policies. The highest-ranking official was Chief of the Reich Chancellery Hans Lammers, who had been a National Socialist since 1922. The author and signatory of many of the "legal" decrees that aided the Nazi consolidation of power, like the Enabling Act and the Reich Defense Law, Lammers was involved in everything from the exploitation of occupied territories to directives on captured pilots.[81] State Secretary Otto Dietrich was Joseph Goebbels's rival in the Ministry of Propaganda. From his post as Minister of Public Enlightenment, Dietrich orchestrated the misinformation campaigns that preceded each invasion. German newspapers were ordered to print headlines like Concentration of Czech Troops on the Borders of Sudeten-Land.[82] "In everything it must be established that the Jews are to blame! The Jews wanted war!" wrote Dietrich. "Naturally, those reports that do not lend themselves to anti-Semitic propaganda must be adapted for use as anti-Semitic propaganda."[83] Reich Peasant Leader and Minister of Food and Agriculture Richard Darré was the author of the "blood and soil decree."[84] In a letter Darré bragged that he had "created the prerequisites which made it possible for the Führer to wage his war as far as food is concerned."[85]

The third group of defendants were involved in Hermann Goering's "Four-Year Plan." When the Office of the Four-Year Plan took control of the economy in 1936, former industrial engineer Paul Koerner was named State Secretary for the Four-Year Plan.[86] *Reichsmarshall* Goering stated that in "all current business concerning the Four-Year Plan, I shall be represented by State Secretary Koerner."[87] During the 1940s, Koerner shifted his focus to exploiting the resources of occupied territories and sat on the

Central Planning Board with Albert Speer and Walter Funk.[88] The fourth group of defendants consisted of bankers involved in a variety of Nazi enterprises. Defendant Karl Rasche had held a top position at the Dresdner Bank, which liquidated seized assets for the Nazis and financed the construction of concentration camps with low- or no-interest loans.[89] Schwerin von Krosigk had been in charge of fiscal mobilization for the Minister of Finance; the fines he imposed against German Jews totaled one billion Reichsmarks.[90] Individuals who could not pay had their property seized and sold. Schwerin von Krosigk was also named a successor in Hitler's will. The other banker, Emil Puhl, had been vice president of the Reichsbank and issued an eight-million-Reichsmark low-interest loan to aid the expansion of the SS. "We agree that the credit in question cannot be considered from the viewpoint of ordinary business," wrote Puhl.[91] The Reichsbank also received seventy-six shipments of dental gold from Auschwitz. By the end of the war, their vaults held thirty-three tons of gold teeth, rings, and glasses.[92]

The SS was represented by Gottlob Berger, Walter Schellenberg, and Edmund Veesenmayer. A former gymnastics instructor, Berger was an ardent anti-Semite, proponent of the Final Solution, and one of Heinrich Himmler's experts on racial selection for the SS. In a wartime article, he wrote, "We the National Socialists believe the Führer when he says that the annihilation *of Jewry* in Europe stands at the end of the fight instigated by the *Jewish* World Parasite against us as his strongest enemy."[93] One of Himmler's favored "twelve apostles," Berger had the most difficulty distancing himself from his unofficial sponsorship of his old comrade, the notorious Oskar Dirlewanger. Berger had interceded to have Dirlewanger released from prison in 1939 to serve under General Franco in the Spanish Civil War. When Dirlewanger returned to Germany, Berger reinstated him as an SS colonel and ordered him to train a regiment of convicted game poachers and criminals to wage antipartisan warfare in Eastern Europe. Even Heinrich Himmler was moved to comment on the Dirlewanger brigade's brutality: "The tone in the regiment is, I may say, in many cases a medieval one with cudgels and such things. If anyone expresses doubts about winning the war he is likely to fall dead from the table."[94] When SS police judge advocate Conrad Morgen issued a warrant in 1942 for Dirlewanger's arrest, his guardian angel, Gottlob Berger, wrote Himmler: "Better to shoot two Poles too many than two too few. A savage country cannot be governed in a decent manner." Awarded the Knight's Cross and given a second battalion, by 1943, Dirlewanger commanded approximately 4,000 men.[95]

Walter Schellenberg was a Waffen SS and former Police Brigadier General who went on to become the head of the military intelligence service of the SS and the Chief of Prisoner-of-War Activities on the eastern front. A close personal friend and advisor to Heinrich Himmler, Schellenberg was a fervent proponent of the Final Solution who oversaw the capture and transportation of thousands of French Jews to Auschwitz. He was also one of the few Nazis to mention "The Final Solution" in writing.[96] Although Schellenberg had gone out of his way to save a number of Jews from certain death in the final days of the war, would this mitigate his guilt? Defendant Edmund Veesenmayer began in the Foreign Office, but as the war progressed, he became more involved in the deportation of Jews in occupied Serbia, Slovakia, and Hungary. After Veesenmayer was appointed Germany's Plenipotentiary in Hungary, his main task was organizing the successful deportation of 381,600 Hungarian Jews to Auschwitz and other concentration camps.[97]

Unlike other contemporary examples of political justice, the Nuremberg trials worked from an unprecedented evidentiary base. Prosecutor Robert Kempner explained, "We had the documents and I had educated young officers, since 1941, on how to find the documents. This was very important from a political point of view because after the First World War the Allies had no documents."[98] Judge Maguire was struck by the quality of the evidence: "Our case is becoming very interesting, we are seeing the pages of history roll out from the confidential records made before the events occurred, and made by the main actors themselves." As in the vast majority of the American Nuremberg trials, documentary evidence alone built a daunting *prima facie* case. The defense could only raise doubts about the meaning of diplomatic correspondence in a dictatorship.

Among the first witnesses presented by the prosecution was Milada Radlova, daughter of Czechoslovakian President Emil Hacha. When President Hacha was summoned to Berlin in 1939 to discuss the future of Czech territory (Bohemia and Moravia), Radlova traveled with him. She described an ominous late-night meeting with Hitler and Goering in the Reich Chancellory. According to Radlova, the Nazi leaders threatened to destroy Prague if Hacha did not capitulate.[99] Further evidence on the pattern of German conquest was provided by Austrian officials forced out during the Anschluss. Besides giving valuable evidence, these witnesses humanized the events.

Next, the tribunal flew to Vienna, deep in the Russian zone of occupation, to take the deposition of former Austrian President Wilhelm Milkas, who was too sick and frail to travel to Nuremberg. Judge Maguire was impressed by "the dramatic and tragic story of the fall of Austria, the delivery of the ultimatum, the actions of Keppler who was Hitler and Goering's agent in the affair, the forced resignation of Schuschnigg . . . the forced appointment of Seyss-Inquart."[100] The Nazis had coupled diplomatic demands with threats of force on Austria, but they staged a bloodless coup; was this "aggression"? There was neither significant resistance nor actual military conflict. Did war crimes require combat? The fate of the aggression charges hinged on basic questions like these. The defense would contend that subversive diplomats like Ernst von Weizsäcker prevented war and should be viewed as heroes. Although they could not forestall the political takeover of nations like Austria and Czechoslovakia, they at least prevented their physical destruction.[101] Encounters with men like Milkas influenced the tribunal; they had not supported the Nazi program until the eleventh hour and, as the ship was sinking, joined the resistance. They had opposed Hitler from the beginning until the end, and they provided standards to measure subsequent claims of resistance.

February 1948 marked yet another intensification in the Cold War. First came the Soviet takeover of Czechoslovakia. Up until 1948, the small nation was not clearly in the grasp of the Soviet Union. In mid-February Klement Gottwald, leader of the Czech Communist Party, eliminated all opposition political parties and strengthened his hold on the government by filling the cabinet with fellow communists.[102] Military resistance was discouraged by the Red Army divisions poised on the border. President Edward Benes and Foreign Minister Jan Masaryk were forced to surrender when a delegation of Soviet officials arrived in Prague. Two weeks later, Masaryk was dead; although official Czech sources claimed he had committed suicide, most in the West believed that he had been murdered.[103]

A second major event occurred in late February: the Soviet Military Governor issued an order limiting access to Berlin, and the next day the Soviets prevented freight from leaving the city.[104] U.S. Military Governor Lucius Clay had worked more closely with the Soviets than any other American official. Clay and Secretary of State James Byrnes remained convinced, even as late as 1947, that cooperation with the Russians was possible, but Washington was moving in a different direction and expected him to follow.[105] As the State Department became more and more involved in the affairs of Germany, General Clay grew less and less comfortable and attempted to resign in July 1947. "I feel that State Department wants a negative personality in Germany. As you know I can carry out policy wholeheartedly or not at all and there is no question left in my mind but that my views relative to Germany do not coincide with present policies," he wrote in a letter to General Eisenhower.[106] Eisenhower shamed his old friend into staying on. According to Jean Smith, editor of the general's papers, "Clay got the message; henceforth, he realized that U.S. policy in Germany would march to a different drummer."[107]

Former Nazi spy Reinhard Gehlen and his operatives were still providing the Americans with estimates of Soviet military capabilities and intentions.[108] Gehlen was playing the Cold War to his advantage by making the United States rely so heavily on his organization. "The agency [CIA] loved Gehlen because he fed us what we wanted to hear," the CIA's former head Soviet military analyst, Victor Marchetti, explained. "We used his stuff constantly, and we fed it to everybody else: the Pentagon; the White House; the newspapers. They loved it too. But it was hyped up Russian bogeyman junk, and it did a lot of damage to this country."[109] One can safely say that Gehlen's estimates were exaggerations, although that was not immediately obvious in 1948.

After the events of early 1948, the Truman administration decided to reinstate the draft. Without an imminent threat to American national security, it was difficult to gain public support. Director of Army Intelligence Stephen Chamberlin met with General Clay in Berlin and told him that the army was having trouble getting the draft reinstated and needed a strong message they could use in congressional testimony. "So I wrote out this cable. I sent it directly to Chamberlin and told him to use it as he saw fit," Clay recalled.[110] The Director of Intelligence received the top-secret cable on March 5. Clay was shocked and dismayed when the message was torn from context and leaked to the media (a portion of the cable first appeared in the *Saturday Evening Post*):

For many months, based on logical analysis, I have felt and held that war was unlikely for at least ten years. Within the last few weeks, I have felt a sudden change in Soviet attitudes which I cannot define but which now gives me a feeling that it may come with dramatic suddenness. I cannot support this change in my own thinking with any data or outward evidence in relationships other than to describe it as a feeling of a new tenseness in every Soviet individual with whom we have official relation. I am unable to submit any official report in the absence of supporting data but my feeling is real. You may advise the chief of staff [Bradley] of this for what it is worth if you feel it is advisable.[111]

"I assumed they would use it in closed session. I certainly had no idea they would make it public. If I had, I would not have sent it." True or not, the cable had had its desired effect. There was panic and alarm among civilians and officials; the money for rearmament was promptly allocated.[112] Historian Michael Howard later observed that a leaked "secret cable" became a new means by which American government officials could influence public opinion. This "was not to be the last occasion on which the American military were to try to influence congressional opinion by an inflated estimate of Soviet intentions and capabilities, but it may well have been the first and most significant."[113]

In its annual assessment of U.S. foreign policy, the State Department's Policy Planning Staff (headed by George Kennan) argued that America's reform and reeducation efforts in Germany had failed. The 1948 "Review of Current Trends in American Foreign Policy" declared: "we must recognize the bankruptcy of our moral influence on the Germans, and we must make plans for the earliest possible termination of those actions and policies on our part which have been psychologically unfortunate." The report singled out the Nuremberg trials as a particular source of irritation: "we must terminate as rapidly as possible those forms of activity (denazification, reeducation, and above all the Nuremberg Trials) which tend to set us up as mentors and judges over internal German problems."[114]

The Nuremberg trials' broadened conception of international criminality was challenged on February 19 when the tribunal in the Hostage case (*U.S. v. Wilhelm List et al.*) handed down their extremely conservative opinion. The Hostage case (Seven) and High Command case (Twelve) charged German generals with violations of the traditional laws of war (Case Twelve included aggressive war and conspiracy charges). The Hostage case accused senior Wehrmacht officers, including Field Marshal Wilhelm List and Lieutenant General Walter Kuntze, both of whom had commanded the Twelfth Army in Yugoslavia and Greece. Also charged was the head of the Second Panzer Army in Yugoslavia during 1942–43, General Lothar Rendulic. The other defendants were high-ranking German officers involved in atrocities against civilians in Yugoslavia, Albania, Norway, and Greece.[115] The court would consider the legality of defendant Maximilian von Weichs's 1941 "Hostage Order," which declared that one hundred Serb civilians would be shot for every German soldier harmed by partisans.[116] Accordingly, entire villages were burned while all the inhabitants were rounded up and slaughtered. Were these reprisals "proportional" to the crimes they sought to punish?

The four-count indictment charged German military leaders with violations of the customary laws of war—the murder and mistreatment of civilians and the destruction of their property. Prosecutor Telford Taylor made the point that this was the first time since the IMT that German officers had been "charged with capital crimes committed in a strictly military capacity."[117] Even Taylor admitted that "We may concede for purposes of argument that the execution of hostages may under some circumstances be justified, harshly as those words may ring in our ears." However, on the question of proportionality, the Germans had gone too far: "the law must be spared the shame of condoning the torrent of senseless death which these men let loose in southeastern Europe."[118]

With Charles Wennerstrum of the Iowa Supreme Court presiding, all of the judges on the tribunal were midwesterners. This geographic distinction was becoming increasingly important, as the majority of the conservative judges came from the Midwest. Just as Judge Brand's opinion in the Justice case provided a model for those sympathetic to a broader view of international criminality, the opinion in the Hostage case became a model for conservative jurists at Nuremberg. The tribunal prefaced their judgment by explicitly narrowing their legal mandate—"it is not our province to write international law as we would have it,—we must apply it as we find it."[119] With many qualifications, the court rejected the idea that partisan or guerrilla forces were protected by the laws of war, and unanimously agreed that these groups fall into the same legal category as spies: "Just as a spy may act lawfully for his country and at the same time be a war criminal to the enemy, so guerrillas may render great service to their country and, in event of success, become heroes even, still they remain war criminals in the eyes of the enemy and may be treated as such." Finally, the tribunal ruled: "a civilian who aids, abets or participates in the fighting is liable to punishment as a war criminal under the laws of war. Fighting is legitimate only for the combatant personnel of a country. It is only this group that is entitled to treatment as prisoners of war and incurs no liability beyond detention after capture or surrender."[120]

Much to the chagrin of those nations occupied by the Third Reich, this tribunal, like the Lieber Code, defined "reprisal" very broadly: "The idea that an innocent person may be killed for the criminal act of another is abhorrent to every natural law. We condemn the injustice of any such rule as a relic of ancient times."[121] Nonetheless, the court concluded: "The occupant may properly insist upon compliance with regulations necessary to the security of occupying forces and for the maintenance of law and order. In accomplishment of this objective, the occupant may, only as a last resort, take and execute hostages."[122] The opinion in the Hostage case branded partisans "*franc-tireurs*" and provided few options for legitimate resistance under military occupation. "We think the rule is established that a civilian who aids, abets, or participates in the fighting is liable to punishment as a war criminal under the laws of war."[123]

The tribunal sentenced both Field Marshal List and Lieutenant General Kuntze to life in prison; two other defendants were acquitted and the rest given prison terms of twenty years or less.[124] The court attempted to address the question of leniency in their opinion: "mitigation of punishment does not in any sense of the word reduce the degree of the crime. It is more a matter of grace than defense."[125] Although the decisions in the Hostage case were very conservative, it would be wrong to assume that they were the result of political pressure. Members of the American military seemed to sympathize with the plight of their German brethren. The once vindictive General Dwight Eisenhower stated in an affidavit that the German antipartisan tactics were not unique: the French briefly had a similar decree "directing the shooting of five German hostages for every French soldier shot by snipers."[126] The judgment in the Hostage case marked a profound shift at Nuremberg. More courts began to adopt a conservative reading of Control Council Law No. 10. Politically it was the safe thing to do because it was in line with America's overall German policy. A conservative position grounded in a positive reading of the laws of war was fast becoming the domain of midwestern judges. By 1948, tension in Nuremberg was growing. The prosecution team consisted of many Harvard Law School graduates, liberal New Dealers, and many in the courtroom staff (translators, etc.) were European, and some were Jews. Some of the judges were suspicious and considered these individuals "vindictive." Years later, General Lucius Clay discussed this issue in his oral history: "The British and French didn't have the same feeling towards the Nazis that we did. Neither one had a huge Jewish population that had developed a hatred you could well understand, which was true in this country. I'm not critical of it at all because I can understand how it developed." Clay described the American reconstruction program as "on the whole too vindictive a directive to have long suited the American people, because we're not a vindictive people." According to Clay, "they went too far in their demands for denazification."[127]

During the Hostage case there were contentious exchanges between the prosecution and the bench. Although the issues tended to be trivial, the tone belied something deeper. These long-simmering differences came to an ugly head on February 23, 1948, when the headline of the *Chicago Tribune* read: IOWAN, WAR CRIMES JUDGE, FEELS JUSTICE DENIED NAZIS. Charles Wennerstrum, the presiding judge, condemned the trial as a "victor's justice" and placed the blame on the prosecution staff. "The high ideals announced as the motives for creating these tribunals have not been evident," he said; "the prosecution has failed to maintain objectivity aloof from vindictiveness, aloof from personal ambitions for convictions."[128] The judge went on to claim that the defendants did not receive a full and fair hearing, and if he had been aware of the character of the trials, he "would have never come."[129]

Although "vindictive" probably referred to Robert Kempner, the implicit target of this attack was Chief Prosecutor Telford Taylor. Typically the forty-year-old Brigadier General was a model of professional decorum; this time, he had been pushed too far. Wennerstrum waited until the day of his departure before granting an interview to Hal Faust of the *Chicago Tribune*. A friend of Taylor's in the U.S. Military Government Press Office gave him the text of the article before wiring it to the United States for publication.[130] Ironically, General Taylor's response appeared in *The New York Times* on the same day as Wennerstrum's attack in the *Chicago Tribune*.

Diplomatic historian Thomas Schwartz notes the significance of this geographic distinction:

> The conservative *Chicago Tribune,* with the remarks of Judge Charles Wennerstrum . . . made itself the mouthpiece of the critics of the Nuremberg trials. Wennerstrum's remark that "some of the Nuremberg prosecutors had become Americans only in the last few years" provided further flammable material. This not subtle reference to the role which Jewish immigrants played in the prosecution apparently found its confirmation when it was reported Kempner had tried to intimidate a witness in the Ministries Case.[131]

Taylor countered with a series of well-placed jabs. "If you in fact held the opinions you are quoted as expressing, you were guilty of grave misconduct in continuing to act in the case at all. In giving vent to these baseless slanders you have now fouled your own nest and sought to discredit the very judgment which you and your two distinguished colleagues have just rendered." Taylor took special offense at the charge that the trials were a victor's justice because the final task of rendering judgment was in the tribunal's hands:

Your statement that these trials are teaching the Germans only that they lost the war to tough conquerors would be laughable if its consequences were not so likely to be deplorable. Your own tribunal, thanks to the wisdom, patience and judicial detachment of your colleagues, accorded the defendants a trial which can be an outstanding and sadly needed lesson to the Germans in respect to the rights of an accused person, and an unshakable demonstration that the Nuremberg trials are for justice, not for vengeance. The one great obstacle to your trial having this effect is the wanton, reckless nonsense which you yourself are quoted as uttering.

Taylor said he would have used stronger language if it did not appear that Wennerstrum's behavior "arises out of a warped, psychopathic mental attitude."[132]

This heated exchange reminded many Americans of the trials dragging on in their name. In Congress, Republican Representatives John Taber, Harold Knutson, Francis Case, and William Langer all believed that America's punitive war crimes policies were getting in the way of German reconstruction. Taber contended that when he visited Germany, he found that "700,000 of their most active business people" were not allowed to work because they were "alleged to be Nazis." The congressman did not bother to veil his anti-Semitism: "the trouble is that they have too many of these people who are not American citizens mixed up in those trials, and they are very hostile to Germans." Congressman Knutson asked, "Is it not just possible that these aliens who are employed by the Government to prosecute these cases do not want to let go of a good thing?"[133] The American dispute over war crimes policy was read with the most interest in Germany and was perceived as a further indication of American "doubt" about the trials. General Taylor's prediction that Wennerstrum's charges "will be used by all the worst elements in Germany against the best" proved correct. A growing number of Germans viewed the second-generation critics' political attacks on the war crimes trials as a sign that the Americans were abandoning their reform policies.[134] War crimes historian Frank Buscher writes:

Wennerstrum's remarks to the *Chicago Tribune* were welcomed by German opponents of the war crimes program. Wennerstrum's action, primarily aimed at an American audience, kindled further German, anti-Nuremberg sentiments. For those Germans opposed to the trials, the fact that Americans were publicly debating these trials seemed to indicate a decreasing U.S. commitment to the proceedings.[135]

Proponents of the American Nuremberg trials were fortunate to have a spokesman as able as Telford Taylor. In the coming years he would be called upon numerous times to set the record straight. But more important, neither he nor General Clay caved in to growing political pressure to cut the proceedings short. Despite February's tumultuous events, the Ministries case moved forward at full speed. The prosecution presented its case throughout January, February, and March of 1948, introducing 3,442 documentary exhibits and the testimony of 70 witnesses. The court did its best to speed the proceedings and held night and weekend sessions.[136]

Despite the geopolitical shifts, Judge Maguire remained unswayed.[137] In words that could have come from Robert Jackson himself, he wrote: "The goal sought is to set out by judicial process standards of International law and justice which it is hoped will be listened to and form finally an enlightened world opinion which will tend to prevent others from doing these things which we all know to be wrong."[138] This view was not shared by all of the tribunal's members.

The first sign of a divergence of opinion within the tribunal came when Dr. Kubuschok of the defense offered a motion to dismiss Count 4 of the indictment (Crimes Against German Nationals 1933–1939) on the ground that it fell outside the court's jurisdiction. According to a "positivist" reading of the laws of war, the Nazi persecution of German Jews was not a war crime because it did not occur during wartime and the acts were committed by Germans against their own nationals. They might have been violations of German constitutional law, but they were not violations of a conservative reading of the laws of war. This was a major challenge, a test to see how this individual tribunal intended to interpret Control Council Law No. 10. In the Justice case, the court broadened the laws of war to include these acts. Their opinion read:

It no longer can be said that violations of the laws of war are the only offenses recognized by common international law. The force of circumstance, the grim fact of world-wide interdependence, and the moral pressure of public opinion have resulted in recognition that certain crimes against humanity committed by Nazi authority against German nationals constituted violations not alone of statute but also of common international law.[139]

Though opposed by the other two members of the tribunal, Judge Maguire did not want to dismiss the charge and wrote to his old friend James Brand, the presiding judge in the Justice case, about the disagreement.

Brand wrote back, "especially glad to hear that you did not go along with your colleagues in their narrow construction of crimes against humanity committed by a government against its own nationals."[140] As he had done in his own case, Brand shrugged off the charges of retroactivity: "I believe that it is too late in history for anyone to claim that governmentally organized persecution on racial, religious, or political grounds may not become a matter of international concern justifying punishment."[141] Judge Maguire was ultimately outnumbered and overruled; on March 26, 1948, Count 4 was dismissed. This was only a preview of the legal battles to come.

By the time the prosecution finished presenting their case, it was obvious that Judge Powers viewed his role and that of the court differently from Judge Maguire. If James Brand was Robert Maguire's role model, Charles Wennerstrum was Leon Powers's role model. During the debate over Count 4, Powers maintained that the acts of persecution had taken place prior to the outbreak of war; thus, they were not war crimes. Former prosecution counsel Walter Rockler offered this description of Powers: "He thought maybe you could convict a man for outright murder at the point of a pistol, but everybody else was innocent."

The prosecution rested its case on March 29, 1948, as the defense prepared to counter the numerous documentary exhibits introduced.[142] By the time the Ministries case reconvened, a verdict had been rendered in Nuremberg's most sensational trial, the *Einsatzgruppen* case. These units were among the most brutal to fall under the black rubric of the SS. The 24 defendants were accused of killing more than a million people.[143] The prosecution's entire case consisted of captured documents that were among the most incriminating documentary evidence ever presented in a war crimes trial. This report from Minsk, Russia was typical: "In the city of Minsk, about 10,000 Jews were liquidated on 28 and 29 July, 6,500 of whom were Russian Jews—mainly old people, women and children." Waldemar Klingelhoefer reported from the Soviet Union in 1944: "Nebe ordered me to go from Smolensk to Tatarsk and Mstislavl to get furs for the German troops and liquidate part of the Jews there. The Jews had already been arrested by order of the *Hauptsturmfuehrer* Egon Noack. The executions proper were carried out by Noack under my supervision."[144] The weight of the evidence was such that the prosecution called no witnesses and prosecutor Ben Ferencz took only two days to present the 253 captured documents.[145] The political tides might have been turning, but there were certain Nazi acts that were considered crimes under any circumstances.

Defendant Otto Ohlendorf gained a great deal of notoriety for his testimony at Nuremberg's IMT. When asked how many Jews his troops killed in Crimea and the Ukraine, Ohlendorf calmly admitted, "Ninety thousand." He claimed that the killings were committed out of military necessity because the Nazis were trying to establish "permanent security"; that was the reason the children were also killed. Ohlendorf explained: "people who would grow up and surely, being the children of parents who had been killed, they would constitute a danger no smaller than the parents."[146] When defendant Walter Blume was asked whether he knew the killing of civilians was contrary to the laws of war, he replied, "I already stated that for me the directive was the Fuehrer Order. That was my war law." Blume added a Cold War–inspired dig: "I was also fully convinced and am so even now, that Jewry in Soviet Russia played an important part and still does play an important part, and it has the especial [sic] support of the Bolshevistic dictatorship."[147]

In his closing statement, Telford Taylor outlined the five common defense arguments (reprisals, superior orders, no personal participation, military necessity, and the obsolescence of the laws of war).[148] Judge Musmanno's voice was charged with emotion as he read the verdict: "Although the principal accusation is murder and, unhappily, man has been killing man ever since the days of Cain, the charge of purposeful homicide in this case reaches such fantastic proportions and surpasses such credible limits that believability must be bolstered with assurances a hundred times repeated."[149] The court deemed the atrocities "so beyond the experience of normal man and the range of man-made phenomena" that only the most exhaustive trial "could verify and confirm them."[150] The tribunal handed down the sternest rulings of all the American Nuremberg trials: thirteen death sentences, two life terms, five prison sentences, and one acquittal. The judges seemed especially incensed by the fact that cultured Europeans, like the former economist Ohlendorf, were capable of such horrifying acts and made this a justification for the severity of the sentences: "The defendants are not untutored aborigines incapable of appreciation of the finer values of life and living. Each man at the bar has had the benefit of considerable schooling. Eight are lawyers, one a university professor. . . . One, as an opera singer, gave concerts throughout Germany before he began his tour of Russia with the *Einsatzkommandos*."[151]

The court also addressed the Cold War–inspired defense arguments that equated Allied city bombing with the crimes of the Einsatzgruppen. "Then it was charged that the defendants must be exonerated from the charge of killing civilian populations since every Allied nation brought about the death of non-combatants through the instrumentality of bombing." According to the opinion, whatever suffering German civilians had been subjected to was unfortunate collateral damage: "Any person, who, without cause, strikes another may not later complain if the other in repelling the attack uses sufficient force to overcome the original adversary. That is a fundamental law between nations as well."[152] The tribunal pointed out an important fact that clearly distinguished U.S. atrocities from those of the Third Reich—when Germany and Japan surrendered, the killing from above stopped. "The one and only purpose of the bombing is to effect the surrender of the bombed nation. The people of the nation through their representatives may surrender and with surrender, the bombing ceases, the killing is ended." In the case of the Third Reich, in most instances, after surrender, the numbers of civilians killed increased. "With the Jews it was entirely different. Even if the nation surrendered they still were killed as individuals."[153] An important objective of the Nuremberg trials had been to create an irrefutable record of Nazi atrocities, and the subsequent American trials seemed to be on their way to accomplishing this. However, few of the war crimes were as straightforward as those of the Einsatzgruppen.

The case of Ernst von Weizsäcker was anything but clear. When German legal theorist Carl Schmitt was being interrogated at Nuremberg, he was asked by Robert Kempner what he thought of the fact that von Weizsäcker's initials appeared on so many incriminating documents. Schmitt appeared genuinely surprised:

KEMPNER: How do you explain that a diplomat like von Weizsaecker, as a state secretary, signed hundreds of such things?
SCHMITT: I would like to give you a nice answer. The question has great significance, a distinguished man like von Weizsaecker. . . . Only I must protect myself.[154]

With the exception of Alfried Krupp, Ernst von Weizsäcker launched the most sophisticated defense effort of the later Nuremberg trials. The German diplomat's five-man team was compromised of Helmutt Becker, American Warren Magee, Albrecht von Kessel of the German Foreign Office, Sigismund von Braun, and the defendant's son, Richard von Weizsäcker. Ernst von Weizsäcker's lawyers claimed that the former State Secretary was "a Christian, an honest diplomat, a true patriot." The defense would argue that he had accepted the job of State Secretary as a "nonenrolled member" of the active German resistance.[155] They did not contest the fact that his initials were on a number of incriminating documents and instead argued that "political conditions under the Hitler dictatorship diminish the value of documentary evidence."[156] Under this reading of the law, things meant the exact opposite of what they appeared to mean. The defense contended that "a diplomatic document cannot be understood without expert interpretation and full knowledge of the historical and political facts." The prosecution derided the strategy as the "Dr. Jekyll and Mr. Hyde" defense.[157]

Ernst von Weizsäcker reached a personal and professional crossroads in 1938, when he was offered the job of State Secretary, officially second only to Joachim von Ribbentrop in the foreign policy establishment. Attorney Helmutt Becker attempted to portray his client as a leading member of the "political resistance" who used his position in the Foreign Office to soften the blow of Hitler's policies through the power of appointment, and by leaking information about Hitler's plans to diplomats from other nations.[158] Von Weizsäcker stated that more than anything else, he had wanted to prevent the outbreak of war. His son would later ask, "What price must a man pay for deciding not to abandon his post—and thus collaborate—in order to exert some influence from his position so as to change policy into something more acceptable and bring about change, or at least to prevent worse?"[159] In the end, the defense conceded that Ernst von Weizsäcker failed in his effort to preserve the peace but argued that he should be judged by his intentions. The diplomat's defense team rejected the prosecution's narrow definition of resistance.[160] Some of the strongest evidence supporting von Weizsäcker's case was the testimony of the members of the British Foreign Office with whom he claimed to have negotiated in 1938–39.[161] One British diplomat who stepped forward on his behalf was the former British Foreign Secretary Lord Halifax.

How would the former State Secretary justify his central role in the German takeover of Czechoslovakia in 1939? Not only did von Weizsäcker demand concessions from the Czechoslovakian government for that nation's German population, he also instructed the leader of the Sudeten German Party, Konrad Heinlen, to reject the government's overtures in order to provide the Nazis with a pretext for intervening.[162] When President Emil Hacha was summoned to Berlin, he was ordered to sign an agreement incorporating Bohemia and Moravia into the Reich. If Hacha refused, Czechoslovakia faced invasion.[163]

The defense would have the most difficult time with the charges of crimes against humanity. The evidence consisted of a March 9, 1942 letter from Heinrich Himmler informing the Foreign Office of his intention to deport a thousand French Jews to Auschwitz. Von Weizsäcker was asked, point-blank, whether he had any objections—he had none. Two days later, a second request, to send another five thousand French Jews, arrived. The German embassy in Paris replied again, "no objection." The response was initialed by defendants von Weizsäcker and Ernst Woermann. During cross-examination Ernst von Weizsäcker claimed that he considered Hitler's persecution of the Jews "from its inception to be a violation of all the rules and laws of Christianity. . . . As far as I was concerned, it was always a higher aim and interest which was of decisive importance; that is to work within the office in favor of peace and to overthrow the Hitler regime, because without peace and without the overthrow of the Hitler regime, the Jews could not be saved anyway."[164]

When the Nazis occupied Rome in 1943, Ernst von Weizsäcker was named ambassador to the Vatican. His main duty was to preserve a Faustian pact between the Third Reich and the pope: the Nazis would respect the Vatican's "extraterritoriality" if Pope Pius XII remained silent about the Final Solution.[165] This pact was tested in the fall of 1943 when the SS began to round up Rome's Jews for deportation to Auschwitz. Ernst von Weizsäcker wrote Berlin in late October to report on the deportation:

> The Pope, although under pressure from all sides, has not permitted himself to be pushed into a demonstrative censure of the deportation of the Jews of Rome. Although he must know that such an attitude will be used against him by our adversaries . . . he has nonetheless done everything possible even in this delicate matter in order not to strain relations with the German government and the German authorities in Rome. As there apparently will be no further German action taken on the Jewish question here, it may be said that this matter, so unpleasant as it regards German-Vatican relations, has been liquidated.[166]

Irrespective of his intentions, had Ernst von Weizsäcker crossed several ethical points of no return? How far could the defense of necessity stretch?

What made the aggression charges relevant in this case was that the Nazis had gone to great pains to provide pretexts justifying each invasion. It was not as if the Germans had announced their intention to dominate Europe and employed only brute military force to achieve that end. The Nazis coupled bad-faith diplomacy with military strength; the result was a brutally effective foreign policy. The majority of the defendants charged with crimes against peace were members of the Foreign Office. Weizsäcker and Woermann were stationed in the main office, while Keppler, Veesenmayer, Ritter, and Erdmannsdorf served as their field operatives. The latter group did the advance work for nearly all of the German invasions. As Telford Taylor remarked in his opening statement, "These German diplomats of aggression, however, wore the mantle of diplomacy to cloak nefarious policies which were solely directed towards the realization of the criminal aims of the Third Reich. Their conduct violated every cardinal principle of diplomacy."[167] Austrian Nazi leader Seyss-Inquart was furnished with a telegram asking the Germans to "send troops to put down disorder."[168] The takeover of Czechoslovakia was done in the name of the violated civil rights of Sudeten Germans and was justified by similar claims of aiding oppressed Germans and reclaiming long-lost territory. Once again, staged border incidents made it appear as if the Nazis were coming to the aid of beleaguered German ethnic minorities in foreign countries. Belgium, Holland, Luxembourg, and France were all accused of violations of neutrality.[169] The invasion of Russia was described as a preventative war.

By far Ernst von Weizsäcker's strongest support came in the form of testimony and depositions from credible character witnesses who claimed that he had been in touch with Admiral Wilhelm Canaris and other resistance leaders. Hans Gisevius submitted an affidavit claiming that von Weizsäcker spoke with General Beck, Lord Mayor Goerdeler, Admiral Canaris, General Oster, and Ambassador Ulrich von Hassell about the "overthrow of the regime."[170] Other dignitaries who testified on his behalf included Niels Bohr, Karl Barth, and General Canaris's widow. Despite a terminal illness, Bishop Eivind Bergrav, a leader of the Norwegian resistance who had been captured and imprisoned by the SS, came to Nuremberg to testify in support of the former State Secretary: "I did this because of my strong feeling of the duty of helping the Tribunal to create full justice toward this man, and because it is my conviction that he is a man who has always been as much opposed to the Nazi regime as I myself have been."[171]

The trial was again interrupted by the Cold War on June 24, 1948, when the Soviets cut all access to Berlin. For several weeks it seemed that the United States and the USSR might go to war. The Military Governor no longer needed to be convinced of a Soviet threat. General Clay sent a top-secret cable on July 19: "the world is now facing the most vital issue that has developed since Hitler placed his political aggression under way. In fact the Soviet government has a greater strength under its immediate control than Hitler had to carry out his purpose. Under the circumstances which exist today only we can exert world leadership. Only we have the strength to halt this aggressive policy here and now."[172]

The Berlin blockade affected the Nuremberg trials in two ways: there was continued pressure from the War Department to bring the proceedings to a close, and the Cold War had entered the courtroom. Visiting American politicians applied direct pressure on trial officials. Prosecutor William Caming recalled that

> Visiting Congressmen clearly conveyed the sentiment to the politically sensitive Military Government of the U.S. Zone under General Lucius Clay. That sentiment was also bluntly asserted to the prosecution staff and to the judges in private conversations and in the form of regret that the real enemy, Russia, was growing stronger and the trials were further weakening efforts to restore Germany to the necessary economic viability that would permit her to serve as a bulwark against communism.

Caming also mentioned a change in "the prosecutory climate": "The defendants and their counsel harped on the themes that the USA had made a grave mistake in intervening before Germany destroyed Russia; Bolshevism and its enmity to the West were the real threats."[173] After the Berlin blockade, the final resting place of many defense arguments was a combination of *tu quoque* and "we told you so." However, by 1948 these arguments had more resonance than similar objections leveled at the IMT in 1946. The Cold War rhetoric, coming from "responsible American statesmen," confirmed the darkest suspicions of German nationalists and die-hard Nazis. The Germans were masterfully playing the politics of the Cold War to their short-term advantage, displaying what Jörg Friedrich calls "retroactive opportunism."[174]

Defendant Hans Lammers's lawyer was none other than Alfred Seidl, who had gained notoriety during the IMT for releasing the secret portions of the Hitler–Stalin Pact. Seidl described Lammers as the "notary public" of the Reich. Although the defendant's signature appeared on the Enabling Act and other important pieces of Nazi legislation, according to his lawyer, this meant little. It was an inversion of the *respondeat superior* defense: Seidl maintained that Lammers was not an "active" participant in the enforcement of these decrees, only their author.[175] The defense attorney made the most of the opportunities provided by the escalating Cold War and offered this justification of Operation Barbarossa: "The development of international relations after the conclusion of World War II . . . has proved, in a way that could have hardly been expected or seemed possible, how justified Dr. Lammers was in his assumption."[176]

The Chief of Prisoner-of-War Activities, Gottlob Berger, had a difficult time covering up his wartime actions. Under cross-examination, Berger claimed that he had not heard of the Final Solution until after his capture. When the prosecution placed him at Posen in 1943 during Himmler's famous speech on the Final Solution, his counsel claimed that Berger "does not think the word 'extermination' was used with regard to Jews."[177] In the end, his attorney simply invoked the Cold War and asked rhetorically: "Was it really only a craze for the 'master race' which claimed the blood of millions of people? Are there not still forces at work, the same as there were ten years ago—ideology which, in conjunction with military power of a dimension not even recognized today, are stretching out their claws to pull down everything in the turmoil of wild chaos?"[178] Berger's lawyer believed that the Cold War now mitigated his client's guilt: the "struggle against Bolshevism was the leading motive of Berger's SS policy and it is on these grounds that the American prosecutor-in-chief is today indicting him on the charge of crimes against humanity. Perhaps the prosecution is unaware of the weakness of its position, but it may not be aware of the entire foundation on which it bases this charge, and events may take place tomorrow that force the prosecutor's own land to tread the same path in the near future."[179]

Those who had not violated the traditional laws of war had a much easier time defending themselves. Although former Propaganda Minister Otto Dietrich had led a radio "Campaign against world Jewry," his attorney attributed this action to "wartime passions."[180] Von Krosigk, Puhl, and Rasche—the bankers who had helped finance the German rearmament and war effort—used a similar strategy. While they admitted that they had aided the rearmament, they questioned whether this was a crime. Even though Karl Rasche had been the chairman of the board of the Dresdner Bank and a member of Himmler's "Circle of Friends" who had actively participated in the economic plunder of Czech banks, his defense attorneys completely rejected the idea of a criminal conspiracy and assumed that the court would do the same.[181] The IMT had acquitted banker Hjalmar Schacht and in the American trials the white-collar criminals received light sentences (in the Flick and Farben cases, and to a lesser extent in the Krupp case).[182]

Of all the American Nuremberg trials, the Flick (Five), Farben (Six), and Krupp (Ten) cases were the most dependent on a broadened conception of international criminality. The directors of the industrial companies were charged with playing a vital role in the German rearmament and war effort. The most conventional charge against them was mistreating slave labor, which the Hague Conventions expressly prohibited.[183] The entire board of directors (*Vorstand*) and its chairman, Hermann Schmitz, were indicted in the Farben case. In addition to the novel crimes against peace count, the twenty-three industrialists were charged with plunder and spoliation, slavery and mass murder, conspiracy, and membership in a criminal organization.

The prosecution maintained that the "Four-Year Plan was a 75 percent Farben project."[184] Defendant Carl Krauch had been a confidant of and important advisor to Hermann Goering.[185] The I. G. Farben Company constructed and operated a "Buna," or synthetic rubber plant, on the premises of Auschwitz. The defendants sat on the board of directors and played integral roles in Germany's rearmament and the Four-Year Plan. Other defendants included the chairman of the board, Hermann Schmitz, and board members Georg von Schnitzler and Fitz Ter Meer.[186] The prosecution attempted to prove that most of the defendants had visited the I. G. Farben factory at Auschwitz and knew that inmates were being systematically killed and horribly mistreated. Defendants Ambros, Buetefisch, and Duerrfeld were all heavily involved in the Farben Auschwitz project. Defendant Ter Meer regularly discussed the allocation of slave labor with Auschwitz commandant Rudolf Hoess. Ernst Struss, the secretary of the I. G. Farben board, testified that he had heard from Farben's chief engineer at Auschwitz that inmates were being systematically slaughtered, and "that before the burning, they were gassed."[187] A British POW who survived the ordeal provided especially dramatic testimony: "The population of Auschwitz was fully aware that people were being gassed and burned. On one occasion they complained about the stench of burning bodies." The witness found it laughable that the defendants were now claiming that they knew and saw nothing. "Of course, all of the Farben people knew what was going on. Nobody could live in Auschwitz and work in the plant, or even come down to the plant, without knowing what was common knowledge to everybody."[188] The defense claimed that although defendant Otto Ambros visited the Auschwitz plant eighteen times, he'd had no idea what was going on at the concentration camp. Further damning evidence was the testimony of the head of Farben's internal security, who admitted that he burned more than fifteen tons of incriminating documents in the final days of the war.[189]

Counsel for the accused also offered the defense of necessity. Both Field Marshal Erhard Milch and industrialist Friedrich Flick testified that in Hitler's Third Reich, one had to utilize slave labor to meet production quotas or face the death sentence of "undermining fighting spirit."[190] The defense tried to portray their clients as typical white-collar executives: "Replace I. G. by I.C.I. for England, or DuPont for America, or Montecatini for Italy and at once the similarity will become clear to you."[191] It was another Cold War–inspired *tu quoque* argument, that the correctness of Hitler's policies was "confirmed by the political situation which has developed in recent months in Europe."[192]

The trial ended on May 12, 1948, and the tribunal was left to weigh 16,000 pages of transcripts, the testimony of 189 witnesses, and 2,800 affidavits. It became clear that the decision would be split when Judge Hebert asked for extra time to file a dissenting opinion.[193] When the judgment was handed down on July 29, 1948, the tribunal divided along geographic lines, and once again the conservative push came from midwestern jurists. Judge Curtis Shake of the Indiana Supreme Court and Judge James Morris of the North Dakota Supreme Court were unconvinced by the evidence and cleared all the defendants of the charges of crimes against peace and conspiracy to commit crimes against peace: "The prosecution, however, is confronted with the difficulty of establishing knowledge on the part of the defendants, not only of the rearmament of Germany but also that the purpose of rearmament was to wage aggressive war. In this sphere, the evidence degenerates from proof to mere conjecture."[194] The majority also accepted the defense of necessity: "There can be little doubt that the defiant refusal of a Farben executive to carry out the Reich production schedule or to use slave labor to achieve that end would have been treated as treasonous sabotage and would have resulted in prompt and drastic retaliation."[195] The sentences in the Farben cases were, as prosecutor Josiah DuBois said, "light enough to please a chicken thief." Not only did the tribunal acquit 10 of the 23 defendants, none of the convicted was sentenced to more than 8 years.[196]

The dean of the Louisiana State University Law School, Paul Hebert, concurred with most of the court's findings, but only in deference to the rulings of the IMT. He accused the majority of having "misread the record in too complete an exoneration and an exculpation even of moral guilt to a degree which I consider unwarranted."[197] He carefully qualified his dissenting opinion:

> I do not agree with the majority's conclusion that the evidence presented in this case falls so short of sufficiency as the Tribunal's opinion would seem to indicate. The issues of fact are truly so close as to cause genuine concern as to whether or not justice has actually been done because of the enormous and

indispensable role these defendants were shown to have played in the building of the war machine which made Hitler's aggressions possible.[198]

Judge Hebert believed that the defendants took "a consenting part in the commission of war crimes and crimes against humanity," reasoning that I. G. Farben Industries "has been shown to have been an ugly record which went, in its sympathy and identity with the Nazi regime, far beyond the activities of . . . normal business." Hebert believed all the defendants to be guilty under Count 3: "In my view, the Auschwitz project would not have been carried out had it not been authorized and approved by the other defendants, who participated in the corporate approval of the project knowing that concentration-camp inmates and other slave labor would be employed in the construction and other work."[199] Judge Hebert pointed to the defendants' clear violation of even the customary laws of war: "Under the evidence it is clear that the defendants in utilizing slave labor which is conceded to be a war crime (in the case of non-German nationals) and a crime against humanity, did not, as they assert, in fact, act exclusively because of the compulsion or coercion of the existing Governmental regulations and policies."[200]

Industrialist Alfried Krupp and executives from his company faced similar charges. The forty-year-old Krupp was named sole owner of the Krupp Armament Works by a 1943 Reich decree called the "Lex Krupp." He and eleven other company executives were indicted for leading the "secret and illegal rearmament of Germany for foreign conquests."[201] As in the Farben case, the indictment included crimes against peace and conspiracy counts in addition to spoliation and forced labor charges.[202] The prosecution contended that the Krupp works had played an important role in Hitler's secret rearmament plan. After the prosecution presented its case, the defense introduced a motion to drop Counts 1 and 4—crimes against peace and conspiracy to commit crimes against peace.[203] The tribunal acquitted all the defendants of these counts, following the IMT's acquittal of Schacht and Speer for the same charges. This was yet another blow to the aggression precedent. Judge Wilkins wrote, "although the evidence with respect to some of them was extraordinarily strong, I concurred that, in view of Gustav Krupp's overriding authority in the Krupp enterprises, the extent of the actual influence of the present defendants was not as substantial as to warrant finding them guilty of Crimes Against Peace."[204] Judge Anderson of Tennessee agreed, contending that the crimes against peace charge was only for "leaders and policy makers," not "private citizens" who participate in the war effort. The defendants argued that they had mistreated slave labor due to military necessity. The court rejected this on the grounds that the defendants were not "acting under compulsion or coercion exercised by the Reich authorities within the meaning of the law of necessity," although it acknowledged that the defendants were "guilty of constant, widespread and flagrant violations of the laws of war relating to the employment of POWs."[205] The tribunal sentenced Alfried Krupp to twelve years in prison and forced him to forfeit all his personal property while sentencing the other defendants to less than ten years each and acquitting one. Judge Anderson filed a dissenting opinion and claimed that the sentences were too severe.[206] After February 1948, the sentences handed down at Nuremberg grew increasingly lenient. This was due to a combination of Cold War pressure and legitimate discomfort with the radical implications of Control Council Law No. 10.

Judge Robert Maguire had assumed that his Nuremberg stay would be no longer than six months. By the summer of 1948, he had been in Germany for 9 months, the end was nowhere in sight, and the novelty had worn off. "Our case moves on but so slowly. We are doing everything we can to hurry it but even so we are not moving or making as much progress as I could wish."[207] When his trial finally ended, the transcript ran to more than 28,000 pages, with more than 9,000 documentary exhibits.[208] The majority of the courtroom portion of the case was finished on October 7, 1948.

While the Ministries case was in recess, the International Military Tribunal for the Far East handed down the verdicts in the Tokyo trial on November 12. After an acrimonious two-and-a-half-year proceeding, the eleven-man court reached yet another split decision. The Cold War had also taken a toll on the IMTFE. As early as February 1948, the State Department's George Kennan had warned American leaders that the United States needed to protect Japan from the "penetration and domination" of communism. Kennan was as strongly against the Tokyo trial as he had been against the Nuremberg trials. After a March 1948 visit to Japan, he considered the IMTFE "profoundly misconceived from the start." In a secret report to the Policy Planning Staff, he described the trial as "*procedurally* correct, according to our concepts of justice, and at no time in history have conquerors conferred upon the vanquished such elaborate opportunities for the public defense and for vindication of their military acts." However, to Kennan this was window dressing, because these were "political trials . . . not law."[209]

Again the IMTFE was forced to confront the unresolved issues that lay at the heart of the London Agreement Charter. By 1948, this was an old debate with new players. The points of contention (with some slight deviations) were the same as those debated inconclusively in Washington and London in 1944 and 1945 and in Nuremberg from 1945 to 1949 (conspiracy to commit aggression, individual responsibility for acts of state, the criminality of aggressive war, the *ex post facto* character of the law, and the existence of negative criminality). By a majority of eight to three, the IMTFE sentenced seven to death, sixteen to life in prison, and two to lesser prison terms, and acquitted none.[210]

All three dissenters agreed that the trial's integrity was compromised by the failure to indict Emperor Hirohito. As John Dower points out in *Embracing Defeat*, the defendants went to great pains to protect the emperor. France's Justice Bernard concluded that "a verdict reached by a Tribunal after a defective procedure cannot be a valid one."[211] Although Australian Chief Judge Webb concurred with the majority opinion, he wrote, "the leader of the crime, though available for trial, had been granted immunity." Justice Bernard argued that it was unfair to judge Emperor Hirohito "by a different standard" and considered the defendants mere "accomplices."[212] Justice Röling questioned the validity of the Kellogg-Briand Pact as a precedent for criminalizing aggression. Although he did not reject the aggressive war charges, the Dutch jurist argued that "no capital punishment should be given to anyone guilty of crimes against peace only."[213] Röling stated, "No soldier should ever be found guilty of the crime of waging an aggressive war simply for the reason that he performed a strictly military function. Aggression is a political concept and the crime of aggression should be limited to those who take part in the relevant political decisions."[214]

The most extreme argument in all the war crimes decisions of the post–World War II period came from Justice Radhabinod Pal of India, who accepted the contention that Japanese foreign policy of the 1930s and 1940s constituted self-defense. Based on this and a radical interpretation of the laws of war, Pal found all of the accused not guilty on every count of the indictment.[215] The implicit and explicit target of his attack was the victorious Allied powers. He mocked the word "aggressors" as a "chameleonic" international legal device used to justify a successful war. The Indian judge had spent most of his adult life opposing British colonial rule at home and believed that the international political situation was inherently unjust because it was established and maintained by force and on the backs of indigenous people throughout the world. To Pal, the real crime was not totalitarianism, but imperialism: "The part of humanity which has been lucky enough to enjoy political freedom can now well afford to have the deterministic ascetic outlook of life," he wrote, "and may think of peace in terms

of the political status quo."[216] The duality in the American-inspired standards of international law was obvious: "I would only like to observe once
again that the so-called Western interests in the Eastern Hemisphere were
mostly founded on the past success of these Western people in 'transmit-
ting military violence into commercial profit.'"[217] Pal took up the cause of
the peoples who had been traditionally labeled "barbarian" or "savage" and
slaughtered like infected livestock: "To them the present age is faced with
not only the menace of totalitarianism but the ACTUAL PLAGUE of imperialism."[218] As for the conspiracy to commit aggressive war, Pal felt that "the
story here has been pushed, perhaps, to give it a place in the Hitler series"
and considered the Bataan Death March and Rape of Nanking "isolated incidents."[219] If killing civilians was a war crime, then what was the legal status of those Allied air commanders who knowingly ordered the deaths of
hundreds of thousands of Japanese civilians? "It would be sufficient for my
present purpose to say that if any indiscriminate destruction of civilian life
and property is still illegitimate in warfare, then, in the Pacific war, this decision to use the atom bomb is the only near approach to the directives
of the German Emperor during the First World War and of the Nazi leaders during the Second World War. Nothing like this could be traced to the
credit of the present accused. . . . Future generations will judge this dire decision."[220] Judge Pal's dissent argued that "natural law" was a Western notion, totally irrelevant to Asian defendants, and viewed the Allied attempt
to criminalize aggression as a means by which they could maintain the status quo, or in his words, "repent of their violence and permanently profit
by it."[221]

Hideki Tojo accepted his death sentence with the same stoic indifference
that Yamashita had exhibited in Manila. Like the Sioux braves in Minnesota who sang and chanted on their way to the gallows, the Japanese officers
faced death as warriors. War to them was not a matter of winning or losing,
it was a matter of living or dying. In his final statement, Tojo confirmed,
"The sentence so far as I am concerned is as deserved." He made clear that
he was happy to sacrifice his life for Emperor Hirohito: "At least, through
the trial, nothing was carried up to the Emperor and on that point I am being comforted." On the day of sentencing, the American prosecutor Joseph
Keenan enjoyed a three-hour lunch with Hirohito.[222]

After another two-week break, the Ministries case reconvened on November 9, 1948, to hear two weeks of final arguments. The High Command
case had finished in late October; the Ministries case was the final trial,
the last vestige of a bygone era.[223] Robert Maguire anticipated returning to

Portland in January 1949, but once the court adjourned and the judges began to debate the verdicts, it was evident that the division between Powers and the other two judges would manifest itself in the tribunal opinion. To match the extent and vigor of Judge Powers's dissent, the majority opinion had to be fortified, and this extra labor added several months to Maguire's stay in Europe.

Though the Nuremberg trials were no longer front-page news in 1949, curiosity was growing about the last trial. The defendants entered the courtroom of the Palace of Justice on April 12 and the first verdicts read concerned the controversial crimes against peace (aggression) charge. Not only had there been no convictions for crimes against peace since the IMT, the charge had been rejected in the Farben, Krupp, and High Command cases. This was the prosecution's last hope to gain a conviction to bolster the IMT's weak precedent.[224] When Judge Christianson began to read the majority opinion, *Stars and Stripes* reported, "there was a sensation in the courtroom."[225] Even before he got to the charges against the individual defendants, it was obvious that the court had taken the broadest reading of their mandate. Because this was the final trial, there was additional evidence available (the minutes of the Wannsee Conference, the records of the Einsatzgruppen, the Four-Year Plan, and the German Foreign Office) that painted a more graphic picture. The majority opinion began on this point:

> Hundreds of captured official documents were offered, received and considered, which were unavailable at the trial before the International Military Tribunal, which were not offered in any of the previous cases before United States Military Tribunals, and the record here presents, more fully and completely than in any other case, the story of the Nazi regime, its program, its acts.[226]

The majority opinion argued that deliberate policies of conquest had long been violations of the customary rules of war and traced the precedents back to Caesar, Frederick the Great of Prussia, Philip II of Spain, Edward I of England, Louis XIV of France, and the colonial powers of the nineteenth and twentieth centuries. According to Maguire and Christianson, "Every and all of the attackers followed the same time-worn practice. The white, the blue, the yellow, black and red books had only one purpose, namely, to justify that which was otherwise unjustifiable."[227] The judges asked an important question that highlighted the weakness of the defense arguments: "But if aggressive invasions and wars were lawful and did not constitute a breach of international law and duty, why take the trouble to explain and justify? Why inform neutral nations that war was inevitable and excusable and based on high notions of morality, if aggressive war was not essentially wrong and breach of law?"[228]

The majority rejected the pleas of superior orders and sovereign immunity on the grounds that to grant "such immunity is to shroud international law in a mist of unreality. We reject it and hold that those who plan, prepare, initiate, and wage aggressive wars and invasions . . . may be tried, convicted and punished for their acts."[229] The opinion also went to special pains to reject the many Cold War–inspired *tu quoque* arguments. The tribunal conceded that the Soviets had been fully complicit in the invasion of Poland; however, this in no way exonerated Germany:

> But if we assume, *arguendo,* that Russia's action was wholly untenable and its guilt as deep as the Third Reich, nevertheless, this cannot, in law, avail the defendants of the guilt of those of the Third Reich who were themselves responsible. . . . It has never been suggested that a law duly passed becomes ineffective when it transpires that one of the legislators whose vote enacted it was himself guilty of the same practice.[230]

In keeping with this broad reading of Control Council Law No. 10, the court found five men guilty of crimes against peace, the first convictions for aggression since the IMT.[231]

Despite the efforts of his five attorneys and high-profile character witnesses, Ernst von Weizsäcker's resistance, in Christianson and Maguire's judgment, was too little, too late. The majority asked "how a decent man could continue to hold office under a regime which carried out and planned wholesale barbarities of this kind."[232] They also called his "Jekyll and Hyde" strategy "a defense readily available to the most guilty . . . not novel, either here or in other jurisdictions."[233]

The majority opinion found von Weizsäcker's failure to mention his links with the resistance until 1948 "suspicious," and his performance on the witness stand also damaged his case. Although the former diplomat easily summarized the details of the Hitler–Stalin Pact from memory during the IMT, when his own trial began, his memory began to falter. This irony was not lost on the tribunal majority: "The exceeding caution observed by the defendant on cross-examination and his claims of lack of recollection of events of importance, which by no stretch of the imagination could be deemed routine, his insistence he be confronted with documents before testifying about such incidents, were not calculated to create an impression of frankness and candor."[234] Maguire and Christianson were unswayed by the defendant's repeated claims of resistance, remarking that "he was not a mere bystander, but acted affirmatively and himself conducted the diplomatic negotiations both with victims and the interested powers, doing this with full knowledge of the facts; silent disapproval is not a defense to action."[235]

Finally, the court ruled that good intentions did not "render innocent that which is otherwise criminal, and which asserts that one may with impunity commit serious crimes, because he hopes thereby to prevent others, or that general benevolence towards individuals is a cloak or justification for participation in crimes against the unknown many."[236] Judges Maguire and Christianson gave an example of the defendant's dishonesty on the stand: his statement that "he thought Auschwitz was merely a camp where laborers were interned, we believe tells only part of what he knew, and what he had good reason to believe."[237] The German diplomats were well aware of the Einsatzgruppen's activities: "The Foreign Office regularly received reports of the Einsatzgruppen operations in the occupied territories. Many of these were initialled by Weizsaecker and Woermann. They revealed the clearing of entire areas of Jewish population by mass murder, and the bloody butchery of the helpless and the innocent, the shooting of hostages in numbers wholly disproportionate to the alleged offenses against German armed forces; the murder of captured Russian officials and a reign of terrorism carried on with calculated ferocity, all told in the crisp, unimaginative language of military reports."[238]

Ernst von Weizsäcker and Ernst Woermann were found guilty of crimes against peace for their roles in the Nazi takeover of Czechoslovakia. Wilhelm Keppler was convicted for his participation in the invasions of Austria and Czechoslovakia, Woermann for aiding the invasion of Poland, and Koerner for his role in the war against the Soviets. The tribunal majority rejected the defense argument that America's Cold War policy justified Operation Barbarossa: "It was plain aggression."[239] Hans Lammers was the only nondiplomat found guilty of aggression for his part in the invasions of Czechoslovakia, Poland, Norway, Holland, Belgium, Luxembourg, and the Soviet Union. The defendants found guilty of crimes against peace were the type of fifth columnists that the authors of the Nuremberg indictment had had in mind when they broadened the definition of war crimes.[240]

When his turn to read a portion of the majority opinion came, Judge Powers stated that his "participation in the reading is merely for the purpose of helping out with the physical task of reading this opinion. It should not be construed as anything so far as my approval is concerned."[241] In his dissent Powers took a conservative interpretation of the court's mandate: "I violently disagree with the opinion that we are engaged in enforcing International law which has not been codified, and that we have an obligation to lay down rules of conduct for nations of the future," he contended. "It is not for us to say what things should be condemned as crimes and what things should not. That has all been done by the lawmaking authority."[242] Powers dissented on all the crimes against peace convictions for the simple reason that "there was no possible basis for claiming that a mere invasion was contrary to international law."[243] Based on this reading he found von Weizsäcker not guilty for two reasons: "One, the invasion of Czechoslovakia was not a crime against peace. Two, he took no part in bringing about or initiating such an invasion." The dissent also cleared Keppler, Lammers, Woermann, and Koerner of any criminal wrongdoing.[244]

For the next two days the verdicts on the various counts of crimes against humanity (3 through 8) were read. The tribunal majority found 14 defendants guilty under at least one count.[245] Ernst von Weizsäcker was found guilty of crimes against humanity for his failure to object to Himmler about the deportation of 6,000 French Jews to Poland. Judge Powers argued that von Weizsäcker and Woermann had not been able to protest because "No grounds . . . based on foreign politics existed for objection." Not only did Powers accept the defense of necessity, but he also mocked the majority's logic: "But the Opinion seems to hold, especially as to WEIZSAECKER, that even in such a situation, he should have taken advantage of the opportunity to deliver a lecture to Ribbentrop on International Law and on morality."[246]

SS General Gottlob Berger was found guilty under Count 3 (war crimes) for the execution of French General Maurice Mesny, a reprisal for a German general killed by French underground forces. The tribunal majority found it "impossible to believe Berger's testimony that he knew nothing of the plans to destroy the Jews or that he never heard of the 'final solution' until after the war" in view of the documentary evidence. However, the court accepted the defendant's plea that during the final months of the war, he saved the lives of "American, British, and Allied officers and men whose safety was gravely imperiled by orders of Hitler that they be liquidated or held as hostages. Berger disobeyed the orders and intervened on their behalf and in doing so placed himself in a position of hazard."[247] Gottlob Berger was found guilty of transporting Hungarian Jews to concentration camps and recruiting concentration camp guards. Finally, Walter Schellenberg was found guilty of helping to create the Einsatzgruppen and preventing Jewish immigration to Belgium "in view of the final solution which is sure to come."[248]

Like the defendants in the Justice case, Hans Lammers was convicted for drafting and implementing Nazi legal policies. "Lammers was not a mere postman," the majority opinion stated, "but acted solely without objection as a responsible Reichminister carrying out the function of his office." He not only knew of the policy but also "approved of it, and took an active, consenting and implementing part in its execution."[249] Edmund Veesenmayer was convicted for war crimes, crimes against humanity, and slave labor for forcing the Hungarian government to deport more than 300,000 Hungarian Jews to concentration camps like Auschwitz.[250] Otto Dietrich was found guilty for providing the anti-Semitic drumbeat that justified the German campaign against the Jews. Gustav Adolf Steengracht von Moyland was convicted for preventing Jewish immigration and aiding in the extermination of Hungarian Jews. Wilhelm Keppler and Hans Kehrl were found guilty of "resettling" Jews to make room for ethnic Germans, and Richard Darré for removing thousands of Polish and Jewish farmers.[251] Bankers Lutz Graf Schwerin von Krosigk and Emil Puhl were convicted of laundering confiscated property and financing the construction of the concentration camps. Regarding Puhl's guilt, the tribunal majority wrote, "The defendant contends that stealing the personal property of Jews and other concentration camp inmates is not a crime against humanity. But under the circumstances which we have here related, this plea is and must be rejected."[252]

Judge Powers dissented on many of the crimes against humanity convictions: "Where a finding of guilt is justified, the opinion so exaggerates the guilt, that I cannot concur in it."[253] He argued that the defendants were guilty of association rather than personal action and cleared diplomats von Weizsäcker and Woermann of criminal wrongdoing because they did not personally commit crimes. Similarly, Powers rejected the convictions of von Moyland, Dietrich, Veesenmayer, von Krosigk, and Puhl: "Many of the acts such as Jewish fines took place before the war began and are not within our jurisdiction. It cannot be a crime against humanity because merely depriving people of their property is not such a crime."[254] By the time the tribunal finished handing down its decision, Judge Powers had dissented on 37 of the 49 convictions. His 124-page opinion opposed all the guilty verdicts other than those for the use of slave labor and membership in the criminal organizations. The judge from Iowa argued that the convictions were a gross misapplication of international law and that it was better to free high-ranking Nazis than to establish misleading precedents.[255]

The sentences were handed down on April 15, 1949 and once again, they did not match the tone of the opinion. While not as lenient as those of the Farben and Flick cases, given the status of the defendants and the body of evidence against them, the sentences were light:

Ernst von Weizsäcker: 7 years.

Gustav Adolf Steengracht von Moyland: 7 years.

Wilhelm Keppler: 10 years.

Ernst Bohle: 5 years.

Ernst Woermann: 7 years.

Karl Ritter: 4 years.

Otto von Erdmannsdorff: Acquitted.

Edmund Veesenmayer: 20 years.

Hans Lammers: 20 years.

Wilhelm Stuckart: Acquitted due to illness.

Richard Darré: 7 years.

Otto Meissner: Acquitted.

Otto Dietrich: 7 years.

Gottlob Berger: 25 years.

Walter Schellenberg: 6 years.

Lutz Graf Schwerin von Krosigk: 10 years.

Emil Puhl: 5 years.

Karl Rasche: 7 years.

Paul Koerner: 15 years.

Paul Pleiger: 15 years.

Hans Kehrl: 15 years.[256]

It appeared that the tribunal majority rejected von Weizsäcker's defense of necessity, but the question was reopened after the judgment was read; the tribunal allowed all of the convicted to file "Motions for the Correction of Alleged Errors of Fact and Law." Among other things, their motions attacked the court's legal legitimacy. "The Tribunal as a whole was never legally established and its said decision and judgment constitutes an arbitrary exercise of military power over each of the said defendants, in violation of the laws of nations and agreements made by the belligerent powers and other countries appertaining thereto."[257]

Because of the court's split decision, the Ministries case was hailed by trial supporters and critics alike. For Brigadier General Telford Taylor, the final year had been a long one; the decisions in the Ministries case provided a limited measure of vindication. Impressed by the strongly reasoned 835-page majority opinion, Taylor praised the resolve of the court's concurring members, asserting that "today's judgment, more severe than many of those which have been handed down previously, is perhaps more important than those which went before. It was decided long after the excitement of the war which ended nearly four years ago."[258] The Chief Counsel believed that the case was both important and redemptive because it "proves that we still mean in 1949 what we meant in 1945."[259] There was also praise for the judge from Iowa. General counsel for I. G. Farben and former Nuremberg defendant August von Knieriem described Powers's dissenting opinion as "extensive and carefully motivated." Carl Haensel, a leading Nuremberg defense counsel, viewed the dissent as the high point of the Ministries case: "The leading event of the day of judgment was the news of Judge Powers' Dissenting Opinion. Judge Powers declared that in his Opinion the majority of the defendants should be acquitted."[260]

CHAPTER 5

NUREMBERG:

A COLD WAR CONFLICT OF INTEREST

ROBERT MAGUIRE AND WILLIAM CHRISTIANSON'S EXTENSIVE majority opinion helped to bolster the reputation of the American Nuremberg trials. Because the two judges convicted defendants under the revolutionary charge of crimes against peace, the American war crimes effort appeared to end with a small victory for the prosecution. The majority opinion in the Ministries case would serve to offset the judgments of the Krupp, Farben, and High Command cases. Although the tone and tactics of the prosecution might have seemed "vindictive" when measured by German or Continental legal standards, on the whole the Nuremberg judgments were very conservative; all of the capital sentences in the *Einsatzgruppen* case, the Medical case, and the Pohl case were for violations of the traditional laws of war. The overwhelming majority of the judges rejected or avoided the contentious, or as some might argue *ex post facto*, aggression and conspiracy charges.

From the vantage point of more than half a century later, the judgments in the American Nuremberg trials appear quite lenient. Years afterward, Robert Maguire wrote, "One thing I think can be said without question, is that so far as the courts were concerned, the attitude was the opposite of emotional, and that they earnestly endeavored, and I think succeeded, in being entirely objective toward the defendants and evidence."[1] If this was one of the "harshest" jurists at Nuremberg, what of the others? Maguire confirmed the trend toward leniency: "I think that it may be fairly said that not only was every attempt made to give the defendants a fair trial and every opportunity to defend themselves, but that the judges in various cases probably leaned backwards in protecting their rights."[2]

The guilt or innocence of Ernst von Weizsäcker has continued to be debated to this day. His son, former West German President Richard von Weizsäcker, blames the failure of his father's complicated defense on the provincial American judges who were "not even familiar with the details of European and German history." However, the loyal son goes too far when he declares that his father has been absolved by modern historians.[3] But is it that simple? While German diplomatic historian Klemens von Klemperer agrees that Ernst von Weizsäcker may have been part of the resistance, he describes the former State Secretary's behavior as "that of a tired servant of the old school rather than that of an outraged man of principle; it was resistance devoid of firm resolve and conviction."[4] "Diplomats had deported foreign Jews because they did not want the Nazis to suspect them of subversion and undermine their position in clandestine peace talks," writes German historian Jörg Friedrich, who goes on to mock von Weizsäcker's defense as "retroactive opportunism."[5] For example, of the approximately 1,200 Roman Jews that Ernst von Weizsäcker helped to deport to Auschwitz, only 14 men and one woman survived World War II.[6]

The case took a strange twist in May 1949, when a Senate Armed Services Committee led by Connecticut Senator Raymond Baldwin began an investigation of the Malmedy Massacre. Much to the delight of his German American constituency, freshman Senator Joe McCarthy of Wisconsin offered his services to the committee; when the first session began on May 4, McCarthy attacked the conviction of Ernst von Weizsäcker and the opinion of judges Maguire and Christianson.[7] According to McCarthy, von Weizsäcker was "the most valuable undercover man which the Allies had in Germany, starting in 1936." His innocence was a well-established fact: "Apparently the evidence is all uncontradicted, there is no question about it." McCarthy argued that the Nuremberg sentences would "do tremendous damage" to the American position in Germany and "make it impossible for us to have any kind of intelligence in the prospective opposition of other nations, potential enemies." The senator called for an investigation into the Ministries case: "I think this committee should see what type of morons— and I use that term advisedly—are running the military court over there. There is something completely beyond conception, and I would like to ask the Chair to go into the matter, and in effect notify the world at this time that the American people are not in approval of this complete imbecility in that area."[8]

In a strategy that later brought McCarthy both fame and censure, he claimed to be on the verge of exposing a massive cover-up of the "Gestapo" tactics of the U.S. Army. Army interrogator Perl was brought before the committee. "I think you are lying. I do not think you can fool the lie detector," McCarthy said to Perl. "You may be able to fool us." A lawyer himself, Perl responded caustically, "If it is so reliable, we should have used it from the beginning. Why a trial at all? Get the guys, and put the lie detector on them. 'Did you kill this man?' The lie detector says, 'Yes.' Go to the scaffold. If it says, 'No,' back to Bavaria."[9] McCarthy's dramatic attack on the Baldwin committee drew much attention, especially in Germany. Although the subcommittee concluded that there had been some abuses, its report came down hardest on the trial critics.[10] "More at stake than the Army's conduct in this particular matter," wrote historian Frank Buscher, "the subcommittee warned . . . that the 'attacks' on the war-crimes trials in general and the Malmedy case in particular were meant to revive German nationalism and to cast doubt upon the U.S. occupation of Germany as a whole."[11] The clamor over the Malmedy trials had a catalyzing effect on many Germans, who saw these exchanges as a green light of sorts. It was now permissible to attack American war crimes policy in a more inflammatory way with the justification that they were merely emulating the tactics of "responsible American statesmen."[12]

Once Germany became the fulcrum of the American plan for the reconstruction of Europe, the question of Landsberg Prison and the fate of the war criminals took on new significance. By 1949, conservative American politicians like Francis Case, Harold Knutsen, John Taber, William Langer, and John Rankin were concluding that alleged improprieties in the Malmedy trial discredited the findings of all the American war crimes tribunals. According to Frank Buscher, by the end of the 1940s, these conservative Republicans had succeeded in establishing "a new Nuremberg philosophy," and many in the United States "had come to accept the conservative argument that the convicted Nazi perpetrators were not criminals, but instead were the victims of the Allied war crimes program."[13]

When judges Maguire, Christianson, and Powers ruled on a series of post-trial defense motions on December 12, 1949, they rejected all but three. Judge Maguire reversed his position on the most significant verdict of the Ministries case and joined Judge Powers in opposing the convictions of

Ernst von Weizsäcker and Ernst Woermann under crimes against peace. The new tribunal majority of Maguire and Powers announced, "After a careful examination of the entire record concerning his conviction with the aggression against Czechoslovakia, we are convinced that our finding of guilt as to that crime is erroneous. We are glad to correct it. The judgment of guilt against the defendant von Weizsaecker as to Count I is hereby set aside and he is hereby acquitted under Count I."[14] Presiding Judge Christianson vehemently dissented from the modification of Ernst von Weizsäcker's sentence from seven to five years, not to mention the reversal of a precedent like the aggression conviction: "A re-examination of the evidence with respect to the actions of defendant von Weizsaecker in connection with the aggression against Czechoslovakia deepens my conviction that said defendant is guilty under said count one." Ministries case prosecutor William Caming had a high regard for Judge Maguire, but to this day remains baffled by his post-trial action. "Judge Maguire's Memorandum Opinion is embarrassingly vague and devoid of any rationale for his change of heart. I can only surmise what the impelling personal factors were," he wrote.[15] The pressure to release von Weizsäcker only increased after his aggressive war conviction was overturned. Former German resistance leader Theo Kordt wrote Lord Halifax in late 1949, describing the von Weizsäcker case as "a new Dreyfuss case" and strongly supporting the former state secretary's claim that he had accepted the job of State Secretary in 1938 in order to prevent war.[16]

Although the "vindictive" policies of the Nuremberg trials and JCS 1067 summoned memories of Versailles, the analogy between the two settlements was a false one. However, as Jörg Friedrich points out, rationality, law, and facts had little place in the debate over German war criminals during the 1950s: "The Nuremberg prosecution, well supplied with documentary evidence, succeeded in refuting these nonsensical excuses and winning convictions. However, the public was not won over." The criminal guilt that the trial planners hoped would serve as "a wedge between the public and the defendants turned out to form a link between them."[17] Many Germans found not just the actual punishment but also the manner in which it came objectionable. By 1949, there was a deep reservoir of German resentment over the subject of war crimes that had yet to be tapped.

During the second phase of American World War II crimes policy (1949–53), American and West German leaders fashioned two American policies—one public and one private. The public one was designed to defend the legal validity of the American trials from widespread German attacks, while the private policy sought to release war criminals as quickly and quietly as the political and legal circumstances would allow. The problematic details surrounding the early releases would occupy the State Department's legal advisors until the last German war criminals were released in the late 1950s. Ironically, the Germans would force the United States to debate the legal validity of the Allied war crimes trials that had been prevented by Article 3 of the IMT's charter in 1945.

The first major step toward the restoration of German sovereignty occurred on September 21, 1949, when the Federal Republic of West Germany was officially established and the Occupation Statute was replaced by West Germany's Basic Law. The former American governing body, the U.S. Military Government, was replaced by the U.S. High Commission for Germany (HICOG), and Clay was replaced by Stimson's former Assistant Secretary of War, John McCloy. Most significantly, American oversight of West Germany shifted from the U.S. Army to the U.S. State Department, and American war crimes policy would soon reflect this change. Throughout 1945, John McCloy had fought passionately for the creation of the IMT and all that it implied. His "certainty and energy" had bowled over even the skeptical British.[18] However, it was now 1949, and the punitive policies of the occupation were no longer compatible with the American program for Germany.

After the establishment of HICOG in 1949, seventy-three-year-old Konrad Adenauer was elected West Germany's first Chancellor. The State Department was satisfied that he was a sufficiently pro-American representative for the German people. Although Adenauer was committed to German integration into the West, the problem created by the imprisoned war criminals was growing into what Frank Buscher describes as "a major obstacle to the achievement of his foreign policy goals."[19]

Though there were continued cries for a reunified Germany, the possibility looked out of the question by 1949, as East Germany had already been militarized by the Soviet Union; its *Volkspolizei* (People's Police) had more than fifty thousand Soviet-trained members.[20] Because the United States had demobilized so rapidly after the war, the Soviets had what appeared to be a huge superiority in conventional forces in Europe. As early as 1949, some of America's most influential foreign policy makers felt that rearming West Germany was inevitable because the United States had barely twelve army divisions, while the Soviets had twenty-four and another seventy in reserve.[21] Rearmament fulfilled the darkest geopolitical prognostications of right-wing German nationalists and unrepentant Nazis who had said all along that the Soviet Union was the true enemy of Western civilization. By

1949, a fast-growing segment of the West German population considered *all* the war crimes trials to be a form of political theater with no basis in either fact or law. The Nuremberg trials had become a hugely important symbolic issue, a contemporary version of the Treaty of Versailles' "shame paragraphs."[22] The attacks on Nuremberg were the same as in 1945, but the international political context had changed; now West German goodwill and cooperation were vital to the American plan for Western Europe.

By 1950, all the war criminals convicted by American courts in Germany were incarcerated in Bavaria's Landsberg Prison.[23] Of the 185 men charged in the American Nuremberg Trials, 177 were tried, 35 acquitted, 24 sentenced to death, 20 sentenced to life, and 98 given other prison terms; 4 committed suicide. In the Dachau and other concentration camp trials conducted by the U.S. Army, 1,672 were charged, 256 acquitted, 426 sentenced to death, 199 sentenced to life, and 791 given other prison terms. In the United Kingdom trials, 1,085 were charged, 348 acquitted, 240 sentenced to death, 24 sentenced to life, and 473 given other prison terms. In the French trials, 2,107 were charged, 404 acquitted, 104 sentenced to death, 44 sentenced to life, and more than 1,000 given other prison terms. There are only the sketchiest details of the Soviet trials. Of 14,240 who were charged, 142 were acquitted, 138 sentenced to death, and more than 13,000 given other prison terms.[24]

Because the Nuremberg trials had no appellate court to review the sentences, John Raymond, Alvin Rockwell, and other members of the legal staff of the U.S. Military Government reviewed the sentences of both the Nuremberg and the Army trials on an ad hoc basis. Up until 1949, General Clay had the final word on the fate of the war criminals. Because the trials were being severely criticized in the United States, he took the sentence confirmation process very seriously, knowing that his decisions were going to be attacked from all sides.

German trial critics did not merely seek clemency; they wanted an apology to assuage their violated sense of honor. Many German veterans considered the war crimes convicts prisoners of war, whose main crime was losing.[25] Due to a Senate investigation, Lucius Clay had been unable to carry out all the Nuremberg death sentences, and they were inherited by John McCloy when he took office as High Commissioner in 1949 (those convicted by the army at Dachau were under the jurisdiction of Army Commander-in-Chief Thomas Handy). German criticism of the American war crimes program weighed heavily on McCloy. From his first day as High Commissioner, he was barraged with thousands of letters, telegrams, and postcards begging clemency for those imprisoned at Landsberg, but his largest problem was the handful of men scheduled for execution.[26] These convicts had exhausted all channels of appeal and awaited his final decision.

John McCloy refused to admit that politics influenced his treatment of the German war criminals. Until his death in 1989, he doggedly maintained that these were apolitical "legal" decisions.[27] The High Commissioner established the Advisory Board on Clemency for War Criminals (also referred to as the Peck Panel) in 1950. He provided this faulty justification for his decision to re-review sentences that already had been both reviewed and confirmed by General Clay: "The availability to the individual defendant of an appeal to executive clemency is a salutary part of the administration of justice. It is particularly appropriate that the cases of defendants convicted of war crimes be given an executive review because no appellate court review has been provided."[28]

It was becoming increasingly clear that many West Germans still did not accept the legal validity of the American war crimes trials. Among the first to take up the defense of the war criminals were the leaders of Germany's Catholic and Protestant churches. Jörg Friedrich points to the irony of the German clergy's position: "The same bishops who had witnessed the murder of more than 4,000 priests and nuns by Nazi courts and kept silent about the deportation and gassing of Jewish converts, now felt the need to confront the occupation authorities with biblical rigor."[29] In a letter responding to a plea for a war crimes amnesty from Bishop Fargo A.J. Muench, the Regent of the German Apostolic Nunciature in Germany, High Commissioner McCloy expressed irritation: "I have been somewhat disturbed, however, in examining these petitions, by what appears to be a persistent tendency to question the legal basis for the prosecutions and the judicial soundness of the judgements." He unequivocally rejected the bishop's call for an amnesty because it would "be taken as an abandonment of the principles established in the trials of the perpetrators of those crimes."[30]

In late January, McCloy set about establishing the Advisory Board on Clemency for War Criminals to consider the petitions of German war criminals convicted by American courts. Although State Department Assistant Legal Advisor for German Affairs John Raymond agreed that an "impartial board" review would relieve public pressure, he was one of the members of General Clay's review board and believed that the vast majority of the death sentences should stand. Most of the prisoners facing the death penalty had been Einsatzgruppen leaders and General Clay had taken special care in reviewing their death sentences.[31] Clay explained, "When you have the responsibility of whether someone is going to die, before you sign a paper you worry about it an awful lot. And I never signed any of those papers without going through the trial record from A to Z. And if there was any doubt, *any doubt*, I commuted the sentence."[32]

Former Nuremberg prosecutor Telford Taylor publicly challenged the decision to review the sentences in a February 2, 1950 *New York Post* article entitled, "Stalling Baffles U.S. Prosecutor." From his law office in New York City, Taylor announced that the "retreat from Nuremberg is on"; he feared that another sentence review would only benefit "those who have wealthy and powerful influences behind them."[33] The next day, Michael Musmanno, the judge responsible for the majority of the death sentences, bolstered Taylor's views in a *Post* follow-up. The judge in the Milch, Pohl, and Einsatzgruppen cases called the death sentences "eminently just and proper" and reminded the public that Otto Ohlendorf and the other twenty-two defendants were responsible for ordering and overseeing a "total number of killings amounting to 1,000,000."[34]

Secretary of State Dean Acheson, in a February 8 cable, warned High Commissioner McCloy that the proposed sentence reviews would reopen the debate over the legal legitimacy of the Nuremberg trials: "Boards of the caliber you suggest would be bound to attract attention and might tend to create impression that legal basis, and procedure of Nuremberg trials under review, or at least be construed as indication of doubt RE Pohl and Ohlendorf cases."[35] McCloy heeded this advice, and by May 1950, two American war crimes clemency boards had been created. The American Nuremberg trials would be reviewed by a three-man committee that would report to John McCloy, while the Dachau and Army cases would be reviewed by Texas Supreme Court Justice Gordon Simpson, who would report to Army Commander-in-Chief General Thomas Handy.[36]

The legal expert for the High Commission's clemency board was former New York Supreme Court Justice David Peck. Questions about parole and incarceration were handled by the former chairman of the New York Board of Parole, Fredrick Moran.[37] The third member of the board was State Department legal advisor Conrad Snow. Their official task was to equalize sentence discrepancies among the Nuremberg tribunals; theoretically the board was authorized only to reduce sentences, not to challenge the legal basis of the decisions. The Peck Panel spent the summer of 1950 in Munich, reading the judgments of the various courts.

Questions about German rearmament led to a deadlock among the Truman administration's policy makers. The President was not blind to the implications of putting weapons back into the hands of German soldiers. He was quick to remind "the experts" that Germany had taken a 100,000-man paramilitary organization and transformed it into the greatest fighting force in modern history.[38] The stalemate over the West German army continued until, once again, "international communism" lived up to American expectations.

During the early morning of June 25, the State Department in Washington received a cable from the U.S. ambassador in Seoul, Korea: "North Korea forces invaded the Republic of Korea territory at several points this morning. . . . It would appear from the nature of the attack and manner in which it was launched that constitutes an all-out offensive against ROK." Initially, North Korean forces overran the South with ninety thousand troops and Soviet-made T-34 tanks.[39] Some of the darker minds in the U.S. government believed that the action had been ordered by Moscow and that once American forces were mired in Korea, the Red Army would launch a Western offensive. President Truman condemned the invasion in the strongest terms, arguing that "Communism was acting in Korea just as Hitler, Mussolini, and the Japanese had acted 10, 15, 20 years earlier. If this was allowed to go unchallenged it would mean a Third World War."[40] By September 1950, the United States had troops in Korea, and the "conflict" had turned into a full-scale war. Truman's decision to back his rhetoric with U.S. ground forces changed the diplomatic landscape throughout the world, but nowhere more than in Germany. The situation was further complicated by the fact that the West Germans were about to be asked to rearm and possibly fight East Germans.

There was a consensus among the State Department's elite that Germany needed to be rearmed.[41] High Commissioner McCloy recognized this and, like Clay before him, issued a dramatic "top secret" warning to Washington. In a cable, McCloy wrote, "If no means are held out for Germans to fight in an emergency my view is that we should probably lose Germany politically as well as militarily without hope of regaining. We should also lose, incidentally, a reserve of manpower which may become of great value in event of a real war and could certainly be used by the Soviets against us."[42]

Secretary of State Acheson and High Commissioner McCloy decided to make Germany part of the Western European Defense Force (EDF), which had been created by representatives of the European powers who had already appointed Dwight Eisenhower Supreme Commander. One of Eisenhower's first assignments was to raise a German army.[43] The man who had once recommended executing the entire German General Staff now actively supported rearmament. Neither England nor France was overly enthusiastic about the idea, but considering the size of the U.S. military commitment in Korea and the amount of American economic aid to Europe, they couldn't afford to voice much opposition. Members of the High Commission met with Chancellor Adenauer to discuss the creation of seven German divisions by the mid-1950s.[44] The Truman administration, the State Department, and Adenauer were all in favor of rearmament, but both nations had huge domestic obstacles to overcome.[45] Both needed the approval of their domestic constituencies and the governments of Great Britain and France before they could implement any new plan.[46] Once it became official that West Germany would be rearmed, questions pertaining to the war criminals took on new significance as West German leaders from all political parties pointed to America's paradoxical role as occupying ally.

The system of war crimes trial review instituted by the High Commissioner was, like its predecessor, ad hoc. There was little procedure to follow, so McCloy's board created their own. Although they were able to review the judgments in each of the twelve American Nuremberg trials, they could not consider the documentary evidence or the actual trial transcripts. It was an impossible task for three men: the transcripts in the Ministries case, for example, ran to twenty-eight thousand pages, with an additional nine thousand documentary exhibits.[47] By the summer of 1950, the Peck Panel was hard at work. Despite the official pronouncements of impartiality, there were very basic ways the review process favored the German war criminals. Fifty lawyers representing the majority of the prisoners were brought before the board. Not only were the judges and prosecutors who had tried the cases conspicuously absent, but unlike in ordinary parole hearings, they did not even know that the sentences were being re-reviewed.[48]

The panel presented its final report to the High Commissioner on August 28. Several members of the HICOG staff expressed reservations about their recommendations. State Department legal advisor John Raymond considered some of the individual decisions excessively lenient and believed that they called the original verdicts into question. "The basic difference in the approach adopted by the Board from the one that we took in reviewing cases is that the Board did not feel bound by the findings drawn as conclusions from the facts, whereas we accepted all the findings of the tribunals," he wrote in a confidential memo. Raymond believed that the "reduction from death to eight years is perhaps going too far."[49] Robert Bowie, High Commissioner McCloy's trusted legal advisor, also had misgivings about the Peck Panel's final report: "I have carefully reviewed the recommendations of the Board and believe that in a number of cases the reductions recommended are excessive. I have serious doubts as to the validity of the 24 recommendations of the Board which seem to me to fail to give sufficient recognition to the seriousness of the crime for which the individuals concerned were sentenced by Tribunals."[50] Like Acheson, Bowie realized that the issue had moved beyond the legal realm and worried lest "the report as a whole create the impression of a repudiation of the Nuremberg trials."[51] In November, Secretary of State Acheson informed President Truman that some of the death sentences would probably be upheld and learned the "President thought that the action proposed was correct."[52]

By late 1950, word of the impending sentence reviews reached the United States, and John McCloy was attacked from all sides. Senator William Langer made the most absurd analogy and compared the Nuremberg trials to Stalin's purge trials on December 18: "These war-trials were decided on in Moscow and they were carried on under Moscow principles. These trials were essentially the same as the mass trials held in the 1930s by Stalin when Vyshinsky used treason trials to liquidate his internal enemies. At Nuremberg the Communists used the war crimes trials to liquidate their external enemies. It is the Communists' avowed purpose to destroy the Western World which is based on property rights." Langer added a new dimension to the critique by claiming that the cases against the industrialists were part of a communist plot "aimed directly at property rights. It was intended to try the accused as aggressors, convict them as having started the war, and then confiscate their property as a penalty." Under questioning from Senator McCarran of Nevada, Senator Langer made a rather dramatic and embarrassing factual error that exposed his complete ignorance about the trials he was attacking so aggressively. Langer had confused the denazification proceedings with the American Nuremberg trials, claiming that "the second Nuremberg trials we sent from all over the United States judges to try between two million and three million Germans who were arrested and tried at what were called the denazification trials."[53]

John McCloy spent the remainder of 1950 wrestling with his final decisions as German nationalists continued to lobby for an amnesty on war crimes.[54] Of all McCloy's duties as High Commissioner, this would be the most difficult. He met with a West German parlimentary committee that included Hermann Ehlers, President of the Bundestag Heinrich Hoefler, Carlos Schmid, Jacob Altmaier, Hans von Merkatz, and Franz Josef Strauss for two and a half hours in January.[55] These leaders pointed out that West Germany's freshly minted constitution "prohibited the death penalty."[56] By this time McCloy had lost his patience, and the man accused of having a "pathological love for Germany" had been pushed too far.[57] According to *The New York Times,* the High Commissioner stated, "I did not know any good German soldier had lost his honor," and reminded the Germans who was holding the cards. "Of this threat Mr. McCloy feels that the Americans would rather not have the Germans if their cooperation depended upon the justification of war crimes or negligence to exact the penalty for them."[58] With rearmament now certain, unrepentant Nazis like Hitler's former bodyguard, Otto "Scarface" Skorzeny, recognized the new bargaining power of German veterans. The Nazi folk hero flexed from his luxurious sanctuary in Madrid: "In good faith, even with a certain amount of enthusiasm, we have put ourselves at the disposal of the Americans. Yet I repeat in the name of all German officers who are working for the future victory of the West, if Peiper dies we will no longer lift a finger to help but will yield to the opposing point of view."[59]

HICOG released *Landsberg: A Documentary Report* on January 31, 1951. It included the statements of the Peck Panel, Judge Simpson, High Commissioner McCloy, and General Thomas Handy. McCloy followed the majority of the board's recommendations; he freed one third of the Nuremberg prisoners and commuted all but five of the outstanding death sentences.[60] The primary beneficiaries of the High Commissioner's generosity were German businessmen: with one stroke of his pen, all of the remaining lawyers, executives, and industrialists convicted in the Farben, Flick, and Krupp trials were freed.[61] Ernst von Weizsäcker had already been released from prison; Ministries case defendant Gottlob Berger had his sentence reduced from twenty-five to ten years.

The most controversial of all John McCloy's decisions was in the case of Alfried Krupp.[62] After a nine-month trial, Krupp had been found guilty of playing a leading role in running his family's company, which built factories on the grounds of concentration camps and used slave labor provided by the SS. In an otherwise lenient judgment, Krupp was sentenced to twelve years and stripped of all industrial and financial holdings on July 31, 1948.[63] High Commissioner McCloy expressed his extreme discomfort with the tribunal's command to seize Krupp's property: "This is the sole case of confiscation decreed against any defendant by the Nuremberg courts." McCloy believed that singling Krupp out "constitutes discrimination against this defendant unjustified by any considerations attaching peculiarly to him. General confiscation of property is not a usual element in our judicial system and is generally repugnant to American concepts of justice."[64]

The duality in American war crimes policy became clear for all to see on February 3, 1951, when Krupp was set free and his property was restored. His release created "the impression" that the United States was reversing its position on war crimes; regardless of American rhetoric, it was back to business as usual.[65] "In 1924 I warned the Bavarian Government against the release from Landsberg prison of a certain Adolf Hitler and a certain Rudolf Hess," wrote Nuremberg prosecutor Robert Kempner. "Today I want to go on record with a warning that the premature opening of the Landsberg gates will loose against society totalitarian subversive forces that endanger the free world."[66]

Suffice it to say, the Landsberg decisions had just the effect that the State Department had anticipated. Nazi apologists who had argued all along that the war criminals were political prisoners felt vindicated. Several segments of the German population stepped up a well-organized campaign for a "war crimes amnesty," their most pressing concern now the fate of the men awaiting execution.[67] Although High Commissioner McCloy and his army counterpart General Handy spared the lives of twenty-one war criminals, seven were still scheduled to hang.[68] General Clay had carefully reviewed five of those death sentences in 1948 and was absolutely convinced that the convicts deserved them. The most infamous of those awaiting execution was Otto Ohlendorf, the man who led Einsatzgruppen D into Russia in 1941. In one year they killed roughly ninety thousand civilians in one year.[69] The tribunal found Paul Blobel responsible for overseeing more than sixty thousand murders.[70] Werner Braune was commander of the unit that committed the Simferopol massacre. Erich Naumann was in charge of a unit that operated on the Russian front for sixteen months.[71] The fifth defendant to be executed was the notorious concentration camp administrator Oswald Pohl. The two convicts under the U.S. Army's jurisdiction, Georg Schallermai and Hans Schmidt, had been particularly sadistic concentration camp guards at Mühldorf and Buchenwald.[72]

The final section of the *Landsberg Report* included the decisions of the U.S. Army in the Malmedy and other trials. Headed by Texas Supreme Court Justice Gordon Simpson, the European Command War Crimes Modification Board, created by General Handy, had a similar task as the Peck Panel, which was to grant clemency where grounds existed.[73] On the whole, the U.S. Army was reluctant to issue wide-ranging war crimes amnesties and was significantly less lenient than John McCloy and the State Department.[74] After reviewing the sentences of the perpetrators of the Malmedy Massacre, Handy reduced all of the death sentences to life in prison and reduced 349 of 510 prison sentences; as a result, 150 men were immediately freed. "The crimes are definitely distinguishable from the more deliberate killings in concentration camps."[75] However, Handy remained convinced that Kampfgruppe Peiper had committed the atrocity and that Joachim Peiper had ordered it.

American statesmen had hoped that these generous acts of clemency would mollify the German people, but ultimately *The Landsberg Report* had the opposite effect. No amount of strategic legalism could hide the fact that the American retreat from Nuremberg had begun, and acts like the reduction of Einsatzkommando Heinz Hermann Schubert's death sentence to ten years spoke more loudly than legalistic distinctions between clemency and parole. Instead of accepting guilt for the crimes of the Third Reich, German nationalists stepped up their attacks on American war crimes policy and focused on the legal validity of the Nuremberg trials.[76]

John McCloy was caught in a public relations crossfire in both Germany and the United States. Like his American lawyer-statesmen predecessors, the high commissioner instinctively believed that what could be justified legally did not have to be justified morally. The third-generation American lawyer-statesman, like Elihu Root before him, would interpret law to suit the needs of a rapidly changing American foreign policy. However, when McCloy attempted to treat the war crimes issue as a one-dimensional legal problem, it blew up in his face. In stark contrast to his disregard for civil rights of Japanese-American citizens during World War II, the fate of Germany's worst convicted war criminals was a matter of the greatest concern. At the time of the Japanese internment, McCloy described America's most sacred document, the Constitution, as "just a scrap of paper."[77]

West German lawyers were succeeding in shifting the focus away from the crimes of the convicted and forcing the Americans to defend the basic legal validity of their trials, German nationalists changed the very nature of the debate. After nearly five years of occupation and reeducation, they refused to make any distinction between those who deserved and those who did not deserve punishment.[78]

Ironically, the question of the trials' legal validity—unchallengeable at Nuremberg due to Article 3 of the London Agreement Charter—would now be debated by American officials and West German lawmakers and politicians. By the early 1950s, the Adenauer administration and the German Foreign Office were trying both to reject the legality of the Allied war crimes trials and to secure the premature releases of the imprisoned war criminals. The prisoners now had a powerful and well-connected group, called the *Heidelberg Juristenkreis*, lobbying on their behalf. Important members of the Kreis included former Nuremberg defense lawyer Otto Kranzbühler, representatives from Germany's Catholic and Evangelical churches, politicians, and leading German jurists.[79] Founded by former Nuremberg prosecutor and Bundestag representative (CDU) Eduard Wahl, the Kreis sought not only the release of the war criminals but also full legal pardons.[80] "When the trials were finished in 1949," said Kranzbühler, "me and a lot of other lawyers who had taken part in those trials felt the obligation to see to it that the defendants sentenced would get out as soon as possible and that the principles of these trials would not be recognized by the coming German government."[81] Just as he had found a way to evade Article 3 and enter Admiral Nimitz's testimony at the IMT, the German lawyer would find a way to reject the legal validity of the Allied war crimes tribunals.

The Juristenkreis held regular meetings with both Konrad Adenauer and American officials. The group not only served as a clearinghouse for information but also drafted the Adenauer administration's proposed solution to the war crimes problem.[82] In a strategy meeting, Chancellor Adenauer instructed Kranzbühler to "see to it that the leading politicians of the [German] states will follow your views. You have to see them and instruct them."[83]

The Essen Amnesty Committee was a more radical right-wing war criminal advocacy group with a much different approach. Led by another former Nuremberg defense attorney, now Bundestag representative, Ernst Achenbach and Freiburg law professor Friedrich Grimm, the committee opposed rearmament and Western integration, and sought a "tabula rasa" on war crimes in the form of an unconditional amnesty. John McCloy would later describe some of its members as representatives of Germany's "right-wing lunatic fringe."[84]

By 1951, it was not just nationalists and neo-Nazis who were dismissing the American war crimes proceedings as a "victor's justice."[85] After the Landsberg decisions, letters and petitions continued to flood the offices of General Handy and High Commissioner McCloy urging the American representatives to stay the final executions of German war criminals. The powerful and educated appealed to them on the grounds of Christian charity. "Stile Hilte" leader Princess Helene von Isemberg pled to McCloy in one letter: "Jesus Christ has given the high doctrine to mankind: Forgive us our fault, as we forgive our enemies. Please, be a Christ, Sir."[86] In one of thousands of letters, a West German postal inspector best captured the spirit of the new debate. He urged the United States to free all war criminals so that: "West Germany will then be a *reliable and strong friend* of the western countries. The Russians fear *American equipment* and the *German soldier* most of all."[87] Many in the State Department recognized very early that logic and legal concepts would not placate a large segment of the German population. To nationalists, Nazis, and professional military men, the Third Reich had been vindicated by the postwar action of the United States. Former Nazis spoke of Hitler's historic mission to organize the people of Europe to wage a war against Bolshevism. At Nuremberg some had argued that Operation Barbarossa had been a justified defensive action. In the Bundestag debates of the early 1950s, German lawmakers made an interesting semantic shift. They began to refer to the war criminals (*Kriegsverbrecher*) as "war sentenced" or "sentenced because of war" (*Kriegsverurteiler*).[88]

The numerous German veteran organizations shared one goal in 1951: they would all fight to save the men on Landsberg's death row. Membership in the SS had been ruled a criminal offense by the IMT at Nuremberg and the Basic Law ensured that former members were disqualified from obtaining military service pensions.[89] Former SS General Otto Kumm created an assistance group for fellow former SS members called the Mutual Aid Society (*Hilfsgemeinschaft auf Gegenseitigkeit*).[90] Its leaders constantly rallied for the release of German war criminals in Allied custody, proclaiming that as a result of the widespread acts of clemency, the United States had repudiated all its war crimes decisions. This was part of a larger effort to prove that the German war criminals had been unjustifiably persecuted. Although groups like the *Stahlhelm* were loyal to Bonn, they too were extremely critical of the judicial treatment of Germans in Allied courts.[91] Both Chancellor Adenauer and High Commissioner McCloy recognized the important swing vote that these seemingly extreme groups would cast.[92]

Many German veterans felt that American "stupidity" in dealing with the Soviet Union had placed "all of Europe in jeopardy."[93] Former German Field Marshal and war crimes convict Albert Kesselring became one of the veterans' prominent spokesmen. Originally sentenced to death by a British military court for reprisals that he ordered against Italian partisans, Kesselring was released from Werl Prison in 1952. In an appeal to U.S. General Matthew Ridgeway, he implored his American counterpart to look beyond petty spites of politicians and to see the larger issue:

Sir, as officer to officer, I appeal to you, in whose hands the fate of many Germans lies. Help the German people cooperate enthusiastically in the fulfillment of the European cause so that they may eagerly comply with their inevitable historical obligation. Europe—indeed the whole western world— should not break down as a consequence of contrasts and conflicts with [sic] could be eliminated. You will be convinced as I am, of the fact that politics has its limits in military matters and vice versa, and that the war criminal cases should be separated from political matters and placed under the former uniform jurisdiction.[94]

After twenty months in British custody, German General Otto Remer was released and founded the far right *Socialist Reich Partei*. Remer not only denied the Holocaust, he claimed that the ovens had been built after the war and that the concentration camp films were fakes. Remer derided West Germany's American-inspired "shit democracy" and "chewing gum" soldiers. He violently opposed the American rearmament plan and happily offered to show the Soviets the way to the Rhine. SRP deputy Fritz Rossler pointed sarcastically to the duality of America's rapidly changing German policy: "First, we were told that guns and ammunition were poison and now this poison has been changed to sweets which we should eat. But we are not Negroes or idiots to whom they can do whatever they want. It is either they or us who should be committed to the insane asylum."[95]

The State Department's public opinion surveys in the weeks following the Landsberg decisions demonstrated that the much-vaunted "lessons" of Nuremberg had been lost on war-weary Germans. The U.S. High Commission released a confidential report entitled "West German Reactions to the Landsberg Decisions" on March 6, 1951. Residents of German cities were asked their opinions of the American clemency decisions, and public opinion in the four Allied zones of Germany was split nearly 50–50. The report concluded that the legal considerations behind the American decisions "completely failed to impress the German public"; the primary reason those surveyed gave for American leniency was that "They realize the injustice of the trials."[96] "A fairly general public view seems to be that all the decisions were a political maneuver rather than an expression of American justice."[97] The State Department's Office of Public Affairs surveyed German *Buergermeisters'* (mayors') about the Landsberg decisions and concluded: "They apparently do not appreciably depart from the general urban public in their interpretations of American motivations in moderating the sentences." The only conclusive thing the surveys demonstrated was that the "lessons" West Germans had learned from the Nuremberg trials were not the ones that their American "reeducators" had hoped to teach them.[98]

As early as 1951, legalistic distinctions like the one between amnesty and parole were lost on the majority of West Germans, who interpreted the American sentence reviews as cynical and politically expedient. Moreover, it was not as if the German public had ever accepted the decisions of the Nuremberg trials. The State Department would use strategic legalism to ameliorate the original sentences; in this case, the mechanism, or as the State Department legal advisors described it, the "device," was an ever-decreasing set of standards for clemency and parole.[99]

A number of pamphlets demanding a reversal of the death sentences appeared in 1951. The most dramatic was authored by former concentration camp administrator SS General Oswald Pohl. One of the convicts facing the hangman's noose, Pohl addressed this open letter, entitled "Germany's Dreyfus Affair," to former SS General Karl Wolff, who surrendered to the Allies in 1945 and worked with prosecutors at Nuremberg allegedly in exchange for immunity. Pohl compared his former comrade to the traitor in the Dreyfus Case: "But you in my eyes, have behaved yourself like the traitor, Esterhazy who was likewise responsible for Dreyfus' conviction." This pamphlet and others in defense of Pohl, Ohlendorf, and other Landsberg death row inmates was published by the Universal Union, a pro-amnesty group led by Frederick Wiehl, Oswald Pohl's attorney.[100] However, these crude tactics were far less successful than the more sophisticated efforts of the politically well-connected Heidelberg Juristenkreis.

Although High Commissioner John McCloy was slow to recognize it, he was forced to realize that no argument would placate certain segments of the German population.[101] Instead of quelling a mounting wave of criticism concerning the treatment of war criminals, the Peck Panel Report created controversies on two continents. In a February 1951 *Nation* magazine article, "Why Are We Freeing the Nazis?" Eleanor Roosevelt called attention to the premature release of prominent war criminals. After the article appeared, the High Commissioner defended his decisions in a letter to the former First Lady published in the U.S. High Commission's *Information Bulletin*: "As for the Krupp case. I find it difficult to understand the reaction on any other basis than the effect of a name. After a detailed study of this case, I could not convince myself that he deserved the sentence imposed on him. There was certainly a reasonable doubt that he was responsible for the policies of the Krupp company, in which he in fact occupied a somewhat junior position."[102] John McCloy could see no justification for taking Krupp's property: "No other person had his property confiscated—

not even the worst mass murderers. Why then single this man out for a type of punishment which, as Justice Jackson has pointed out, was entirely foreign to American tradition?"[103] McCloy vehemently denied that politics played a role in his decisions. "What really smarts with me is the suggestion that these decisions were the result of 'expediency,' i.e. that they were timed to gain a political objective. . . . If we were moved by expediency would it have been reasonable to release a man with such a world resounding name as Krupp."[104]

Once again, former Nuremberg prosecutor Telford Taylor defended the trials and called McCloy's misstatements "so serious that they should not be allowed to stand uncorrected." The High Commissioner had not helped his own case by making very basic factual errors that Taylor was quick to point out:

> Mr. McCloy states at the outset of his letter . . . 'I inherited these cases from General Clay who, for one reason or another had been unable to dispose of them finally.' This statement is 87–1/2% incorrect. The judgments pronounced at Nuremberg were to be final, but the sentences were subject to reduction at the discretion of the Military Governor. In eleven of the twelve cases, General Clay exercised his responsibilities, and reviewed the sentences prior to his resignation as Military Governor.[105]

The former Chief Counsel went on to emphasize how one-sided the High Commissioner's review had been:

> The Board read the judgments in all twelve cases (but apparently not the records), and heard fifty lawyers representing the criminals confined at Landsberg Prison. No representative of the prosecution was heard, or invited to appear, before either the Clemency Board or Mr. McCloy.[106]

Nuremberg prosecutor Sir Hartley Shawcross, now British Attorney General, attacked the Landsberg decisions as "political expediency" based on "the wholly false view that these sentences were no more than vengeance wreaked by the victors upon the vanquished." The American clemency action would undermine "the validity of what has been done." Shawcross rejected the argument that the Cold War somehow justified a shift in war crimes policy: "These Nazis were and are no friends of ours simply because they fought against the Russians during the war. Nothing could do a greater disservice to our cause, at a time when Germany is being led back into the international life of Europe, than at the same time to whitewash the Nazis and what they stood for."[107]

High Commissioner McCloy took grave exception to the charge that his decisions were politically motivated: "In view of my substantial part in originating the concept of Nuremberg and in setting up the machinery, any suggestion that my decisions reflect any lack of sympathy for the basis of these trials is as incorrect and unfounded as the implication that my decisions were motivated by considerations other than justice and clemency."[108] However, it was no longer a question of getting the war criminals freed; a steadily growing number of Germans continued to attack the legal validity of the trials themselves. McCloy's decisions were seen not as benevolent acts of clemency within a modern legal system but as the cynical abandonment of a failed policy.

The wives of the condemned German war criminals visited their loved ones for the final time on May 25, 1951; while some wept openly, Elonora Pohl, wife of Oswald Pohl, maintained her composure inside Landsberg Prison but collapsed from a nervous breakdown just outside the gates.[109] After High Commissioner McCloy received the word from Washington, Blobel, Braune, Naumann, Pohl, Ohlendorf, Schallermaier, and Schmidt were quietly hanged on June 7.[110] When the funeral of Einsatzgruppen leader Otto Ohlendorf took place a few weeks later, representatives from all of Germany's right-wing parties attended. When the casket was lowered into the grave, the mourners gave the Nazi salute.[111] One wreath bore the following slogan: "No more beautiful death in this world than to be struck down before the enemy."[112]

The early public opinion polls conducted by the State Department's Bureau of Public Affairs afterward drew the same conclusion as the pre-execution polls. In the Wuerttemberg-Baden area, "Many papers argue that the commutation of sentences is proof that something was wrong with the sentences." According to Jörg Friedrich, "The public uproar over the hanging of these blood tainted butchers underlined Nuremberg's failure."[113]

[All photos courtesy of Constance and Joseph Wilson.]

Ernst von Weizsäcker.

Ernst von Weizsäcker with Adolf Hitler.

Ernst von Weizsäcker *(second from right)*.

Ernst von Weizsäcker discusses the details of the Munich Agreement with
British Prime Minister Neville Chamberlain, Berchtesgaden, 1938.

State Secretary Von Weizsäcker greeting Japanese officials in 1941.

Adolf Hitler awards a medal to a German sailor, as defendant Bohle looks on.

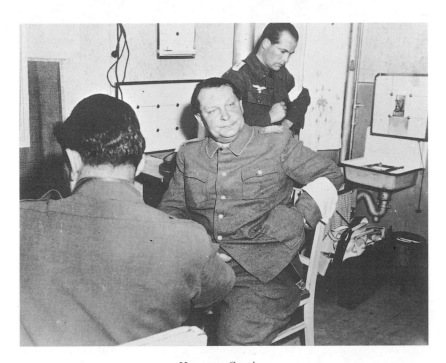

Hermann Goering.

Tribunal IV: *(left to right)* Leon Powers, William Christianson, Robert F. Maguire.

Ernst von Weizsäcker confers with his defense team.

Ministries Case defendants:
(left to right, front row)
Ernst von Weizsäcker, Steengracht von Moyland, Wilhelm Keppler,
Ernst Wilhelm Bohle, Ernst Woermann, Karl Ritter,
Otto von Erdmannsdorf, Edmund Veesenmayer, Hans Lammers,
Wilhelm Stuckart, Richard Darré;
(second row)
Otto Dietrich, Gottlob Berger, Walter Schellenberg, Schwerin von Krosigk,
Emil Puhl, Karl Rasche, Paul Koerner, Paul Pleiger, Hans Kehrl.

CHAPTER 6

THE RAPID LIQUIDATION OF THE

WAR CRIMES PROBLEM

WITH THE LAST EXECUTIONS OF WAR CRIMINALS OVER, TALKS about the complete restoration of West German sovereignty were well under way by the fall of 1951. Once again, the continued incarceration of war criminals proved to be one of the most difficult points of contention between American and West German leaders. Attorneys of the *Heidelberg Juristenkreis*, led by former Nuremberg defense attorney Otto Kranzbühler, approached Carlo Schmid, chairman of the Bundestag's subcommittee on POWs, with a plan to reject the legal validity of all Allied war crimes trials.[1] Schmid passed the *Juristenkreis* plan on to Konrad Adenauer with the additional demand that all the prisoners who had served one third of their sentences should be released. On November 19, the subcommittee also introduced a resolution calling for an amnesty on war crimes and a transfer of the prisoners to West German custody.[2]

Although the Americans were eager to turn the war criminals over to German authorities, it was not so simple. The State Department was fully aware that if the West German government wanted to assume physical custody of the convicts, they would have to recognize the legal validity of the original sentences.[3]

Chancellor Adenauer met with the recently reelected British Prime Minister, Winston Churchill, in late December 1951. Although Churchill offered to turn the British war crimes prisoners over to the Federal Republic, he made it very clear that if the Germans wanted to take them, they would have to acknowledge the legality of the sentences.[4]

High Commissioner McCloy met with Adenauer to discuss the war crimes, and while the German leader endorsed the plan for a mixed clemency board, he told McCloy that he was prepared to accept this solution as long as that Germany would not be required to recognize the Nuremberg judgments.[5] McCloy asked who would take control of the German prisoners once the contractual agreements to end the Allied occupation went into effect. Adenauer replied that West Germany could, McCloy told the Chancellor that he had "not fully thought this through," and pointed out "the difficulty of finding justification under Ger law to hold these individuals in custody without recognition of validity of these sentences."[6]

By early 1952, the German Foreign Office realized the implications of a custody transfer. As historian Frank Buscher has noted, recognizing the validity of the Nuremberg trials would be tantamount to an official German recognition of the judgments and the verdicts, something that the German diplomats wanted to avoid at all costs.[7] In conversations with German politicians, Adenauer stated firmly that he would refuse to recognize the Allied verdicts and that he would demand another sentence review board.[8]

Although Adenauer supported the Heidelberg Juristenkreis plan for an international clemency board composed of Germans and Americans, a number of problems remained. John McCloy was able to prevent the uproar over the Landsberg decisions from derailing American foreign policy, but the State Department's strategic legalism was beginning to look increasingly pale in the stark light of the Cold War. Many West Germans found it odd that the United States was now excitedly making provisions for a new German army while military leaders like Erich von Manstein, Wilhelm List, Walter Kuntze, Hermann Reincke, Erhard Milch, Herman Hoth, Georg von Kuechler, Hans von Salmuth, and Walter Warlimont remained in prison.[9] State Department officer Charles Thayer pointed out the problem of imprisonment of German soldiers in a March 1952 secret report: "The case of the top-ranking generals, in particular, seems to enter into almost all discussions of a German defense contribution."[10] If anything, American leniency on the war crimes question had reopened it, and now many West Germans demanded an amnesty on war crimes as a precondition for rearmament. Thayer wrote, "Release of war criminals is frequently stated to be condition for any German participation in a defense effort, and release of prisoners who are held for alleged war crimes is a condition for defense participation posed by the government coalition in the Bundestag debate on February 8."[11]

In an effort to prevent German rearmament, on March 10, Soviet leader Josef Stalin offered to withdraw the Red Army from East Germany, re-unify Germany, and hold free elections. Although the Soviet leader's proposal was rejected, it did strengthen the West German bargaining position with the United States. As the final ratification process for the agreements to end the occupation neared, the Heidelberg Juristenkreis continued to push the West German government to reject the legal validity of the Allied war crimes trials.[12] Otto Kranzbühler urged Konrad Adenauer and the German Foreign Office to act so "that the principles of these trials would not be recognized by the coming German government."[13] According to Kranzbühler, in a private meeting, he and Eduard Wahl "convinced Adenauer . . . that it was about accepting war guilt or not—accepting special law only for Germans and not for anybody else which no government could really do. Adenauer agreed with that and it was astonishing."[14]

The contracts restoring West German sovereignty were signed by the Allies on May 26 and 27, 1952, in Bonn and thus came to be known as the Bonn Agreements. West Germany's official position on the Allied war crimes tribunals can be found in articles 6 and 7 of the treaty's "Convention on the Settlement of Matters Arising out of the War and Occupation." Article 6 established a six-man committee, composed of one representative from each Allied power and three Germans, to make further parole and clemency recommendations "without calling into question the validity of the convictions." Article 7, section 1 appears to be a straightforward endorsement of the legal validity of all the Allied war crimes trials: "All judgments and decisions in criminal matters heretofore or hereafter rendered in Germany by any tribunal or judicial authority of the Three Powers or any of them shall remain final and valid for all purposes under German law and shall be treated as such by German courts and authorities." However, buried in Article 6, section 11 is an exception: "The provisions of Article 7 of this Chapter shall not apply to matters dealt with in this Article."[15] In other words, the Article 6 clemency board did not have to accept the validity of the Allied courts' decisions.

"It was drafted after we had a conference with Adenauer," explained Otto Kranzbühler. "A good lawyer would never do it that way, to put the exception in a different place than the rule. But it was intended to conceal. Nobody took notice of it, no press mentioned it." Historian Frank Buscher argues that the confusion created a "constitutional gray zone that made it possible for the lawmakers to couch their obvious biases in legalistic terms. As a result, they could freely attack the Allies for allegedly violating the provisions of the Federal Republic's constitution when extraditing and executing German citizens."[16] To Buscher, the debate over sentence validity provides further evidence that the American reeducation efforts in Germany had failed. "The philosophy of the *Bundestag* was that the inmates of Landsberg, Werl, and Wittlich were almost exclusively honorable soldiers, who had merely followed orders. Such views, held by the Federal Republic's political elites, were bound to influence the thinking of the general public sooner or later."[17] During McCloy's final press conference as High Commissioner in 1952, he said that he was optimistic about West German democracy, but warned his audience not to expect the United States to simply trade war criminals for German rearmament.[18]

Two million West German veterans adopted a resolution calling for a war crimes amnesty on July 14, 1952; it was also adopted by German veteran organizations: the Association of Former Fighter Pilots, the Air Force Circle, the German Association of War Wounded, the Association of German Soldiers, the Association of Former Members of the German Africa Corps, and others. Gottfried Hansen, the chairman of the Union of German Ex-Soldiers, wrote to U.S. General Matthew Ridgeway and called for a "speedy and satisfactory solution" to the war crimes problem in the form of a general amnesty. Hansen announced that "no German can be expected to don a Military uniform again until the question of 'war criminals' has been satisfactorily settled."[19] According to historian Jörg Friedrich, the rearmament question fundamentally altered America's relationship with the Federal Republic of Germany: "They could not be allies and prison guards at the same time. There was no choice but to pardon and integrate the convicted."[20]

By 1952, the German press had erased all distinctions among the various categories of war criminals. Eli Debevoise, General Counsel for the U.S. High Commission, issued a secret report on the problems this posed on September 6: "Through the device of lumping all prisoners into the category of soldiers and all common crimes as 'war crimes,' the press has been able to thoroughly mislead and confuse the German public." The report concluded that there was a German campaign "aimed at unraveling loose threads in the fabric of action taken by the Allies on war criminals, and thus progressively unraveling the fabric."[21]

High Commissioner Walter Donnelly announced the latest and most depressing German public opinion poll to date. According to the State Department's August survey, only 10 percent of the West Germans polled

approved of the handling of the war criminal issue, while 59 percent dis-
approved. Those screaming the loudest were not the ill-informed and the
downtrodden: "Most widely disapproving are opinion leading population
elements—men, better educated, and economically better situated." "Outright release of the Ger generals now held prisoner by Western powers is
the remedy most frequently suggested by those disapproving of the present treatment."[22] The biggest short-term problem facing the Americans was
putting the Mixed Clemency Board created by Article 6 of the Bonn Agreements into action, because first the agreements had to be ratified by all three
European Defense Community powers. The West German government was
becoming agitated because a board had not yet been established. The Bundestag debated the war crimes question for more than two hours on September 17. West German lawmakers vociferously attacked Allied policy;[23] ironically, the Communists were the only party that did not attack the trials.[24]
Despite German dissatisfaction over prisoner releases, the number of war
criminals in Allied custody was declining steadily. In less than one year (December 15, 1951 to September 13, 1952), the population of Landsberg Prison
was reduced by 25 percent (from 458 to 338).[25] Because the establishment
of the Article 6 Mixed Board was held up by the ratification of the EDC
Treaty in the French Assembly, the Heidelberg Juristenkreis suggested the
creation of an interim board to review cases until the Article 6 Board could
be convened.[26]

Rearmament plans gained new momentum when General Dwight David
Eisenhower was elected President of the United States in November 1952.
His Secretary of State, John Foster Dulles, was a third-generation American lawyer-statesman, the grandson of American diplomat John Foster, the
nephew of Secretary of State Robert Lansing, and brother of American spymaster Allen Dulles.[27] Thus he came to his conservatism quite naturally,
and his appointment would have a profound impact on the future treatment of German war criminals.[28]

The new Secretary of State traveled to Bonn in early February 1953 to
meet with West German leaders and discuss the issue of the war criminals.[29]
By 1953, the State Department conceded that the Nuremberg trials had
failed to "reeducate" West Germans: "From the political point of view, the
crux of the war criminals problem in Germany is the refusal of a large number of Germans to accept the principles underlying the trials or the findings
of the trials."[30]

German Chancellor Konrad Adenauer visited the United States in
April to attend the Washington Foreign Ministers Conference. The State

Department knew that he intended to press for the release of more war criminals. A preconference memo described the American policy initiative: to prevent "the subject of war criminals from adversely affecting U.S.–German relations or a German defense contribution."[31] The memo acknowledged that the German attitude toward the trials remained "a problem of continuous difficulty."[32] According to the State Department, rationality and empirical facts meant little to West Germans: "Their attitude is strongly emotional and is not influenced by argument or by objective presentation of the facts. They persist in believing ... that most war criminals are soldiers who have been punished for doing what all soldiers do or may be ordered to do in time of war, and that only a small minority of the prisoners are guilty of atrocities or common crimes."[33] Above all, the White House and the German Chancellor wanted a parole board before the September 1953 elections in Germany.

In the first meeting of the Foreign Ministers Conference, Adenauer pointed to the considerable "psychological and public opinion problems in Germany connected with the war criminal issue."[34] The new High Commissioner James Conant said the United States hoped to have either a mixed parole board or a clemency board before the German elections, but suggested that "little publicity be given to these plans and that public references be made in only general terms."[35] Secretary of State John Foster Dulles "reiterated to the Chancellor that the U.S. would review the policies of its military authorities with a view to a more liberal treatment of war criminals." On the parole board question, Dulles "reassured the Chancellor that we anticipated the establishment of the joint parole board or commission prior to general EDC ratification."[36] After the meetings, Adenauer announced that he was "extraordinarily satisfied" with the progress made.[37]

During the summer of 1953, a State Department memo warned that the continued imprisonment of convicted war criminals could hurt Adenauer's CDU (Christlich-Demokratische Union/Christian Democratic Union) Party in the upcoming election, not to mention have an "adverse effect upon a German defense contribution."[38] Because the EDC Treaty faced an uncertain future in the French Assembly, the Mixed Board remained unconvened. Secretary of State Dulles discussed the war criminal problem with President Eisenhower in June. They would attempt to persuade the French to accept the board outlined in the contractual agreements, but if this failed, the United States would establish a parole system for the German war criminals in its custody.[39]

In July, a week before the Allied Foreign Ministers met in Washington, the French High Commissioner offered a way around the ratification impasse. André Francois-Poncet suggested that each Allied nation create temporary boards modeled on the Article 6 Mixed Board to review their respective war crimes sentences. The three powers agreed to the plan on July 11 and less than a week before the German elections, the Interim Mixed Parole and Clemency (IMPAC) board was convened.[40] It would rule on American war crimes cases until the treaties establishing the Mixed Board were ratified. The IMPAC board had been created by a joint order of the U.S. High Commission for Germany and the Supreme Commander of the U.S. Army in Europe on August 31, 1953.[41] It consisted of three Americans and two Germans and functioned like a traditional parole board; prisoners were allowed to plead their cases twice a year. The interim board's chairman, Henry Lee Shattuck, was an attorney from Boston. The other two Americans were Army Major General Joseph Muller and a career State Department officer, Edwin Plitt. German representatives Emil Lersh and Hans Meuschel were former high court judges.[42]

New nonjudicial mechanisms helped further loosen parole standards; credit for time served was again increased and the parameters for medical parole were broadened with new provisions added for physical health, mental health, old age, and the condition of the prisoner's family.[43] Eligibility for parole on life and death sentences was reduced to fifteen years from the day of arrest.[44] When the interim board was established, 312 prisoners remained in Landsberg prison; 281 were under army jurisdiction, and 71 of those were serving life sentences. Only 31 of the war criminals convicted by the United States at Nuremberg remained in custody.[45]

During the final days of his election campaign, Adenauer took a firm stand on the fate of the convicted war criminals. Not only did he demand the release of all those in Allied custody, he pushed several bills through the Bundestag granting economic benefits to former SS members and Nazi officials.[46] The Chancellor realized the importance of being on the "right" side of the issue and even visited Werl Prison (where prisoners tried and convicted by the British were jailed), shook hands with the prisoners, and assured them that he was doing his best to get them released.[47] This active commitment to the German war criminals and his unrelenting pressure on the U.S. government won him the support of the nation's veterans. Representatives from the powerful German military organizations urged their members to support the CDU Party, and Konrad Adenauer was reelected.[48]

After the German leaders produced the political results both sides desired, they sought compensation. In a letter to American war crimes officials urging the release of more prisoners, Dr. Friedrich Middelhauve, vice president of the Free Democratic Party (FDP), made it clear that now the time had come for the United States to capitulate on the subject of war criminals:

The Free Democratic Party of West Germany is the motor of German-American teamwork. It constitutes a strong bulwark against Communist infiltration, radicalism from the left and the right. It helped democracy win in West Germany on September 6, 1953 by 3,000,000 votes. Say action should be taken, you can't afford delay: Let your congressman awaken through you—so act to-day! YOUR POSITIVE DECISION—A BLOW TO BOLSHEVISM.[49]

By 1953, the main concern for American officials in charge of implementing war crimes policy in Germany was keeping the paroles as quiet as possible. Chief U.S. Parole Officer Paul Gernert reported to High Commissioner Conant that the German press had helped by not publicizing the release of prominent convicted war criminals.[50]

In January 1954, the U.S. embassy in Japan reopened the entire war crimes debate by suggesting a general amnesty for lower-level Japanese war criminals. Ambassador John Allison sought a political solution to the Japanese war crimes problem. If that proved impossible, he suggested "an accelerated parole process to ensure the release of those prisoners within two years." Although the two war crimes programs had been very different, they were inextricably connected. According to historian John Dower, the Japanese war crimes trials failed to reform and reeducate, much like the German trials: "Defendants who had been convicted and sentenced to imprisonment became openly regarded as victims rather than victimizers, their prison stays within Japan made as pleasant and entertaining as possible." At Japan's Sugamo Prison, there were 114 performances staged for the convicts' entertainment in 1952 alone.[51]

In a secret memo to the U.S. embassy in Bonn, State Department Officer John Auchincloss reminded his superiors that whatever was done in Japan would have "extensive repercussions in Germany" and predicted very negative side effects. Not only would such a major concession cast a dark shadow over the legacy of the war crimes trials, it would bolster the far right in Germany and cause both congressional and public opinion problems.[52] Auchincloss warned his superiors that "The appearance of a political solution would have, in effect, the same disadvantages of a real political solution, and we should not underestimate what these disadvantages would be. The United States would have put itself in the position of disregarding the principles involved in the original trials, and this would undermine, in retrospect, the entire war crimes program."[53]

John Auchincloss was not a traditional American lawyer-statesman; he did not believe that what could be justified legally did not have to be justified morally. He even raised the traditionally taboo question of principle: "The men now serving sentences for war crimes are doing so because we believed at one time that they deserved to be punished for what they did," he wrote. "Do we still believe this, or do we not? If we do not, then we should release the men as soon as possible." Finally, Auchincloss sought a clarification of American war crimes policy: "We should reexamine our basic position in order to see whether we believe in what we have done, before we proceed to undo it. If we believe in it, we should stick to it, for to act against it would be cynical, if our purpose were to gain a political advantage, or weak, if our purpose were to avoid political pressure."[54] A meeting of American war crimes officials was scheduled in Washington for early 1954.

The war crimes summit was held at the State Department on February 16. The attendees included U.S. Ambassador to Japan John Allison, State Department legal advisors John Raymond and John Auchincloss, former Peck Panel member Conrad Snow, and legal advisors from both Germany and Japan. Ambassador Allison opened the meeting with the shocking admission that "the question of war criminals in Japan was becoming a farce in view of the Japanese Government's laxity of control over the prisoners who were permitted to attend baseball games and other activities in Tokyo."[55] John Raymond argued strongly that granting amnesty would undermine the entire legal basis of the war crimes trials: it would have the effect of wiping out the crime. However, parole or clemency "fell into a different category and did not necessarily prejudice the legal basis of the trials."[56] Although Secretary of State Dulles officially rejected the proposed amnesty on May 26, he did agree to "change the ground rules" by reducing parole eligibility for those war criminals originally sentenced to death from fifteen to ten years.[57]

The French National Assembly killed the EDC Treaty in August and the Allies had to find another way to rearm West Germany. Winston Churchill urged President Eisenhower to absorb the new German army into NATO forces.[58] Meanwhile, German veterans' groups like the *Stahlhelm* continued to argue that West Germany should refuse to rearm until all the war criminals had been set free.[59] German disdain for the Nuremberg trials and the "vindictive" policies of the occupation had hardened by 1955. In a letter to State Department legal advisor John Raymond, HICOG's head of prisons, Richard Hagan, reported a conversation with a former Nuremberg defense lawyer who was now a representative of a German POW group. He admitted to Hagan that even if the United States freed all of the German prisoners, "there would be no end to the war criminal problem until in the German mind each act has been justified."[60]

The Federal Republic of Germany regained its full sovereignty on May 5, 1955, when the Paris Treaties took effect. What that translated to in clear language was that men sentenced to death in 1948 would soon be eligible for parole. Nonetheless, America's lenient war crimes policy won no goodwill from West German politicians. Eric Mende, one of the most powerful members of Adenauer's coalition, announced on July 25 that it would be impossible to recruit decent officers for the new German army "unless a substantial number of war criminals are released." He was echoing the views of former *Wehrmacht* generals like Hans Speidel and Adolf von Heusinger—who had both served as military advisors to the Federal Republic of Germany.[61] According to Frank Buscher, instead of accepting responsibility for Nazi Germany's atrocities, "legislators of almost all parties portrayed the Allies as the villains and the violators of the law."[62]

The parole of German war criminals was further accelerated by yet another revision of parole requirements in July, after President Eisenhower approved a new recommendation that prisoners with sentences over 30 years (including life) should be considered eligible for parole after serving 10 years.[63] By July 1955, the United States held fewer than 100 war crimes prisoners at Landsberg, and only 10 were Nuremberg convicts.[64] When the Interim Mixed Parole and Clemency Board ceased functioning on August 1, 1955, the United States had released almost 90 percent of the convicted war criminals in its custody and the European Allies were not far behind with clemency programs of their own.[65]

There was a crisis brewing over the pending parole of Malmedy Massacre convict Sepp Dietrich. Because he had been tried by the U.S. Army, he was an Army prisoner and there was little the State Department could do. High Commissioner Conant had always followed the IMPAC board's recommendations, but when it came to the German soldiers involved in the Malmedy Massacre, Army leaders had consistently refused to consider early releases. It is important to remember that General McAuliffe, the man now in charge of the German prisoners, had been surrounded by the Nazis at Bastogne in 1944 and had refused to surrender.[66] Parole boards had twice unanimously recommended that Dietrich be paroled, but both recommendations were turned down.[67]

Once West Germany regained national sovereignty and the first military legislation was introduced in the Bundestag, public interest in the war criminals was revived.[68] The unpleasant fact was that most of the country's political and religious elites were now more intent than ever on an unconditional war crimes amnesty. Representatives of Germany's leading political parties (CDU, FDP, BHE, and DP) appealed to the former occupation powers "to release the prisoners they still hold."[69] Even the leaders of Germany's Catholic and Protestant churches called for an amnesty. It was clear that in order to resolve the contradiction of the "occupying ally," the United States would release the remaining "hard core" war criminals.

The long-awaited and much-anticipated Mixed Clemency Board was established on August 11, 1955. The Mixed Board (also referred to as the Article 6 Board) was responsible for reviewing the parole applications of the remaining forty-four "hard core" war criminals in Landsberg Prison. The six-man board was composed of three Germans and one member from each of the Allied countries. Career State Department officer Edwin Plitt was appointed the American member.[70] The board was supposed to be an independent judicial body, and each Allied representative was supposed to rule according to his conscience.

In late 1955, Malmedy Massacre convict Sepp Dietrich was granted parole. When word of this symbolically significant release reached the United States, there was a major public outcry.[71] Senator Estes Kefauver called Dietrich's release a "serious error" and requested a Senate investigation. The State Department in Bonn was startled by the implications of an inquiry into American war crimes policy. High Commissioner Conant immediately attempted to contain the public relations damage and wrote Secretary of State Dulles, "U.S. public reaction Re Dietrich case has reached a point where it may endanger American-German relations to such a degree that I am bringing the matter to your personal attention." The State Department believed that "Any Senate investigation of this case, which would necessarily bring into question Allied policy on war criminals, could do great damage." Conant felt "it essential that a full message be sent to Senator Kefauver. . . . Same statement should be to other Senators who have indicated interest."[72]

While the second phase of American war crimes policy failed to appease German veterans, it succeeded in infuriating American veterans.

Commander of the Veterans of Foreign Wars Joseph Lombardo called for not only a Senate investigation but also the resignation of American Mixed Board Member Edwin Plitt and an investigation into why he had voted in favor of Dietrich's early release.[73] This request was especially problematic because the decisions of the Mixed Board, when unanimous, were final and not subject to the instructions of the members' respective governments. By November 28, the controversy over Dietrich's release was bolstered by American Legion National Commander J. Addington Wagner's call for Plitt's resignation.[74]

Above all, the State Department wanted to avoid a public inquiry into the Mixed Board's inner workings. Once again, American war crimes policy was losing a two-front public relations battle and once again, an American diplomat was caught in the crossfire. High Commissioner Conant wrote to Secretary of State Dulles asking for his "personal attention" to the war crimes problem. According to Conant, the ongoing controversy surrounding the vote of the American member, Edwin Plitt, was "damaging German-American relations." He recommended that Dulles personally put this fire out with "Serious effort through personal conversation or otherwise to convince Wagner, American Legion, Murphy of VFW and Senator Kefauver that their criticism is unjustified" and that Plitt's vote to parole Dietrich was "in accord with the policy of the U.S. Government."[75]

In early December, a State Department brief on how to justify Sepp Dietrich's parole was prepared for the Secretary of State. The defense would not be based on the details of the individual case; instead, it would stress that parole, unlike clemency, is a conditional release. As State Department legal advisor John Raymond had suggested, Dulles would stress that the Mixed Board was "an independent body" whose rulings, when unanimous, were binding. Again, the Secretary of State was instructed to keep his responses general and focus on the "independence" of the Mixed Board.[76] However, this defense was unconvincing in Edwin Plitt's case because he was a career employee of the State Department, the agency responsible for American war crimes policy.

With the outcry over Dietrich far from over, the impending release of his comrade Joachim Peiper was about to compound the State Department's problems.[77] The controversy over Dietrich's release dragged into 1956 as the calls for the dismissal of the American Mixed Board member grew louder. Ironically, now Plitt was being defended by prominent German Nuremberg critics like the Papal Nuncio Bishop Fargo, who was incensed by the injustice "done to a red-blooded American such as I know Mr. Plitt to be."[78]

The British Foreign Office weighed in on January 20.[79] The British felt that "Publication of the considerations underlying a recommendation of the Board could scarcely avoid the casting of doubt on the validity of the original convictions; this is expressly forbidden by the terms of the Bonn Conventions."[80] The State Department continued to refuse to release the details of the board's decisions, arguing that the Mixed Board was not an arm of the State Department but rather "a quasi-judicial body, and that the purpose of giving its members freedom of action was to enable them to exercise an objective judgment based on the facts of the individual case."[81] These legalistic justifications did little to dispel the impression that the Mixed Board was another strategic legalist shakeout mechanism. By early 1956, the State Department needed a scapegoat and Plitt would serve nicely. The State Department announced that he would be replaced on the Mixed Board by former New Hampshire judge, Senator Robert Upton. This helped to restore some of the Mixed Board's credibility in the United States but had the opposite effect in West Germany, where Edwin Plitt had been regarded highly by his German colleagues. And why not? He had certainly proved willing to carry out an accelerated parole system designed to release German war criminals.[82]

In early March, the legal advisors from the State Department began to brace for the outcry over the release of Malmedy Massacre ringleader Joachim Peiper.[83] When Senator Upton arrived in Germany in late March 1956 to assume Edwin Plitt's seat on the Mixed Board, he soon learned that his colleagues had granted Peiper parole. The only thing standing between Peiper and his freedom was the board's approval of his parole plan. Although Upton accepted Peiper's release as a *fait accompli,* he immediately set about distancing himself from the decision. In a letter to State Department legal advisor John Raymond, Upton made it very clear to the State Department that he would not assume responsibility: "In any press release by the Department concerning this case I expect you to make it clear that the action authorizing the parole of Peiper was taken before I became a member of the Board." More ominously, Upton expressed strong misgivings about the Mixed Board's view of the parole process and believed that his European colleagues saw parole as little more than a "device" to release war criminals.[84] Although the State Department had sought an independent jurist to boost the Mixed Board's reputation, the new American member was turning out to be more than they had bargained for.

Because Joachim Peiper had now served ten years, he could be released. According to Peiper's parole application, he had been offered a job by the

German automotive company Porsche. His parole plan was approved by the Mixed Board by a vote of five to one, the lone dissenting vote coming from the American member.[85] In his minority report, Senator Upton wrote: "I began an intensive study of the case from which I concluded that Col. Peiper ought not presently to be granted parole. The records before me clearly established that the shooting down of prisoners of war and civilians during the Ardennes offensive was confined to the combat group commanded by Colonel Peiper."[86]

The senator wrote State Department legal advisor John Raymond to object to his colleagues' use of parole to release war criminals irrespective of their crimes. "A majority of the Board apparently are disposed to hold that on applications for parole by a war criminal eligible for parole the nature of the offense is not considered in determining whether, if parole is granted, the applicant would have been sufficiently punished. In other words, these members hold that if eligible for parole a war criminal has expiated his crime." Robert Upton considered this absolutely improper and "contrary to the procedure of Parole Boards generally, but probably conforms to the procedure which was here in the Interim Mixed Board."[87]

Between January 31, 1953 and January 31, 1955, the United States had released 82 percent of the convicts in Landsberg Prison, and the European Allies were pursuing clemency programs of their own.

German War Criminals in Captivity[88]

In Confidential	8/31/53	1/31/55	% Released
U.S. Army	281	34	87.9
U.S. Embassy (Nuremberg)	31	7	77.4
British (Werl)	82	27	67.0
French	72	18	75.0

Prior to West German Chancellor Konrad Adenauer's visit to Washington in June 1956, the State Department reported a conversation with the West German Foreign Minister, who informed them that Adenauer wanted the United States to "speed up releases from Landsberg" and to relax the conditions of those now on parole. Even though the United States had released all but a handful of war criminals, the foreign minister claimed to be "gravely concerned" over the Mixed Board's "slow progress."[89] It was now clear that the West German government would not rest until all war criminals in Western captivity were released.

Anticipating Chancellor Adenauer's request for more war criminal releases, State Department officers John Raymond and John Auchincloss prepared a position paper entitled "German War Criminals Held By the United States."[90] Although the State Department was prepared to release more war criminals, they ruled out an unconditional amnesty. Robert Upton announced his resignation after less than three months on the Mixed Board on June 11, 1956 and once again, he expressed dissatisfaction with the German members' view that the nature of the offense was not to be considered.[91] Upton made it clear that the State Department's description of the Mixed Board as a traditional parole board was not accurate: "In Germany the Board has come to be regarded as an instrumentality for the release of war criminals rather than an agency for the exercise of clemency or parole in deserving cases."[92] He stated that this "resulted in frequent disagreements among the members of the Board."[93]

Senator Upton met with State Department legal advisor John Raymond to discuss the future of American war crimes policy in late July 1956. Upton offered a plan that would rid the United States of the war crimes problem once and for all by marrying a clemency program to the existing parole program. Once paroled prisoners demonstrated "that they are once again law-abiding citizens able to behave themselves," their sentences would be reduced to time served.[94] Upton met with Raymond, John Auchincloss, and the new American Mixed Board member, Spencer Phenix, in Washington on July 31. This time the Americans were taking no chances. Phenix was a veteran State Department officer who had been involved in everything from drafting the Kellogg-Briand Treaty to arbitrating post–World War I debt, working for the OSS during World War II, and the CIA's National Committee for a Free Europe. From the beginning, Phenix stated very plainly that if American war crimes policy needed a scapegoat, he would fall on his sword. Since the members of the Mixed Board were "independent of government instructions," there was already an arm's length relationship between the department and the American board member. Phenix understood that the objective of the final phase of American war crimes policy was to release the remaining prisoners and was prepared to go to greater lengths to free war criminals than his predecessors.[95]

The newly appointed American Mixed Board member offered his appraisal of American policy in two memos on February 8, 1957. Memo A was a statement about the present American position. Although many had been freed, these had been conditional, probationary releases. If the United States did not change course, the Mixed Board "would continue in operation until the deaths of the six individuals serving life terms, or, barring prior death, until 1985." Phenix saw nothing to be gained by such a "dull and profitless operation." Although he considered turning the prisoners over to the Federal Republic, he noted that the German government's refusal to recognize the validity of the convictions "constituted a bar to the transfer of any penal responsibility to the German authorities." Memo A concluded with a recommendation "to re-examine the present parole procedure with a view to its termination within a reasonable period."[96]

Spencer Phenix's Memo B was an example of strategic legalism *par excellence,* or as he put it, "a statement of what I am prepared to do as the American member of the Mixed Board to facilitate a relatively prompt settlement of the problem." Phenix called for the "rapid liquidation of the war crimes problem" and suggested continued reliance on the strategic legalists' favorite post-trial, nonjudicial "device"—another reduction in the parole requirements. If that failed to win approval, he suggested transferring authority over the prisoners to the Federal Republic of Germany.[97] If the Germans' only objection was the sentence validity problem, he could find a clever way around this long-standing impasse: "it should not be difficult to incorporate in any exchange of notes recording agreement between the two governments some saving paragraph which would cover that point." An old hand at the strategic legalist game, Phenix offered this illustration: "Many years ago I negotiated the settlement agreement between British and American Governments covering the 'Disposal of Certain Pecuniary Claims Arising out of the Recent War,' signed 19 May 1927." The discussions centered around cargo and ship seizure, detentions and confiscation. During the negotiations, the British found the subject "at least as sensitive as the German Government finds the war criminal problem." To get around this, Phenix drafted notes "exchanged recording the agreement." The notes reserved "the right of each government to maintain in the future such a position as it may deem appropriate with respect to the legality or illegality under international law . . . it being specifically understood that the juridical position of neither government is prejudiced by the present agreement." At the time, the British believed that this solution provided them with "sufficient political insurance." Phenix did not see why the German Government would not accept a similar solution that would allow both West Germany and the United States to justify the final war criminal releases any way they saw fit.[98]

In Memo B, the new American board member stated very plainly, "I am prepared to suggest to the Mixed Board the adoption of the following procedure for the rapid liquidation of the war crimes problem." Under this plan, the Mixed Board could recommend the reduction of sentences "to actual time served in prison, on parole, and on good conduct time" and terminate the sentence. Phenix believed that the German government "will be so pleased with the almost immediate termination of the sentences . . . that they will be willing to accept without further argument or discussion responsibility for the 'custody and carrying out of the sentences' of the remaining 92."[99] In a cover letter attached to the two memos, he stated very plainly that he was prepared to shoulder any and all blame and responsibility. Phenix asked only that the State Department not only to "keep its hands officially out of the war criminal problem" but also to "disclaim all responsibility for the decisions of the American member, scrupulously refraining from attempting to explain or justify his action."

Phenix requested a meeting in Washington with State Department legal advisor John Raymond. "Without in any way passing the buck of responsibility back to the Department," wrote Phenix, "I could be given an informal indication that the procedure I have suggested in Memorandum 'B' is not unacceptable per se or inconsistent with the Department's basic policies." He hoped that he could "get this bothersome problem quietly out of the way where it will no longer complicate international relations."[100] Raymond attached a handwritten note to the memo: "Very interesting food for thought. My preliminary reaction is to agree with the first three pages of Memo B."[101]

Spencer Phenix met with Raymond and State Department officials in Washington on March 11 and 12 to discuss the plan outlined in Memo B. The strategic legalist mechanism was "an appropriate petition" stating that the "ultra hardcore" convicts had been "rehabilitated." Because of Phenix's "independent status" as a member of the Mixed Board, he did not seek the State Department's consent, only a wink and a nod, "to avoid causing any conflict with policy which the Department might have under consideration." Although the department representatives would neither "approve nor disapprove the proposed plans," they believed "that the plans did not appear to give rise to any conflict with Departmental policies."[102]

During the Mixed Board's April 10, 1957 meeting, Phenix presented his plan to the German members, who were "entirely satisfied by the action taken by the Board which, I feel, has now done its part in pointing the way to a practicable solution of the problem."[103] Anticipating criticism from the U.S. Army, Phenix spoke to the Army Judge Advocate General about the board's unanimous decision to release Joachim Peiper. Phenix believed that the army, like the State Department, would be happy to have him as a scapegoat.[104]

The American Mixed Board member also met with representatives of the Heidelberg Juristenkreis, the war crimes lobbying group led by Eduard Wahl and Otto Kranzbühler. "What really concerns the Heidelberg authorities seems to be their continued responsibility for the Landsberg prisoners," Phenix wrote. "The Heidelberg Group expressed the opinion that if the Germans refused to accept unqualified custody the next best solution would be to negotiate an agreement whereunder Germany assumed all operational responsibility for the non-paroled prisoners." Phenix told John Raymond that the Mixed Board would make no public announcement of Peiper's release and "expressed the hope that the Foreign Office will also refrain from publicity at this time. The disadvantages of publicity were pointed out to me by the Heidelberg authorities who quickly agreed and, I am sure, the Department is of the same opinion."[105]

In late April, Richard Hagan, the U.S. parole official in Germany, wrote to the State Department legal advisor to report that there were only 18 prisoners remaining in Landsberg Prison and 193 on parole. Spencer Phenix reported to Raymond on May 13, that the sentences of 74 individuals paroled for good conduct had been "reduced to time already served." Under Phenix's Memo B plan, the United States had reduced their case load from 300 to 148; "15 are confined in Landsberg, four are on medical parole, one is on good conduct release and 128 are on parole." Phenix estimated the number of "hard core" cases to be 9.[106] By the end of 1957, only four convicts remained in Landsberg Prison with thirty-six still on parole. According to the State Department, the last four prisoners were "the ultimate hard core," and even Phenix believed it highly improbable that the board would unanimously recommend parole.[107]

Ernst Biberstein, Waldemar Klingelhoefer, and Adolf Ott had been sentenced to death on April 14, 1948, but the Peck Panel spared their lives in 1951.[108] The remaining German war criminals in U.S. custody made the men of *Kampfegruppe* Peiper look like choirboys. During their trial, the prosecution took only two days to present its case, which consisted entirely of their own reports. Biberstein admitted, "I personally superintended an execution in Rostov which was performed by means of a gas truck." Ott was equally candid: "I have already said . . . every Jew who was apprehended had to be shot. Never whether he was a perpetrator or not."[109]

Due to the extreme nature of the defendants' crimes, the Mixed Board could not easily grant them parole. During the April 29, 1958 board meeting, the German Foreign Office presented parole requests for these prisoners. While the board unanimously denied parole, they moved to approve individual clemency requests and "it was recommended unanimously that the sentences of the four be reduced to time served." The Mixed Board submitted their formal recommendations to the U.S. ambassador and the U.S. Army. Phenix informed Raymond that the United States had only 31 parolees left under American jurisdiction. The board had already received the "appropriate petitions" from 269 convicts and reduced their sentences to time served.[110]

Secretary of State John Foster Dulles received a cable from the U.S. Embassy in Bonn on May 6 announcing that the "sentences of four remaining prisoners confined Landsberg (three Embassy Biberstein, Ott, Sandberger, one Army Brinkmann) have been commuted to time served."[111] The gates of Landsberg prison swung open for the final time on May 9, 1958 as the last four German war criminals in American custody were released.[112] Spencer Phenix reported to John Raymond on May 13: "It is only fair to say that circumstances played a more significant part than I did. In any case it is pleasant to feel that this diplomatic pebble has been removed from the State Department's shoes."[113] A few weeks later, Raymond offered Phenix "his sincere congratulations on the very capable manner in which you have discharged an exceedingly difficult and delicate assignment."[114] Spencer Phenix had found the final solution to the American war crimes problem.

CONCLUSION

FINALLY, WE ARE LEFT WITH TWO MYTHS: THE AMERICAN MYTH OF the redemptive trial and the German myth of harsh victor's justice. The outcome of the Nuremberg trials does not affirm the contention that political justice is, by its very nature, illegitimate—if anything, America's post–World War II war crimes policies show the many types and gradations of political justice. What is most often overlooked, especially about the American Nuremberg Trials, is the leniency of most of the original sentences. Originally convicted and sentenced to twenty and twenty-five years respectively in the Ministries case, high-ranking Nazis like Hans Lammers and Gottlob Berger were both released from Landsberg Prison in December 1951.[1] As for the "ex post facto" laws like those concerning "aggression," all of the Nuremberg courts proved reluctant to apply, much less convict under, these controversial new laws. In the industrialist cases, several of the courts were almost unwilling to punish executives whose companies had demanded, utilized, and egregiously mistreated slave labor. The more systematic killing of millions of civilians was a massive violation of both customary military practice and the codified laws of war, not to mention the fact that it was done with a cold-blooded precision that was unique in human history. The Nuremberg trials left a complex and mostly sensible set of military and political standards that were not upheld in the post–World War II era.

It was not enough for American leaders to simply defeat and destroy the Third Reich; they also insisted on reforming their vanquished foes. The assumption that the Germans would denounce their former leaders and embrace their conquerors' value system was erroneous. During the 1950s, die-hard Nazis were allowed to exploit the Cold War and in the end considered themselves unjustifiably persecuted. The most important agents of "persecution" were America's punitive occupation policies, and above all, the Nuremberg trials.

The war crimes trials' initial credibility problems were exacerbated by American leniency—a second policy that contradicted the original, punitive occupation policy (JCS 1067). As a result of this dramatic shift, a very basic debate was reopened. Instead of discussing the shocking atrocities committed by many of the high-ranking convicts, American officials were forced to defend the basic legal legitimacy of the trials. Frank Buscher attributes the shift in German attitutde to the hard line taken by West German lawmakers on the sentence validity question in the early 1950s: "Most importantly, during the period beween the creation of the Federal Republic and the attainment of sovereignty, the parliament stubbornly refused to accept any responsibility for Nazi Germany's atrocities and war crimes. Instead, legislators of almost all parties portrayed the Allies as villains and violators of the law."[2] It was ironic, as Jörg Friedrich points out, that the convicted war criminals do not want to be "judged by their standards or treated according to their own methods."[3] Strategic legalism in the form of nonjudicial, post-trial sentence reductions allowed the State Department to shift the direction of American war crimes policy without officially contradicting JCS 1067. However, American actions spoke far louder and more eloquently than the State Department's dissembled words. American public opinion polls showed the German public split nearly 50/50 in their opinions of Nuremberg's IMT in 1946, but by the early 1950s West German public opinion had turned sharply against the trials.[4]

However, just as the Allies were releasing their last convicted war criminals in the late 1950s, something amazing did occur. In 1958, the West German government opened the Central Office of the State Ministries for the Investigation of National Socialist Crimes of Violence in Ludwigsburg. The West German government began to try concentration camp staff and *Einsatzkommandos* for violations of German law during World War II. Although men like Treblinka commandant Franz Stangl were sentenced to long prison terms, many West Germans found it odd that their government had chosen to move so far down the chain of command in their own trials. Between 1958 and the end of 1985, West German courts convicted 992 Germans for wartime atrocities. However, many of the sentences were extremely lenient. Historian Jeffrey Herf explains how the American and Allied war crimes clemencies of the 1950s undermined the subsequent German trials: "these decisions had a profoundly negative impact on subsequent trials in German courts because higher-ranking officials who had been amnestied in 1951 offered testimony in trials in the 1960s against lower-raniking officials who bore less guilt. As a result, it became more difficult to gain convictions in these later cases."[5] "They had too many friends," the late Nuremberg prosecutor Robert Kempner explained to the author in a 1988 interview. "The man who wanted parole told their people, 'If you don't sign good things about the parole business, I will tell about you'—very simple— 'I will tell about you.'" Kempner offered this telling anecdoate about the German trials:

> I was sitting with the Chief German Justice during the Auschwitz case as a spectator. You saw Veesenmayer as a witness for the defense and he was a free man. . . . He told the court stories and this judge next to me asked me, "Who is this man?" and I said, "This is a very nice acquaintance of mine, he was only responsible for 400,000 Jews." "Why is he running around?" I said, "Because he is a defense witness for the Auschwitz case." Veesenmayer came back when he was through and he stopped at me and said, "How are you?" and I said, "We have both grown older." Later I talked with a reserve judge and he said, "It is very bad for us, Veesenmayer is running free and we should judge about the little SS men who killed only two."[6]

Although Edmund Veesenmayer was sentenced to twenty-five years in the Ministries case, he too was released in December 1951.

The idea that the U.S. government took a firm position on the subject of war crimes and in the process, "reeducated" postwar Germans and Japanese was and remains a comforting myth. The United States proved unwilling to uphold sentences that were jsutified and in many cases lenient. Soldiers who individually killed civilians by the thousands, judges who twisted the law to suit the whims of despots, diplomats who were caught double dealing, bankers who laundered the booty ov the dead, industrialists who used and abused slave labor, and doctors who mutilated living humans in the name of science—to name only a few—deserved to pay a heavy price for such acts.

During the Cold War, the superpowers defied international authority and took cynical, strategic legalism to new heights. Although there were prominent exceptions, like the Eichman trial (1961) and the Calley and Medina trials (1971), on the global level—international law, the Nuremberg Principles, the Hague Conventions, even the customary laws of war—provided little protection for civilians caught on the wrong side of the political dividing line in places like Vietnam, Cambodia, East Timor, Afghanistan, and El Salvador, to name only a few.

Actually, the tragic fate of Cambodia clearly demonstrates the weakness of international law during the Cold War. After the Vietnamese toppled the Khmer Rouge in 1979, it soon becamse clear that Pol Pot's regime had systematically carried out some of the worst atrocities since World War II. Did the Untied States call for the prosecution of Pol Pot, Ieng Sary, Khieu Samphan, and other Khmer Rouge leaders? No, quite the opposite: in 1979, Cyrus Vance, the Carter administration's UN representative, voted to allow the deposed, genocidal regime to retain its seat in the UN General Assembly. After the decision, a senior U.S. official justified the decision to journalist Nayan Chanda: "The choice for us was between moral principles and international law. The scale weighed in favor of law because it served our security interests."[7] Deposed Khmer Rouge leader Ieng Sary put it most succintly in a 1981 interview: "First are the aggressors and expansionists headed by the Soviet Union. . . . It is good that the USA and China are agreed here. We too are on this team!"[8]

The cynicism of American strategic legalism reached new heights in 1985, when the International Court in the Hague agreed to hear the Nicaraguan Sandinista government's case against the United States for mining its harbors and illegally supporting the Contra guerrillas. Rather than contest the changes, the Reagan administration simply withdrew from the International Court's jurisdiction for a two-year period. Although the court ultimately ruled against the United States, this had little effect on Reagan's secret war in Central America and provided a graphic illustration of Thucydides' famous maxim from the Melian dialogue, "the standard of justice depends on the equality of power to compel and that in fact the strong do what they have the power to do and the weak accept what they have to accept."[9]

Former U.S. Senator Daniel Patrick Moynihan argues that by 1990, there was "a certain disorientation in American foreign policy," which grew out of "our having abandoned, for practical purposes, the concept that international relations can and should be governed by a regime of public international law." Though alarmed by America's decision to shed all international legal pretense, Moynihan was more bothered by the fact that "this idea had not been succeeded by some other reasonably comprehensive and coherent notion as to the kind of world order we do seek, or which at all events we do accept and try to cope with."[10] This lack of vision became most apparent after the collapse of the Soviet Union and the end of the Cold War.

The post–Cold War world confronted American leaders with any number of daunting challenges and in the process exposed the limits of American power and vision on the most pressing questions of our time. Although Nuremberg's International Military Tribunal continues to provide an important symbolic model for human rights advocates, the end of the Cold War saw genocidal civil wars in Rwanda and Bosnia vie for the West's increasingly fragmented and unfocused attention. Most shocking about the "postmodern" wars of the 1990s was that the line between soldier and civilian had all but vanished. Michael Ignatieff goes so far as to argue that in "postmodern" conflict, "war crimes and atrocities" became "integral to the very persecution of war."[11]

The strategic legalism of the Reagan and Bush administrations during the final years of the Cold War was transformed into a more timid, therapeutic form of legalism under the Clinton administration. With genocides in Rwanda and former Yugoslavia, the mantra "Never Again" became, in the words of President William Jefferson Clinton, "I am sorry." At the time of Rwanda's hundred-day massacre (claiming between 700,000 and 900,000 lives and sparking civil war in the Congo), his administration did not push for UN intervention, downplayed clear warnings, and even quibbled over using the word "genocide" to describe the clearest example since World War II.[12] However, this did not deter President Clinton from making a postgenocide airport stop in Kigali to apologize to Rwandans for his error in judgment. More distressing than Clinton's day-late, dollar-short "concern" was the growing acceptance of the idea that it was permissible to stand aside and watch knowingly as genocide was carried out on live television as long as it was likely that a dozen or so ringleaders would be solemnly indicted and tried by an international tribunal in the not-too-distant future. As Michael Ignatieff observes: "The two tribunals were created in 1993 and 1994 by Western governments who had done little or nothing to stop the crimes the tribunals were set up to punish. Instead of armed intervention, the international community promised the victims justice, in the form of a prosecutor, a panel of judges, and a secretariat of investigators and lawyers."

The duality—the yawning chasm between American rhetoric and foreign policy, the very thing that so infuriated postwar Germans—continues to widen. George Kennan observed, "And thus, extravagantly do we, like a stern school master clothed in the mantle of perfect virtue, sit in judgment over all other governments, looking sharply down the nose of each of them to see whether its handling of its domestic affairs meets our approval."[13]

During the 1990s the American duality was alive and well in the persons of Secretary of State Madeline Albright and U.S. Ambassador for War Crimes David Scheffer. Their public relationship is not unlike that of President Woodrow Wilson and his Secretary of State Robert Lansing. While Albright has strongly advocated the enforcement of international criminal law and urged the prosecution of everyone from Pol Pot to Slobodan Milosevic, her top war crimes official has proven considerably more conservative. In 1998 the American duality was forced into the stark light of the Roman summer. Many of the world's international legal luminaries had gathered to hammer out the details of the UN's long-awaited international criminal court at the Rome Conference. Finally, much to the dismay of human rights groups and international law advocates, the United States sided with China, Iraq, Algeria, India, and Israel and refused to join the one hundred other nations signing the treaty to create a permanent international criminal court. Once again, the American delegates wanted one set of international laws for the rest of the world and another, more flexible set for the United States. In January 2000, Jesse Helms, chairman of the Senate Foreign Relations Committee, met with the UN Security Council and issued an ominous warning: "A UN that seeks to impose its presumed authority on the American people, without their consent, begs for confrontation and—I want to be candid with you—eventual U.S. withdrawal."[14]

Fifty years after the United Nations adopted the "Nuremberg Principles," there remains a great deal of confusion surrounding the issues raised by these revolutionary trials. Though they certainly served as a warning to rogue political leaders that under the right set of political circumstances they might find themselves held accountable, other aspects remain far less certain. It took the UN three decades to try one war criminal in Cambodia. One has to ask whether it is possible to enforce a Nuremberg-based set of international laws under tense, armed, diplomatic compromises like the Dayton Accords and the Paris Agreements.

Given the fate of international law since Nuremberg, the time has come to reconsider the legacy of the Nuremberg trials as more of an anomaly than a paradigm. Human rights and war crimes prosecutions only become considerations for U.S. foreign policy when they correspond with larger policy objectives, or more commonly, when they turn into public relations problems. Lurching from global crisis to global crisis, we live in an age when strategic, much less moral, doctrines have been replaced by psychobabble, public opinion polls, and that great arbiter of justice, CNN. Today, Telford Taylor's description of America "as a sort of Steinbeckian 'Lennie,' gigantic and powerful, but prone to shatter what we try to save" has never seemed more fitting.[15]

The early to mid-1990s were heady times for those who believed that Nuremberg-derived system of international criminal law would soon take root. However, at the end of the decade and the bloodiest century in recorded history, the so-called "international community" has grown increasingly indifferent to and accepting of the horrors suffered by its most powerless, politically insignificant members. Laws of war professor Jonathan Bush described the phenomenon: "What was most troubling about this early 1990s feeling was that it overvalued what trials can do and completely missed the point of what Nuremberg did and didn't do."

Today, despite the most comprehensive set of laws governing war and international relations in human history, the oldest and most basic distinction, the one between soldier and civilian, is fast disappearing. A nineteenth-century German historian calculated that from 1496 b.c. to a.d. 1861, a span of 3,357 years, only 227 had been years of peace while 3,130 had been years of war. For every year of peace there had been thirteen years of war.[16] As Sven Lindqvist suggests in his book *Exterminate All the Brutes*, "You already know enough. So do I. It is not knowledge that we lack. What is missing is the courage to understand what we know and draw conclusions."[17] Having just concluded the bloodiest century in the history of man, is it enough to seek salvation in new codes of international criminal law? More laws are not necessary; what is necessary if we are to avoid an even bloodier twenty-first century is the will to enforce the laws that exist.

(2000)

POSTSCRIPT

THE NEW AMERICAN PARADIGM

TODAY, THE NUREMBERG TRIALS AND THE PRINCIPLES THAT they spawned seem like quaint memories from a long-bygone era. The 9/11 attacks and the ensuing "Global War on Terror," forced America's international legal duality out into the open for all to see. Weeks after 9/11, senior Justice Department lawyers convinced President Bush that the "War on Terror" was a new kind of war requiring "a new paradigm" that would render the Geneva Convention's strict limitations on the treatment of enemy prisoners "obsolete."[1]

Unlike previous American presidents who claimed to support international law when the outcome was favorable to the United States, President Bush explicitly rejected both long-standing, codified laws of war like the Geneva Conventions and older customary distinctions such as that between soldier and civilian.[2] The Bush administration pushed aside the military professionals and argued that there were no limits—constitutional or congressional—on presidential authority.[3]

Brazen disregard for the laws of war was soon elevated to a matter of principle as America began a sordid affair with what Vice President Cheney described as "the dark slide." Even though the U.S. Second Court of Appeals compared torturers to slave traders in a 1980 opinion, by the summer of 2002 the United States had redefined torture to include only those acts that resulted in death or organ failure. According to the new American definition, not even John McCain's treatment at the hands of the North Vietnamese met the new standard.[4]

President Bush officially declared war on international criminal law when he unsigned the Rome Statute establishing the International Criminal Court in July 2002. Conservatives viewed the ICC and the concept of "universal jurisdiction" as a kind of inverse strategic legalism or "lawfare." According to Brigadier General Charles Dunlap, lawfare used the law instead of military force "to achieve an operational objective."

A new federal law called the American Service-Members' Protection Act (better known as the Hague Invasion Act), passed in August 2002, authorized the President to use "all means necessary and appropriate to release US prisoners of the ICC." The Bush administration also began suspending aid to countries that refused to give U.S. citizens immunity before the ICC. Initially the Bush administration took the position that neither the federal War Crimes Act nor the Geneva Conventions constrained U.S. forces in Afghanistan. Because the United States deemed that nation "a failed state," they could define both Al Qaeda and the Taliban as "illegal enemy combatants" unprotected by common Article 3 of the Geneva Convention.[5]

It was one thing for American Special Forces teams to play fast and loose with the laws of war on hot battlefields in the Pashtu frontier, where the irregular nature of the foe merited such an approach. However, by the time the war shifted to Iraq, "torture's perverse pathology" had taken root, and now army reservists were applying similar standards during the invasion of a sovereign nation. According to historian Alfred McCoy, not only does torture fail to provide reliable intelligence, it also "leads to both the uncontrolled proliferation of the practice and long-term damage to the perpetrator society."[6]

Although the term "enemy combatant" was used as a strategic legal mechanism to get around international humanitarian law, when all else failed, the Bush administration invoked simple messianic unilateralism. "Good" and "Evil" became the new "metrics" for a vague new American foreign policy whose exponents claimed to be on a crusade to rid the world of "Evil" and to spread "Freedom."[7] Very suddenly, colonialism, crusades, nuclear weapons, and prayer breakfasts were all the rage for ambitious post–9/11 D.C. Republicans. Not only did America's evangelical President describe the War on Terror as a "Crusade," he claimed "God" had told him to strike at Al Qaeda and Saddam Hussein.[8] However, this Judeo-Christian inspired, reflexively anti-Islam rhetoric and policy proved strategically unsound and worked as a force multiplier for America's enemies. Soon the United States was fighting not only Al Qaeda but also "Islamofascism" and "IslamHitlerites."[9]

After 9/11, human rights utopians were immediately replaced by proud neo-imperialists who called for a unipolar world, with America striking out preemptively against threats both real and imagined. Russian-born *Wall Street Journal* editor, Council on Foreign Relations fellow, and *L.A. Times* columnist Max Boot argued that "Afghanistan and other troubled lands today cry out for the sort of enlightened foreign administration once provided by self-confident Englishmen in jodhpurs and pith helmets." Heavily praised by the mainstream press, Boot's 2002 book, *Savage Wars for Peace*, points to the 1898 U.S. war in the Philippines as a template for the "War on Terror." "In deploying American power, decision makers should be less apologetic, less hesitant, less humble," wrote Boot. "America should not be afraid to fight 'the savage wars of peace' if necessary to enlarge the 'empire of liberty.'"[10] President Bush's Canadian speechwriter, David Frumm, and Iraq War architect, Richard Perle, went so far as to claim that the stakes for the United States in the War on Terror were "victory or holocaust."[11]

The War on Terror's cheerleaders and enablers were not limited to the right. Pro-war columns by liberal hawks like Judith Miller, Michael Gordon, Thomas Friedman, Michael Ignatieff, David Remnick, Jeffrey Goldberg, Peter Beinart, Paul Berman, and Kenneth Pollack helped to sell and justify U.S. policy and conduct. "The press played ball. After 9/11, they rolled over and played dead," said the dean of the White House press correspondents, Helen Thomas. "Really, they asked no questions, they all had to be patriotic. . . . To ask a question was to be unpatriotic, un-American and so forth."[12] Even the onetime human rights advocates at Harvard's Carr Center blew with the wind. Not only did Michael Ignatieff advocate the use of torture, his colleague Sara Sewall advised the U.S. military on counterinsurgency policy, and even Pulitzer Prize–winning journalist Samantha Power, who was quick to point out atrocities in Darfur, remained conspicuously silent about the new American paradigm.[13] It is no coincidence that today all three are politicians or policy makers.

The most incisive criticism of the Bush administration's POW policies came from professional soldiers who were growing increasingly uncomfortable with multiple combat tours ordered by civilian leaders who had never been in a fistfight, much less a firefight. Because the career military lawyers supported Geneva Convention protections for prisoners, they were simply cut out of the policy-planning process.[14] One heavily decorated Vietnam war veteran wrote: "Never before in our country's history has an administration charged with defending our nation been so lacking in hands-on combat experience and therefore so ignorant about the art and science of war."[15] Secretary of State Colin Powell, one of the few Vietnam veterans in the Bush administration, argued forcefully and prophetically that the new American paradigm would "reverse over a century of U.S. policy and practice," and predicted "a high cost in terms of negative international reaction, with immediate adverse consequences for our conduct of foreign policy."[16]

Many American policy makers, pundits, and academics attempted to rationalize the use of torture based largely on the "ticking time bomb" scenarios of television supersleuth Jack Bauer. There was, however, one problem: torture does not provide a steady stream of reliable intelligence, as evidenced by testimony of superterrorist Khalid Sheikh Mohammed. After months of torture and isolation, "KSM" confessed to masterminding thirty Al Qaeda operations and even wielding the knife that decapitated Daniel Pearl.[17]

"We are falling into the trap of imitating the 'evil-doing' which we accuse our enemies of initiating," wrote Rich Arant. A contract interrogator who worked at Abu Ghraib and Afghanistan's Bagram Air Force base in 2003–4, Arant had a revelation one night while questioning a former Afghan Mujahid who had fought against the Soviets and was now in jail because a paid U.S. government informant and well-known Soviet collaborator had fingered him. When Arant told the old soldier he could trust an American to treat him with more respect than the Russians, "this dignified man completely collapsed in tears, unable to speak," wrote Arant. "After my interpreter and I gave him a chance to gather himself, he said, 'I fought Russians, our common enemy, and now you Americans have imprisoned me on the word of a son of the Russians. This is my reward. '" Arant quit shortly thereafter and offered this observation:

> Our leaders have taught us that taking a life on today's battlefield can be a righteous and patriotic act, an act of bravery or self-defense, a "preemptive" necessity in the new age of the war on terror. "Precautionary murder" is the term once used by T. E. Lawrence, Lawrence of Arabia. Former conventions regarding the treatment of prisoners are now considered quaint, obsolete. But a prisoner is as defenseless as a passenger held hostage on an aircraft. There is little honor found in exploiting his fears, no matter how pressing the requirement.[18]

By the time the United States invaded Iraq in 2003, extraordinary rendition, secret prisons, indefinite detention of American citizens, domestic espionage, and watch lists were all accepted as facts of life by a stunned and submissive American population who viewed the havoc wrought in their name from afar. That arm's-length relationship was shattered in 2004 when General Anthony Taguba's report on prisoner abuse at Abu Ghraib was leaked to Seymor Hersh and photographs of American soldiers perversely torturing and humiliating common Iraqi criminals flashed around the world in seconds. Bin Laden himself could not have staged a more successful propaganda coup as smiling, fresh-faced American girls led naked Iraqi men on leashes. One senior policy maker described the perpetrators to me as "the seven soldiers who lost the war."[19]

The Bush administration's response to the Abu Ghraib affair was similar to President Theodore Roosevelt's response to atrocities in the Philippines War or President Nixon's response to the Mai Lai Massacre: the perpetrators were "a few bad apples" and these were "isolated" events.[20]

However, this buffoonery was limited to the Abu Ghraib Seven. This appendix from the Taguba Report speaks for itself: in a sworn statement, a U.S. soldier stationed at Abu Ghraib wrote, "I climbed a yellow ladder . . . to see a light skinned, black male . . . taunt the prisoners by flexing and shouting at them. Right after this, a Caucasian soldier . . . taunted the prisoners of compound 'B' and 'C' by similar means of flexing and shouting at them. This caused the prisoners to become extremely irate, and a short riot ensued that resulted in gunfire" (seven Iraqis were shot).[21]

It did not take long for American POW policy to be denounced by our British allies, the U.S. Supreme Court, federal judges, the International Red Cross, and the American Bar Association. Now there is irrefutable documentary evidence that even American doctors and psychiatrists violate the Geneva Conventions, the Nuremberg medical standards, and the Hippocratic oath. The *New England Journal of Medicine* called the complicity in the interrogation process "a matter of national shame."[22] Military professionals, like former Navy Judge Advocate General, Rear Admiral John Hutson, rejected the few bad apples argument: due to "the range of individuals and locations involved in these reports, it is simply no longer possible to view these allegations as a few instances of an isolated prison."[23]

The Guantanamo Bay camp is in many ways a distraction, a set piece, or as defense attorney Clive Stafford Smith put it, a "lightning rod not only for criticism but also for global attention." Largely ignored is the archipelago of secret prisons around the world where "high-value" detainees are tortured, interrogated, and sometimes killed. FBI agents who visited the Cuban prison were shocked by both the style and the substance of the interrogations. Stupidly brutal, proudly racist, and deeply perverse, the FBI agents witnessed scantily clad female interrogators sexually taunting Muslim captives (one even smeared fake menstrual blood on a suspect).[24] FBI agents watched one "detainee sitting on the floor of the interview room with an Israeli flag draped around him, loud music being played and a strobe light flashing." According to one FBI memo, the theatrics "produced no intelligence."[25]

When it came to war crimes trials for the vanquished, the Bush administration employed traditional, primitive political justice. As a result, it could not even provide an easily convicted thug like Saddam Hussein with a decent show trial. The fallen Iraqi leader's chaotic American-choreographed proceeding saw lawyers murdered, courtroom brawls between defendants and guards, and even an execution video on YouTube before it made the morning papers.[26] The treatment meted out to American and Australian collaborators like Jose Padilla, John Walker Lindh, and David Hicks has been oddly unsystematic, as if the prosecutors were making up the rules as they went along.

The self-contained legal bubble of Guantanamo Bay has become a sort of Orwellian version of Alice's Wonderland where even defendants found not guilty "can be held in perpetuity."[27] The Gitmo military commission was firmly under the control of Vice President Dick Cheney and his political appointee Susan Crawford. Navy Lieutenant Commander Brian Mizer filed a motion in 2008 that charged senior Pentagon appointees with "exercising unlawful command influence" by pressuring prosecutors to charge "high-value" detainees in order to gain "strategic political value" before the 2008 election.[28] The tribunal's top legal official, Brigadier General Thomas Hartman, was removed from his position after judges in three separate cases barred him from participating in trials due to his pro-prosecution bias.[29] Convinced that political interference made fair trials impossible, Colonel Morris Davis, Major Robert Preston, Captain John Carr, and Captain Carrie Wolf all resigned.

Australian David Hicks was the beneficiary of an eleventh-hour political deal that sent the prisoner home in a futile effort to aid Australian Prime Minister John Howard's doomed reelection effort. Although Hicks signed a document claiming that he had not been mistreated by Americans, this statement was contradicted by his earlier affadavit.[30] "The charade that took place at Guantanamo Bay would have done Stalin's show trials proud," said one of Australia's most experienced criminal lawyers, Robert Richter.

"First there was the indefinite detention without charge. Then there was the torture, however the Bush lawyers, including the attorney general, might choose to describe it. Then there was the extorted confession of guilt."[31]

The Bush administration strained to make an analogy between the Nuremberg and Gitmo trials. In the lead-in to the first Gitmo trial, U.S. diplomats received a memo that instructed them to point to the execution of Nuremberg convicts to justify the death penalty at Guantanamo Bay.[32] Brigadier General Hartmann went so far as to claim that the legal protections for Guantanamo Bay defendants "exceed those that were available at Nuremberg."[33] Colonel Morris Davis described one conversation with the Pentagon's top lawyer and recently resigned torture advocate, William Haynes, who tried to describe the Gitmo trials as "the Nuremberg of our time." When Davis reminded him that defendants at Nuremberg were acquitted, Haynes appeared shocked and replied: "Wait a minute, we can't have acquittals. If we've been holding these guys for so long, how can we explain letting them get off? We can't have acquittals, we've got to have convictions."Although the Bush administration and Guantanamo officials continue to compare the Guantanamo Bay military commission to the Nuremberg trials, nothing could be further from the truth. It took Nuremberg's international court less than 13 months to indict, try, and sentence Nazi Germany's top leaders in an imperfect but highly credible procedure. Between late 1946 and 1949, the United States tried another 177 German leaders in 12 more trials at Nuremberg.[34] At no point did the United States monitor the work of the defense attorneys or authorize the use of torture to gain information. No Nuremberg defendants or their lawyers ever alleged that they were tortured. Former Nuremberg prosecutor Henry King found the analogies offensive: "To torture people and then you can bring evidence you obtained into court? Hearsay evidence is allowed? Some evidence is available to the prosecution and not to the defendants?"[35]

The Guantanamo Bay tribunals would have lived up to the worst star chamber expectations were it not for the verdict in the Hamdan case. In a split decision, a six-officer military commission convicted Osama Bin Laden's driver, Salim Hamdan, of the lesser charge of providing material support for terrorism, but acquitted him of the more serious conspiracy charge. The Hamdan case proved once again that even primitive political justice cannot be stage-managed.[36]

Thankfully, not all Americans have given in to the fear. U.S. District Judge John Coughenour tried and convicted Algerian Ahmed Ressam for his plot to bomb Los Angeles Airport. Coughenour did not need a secret military tribunal, or indefinite detention, or to deny the defendant the right to counsel, or to deem him "an enemy combatant." The judge explained, "The message to the world from today's sentencing is that our courts have not abandoned our commitment to the ideals that set our nations apart." According to Coughenour, if the prevailing American view becomes that terrorism renders the Constitution obsolete, "the terrorists will have won."[37]

Former Navy General Counsel Alberto Mora was another who pushed back against the Bush administration: "When you put together the pieces, it's all so sad. To preserve flexibility, they were willing to throw away our values."[38] With the establishment of a new, Democractic administration and a fresh set of international crises causing near-seismic shifts, Americans would be wise to consider the words of American Nuremberg prosecutor Robert Jackson's now famous opening address: "We must never forget that the record on which we judge these defendants today is the record on which history will judge us tomorrow. To pass these defendants the poison chalice is to put it to our own lips as well."[39]

(2010)

NOTES

PREFACE

1. Telford Taylor, *Nuremberg and Vietnam: An American Tragedy* (New York: Bantam, 1971), 1.

2. Richard Goldstone, the first UN war crimes prosecutor at The Hague, told Betsey Pisik of *The Washington Times*, "The most important legacy of Nuremberg was the concept of universal jurisdiction." "World Tribunal vs. Sovereignty," *The Washington Times*, October 26, 1998. "Universal jurisdiction" is the theory that would allow a national or international court to try war crimes perpetrators, regardless of the location of their deeds and the nationality of their victims. Tina Rosenberg, "From Nuremberg to Bosnia," *The Nation*, May 15, 1995; "Tipping the Scales of Justice," *World Policy Journal* 12, no. 3 (Fall 1995): 55–64. Pulitzer Prize–winning journalist Samantha Power and Daniel Goldhagen, author of *Hitler's Willing Executioners*, called for a Senate or International Criminal Court investigation of Senator Bob Kerry's alleged atrocities during the Vietnam War.

3. Tina Rosenberg wrote: "But the tribunals' organizers did intend them as show trials in a positive sense, to reveal Nazi crimes to the world and to encourage ordinary Germans to confront their responsibilities." Roger Cohen concurred in *The New York Times* on April 30, 1995: "A half- century ago, the Nuremberg trials helped lay terrible ghosts to rest and so make possible Germany's central role in the reconstruction of central Europe." However, American Nuremberg scholar Jonathan Bush and German historian Jörg Friedrich both flatly rejected this contention at the conference "Accounting for Atrocities" at Bard College in 1998. According to Jonathan Bush, "[Nuremberg] was the complete failure of what we

would today call civic society, a reeducation in democracy. . . . West Germany . . . is the classic example of peace—and more than that, peace, prosperity, security, good foreign relations, and all that—without justice" (*Proceedings of "Accounting for Atrocities: Prosecuting War Crimes Fifty Years After Nuremberg," October 5–6, 1998* [Annandale-on-Hudson, N.Y.: Bard College Publications, 2000], 11–14). This conclusion was particularly unpalatable during the 1990s. Military law expert Howard Levie also raised questions about using trials for "reeducation": "How much the trials themselves had to do with this transformation from deadly enemies to close friends and partners can only be a matter of conjecture" (*Terrorism in War: The Law of War Crimes* [Dobbs Ferry, N.Y.: Oceana, 1993], 8). See also *Americans as Proconsuls*, ed. Robert Wolfe (Washington: U.S. Govt. Printing Office, 1978), 246.

4. Jonathan Bush offered this dissenting view: "The triumphalism can be put to the side. What was more troubling, I think, was the idea that it overvalued what trials can do, this early 1990s feeling, and it completely missed the point of what Nuremberg did and didn't do" (*Proceedings of "Accounting for Atrocities"* 11)

5. Jonathan Bush, "The Good, the Bad, and the Ugly," *Columbia Journal of Transnational Law* 45, no. 898 (2007): 928.

INTRODUCTION

1. U.S. District Court for the District of Oregon, "In the Matter of the Memorial to Messrs. Robert E Maguire and Charles A. Hart, May 17, 1976" (Portland: Federal Court Reporters), 2.

2. Ibid.

3. Ibid.

4. U.S. District Court for the District of Oregon, "In the Matter of the Memorial to Messrs. Robert E Maguire and Charles A. Hart, May 17, 1976," 13.

5. Telford Taylor, interview by author, tape recording, New York City, 8 April 1987.

6. The Thirty Years War was to the sixteenth century what World War II was to the twentieth; both wrought destruction on an unprecedented scale. It is estimated that half of Europe's German-speaking population was killed by either war or famine during the Thirty Years War. 8,000,000 people are said to have perished, not counting some 350,000 killed in battle" (*The Conduct of War 1781–1961* [New York: Da Capo, 1961], 15). David Kaiser, *Politics and War: European Conflict from Philip II to Hitler* (Cambridge: Harvard University Press, 1990), 83. See also Theodore Rabb, *The Thirty Years War: Problems of Motive, Extent and Effect* (Washington, D.C.: University Press of America, 1981).

    See also Hans Delbrück, *The Dawn of Modern Warfare* (Lincoln: University of Nebraska Press, 1990); J. F. C. Fuller, *The Conduct of War 1781–1961* (New York: Da Capo, 1961); and Jeremy Black, *The Rise of the European Powers 1679–1793* (London: Edward Arnold, 1990).

7. For an excellent modern analysis of sovereignty see George F. Kennan, *Around the Cragged Hill* (New York: Norton, 1993). "Sovereignty was originally a quality at-

tached to the person of a great ruler, normally an emperor or someone equivalent. It was his person, not the country or the people over whom he ruled, who was 'sovereign.' He alone was unlimited in his powers, in the sense that no one else's word could rival his authority. All of his subjects owed him submission and obedience. It was this that made him sovereign" (87). See also David Luban, *Legal Modernism* (Ann Arbor: University of Michigan Press, 1994), 337–338 for an interesting discussion of sovereignty's relationship to legal positivism.

8. Under the act-of-state doctrine during the era of the nation-state, the leader of a sovereign nation was immune from legal prosecution. There were exceptions: for example, rogues like Napoleon who refused to play by the rules were punished. See also John Alan Appleman, *Military Tribunals and International Crimes* (Indianapolis: Bobbs-Merrill, 1954), 54–59. Reinhard Koselleck writes in *Critique and Crisis* (New York: Berg, 1988): "Each sovereign had the *jus ad bellum,* the same right to make war, and war became a means of princely politics, guided by *raison d'etat* and reduced to the common formula of a 'European balance of power'" (43–44).

9. Otto Kirchheimer, *Political Justice: The Use of Legal Procedure for Political Ends* (Princeton: Princeton University Press, 1961), ii.

1. THE END OF LIMITED WAR

1. Michael Howard, *War in European History* (New York: Oxford University Press, 1976), 5. John Keegan, *The Face of Battle* (New York: Penguin, 1976). Howard and Keegan both agree that greed played a more important role than honor in early European warfare. Howard writes, "the increasing codification of the laws of war was due less to any searching of Christian, legal, or Knightly consciences than to a different development indeed: the growing commercialism of war. Ransom and booty were no longer agreeable bonuses, but, for a growing number of belligerents, the major object of their activity" (7).

2. Howard Levie leaves few doubts about the brutality of early European warfare in his encyclopedic study, *Terrorism in War: The Law of War Crimes* (Dobbs Ferry, N.Y.: Oceana, 1993): "In a city taken by storm almost any licence was condoned by the law. Only churches and churchmen were technically secure, but even they were not often spared. Women could be raped, and men killed out of hand. All the goods of the inhabitants were regarded as forfeit. If lives were spared, it was only through clemency of the victorious captain; and spoilation was systematic" (9–10). On ransom and booty in early European warfare, he writes: "The prospect of this free run of his lust for blood, spoil and women was a major incentive to a soldier to persevere in the rigors which were likely to attend a protracted siege" (10). Levie also points out that many early European wars often ended with an amnesty: "In the peace treaties ending the wars of the seventeenth century and thereafter, it became the custom to include in each one an amnesty (or 'oblivion') provision which, in effect, forgave, among other things, any war crimes committed during the course of hostilities which the treaty was intended to bring to an end." Levie

cites Article II of the Treaty of Westphalia and Article III of the 1713 Treaty of Utrecht as examples of "oblivion provisions" (12).

3. Howard, *War in European History*, 5. Howard describes war against the heathens as "*guerre mortale* in which not only the property but the lives of the vanquished were at the mercy of their conquerer." Moreover, when Christian knights were fighting pagans, "no holds were barred, and knights indeed could gain remission from their sins by waging it."

4. Dee Brown, *Bury My Heart at Wounded Knee* (New York: Holt, 1970), 9. For more on American Indian numbers see Colin Galloway's *New Worlds for All: Indians, Europeans, and the Remaking of Early America* (Baltimore: Johns Hopkins University Press, 1998).

5. Richard Drinnon, *Facing West: The Metaphysics of Indian-Hating and Empire-Building* (Norman: University of Oklahoma Press, 1980), xiii. "The basic feature of the white policies is the assault of the strong on the weak, the intention to take their land from them. This phenomenon has taken its most grandiose form in North America. Land-hungry whites crowd in between the weak and partly decayed settlements of the Indians" (Sven Lindqvist, *Exterminate All the Brutes,* trans. Joan Tate [New York: New Press, 1996], 144). Frederick Jackson Turner, "The Significance of the Frontier in American History" (1893).

6. Walter McDougall, *Promised Land, Crusader State* (Boston: Houghton Mifflin, 1997), 17.

7. Edmund Morgan, *American Slavery, American Freedom* (New York: Norton, 1975), 4. See Anders Stephanson, *Manifest Destiny: American Expansionism and the Empire of Right* (New York: Hill and Wang, 1995), 24.

8. The second President of the United States, John Adams, described Indian warfare in a 1775 letter: "The Indians are known to conduct their Wars so entirely without Faith and Humanity that it will bring eternal infamy." Drinnon, *Facing West,* 70.

9. Hugh Brogan, *The Pelican History of the United States of America* (London: Penguin, 1986), 64*n*7.

10. John Keegan, *Fields of Battle: The Wars for North America* (New York: Knopf, 1996), 270. According to Keegan, "Intertribal warfare was a fact of American Indian life long before the coming of the Europeans, as in so many 'hard primitive' societies; Indians fought for honour, revenge, excitement, and in order to replace the casualties of war by seizing and 'adopting' captives from the enemy" (103).

11. Keegan, *Fields of Battle,* 273, 283. Carol Chomsky makes the point that women and children had always been fair game in American Indian warfare in "The United States–Dakota War Trials: A Study in Military Injustice," *Stanford Law Review* 43 (1) (Nov. 1990): 88.

12. Paul Wellman, *The Indian Wars of the West* (New York: Indian Head Books, 1992), 28*n*4.

13. Jill Lepore, *The Name of War: King Philip's War and the Origins of American Identity* (New York: Knopf, 1998), xiv.

14. Lepore, *The Name of War,* xiv.

15. Drinnon, *Facing West,* 331.

16. Drinnon, *Facing West,* 331.

17. Anthony Wallace, *Jefferson and the Indians: The Tragic Fate of the First Americans* (Cambridge: Harvard University Press, 1999), 175. See also Drinnon, *Facing West,* 81.

18. Drinnon, *Facing West,* 87.

19. Drinnon, *Facing West,* 87.

20. Drinnon, *Facing West,* 82 and Peter Parish, *Slavery: History and Historians* (New York: Harper and Row, 1989), 12–13, 26–28. According to Parish, America's slave population grew from 26,000 in 1700 to 2 million by 1830.

21. McDougall, *Promised Land, Crusader State,* 56; Drinnon, *Facing West,* 76. Senator Benjamin Leigh of Virginia was more candid than most when he described the significance of America's westward spread in 1824: "It is peculiar to the character of this Anglo-Saxon race of men to which we belong, that it has never been contented to live in the same country with any other distinct race, upon terms of equality; it has invariably when placed in that situation, proceeded to exterminate or enslave the other race in some form or other, or, failing that, to abandon the country" (Stephanson, *Manifest Destiny,* 27).

22. Drinnon, *Facing West,* 99.

23. Elihu Root, *The Military and Colonial Policy of the United States* (New York: AMS Press, 1970), 320–321.

24. Vine Deloria Jr. and Clifford Lytle, *American Indians, American Justice* (Austin: University of Texas Press, 1983), 4. American Indian historian Vine Deloria Jr. best describes the Indians' ambiguous international legal status: "Marshall, building on this foundation of domestic dependency, interposed a limited sovereignty enjoyed by the Indian nations to prevent the state of Georgia from extending its power over the Cherokee Nation's lands."

25. Chomsky, "The United States–Dakota War Trials," 16–17.

26. Chomsky, "The United States–Dakota War Trials," 16. The Minnesota Indian War of 1862 and the trial that followed were brought to my attention by historian John Willand of North Hennepin Community College in Minnesota.

27. Brown, *Bury My Heart at Wounded Knee,* 38. See also Chomsky, "The United States–Dakota War Trials," 16.

28. Brown, *Bury My Heart at Wounded Knee,* 39.

29. Brown, *Bury My Heart at Wounded Knee,* 39.

30. Brown, *Bury My Heart at Wounded Knee,* 39–40.

31. Brown, *Bury My Heart at Wounded Knee,* 40.

32. Brown, *Bury My Heart at Wounded Knee,* 40.

33. Charles Bryant and Abel Murch, *A History of the Great Massacre by the Sioux Indians in Minnesota* (Millwood, N.Y: Kraus Reprint, 1977), 315.

34. Brown, *Bury My Heart at Wounded Knee,* 43. "The Santees might as well strike first instead of waiting for the soldiers to come and kill them. It would be better to fight the white men now while they are fighting among themselves far to the south."

35. Brown, *Bury My Heart at Wounded Knee*, 44. He warned his militant followers that the whites were "like the locusts. . . . Count your fingers all day long and white men with guns in their hands will come faster than you can count."

36. Brown, *Bury My Heart at Wounded Knee*, 44.

37. Brown, *Bury My Heart at Wounded Knee*, 44.

38. Marion Satterlee, "A Description of the MASSACRE BY SIOUX INDIANS. In Renville County, Minnesota, August 18–19" (Minneapolis: Fisher Paper Co., 1916). This quote came from the section entitled "The Massacre at Redwood Agency," 4.

39. Brown, *Bury My Heart at Wounded Knee*, 45.

40. Kenneth Carley, *The Sioux Uprising* (Minneapolis: The Sioux Uprising Committee of the Minnesota State Historical Society, n.d.), 4. Settler Justina Kreiger was captured by the Sioux and recalled her ordeal in a book written at the time: "One of these inhuman savages seized . . . my niece, yet alive, held her up by the foot . . . while holding her there by one hand . . . he hastily cut the flesh around one of the legs . . . and then, by twisting and wrenching, broke the ligaments and bone, until the limb was entirely severed from the body, the child was screaming frantically, 'O God! O God!'"

41. Carley, *The Sioux Uprising*, 4.

42. Carley, *The Sioux Uprising*, 5.

43. Wellman, *The Indian Wars of the West*, 28n4. As the Lower Agency massacre was in progress, the Santee leader rode into town and became angry because his men were too busy looting and not intent enough on killing (Satterlee, "A Description of the MASSACRE BY SIOUX INDIANS," 4).

44. Satterlee, "A Description of the MASSACRE BY SIOUX INDIANS," 4. The brave ferry boat operator Herbert Millier is called Jacob Mauley in other accounts. Satterlee and others credit him with saving at least forty lives before he was killed.

45. Brown, *Bury My Heart at Wounded Knee*, 45.

46. The Santee made a key strategic error by not pressing their advantage and capturing the American fort. Little Crow was in favor of attacking; however, the young braves wanted to attack the undefended town of New Ulm, loot the storehouses, and capture more civilians. Once again, Little Crow was overruled (Satterlee, "A Description of the MASSACRE BY SIOUX INDIANS," 46).

47. *The New York Times*, August 22, 1862, 1. See also Robert Hays, *A Race at Bay* (Carbondale: Southern Illinois University Press, 1997). This entire book is devoted to *New York Times* editorials on America's "Indian Problem."

48. Brown, *Bury My Heart at Wounded Knee*, 50.

49. Carley, *The Sioux Uprising*, 2–3.

50. Carley, *The Sioux Uprising*, 4.

51. *The New York Times*, August 24, 1862.

52. Richard Ellis, *General Pope and U.S. Indian Policy* (Albuquerque: University of New Mexico Press, 1970), 6.

53. "The horrible massacres of women and children and the outrageous abuse of female prisoners, still alive, call for punishment beyond human power to inflict. There will be no peace in this region by virtue of treaties and Indian faith" (Chomsky, "The United States–Dakota War Trials," 23).

54. Chomsky, "The United States–Dakota War Trials," 23.

55. Brown, *Bury My Heart at Wounded Knee*, 52.

56. Brown, *Bury My Heart at Wounded Knee*, 56–57. After the final battle, Little Crow announced that he was embarrassed to call himself a Sioux because the Americans fought "like cowardly women" (58).

57. Wellman, *The Indian Wars of the West*, 39n3.

58. Little Crow left this message for Sibley on September 7, 1862: "For what reason we have commenced this war I will tell you. It is on account of Major Galbraith. We made a treaty with the government, and beg for what we do get, and can't get that till our children are dying with hunger. It is the traders who commenced it. Mr. A. J. Myrick told the Indians that they could eat grass or dirt. Then Mr. Forbes told the Lower Sioux that they were not men." Colonel Sibley offered this response: "LITTLE CROW—You have murdered many of our people without a sufficient cause. Return me the prisoners under a flag of truce, and I will talk with you then like a man" (Brown, *Bury My Heart at Wounded Knee*, 54).

59. Chomsky, "The United States–Dakota War Trials," 21n44.

60. Brown, *Bury My Heart at Wounded Knee*, 55.

61. Brown, *Bury My Heart at Wounded Knee*, 55.

62. Chomsky, "The United States–Dakota War Trials," 22.

63. Chomsky, "The United States–Dakota War Trials," 23.

64. Chomsky, "The United States–Dakota War Trials," 24.

65. Chomsky, "The United States–Dakota War Trials," 50–51. Godfrey was married to an Indian woman and was reported to have killed seven at New Ulm. According to Carol Chomsky, Godfrey plea bargained for his life and testified in fifty-five cases; of those, eleven ended with death penalties.

66. Chomsky, "The United States–Dakota War Trials," 27. On the first day, the commission sentenced ten to death.

67. Chomsky, "The United States–Dakota War Trials," 23.

68. Brown, *Bury My Heart at Wounded Knee*, 54.

69. *The New York Times,* November 9, 1862, 2.

70. The mood in Minnesota was best summarized by an article in the *St. Paul Press*: "The business has been dispatched with celerity, as many as forty cases having been tried per day in some instances. . . . Besides, no individual injustice is probably done, as ninety-nine hundredths of these devils are guilty, and witnesses in their favor would be as useless as teats on a boar" (*The New York Times*, November 9, 1862, 2).

71. Chomsky, "The United States–Dakota War Trials," 29.

72. Chomsky, "The United States–Dakota War Trials," 29.

73. Chomsky, "The United States–Dakota War Trials," 31.

74. Chomsky, "The United States–Dakota War Trials," 30.

75. Chomsky, "The United States–Dakota War Trials," 32n8.

76. Chomsky, "The United States–Dakota War Trials," 32n8, 33. *The New York Times,* December 12, 1862, reported President Lincoln's reductions: "The President was anxious not to act with so much clemency as to encourage another outbreak of the savages, nor with a degree of severity which should be real cruelty, and therefore at

first ordered only the execution of such Indians as 'had proved guilty of violating females.'"

Reverend Riggs translated President Lincoln's decision to the prisoners on December 22: "Their Great Father at Washington . . . has come to the conclusion that they have each been guilty of wantonly and wickedly murdering his white children. And for this reason he has directed that they each be hanged by the neck until they are dead, on next Friday" (Chomsky, "The United States–Dakota War Trials," 33).

77. Chomsky, "The United States–Dakota War Trials," 34.

78. *The New York Times,* November 24, 1862.

79. Chomsky, "The United States–Dakota War Trials," 36–37.

80. Michel Foucault, *Discipline and Punish* (New York: Vintage, 1977), 7–8.

81. Chomsky, "The United States–Dakota War Trials," 36–37.

82. Carley, *The Sioux Uprising,* 66.

83. Stephen Longstreet, *Indian Wars of the Great Plains* (New York: Indian Head, 1970), 125.

84. Brown, *Bury My Heart at Wounded Knee,* 63–64.

85. Otto Kirchheimer, *Political Justice: The Use of Legal Procedure for Political Ends* (Princeton: Princeton University Press, 1961), 260.

86. Levie, *Terrorism in War,* 13; Geoffrey Best, *War and Law Since 1945* (Oxford: Clarendon, 1994), 41.

87. Francis Lieber, *Lieber's Code and the Law of War,* ed. Richard Hartigan (Chicago: Precedent, 1983), 2. See also Telford Taylor, *Nuremberg and Vietnam* (New York: Bantam, 1971), 21. Lieber had three sons fighting in the Civil War, two Union and one Confederate. Early in the war, Lieber and General Halleck met at Fort Donaldson, where the professor was visiting a son whose arm had just been amputated.

88. Lieber, *Lieber's Code and the Laws of War,* 14.

89. Lieber, *Lieber's Code and the Laws of War,* 21. See also Taylor, *Nuremberg and Vietnam,* 21.

90. Lieber, *Lieber's Code and the Laws of War,* 22. Lieber's own prediction to Halleck that "It will be adopted as a basis for similar works by the English, French, and Germans soon proved true." The Prussians modeled their own code after it in 1870. For a more comprehensive account see Leon Friedman, ed., *The Laws of War* (New York: Random House, 1972), 1:6.

91. Lieber, *Lieber's Code and the Laws of War,* 49.

92. Lieber, *Lieber's Code and the Laws of War,* 50.

93. James McPherson, *Battle Cry of Freedom* (New York: Ballantine, 1989), 854. According to the author, 360,000 Union and 260,000 Confederate soldiers were killed in America's bloodiest war.

94. J. F. C. Fuller, *The Conduct of War 1789–1961* (New York: Da Capo, 1961), 111. Fuller has extreme views on many things, including President Lincoln, calling him "none other than a dictator" (99). Fuller considers the movement toward "people's wars" a return to tribal warfare. David Kaiser blames the Enlightenment and revolutionary political ideologies for the change (*Politics and War* [Cambridge: Harvard University Press, 1990], 211–212). See also Quincy Wright, *A Study of War* (Chicago:

University of Chicago Press, 1969), I:152; Bernard and Fawn Brodie, *From the Cross-bow to the H-Bomb* (Bloomington: Indiana University Press, 1972), 125.

95. J. F. C. Fuller, *Decisive Battle of the U.S.A.* (New York: Da Capo, 1993), 305–308. See also Best, *War and Law Since 1945,* 51 on Sherman's march as precedent setting.

96. Fuller, *The Conduct of War 1789–1961,* 109. The author sees the American way of war as a harbinger of things to come: "For the nineteenth century this was a new conception, because it meant that the deciding factor in war—the power to sue for peace—was transferred from the government to the people, and that peace making was the product of revolution" (108). See also Henry Hitchcock, *Marching with Sherman: Passages from the Letters and Campaign Diaries of Henry Hitchcock* (New Haven: Yale University Press, 1927). Royster believes that contemporary scholars have attached too much importance to his harsh and frank words (Charles Royster, *The Destructive War: William Tecumseh Sherman, Stonewall Jackson, and the Americans* [New York: Knopf, 1991], 358). Royster also does an excellent job of summarizing much of the contemporary historiography on Sherman (352–356).

97. Michael Walzer, *Just and Unjust Wars* (New York: Basic, 1977), 32.

98. Walzer, *Just and Unjust Wars,* 126–128. General Sherman's extremely candid wartime memoirs provide a window into an extremely complex and brutally honest man. "Until we can repopulate Georgia, it is useless to occupy it; but the utter destruction of the roads, houses and people will cripple their military resources. . . . I can make the march and make Georgia howl. . . . I shall feel justified in resorting to the harshest measures, and shall make little effort to restrain my army" (William T. Sherman, *Personal Memoirs of William Tecumseh Sherman* [New York: Library of America, 1990], 2:111).

99. Fuller, *The Conduct of War 1789–1961,* 99.

100. For more on Reconstruction see Eric Foner, *Reconstruction: America's Unfinished Revolution 1863–1877* (New York: Harper and Row, 1988), 603.

101. Friedman, ed., *The Laws of War,* 783.

102. The biographical information comes from a sympathetic Southern account by James Madison Page, *The True Story of Andersonville* (New York: Neale Publications, 1908), 183.

103. Royster, *The Destructive War,* 26, 325–327; Geoffrey Ward, *The Civil War* (New York: Knopf, 1990), 338.

104. Ward, *The Civil War,* 338. For the indictment in the Wirz case see Friedman, ed., *The Laws of War,* 788.

105. McPherson, *Battle Cry of Freedom,* 797.

106. Friedman, ed., *The Laws of War,* 788. I was also fortunate to study this case in Telford Taylor's "Laws of War" seminar at Columbia University Law School in 1992. My analysis draws on Taylor's lectures and our discussions about the case.

107. Friedman, ed., *The Laws of War,* 787.

108. Friedman, ed., *The Laws of War,* 788.

109. Friedman, ed., *The Laws of War,* 789.

110. Friedman, ed., *The Laws of War,* 790.

111. Friedman, ed., *The Laws of War,* 793.

112. Friedman, ed., *The Laws of War*, 786.

113. Friedman, ed., *The Laws of War*, 786.

114. Friedman, ed., *The Laws of War*, 786.

115. Friedman, ed., *The Laws of War*, 786.

116. Levie, *Terrorism in War*, 513.

117. Levie, *Terrorism in War*, 513.

118. Friedman, ed., *The Laws of War*, 798. There are unconfirmed reports that Wirz was offered a plea bargain—if he had agreed to name Confederate President Jefferson Davis as part of a conspiracy to kill Union soldiers, his life would have been spared. This unconfirmed rumor comes from Page, *The True Story of Andersonville*, 220.

119. Friedman, ed., *The Laws of War*, 798.

120. McPherson, *Battle Cry of Freedom*, 802. McPherson best described Wirz, as "a scapegoat for the purported sins of the South" (797).

121. Lieber, *Lieber's Code and the Laws of War*, 22.

122. Lieber, *Lieber's Code and the Laws of War*, 22.

123. Brown, *Bury My Heart at Wounded Knee*, 86.

124. Brown, *Bury My Heart at Wounded Knee*, 86.

125. Brown, *Bury My Heart at Wounded Knee*, 86.

126. Wellman, *The Indian Wars of the West*, 70; Brown, *Bury My Heart at Wounded Knee*, 86; Brogan, *The Pelican History of the United States of America*, 63.

127. Brown, *Bury My Heart at Wounded Knee*, 86.

128. Brown, *Bury My Heart at Wounded Knee*, 86.

129. Brown, *Bury My Heart at Wounded Knee*, 86.

130. Wellman, *The Indian Wars of the West*, 71n and Brogan, *The Pelican History of the United States of America*, 63.

131. Brown, *Bury My Heart at Wounded Knee*, 89.

132. Brown, *Bury My Heart at Wounded Knee*, 89.

133. Brown, *Bury My Heart at Wounded Knee*, 89.

134. Brown, *Bury My Heart at Wounded Knee*, 88 and Wellman, *The Indian Wars of the West*, 72–73. My accounts of the Sand Creek and Wounded Knee massacres owe a great deal to my conversations with Bob Primeaux.

135. Brown, *Bury My Heart at Wounded Knee*, 90.

136. Brown, *Bury My Heart at Wounded Knee*, 90.

137. Brown, *Bury My Heart at Wounded Knee*, 90.

138. Brown, *Bury My Heart at Wounded Knee*, 91.

139. Brogan, *The Pelican History of the United States*, 69.

140. Brogan, *The Pelican History of the United States*, 62.

141. Wellman, *The Indian Wars of the West*, 56–57.

142. Drinnon, *Facing West*, 329.

143. Brown, *Bury My Heart at Wounded Knee*, 297.

144. Brown, *Bury My Heart at Wounded Knee*, 298.

145. Brown, *Bury My Heart at Wounded Knee*, 299.

146. Brown, *Bury My Heart at Wounded Knee*, 299.

147. Brown, *Bury My Heart at Wounded Knee*, 300.

148. Brown, *Bury My Heart at Wounded Knee*, 300.

149. Hermann Hagedorn, *Roosevelt in the Badlands* (Boston: Houghton Mifflin, 1921), 352.

150. Hagedorn, *Roosevelt in the Badlands*, 355. Roosevelt drew what in his mind was a telling parallel. "Turn three hundred low families of New York into New Jersey, support them for fifty years in vicious idleness, and you will have some idea of what the Indians are. Reckless, revengeful; fiendishly cruel, they rob and murder . . . the defenseless, lone settlers on the plains."

151. Brown, *Bury My Heart at Wounded Knee*, 299.

152. Brown, *Bury My Heart at Wounded Knee*, 446.

153. Phone interview with Bob Primeaux, 16 August 1999.

2. THE CHANGING RULES OF WAR AND PEACE

1. Richard Hartigan makes this point in *Lieber's Code and the Laws of War* (Chicago: Precedent, 1983).

2. Hartigan, *Lieber's Code and the Laws of War*, 21. Cynics saw the Russians as using humanitarianism to avoid costly military upgrades. See also Calvin DeHormond Davis, *The United States and the Second Hague Peace Convention* (Durham: Duke University Press, 1975), 4–5. For an American participant's account see Joseph Choate, *The Two Hague Conferences* (1913; reprint, New York: Kraus Reprint, 1969), 5–6. The only stated objective of the conference was to limit new armaments systems and thus preserve the nation's "physical and intellectual" strength for more positive enterprises.

3. The United States delegation included Andrew White, Seth Low, Stanford Newell, Admiral Alfred Thayer Mahan, and Fredrick William Hols.

4. See Adam Roberts and Richard Guelff, eds., *Documents on the Laws of War* (Oxford: Clarendon, 1989), 35–109 for the texts of both the 1899 and 1907 conventions. For a summary see Leon Friedman, ed., *The Laws of War* (New York: Random House, 1972), 152–153.

5. William Hull, *The Two Hague Conferences and Their Contribution to International Law* (Boston: Gwin, 1928), 503.

6. Davis, *The United States and the Second Hague Peace Convention*, 15–16. See also Stanley Hoffman, "The Delusion of World Order," *New York Review of Books* 39 (7) (1992): 37; Friedman, ed., *The Laws of War*, 14; Ann and A. J. Thomas, *The Concept of Aggression* (Dallas: Southern Methodist University Press, 1972); and Julius Stone, *Aggression and World Order* (London: Stevens and Sons, 1958).

7. Hoffman best describes the obvious structural weaknesses of international courts in "The Delusion of World Order": "International society has neither the centralized government, judicial system, and police that characterize a well-ordered state nor the consensus on what constitutes a crime that exists in domestic affairs" (38). See also Friedman, ed., *The Laws of War*, 14; Thomas, *The Concept of Aggression*; Stone, *Aggression and World Order*.

8. Davis, *The United States and the Second Hague Peace Convention*, 25.

9. Davis, *The United States and the Second Hague Peace Convention*, 25.

10. John Keegan, *The First World War* (New York: Knopf, 1998), 17.

11. Choate, *The Two Hague Conferences*, 44. For more on Elihu Root see Richard Leopold, *Elihu Root and the Conservative Tradition* (Boston: Little, Brown, 1954).

12. Drinnon, *Facing West*, xiii.

13. Drinnon, *Facing West*, 240. A messianic justification for the American expansion was offered by Reverend Josiah Strong in his hugely popular 1885 book, *Our Country*. Strong, the head of the Christian Home Mission, described America as "Time's noblest offspring" (Drinnon, *Facing West*, 238) and predicted a "final competition of the races" (Anders Stephanson, *Manifest Destiny* [New York: Hill and Wang, 1995], 80).

14. "While once such people threatened the very continuance of civilization, they now exist only on sufferance." Drinnon, *Facing West*, 239–240.

15. Drinnon, *Facing West*, 238–240.

16. *Selections from the Correspondence of Theodore Roosevelt and Henry Cabot Lodge 1884–1901* (New York: Scribners, 1925), 313. Captain Alfred Thayer Mahan's *The Influence of Sea Power Upon History* was published in 1890 and would have a profound impact on American foreign policy in the coming decade, wrote Thomas Paterson, J. Garry Clifford, and Kenneth Hagan in *American Foreign Policy: A History—1900 to Present*, vol. 2 (Lexington: D. C. Heath, 1988). Mahan's book "became a treasured volume in the libraries of American imperialists like Henry Cabot Lodge and Theodore Roosevelt. Mahan's thesis was direct: a nation's greatness depended upon its sea power. . . . The loop was closed: a great nation required colonies" (163).

17. *Selections from the Correspondence of Theodore Roosevelt and Henry Cabot Lodge 1884–1901*, 205.

18. Leon Wolff, *Little Brown Brother* (London: Longman, 1961), 29.

19. Stephanson, *Manifest Destiny*, 88.

20. Lindqvist, *Exterminate All the Brutes*, 140. Wolff, *Little Brown Brother*, 346, 46, 140. For more on European colonialism in Africa see Adam Hochschild, *King Leopold's Ghost: A Story of Greed, Terror, and Heroism in Colonial Africa* (New York: Houghton Mifflin, 1999).

21. Judith Shklar, *Legalism: Laws, Morals, and Political Trials* (Cambridge: Harvard University Press, 1964), 1.

22. Shklar, *Legalism*, viii.

23. Shklar, *Legalism*, viii.

24. Leopold, *Elihu Root and the Conservative Tradition*, 18. In a letter dated August 10, 1899, Theodore Roosevelt described Root as "a great corporation lawyer and retained by Whitney and the street railway men"; *Selections from the Correspondence of Theodore Roosevelt and Henry Cabot Lodge*, 415.

25. Elihu Root, *The Military and Colonial Policy of the United States* (New York: AMS Press, 1970), 9. For more on Root see Philip Jessup's two-volume biography, *Elihu Root* (Hamden, Conn.: Archon, 1964), and Leopold, *Elihu Root and the Conservative Tradition*.

26. Root, *The Military and Colonial Policy of the United States*, 9.

27. Root, *The Military and Colonial Policy of the United States*, 10. Root dismissed Aguinaldo's claim to Philippine independence: "As well the friendly Indians, who

have helped us in our Indian wars, might have claimed the sovereignty of the West. They knew that we were incurring no such obligation, and they expected no such reward" (39).

28. Sven Lindqvist described the changing justifications for colonial wars: "During the nineteenth century, religious explanations were replaced by biological ones. The exterminated peoples were colored, the exterminators were white." Darwin had seen "the struggle for life" in Argentina in 1832: "Everyone here is fully convinced that this is the most just war, because it is against barbarians. Who would believe in this age such atrocities could be committed in a Christian civilised country?" Lindqvist, *Exterminate All the Brutes,* trans. Joan Tate (New York: New Press, 1996), 115–116. Richard Drinnon, *Facing West: The Metaphysics of Indian-Hating and Empire-Building* (Norman: University of Oklahoma Press, 1980), 236, 157.

29. Elihu Root, "The American Soldier," in *Miscellaneous Addresses* (Cambridge: Harvard University Press, 1916), 12.

30. Wolff, *Little Brown Brother,* 290.

31. Wolff, *Little Brown Brother,* 290.

32. Jessup, *Elihu Root,* 338. Charles Burke Elliott described the Philippines' Moro tribesmen in 1916 as "not open and fair in fight, and frequently resorts to what white men regard as improper methods of attack." The Moros' wavy-bladed Kris knives "are often prized for their service in having killed a great number of persons, and the selling price is established accordingly." Elliott, *The Philippines to the End of the Military Regime* (Indianapolis: Bobbs and Merrill, 1917), 118.

33. Wolff, *Little Brown Brother,* 207.

34. Wolff, *Little Brown Brother,* 207.

35. Wolff, *Little Brown Brother,* 207.

36. Wolff, *Little Brown Brother,* 237.

37. Wolff, *Little Brown Brother,* 237, 253.

38. Herbert Welsh, *The Other Man's Country* (Philadelphia: J. P. Lippincott, 1900), 210.

39. Welsh, *The Other Man's Country,* 210.

40. Welsh, *The Other Man's Country,* 210. See also Wolff, *Little Brown Brother,* 237.

41. Brian McAllister Linn, *The U.S. Army and Counterinsurgency in the Philippines War, 1899–1902* (Chapel Hill: University of North Carolina Press, 1989), 23.

42. Henry Graff, ed., *American Imperialism: The Philippine Insurrection* (Boston: Little, Brown, 1969), 76.

43. It read, "The undersigned, being all staff correspondents of American newspapers stationed in Manila, unite in the following declaration: We believe that, owing to official despatches from Manila made public in Washington, the people of the United States have not received a correct impression of the situation in the Philippines, but that these despatches have presented an ultra-optimistic view that is not shared by the general officers in the field" (Wolff, *Little Brown Brother,* 262).

44. "Barbarians recede or are conquered . . . that peace follows their retrogression or conquest, is due solely to the power of the mighty civilized races which have not lost the fighting instinct." Drinnon, *Facing West,* 299. Roosevelt compared the Philippine situation to the American Indian wars: "The reasoning which justifies

our having made war against Sitting Bull also justifies our having checked the outbreaks of Aguinaldo and his followers."

45. Wolff, *Little Brown Brother*, 303.

46. Wolff, *Little Brown Brother*, 331.

47. Wolff, *Little Brown Brother*, 331.

48. Drinnon, *Facing West*, 321. According to Wheaton, "Unexampled patience was exercised throughout the department in the treatment of these savages, habitually violating all the laws of war as known to civilized nations."

49. Stuart Creighton Miller, *Benevolent Assimilation: The American Conquest of the
Philippines* (New Haven: Yale University Press, 1982), 200; Drinnon, *Facing West*,
322. Captain Connell believed that cleaning up the town would give it "a sem-
blance of civilization."

50. Drinnon, *Facing West*, 323.

51. Miller, *Benevolent Assimilation*, 94–95; see also Wolff, *Little Brown Brother*, 200.

52. Miller, *Benevolent Assimilation*, 204; Wolff, *Little Brown Brother*, 203–204.

53. Miller, *Benevolent Assimilation*, 94–95. See also Drinnon, *Facing West*, 324. General Chaffee commented on General Smith's appointment: "I am told, is an energetic officer, and I hope he will prove so in command of that brigade."

54. Miller, *Benevolent Assimilation*, 220. Wolff, *Little Brown Brother*, 356; Friedman,
ed., *The Laws of War*, 803–804.

55. Friedman, ed., *The Laws of War*, 803–804.

56. Friedman, ed., *The Laws of War*, 804.

57. Miller, *Benevolent Assimilation*, 220.

58. Friedman, ed., *The Laws of War*, 804. Jacob Smith's mission on Samar was "to disarm these people and to keep them disarmed, and any means to that end is advisable." General John Franklin Bell believed that "These people need a thrashing
to teach them some good common sense" (Drinnon, *Facing West*, 325). After receiving news of the executions, Adna Chaffee cabled General Smith: "have you
been having any promiscuous killing in Samar for fun" (Miller, *Benevolent Assimilation*, 227).

59. Drinnon, *Facing West*, 315.

60. Drinnon, *Facing West*, 326–327. Major Littleton "Tony" Waller had served in
Egypt during the Arabian pasha's rebellion against Khedive and in China during
the Boxer Rebellion.

61. Miller, *Benevolent Assimilation*, 207.

62. Drinnon, *Facing West*, 327.

63. Jessup, *Elihu Root*, 342.

64. Miller, *Benevolent Assimilation*, 230; Drinnon, *Facing West*, 327. Waller did not
deny the killings; instead he argued that they fell within the scope of Jacob Smith's
orders.

65. Miller, *Benevolent Assimilation*, 230; Friedman, ed., *The Laws of War*, 803–804.

66. Friedman, ed., *The Laws of War*, 804.

67. Friedman, ed., *The Laws of War*, 801.

68. Friedman, ed., *The Laws of War*, 804.

69. Friedman, ed., *The Laws of War*, 804.

70. Friedman, ed., *The Laws of War*, 804.

71. Friedman, ed., *The Laws of War*, 804.

72. Back in Washington, Root concocted a scheme to have Smith declared "temporarily insane." Chaffee could not persuade the medical officers to back his plan.

73. Friedman, ed., *The Laws of War*, 799–800.

74. Friedman, ed., *The Laws of War*, 799–800.

75. Jessup, *Elihu Root*, 341–342. Morefield Story, Julian Cadman, and Carl Schurz were the most outspoken critics of America's Philippine policy.

76. Root justified any American atrocities under the doctrine of reprisal: "That such soldiers fighting against such an enemy, and with their own eyes witnessing such deeds should occasionally regardless of their orders retaliate by unjustifiable severities is not incredible" (Jessup, *Elihu Root*, 342). Root was also attacked by old friends like General Grenville Dodge for yielding to those who did not understand war. He wrote Dodge on July 21, 1902, "I had very much the same view of the case that you express, but a careful examination of the entire record and evidence was extremely distressing to me" (341).

77. Jessup, *Elihu Root*, 342.

78. Drinnon, *Facing West*, 329. In a personal letter to Senator Henry Cabot Lodge, Root tellingly described the trials in Manila as "the token courts-martial of a total of ten officers" (522).

79. Drinnon, *Facing West*, 522; Telford Taylor lecture at Columbia Law School, February 3, 1993.

80. Wolff, *Little Brown Brother*, 360. Wolff estimates the United States killed approximately 20,000 on the battlefield. However, Philippine civilians were the real victims in this conflict. It is estimated that out of a prewar population of 8,000,000, approximately 200,000 died of diseases like typhus and dysentery. See also Paterson, Clifford, and Hagan, *American Foreign Policy 1900 to Present*, 2:205.

81. Godfrey Hodgson, *The Colonel: The Life and Wars of Henry Stimson* (New York: Knopf, 1990), 50.

82. Daniel Patrick Moynihan, *On the Law of Nations* (Cambridge: Harvard University Press, 1990), 23.

83. Jessup, *Elihu Root*, 470.

84. Davis, *The United States and the Second Hague Peace Convention*, 282–283. See Roberts and Guelff, eds., *Documents on the Laws of War*, 35–109 for the full texts of both the 1899 and 1907 conventions. For a summary see Friedman, ed., *The Laws of War*, 152–153; Davis, *The United States and the Second Hague Peace Convention*, 15–16. See also Hoffman, "The Delusion of World Order," 37 and Choate, *The Two Hague Conferences*, 44.

85. Davis, *The United States and the Second Hague Peace Convention*, 25, 282. According to Fritz Dickman, such schemes robbed Germany of "Her superior military organization, which affords her a headstart in any general mobilization and which may well prove decisive." Andreas Hillgruber, *Germany and the Two World Wars*, trans. William C. Kirby (Cambridge: Harvard University Press, 1981), 35.

86. Hull, *The Two Hague Conferences*, 92.

87. Davis, *The United States and the Second Hague Peace Convention*, 11.

88. Hull, *The Two Hague Conferences,* 87.

89. Jessup, *Elihu Root,* 310.

90. Marc Trachtenberg, *History and Strategy* (Princeton: Princeton University Press, 1991), 77–78. See also Howard, *Restraints on War,* 9; Keegan, *The First World War,* 8. Keegan describes World War I as "the Last Civilized War," contending that "it was, despite the efforts by state propaganda machines to prove otherwise, and the cruelties of the battlefield apart, a curiously civilized war." See also Geoffrey Best, *War and Law Since 1945* (Oxford: Clarendon, 1994).

91. J. F. C. Fuller, *The Conduct of War,* 280. David Kaiser argues in *Politics and War* (Cambridge: Harvard University Press, 1990), "By the twentieth century . . . war had become an aberration, and one which imposed new, unique demands upon the whole society" (280).

92. Described by historian Andreas Hillgruber as a policy in which "military strategy . . . coerced foreign policy" (Hillgruber, *Germany and the Two World Wars,* 8). See also David Calleo, *The German Problem Reconsidered* (New York: Cambridge University Press, 1978), 8. Hillgruber characterizes the German foreign policy style as "crude and overbearing" (8). James Willis comments on the strategic thinking of the German leadership: "The Germans arrogantly placed too much faith in the potency of sheer military force, failing to recognize that such power necessarily had limits" (*Prologue to Nuremburg* [Westport, Conn.: Greenwood, 1982], 9). Alwyn Freeman defines *Kriegsraison* as "the German doctrine of military necessity whose logic conduces inevitably to the abrogation of all restraints upon belligerent activity" ("War Crimes by Enemy Nationals Administering Justice in Occupied Territories," *American Journal of International Law* 41 [1947]: 584).

93. Martin van Crevald, *The Transformation of War* (New York: Free Press, 1991), 42. In 1871, General Helmuth von Moltke devised the first plan for a war with Russia and France. In 1892, Chief of Staff Alfried von Schlieffen calculated that Germany's adversaries had twice the troops and thus began to develop a strategic plan that would help overcome these odds. See also Manuel DeLanda, *War in the Age of Intelligent Machines* (New York: Swerve Editions, 1991), 91 for a comparison to the Battle Cannae.

94. Kitchen, *Europe Between Wars,* 67.

95. Martin Kitchen, *Europe Between Wars* (London: Longman, 1988), 67. Herr von Jagow, German Secretary of Foreign Affairs, announced on April 29, 1913 that "Belgian neutrality is provided for by International Conventions and Germany is determined to respect those Conventions." At the same meeting of the Reichstag, Herr von Heeringen, Minister of War, announced, "Germany will not lose sight of the fact that the neutrality of Belgium is guaranteed by International Treaty." Henri Davignon, ed., *Belgium and Germany: Texts and Documents* (Brussels: Belgian Govt. Publication, 1921), 7. Walzer, *Just and Unjust Wars,* 240. See also Hillgruber, *Germany and the Two World Wars,* 231. Hillgruber, *Germany and the Two World Wars,* 8.

96. Willis, *Prologue to Nuremberg,* 9. This excellent and comprehensive study of the war crimes issue during World War I helped me a great deal, especially in my analysis of the Leipzig trials.

97. For complete documentation of the Belgian charges see Fernand Passelecq, *Truth and Travesty: An Analytical Study of the Belgian Government to the German White Book* (London: Sir Joseph Causton and Sons, 1916), 9. For the German response see the German Imperial Foreign Office, *The Belgian People's War: A Violation of International Law* (New York: Press of John C. Rankin, 1915). For more on the Bryce Report see Niall Ferguson, *The Pity of War* (New York: Basic, 1998), 232, 494.

98. Committee on Alleged German Outrages, *Report on Alleged German Outrages* (New York: Macmillan, 1964), 21–22. See Willis, *Prologue to Nuremberg,* 10, quoting from the 5 September 1914 *London Times.* Asquith described the destruction of Louvain as "the greatest crime against civilization and culture since the Thirty Years' War . . . a shameless holocaust." See David Kaiser on the role of public opinion: "Because of the spread of literacy, political success also depended to a great extent upon the careful management of public opinion and the press" (*Politics and War* 273). See also Paul Kennedy, *The Rise of German-Anglo Antagonism, 1860–1914* (London: Allen and Unwin, 1980).

99. John Keegan, *The Face of Battle* (New York: Penguin, 1976), 260.

100. Keegan, *The Face of Battle,* 285. In *The First World War,* Keegan writes that in the first four months of World War I, 300,000 French were killed and another 600,000 were wounded (6–7). In *War and Law Since 1945,* Best writes, "The First World War very much changed the total context in which the law of war operated and in which alone it can be properly understood. 1919 marks as much of a shock in its history as 1945" (53).

101. Willis, *Prologue to Nuremberg,* 13. The French tried and imprisoned three men for pillaging in 1914; the German government countered by imprisoning six French officers. Their release was pending the release of the Germans convicted of war crimes.

102. Hillgruber, *Germany and the Two World Wars,* 12. Assaults by hot air balloons were a violation of the second Hague Convention, but by war's end each side was attacking cities. This highlighted the dilemma of the laws of war: can a nation be expected to place itself at a strategic disadvantage by unilaterally observing international law?

103. Hillgruber, *Germany and the Two World Wars,* 12.

104. Hillgruber has observed: "Public opinion in other European nations slowly came to sense a threat, less because of the goals of German foreign policy per se than the crude, overbearing style Germany projected on the international stage" (*Germany and the Two World Wars* 12). See also Willis, *Prologue to Nuremberg,* 8. Again the Germans were largely responsible for their own image. The introduction to the German General Staff's *Manual of Land Warfare* contained several telling passages: "No consideration can be given to the dictates of humanity, such as consideration for persons and property, unless they are in accordance with the nature and object of the war."

105. Freeman, "War Crimes by Enemy Nationals Administering Justice in Occupied Territories," 591. Freeman notes: "more objectionable would seem to have been the execution of Miss Cavell within a few hours after the trial, to forestall an ap-

peal." She first met her lawyer in the courtroom and did not know of the charges against her until the arraignment. Willis, *Prologue to Nuremberg,* 28; Telford Taylor, lecture at Columbia University Law School, February 11, 1993; Howard Levie, *Terrorism in War: The Law of War Crimes* (Dobbs Ferry, N.Y.: Oceana, 1993), 225.

106. Willis, *Prologue to Nuremberg,* 27.

107. Willis, *Prologue to Nuremberg,* 27. See also Walter Gorlitz, ed., *The Kaiser and His Court: The Diaries, Note Books and Letters of Admiral Georg Alexander von Muller, Chief of the Naval Cabinet 1914–1918* (London: MacDonald and Co., 1961), 115 and Hillgruber, *Germany and the Two World Wars,* 12.

108. Paterson, Clifford, and Hagan, *American Foreign Policy: A History—1900 to Present,* 2:268. See also Willis, *Prologue to Nuremberg,* 17 and Levie, *Terrorism in War,* 21–22, 66–67, 105–107 on submarines and the laws of war.

109. Paterson, Clifford, and Hagan, *American Foreign Policy: A History—1900 to Present,* 2:268; Gray, *The U-Boat War,* 81–83.

110. Paterson, Clifford, and Hagan, *American Foreign Policy,* 267–268. The British also mined the North Sea and cut off German imports (food and cotton).

111. Willis, *Prologue to Nuremberg,* 29.

112. Willis, *Prologue to Nuremberg,* 30. See also Levie, *Terrorism in War,* 145n20.

113. Edwyn Gray, *The U-Boat War* (London: Leo Cooper, 1973), 243.

114. Gray, *The U-Boat War,* 243.

115. Willis, *Prologue to Nuremberg,* 35.

116. Willis, *Prologue to Nuremberg,* 37, 39. Many American clergymen saw the war as "Armageddon and Wilhelm II as the biblical beast of the last days" (272).

117. Elihu Root, *Miscellaneous Addresses,* 293.

118. Root, *Miscellaneous Addresses,* 288

119. Leopold, *Elihu Root and the Conservative Tradition,* 121.

120. Kaiser, *Politics and War,* 351; Christopher Simpson, *The Splendid Blond Beast: Money, Law, and Genocide in the Twentieth Century* (New York: Grove, 1993), 28. See also Jon Kirakosyan, *The Armenian Genocide* (Madison: Sphinx, 1992); Telford Taylor, *The Anatomy of the Nuremberg Trials: A Personal Memoir* (New York: Knopf, 1992), 13, 18: Ulrich Trumpner, *Germany and the Ottoman Empire* (Princeton: Princeton University Press, 1968). According to David Kaiser: "By the time of the Balkan Wars . . . they had abandoned this principle and determined instead to rebuild the empire upon a basis of ethnic Turkish nationalism . . . and to solve the problem of the Armenian minority by exterminating the Armenians" (351).

121. Karl Schwabe, *World War, Revolution, Germany, and Peacemaking* (Chapel Hill: University of North Carolina Press, 1985), 164.

122. Willis, *Prologue to Nuremberg,* 72, 117. See also Hoffman, "The Delusion of World Order," 37: "Wilsonian liberalism proposed a third principle," wrote Hoffman, "World order would emerge if the world of nation-states was also a world of constitutional governments." Lloyd Ambrosius, *Wilsonian Statecraft* (Wilmington, Del.: Scholarly Resources, 1991), 134. The League of Nations was the institution and collective security was the mechanism that would guarantee the sovereignty and territorial integrity of nations (130). Sally Marks, *The Illusion of Peace* (New York: St. Martin's, 1976), 16.

123. Willis, *Prologue to Nuremberg,* 80. See also Schwabe, *World War, Revolution, Germany, and Peacemaking,* 164.

124. Willis, *Prologue to Nuremberg,* 70.

125. Simpson, *The Splendid Blond Beast,* 23.

126. Michael Marrus, *The Nuremberg War Crimes Trials 1945–1946* (New York: Bedford, 1997), 8–10. This slim volume is a collection of some of the key war crimes documents of the twentieth century.

127. Marrus, *The Nuremberg War Crimes Trials 1945–1946,* 8–10. Even as late as 1919, Lloyd George pressed for the trial (Willis, *Prologue to Nuremberg,* 174).

128. Marrus, *The Nuremberg War Crimes Trials 1945–1946,* 8. See also Levie, *Terrorism in War,* 24–25.

129. Lansing not only invoked the act-of-state doctrine to argue that as a sovereign the Kaiser bore no legal responsibility, he also considered the trial plan a blatant implementation of *ex post facto* law (*The Foreign Relations of the United States: Paris Peace Conference 1919* [Washington: U.S. Government Printing Office, 1945], 568–569). See also Paterson, Clifford, and Hagan, *American Foreign Policy: A History—1900 to Present,* 2:285.

130. Willis, *Prologue to Nuremberg,* 41, 76.

131. Willis, *Prologue to Nuremberg,* 41, 76. See also Schwabe, *World War, Revolution, Germany and Peacemaking,* 163–166.

132. Simpson, *The Splendid Blond Beast,* 24. McDougall, *Promised Land, Crusader State,* says Robert Lansing described the Treaty of Versailles as "thoroughly bad" and the League of Nations as "thoroughly useless" (142). Secretary of State Lansing asked critics: "Had you rather have the Kaiser or the Bolsheviks?" According to Schwabe, *World War, Revolution, Germany, and Peacemaking,* "In short, the American legal experts were not willing to abandon the framework of existing international law" (164).

133. Willis, *Prologue to Nuremberg,* 24. Historian James Willis speculates that President Wilson acceded to British demands on the war crimes issue in order to obtain their support for the Monroe Doctrine amendment: "The close conjunction of decisions makes such a thesis not unreasonable. Wilson compromised on the Kaiser's trial on April 8, and on the evening of April 10, the British helped him override French opposition to the amendment."

134. Marrus, *The Nuremberg War Crimes Trials,* 10.

135. Marrus, *The Nuremberg War Crimes Trials,* 10.

136. See Paul Piccone and G L. Ulmen, "American Imperialism and International Law," *Telos* 72 (Summer 1987): 60.

137. Piccone and Ulmen, "American Imperialism and International Law," 60.

138. Willis, *Prologue to Nuremberg,* 177.

139. Willis, *Prologue to Nuremberg,* 60. The most famous myth was that the General Staff had been stabbed in the back by weak-kneed politicians and that the war crimes accusations were all false. See also 72, 117. Even as late as 1919, Lloyd George pressed for the trial.

140. Willis, *Prologue to Nuremberg,* 60.

141. Taylor, *The Anatomy of the Nuremberg Trials,* 16.

142. Willis, *Prologue to Nuremberg*, 100.

143. Levie, *Terrorism in War*, 27.

144. Levie, *Terrorism in War*, 28.

145. Levie, *Terrorism in War*, 28.

146. John Appleman, *Military Tribunals and International Crimes* (Westport, Conn.: Greenwood, 1971), 54–57. Bismarck offered very pragmatic advice on the treatment of the vanquished. "People insist that, in conflicts between states, the conqueror should sit in judgment upon the conquered, moral code in hand, and inflict punishment upon him for what he has done.... Punishment and revenge have nothing to do with policy. Policy must not meddle with the calling of the Nemesis, or aspire to exercise the judge's office." Mortiz Busch, *Our Chancellor* (New York: Scribners, 1884), 1:99; from Fuller, *The Conduct of War*, 305.

147. Claud Mullins, *The Leipzig Trials* (London: H.F.G Witherby, 1921), 42.

148. Mullins, *The Leipzig Trials* , 99.

149. Mullins, *The Leipzig Trials*, 12. The tribunal admonished the defendants, "Don't imagine that you are going to get rid of this terrible affair by trying to put the blame upon a dead man: that won't do."

150. Friedman, ed., *The Laws of War*, 876.

151. Friedman, ed., *The Laws of War*, 880. The judgment read: "The rule of International Law, which is here involved, is simple and is universally known. No possible doubt can exist with regard to the question of its applicability. The Court must in this instance affirm Patzig's guilt of killing contrary to International Law."

152. Friedman, ed., *The Laws of War*, 868.

153. Mullins, *The Leipzig Trials*, 66–67; Levie, *Terrorism in War*, 31.

154. Friedman, ed., *The Laws of War*, 882. See also Willis, *Prologue to Nuremberg*, 135.

155. Mullins, *The Leipzig Trials*, 162.

156. Willis, *Prologue to Nuremberg*, 135.

157. Levie, *Terrorism in War*, 32.

158. Mullins, *The Leipzig Trials*, 162. Taylor, *The Anatomy of the Nuremberg Trials*, 12, 17.

159. Levie, *Terrorism in War*, 32.

160. Levie, *Terrorism in War*, 516*n*246.

161. "However, with official connivance, and wholehearted public approval, Boldt escaped in November 1921 and Dithmar in January 1922" Levie, *Terrorism in War*, 33.

162. Willis, *Prologue to Nuremberg*, 135.

163. Willis, *Prologue to Nuremberg*, 23.

164. Piccone and Ulmen, "American Imperialism and International Law," 62.

165. Quincy Wright, *A Study of War* (Chicago: University of Chicago Press, 1969), 342.

166. Wright, *A Study of War*, 342. Both Grotius and Gentili recognized the necessity of punishing those who initiated unjust wars.

167. Wright, *A Study of War*, 342.

168. Howard, *Restraints on War*, 11. Howard describes their effort to create not simply laws of war, but laws against war. This was one in a series of treaties written in the late 1920s all aimed at outlawing "aggression."

169. Marrus, *The Nuremberg War Crimes Trials,* 14. See also Finch, "The Progressive Development of International Law," 613.

170. For nearly three hundred years of international relations, war was considered a legally admissible instrument of policy independent (Ulmen, "American Imperialism and International Law," 49). Sally Thomas has argued that the lawful/unlawful distinction was a departure from the concept of just and unjust war. The illegality of war was not a judgment based on "the intrinsic injustice of the cause of war, but of a breach of a formal procedural requirement" (17). Quincy Wright, "International Law and Guilt by Association," *The American Journal of International Law* 43(1949): 753.

171. Hodgson, *The Colonel,* 164.

172. According to Stimson's biographer, Godfrey Hodgson, "Stimson grew up in admiration of men . . . Theodore Roosevelt, Elihu Root, Albert Beveridge, and Brooks Adams" (Hodgson, *The Colonel,* 20, 49).

173. In 1932, as Secretary of State, he condemned the Japanese invasion of Manchuria as a violation of the Washington Conference Treaty of 1922 and the Kellogg-Briand Pact (Hodgson, *The Colonel,* 164).

174. Hodgson, *The Colonel,* 164.

175. Hodgson, *The Colonel,* 164; see also *The New York Times,* August 9, 1932. Paterson, Clifford, and Hagan, *American Foreign Policy: A History—1900 to Present,* 1:339. Stimson was less concerned about the fate of China than "the specter of great powers seizing new empires to rescue themselves from economic depression" (339).

176. Hodgson, *The Colonel,* 158; Paterson, Clifford, and Hagan, *American Foreign Policy,* 2:280. Accordingly, Wilson's *raison d'etat* was "the expansion of freedom." However, "freedom" was defined by the Americans. Although the Treaty of Versailles abolished colonialism, the Americans refused to abandon the Monroe Doctrine. See also Ambrosius, *Wilsonian Statecraft,* 56. Tucker, "Brave New World Order," 26. Piccone and Ulmen, "American Imperialism and International Law," 63. See also Hodgson, *The Colonel,* 158.

177. Piccone and Ulmen, "American Imperialism and International Law," 57, 63. To Schmitt, the American redefinition of "recognition" was of vital importance. "In Schmitt's estimation, such a doctrine had a clearly interventionist character. It meant that the United States could effectively control every governmental and constitutional change in every country in the Western Hemisphere" (63).

178. Paterson, Clifford, and Hagan, *American Foreign Policy: A History—1900 to Present,* 2:375. See also International Military Tribunal, *Trial of the Major War Criminals* (Nuremberg: International Military Tribunal, 1947), 5:322; Ann and John Tusa, *The Nuremberg Trial* (New York: Atheneum, 1984), 21. The conferees felt that the Germans had violated the laws of war so egregiously that simple drumhead justice would not suffice.

179. Whitney Harris, *Tyranny on Trial* (Dallas: Southern Methodist University Press, 1954), 4.

180. Harris, *Tyranny on Trial,* 4. See also Robert Conot, *Justice at Nuremberg* (New York: Carol and Graf, 1983), 9.

181. John Lewis Gaddis, *The United States, Russia, and the Origins of the Cold War* (New York: Columbia University Press, 1972), 8.

182. The entire text of the Moscow Declaration can be found in the Trials of the German War Criminals (Washington, D.C.: U.S. Government Printing Office, 1949). Bradley F. Smith, *The Road to Nuremberg* (New York: Basic, 1981), 8–9. President Roosevelt's style was to deemphasize political questions to prevent divisions in the wartime alliance (39). See also Tusa, *The Nuremberg Trial*, 50–51 and Taylor, *The Anatomy of the Nuremberg Trials*, 34. Bradley F. Smith offers the most comprehensive account of the pretrial debates in *The American Road to Nuremberg: The Documentary Record* (Stanford: Hoover Institution Press, 1982).

183. Frank M. Buscher, *The U.S. War Crimes Program in Germany, 1946–1955* (Westport, Conn.: Greenwood, 1989), 8. Buscher ably summarizes the historiography of the occupation period. See also John Gimbel, *The American Occupation of Germany* (Palo Alto: Stanford University Press, 1968); John Montgomery, *Forced to Be Free: The Artificial Revolution in Germany and Japan* (Chicago: University of Chicago Press, 1967); and Paul Hammond, "Directives for the Occupation of Germany: The Washington Controversy," in Harold Stein, ed., *American Civil-Military Decisions* (Birmingham: University of Alabama Press, 1963). For German views see Walter Dorn, "*Die Debatte über die amerikanische Besatzungspolitik für Deutschland (1944–1945)*" *Vierteljahrshefte für Zeitgeschichte* 20(1972): 39–62; and Gunter Moltmann, "*Zur Formulierung der amerikanischen Besatzungspolitik in Deutschland am Endedes Zweiten Weltkrieges,*" *Vierteljahrschefte für Zeitgeschichte* 15(1967): 299–322.

184. Hans Morgenthau Jr., *Morgenthau Diaries* (New York: Da Capo, 1974), 2:443–444. The American Jewish Conference expressed a similar view in a letter to Secretary of State Cordell Hull: "These crimes cannot go unpunished without destroying the legal and moral foundations upon which our civilization rests." (For the original text see 30–44 and the introduction to the memo from Henry Morgenthau to President Roosevelt, 5 September 1944, in Smith, ed., *The American Road to Nuremberg*, 27–29.)

185. Smith, *The American Road to Nuremberg*, 8. Presidential Memorandum for the Secretary of War, 26 August 1944, in Smith, ed., *The American Road to Nuremberg*, 20–21. It would be generous to say that FDR waffled on war crimes policy: it had been a detail in a two-theater war.

186. Smith, *The American Road to Nuremberg*, 20–21.

187. From Henry Morgenthau Jr. to President Roosevelt (The Morgenthau Plan), 5 September 1944, in Smith, ed., *The American Road to Nuremberg*, 27–29.

188. Smith, *The American Road to Nuremberg*, 28.

189. Taylor, *The Anatomy of the Nuremberg Trials*, 107–111.

190. Robert Abzug, *Inside the Vicious Heart* (New York: Oxford University Press, 1985), 44.

191. Smith, ed., *The American Road to Nuremberg*, 6–8. *The Road to Nuremberg* and *The American Road to Nuremberg* are two different books, both by B. F. Smith.

192. Conot, *Justice at Nuremberg*, 11.

193. Conot, *Justice at Nuremberg*, 13.

194. Secretary of War Henry Stimson to President Roosevelt, 9 September 1944, in Smith, ed., *The American Road to Nuremberg*, 30–31.

195. Smith, ed., *The American Road to Nuremberg*, 31.

196. Smith, ed., *The American Road to Nuremberg*, 31.

197. Tusa, *The Nuremberg Trial*, 60.

198. Memorandum, "Major War Criminals" by British Lord Chancellor Sir John Simon, 4 September 1944, in Smith, ed., *The American Road to Nuremberg*, 33–37. Churchill advocated a similar plan (46). The British were adamant about not redefining war crimes, but as victory neared, this conservative approach fell by the wayside (18).

199. Smith, ed., *The American Road to Nuremberg*, 1. The title of the first chapter is "The Great German War on the Potomac." The Tusas describe the idea for a trial as having "originated in an interdepartmental row in Washington over plans for the future of conquered Germany" (50). Smith describes Roosevelt's treatment of the war crimes question: "The reason for this lack of preparation was simple: Nothing definitive had come down from the White House indicating what Franklin Roosevelt thought should be done with the remains of central Europe once Nazism had been destroyed. The President was still stalling on the question, as he had been stalling since the U.S. entered the war in 1941" (*The Road to Nuremberg* 13).

200. Henry Stimson to Henry Morgenthau, 9 September 1944, in Smith, ed., *The American Road to Nuremberg*, 30. Stimson wrote: "My basic objection to the proposed methods of treating Germany which were discussed this morning was that in addition to a system of preventative and educative punishment they would add the dangerous weapon of complete economic oppression."

201. Henry Stimson to Henry Morgenthau, 9 September 1944, in Smith, ed., *The American Road to Nuremberg*, 30.

202. Tusa, *The Nuremberg Trial*, 61.

203. Kai Bird, *The Chairman: John McCloy, the Making of the American Establishment* (New York: Simon and Schuster, 1991), 258.

204. Tusa, *The Nuremberg Trial*, 50.

205. William Bosch, *Judgment on Nuremberg* (Chapel Hill: University of North Carolina Press, 1970), 9. Many believed that the vindictive tenor of the Treaty of Versailles had fostered a political atmosphere that allowed the seed of National Socialism to germinate and flourish. The twin debacles of the Versailles and the Leipzig trials contained practical lessons for the victors of World War II." This view would later play into the hands of post-World War II German nationalists (Louis Snyder, *The Roots of German Nationalism* [Bloomington: University of Indiana Press, 1978], 175). Karl-Heinz Janssen makes a similar point in "*Versailles und Nürnberg: Zur Psycholgie der Kreigsschuldfrage in Deutschland*"; to Janssen, Nuremberg and Versailles "refers to a continuity, to a link between World War I and World War II—both have negative connotations despite five years of 're-education' and thirty-eight years of political education" (in *Licht in den Schatten der Vergangen-*

heit, eds. Jörg Friedrich and Jörg Wollenberg, Frankfurt/Main: Ullstein Zeitgeschichte, 1987), 26.

206. The Secretary of War to the Secretary of State, 27 October 1944, in Smith, ed., *The American Road to Nuremberg*, 40–41.

207. Tusa, *The Nuremberg Trial*, 52. They describe the Secretary of War's thinking: "He was unwilling to criminalize the entire German nation, but saw a therapeutic value in punishing internationally recognized war criminals" (52).

208. Bird, *The Chairman*, 205. David Wyman, *The Abandonment of the Jews* (New York: Pantheon, 1984), 14. Martin Gilbert, *Auschwitz and the Allies* (New York: Holt, 1981), 94. In 1942 former member of the Polish Foreign Ministry and underground leader Jan Karski disguised himself as a concentration camp guard and entered the Belzec concentration camp. Karski wrote a report of what he had seen and traveled to London and Washington Washington in 1943 and presented his first-hand account to President Roosevelt, Secretary Stimson, and OSS Chief William Donovan. He also met with Felix Frankfurter, whom he hoped would be a natural ally; the Supreme Court Justice was an active Zionist. But after meeting at the Polish embassy, Frankfurter told the Polish ambassador that he could not believe the stories: "Mr. Ambassador, I did not say that this young man is lying. I said that I am unable to believe him." Frankfurter was not alone; Walter Lippman also met with Karski "but, unlike other columnists who heard Karski's story, he—the only Jew among them—decided not to write about it" (206–207). See also "Nazi Mass Killing Laid Bare in Camp," *New York Times*, August 30, 1944.

209. American war crimes prosecutor Colonel Telford Taylor credited a coalition of American lawyer-statesmen and former New Dealers with "the assemblage of all these concepts in a single trial package." Taylor described the backgrounds of the "handful of American lawyers, all but Cutter . . . from New York City. Some of them (Stimson, McCloy) were what today we would call 'moderate' Republicans; several (Rosenman, Chanler, Herbert Weschler) were Democrats. Elitist and generally accustomed to personal prosperity, all had strong feeling of noblesse oblige" (Taylor, *The Anatomy of the Nuremberg Trials*, 42).

210. Taylor, *The Anatomy of the Nuremberg Trials*, 42.

211. *The Foreign Relations of the United States: The Conference at Quebec, 1944* (Washington, D.C.: U.S. Government Printing Office, 1972), 124–125.

212. *The Foreign Relations of the United States 1945* (Washington, D.C.: U.S. Government Printing Office, 1968), 3:1162–1164. Bernays hoped to try "Nazi organizations themselves rather than individuals and to convict them and all their members of engaging in a criminal conspiracy to control the world, to persecute minorities, to break treaties, to invade other countries and to commit war" (1163).

213. Conot, *Justice at Nuremberg*, 12. As Geoffrey Best observes, the worst atrocities of World War II were not war crimes under the traditional laws of war: "International law at that date held it no crime for a government to murder its own subjects. Civilians had, within the past decade, been killed on so many occasions, in such varied circumstances, and under so many pretexts, that there could be real difficulty in distinguishing the more justiciable instances from the less" (*War and Law Since 1945*, 64).

214. "Trial of European War Criminals," Colonel Murray Bernays, 15 September 1944, in Smith, ed., *The American Road to Nuremberg*, 33–34.

215. David Luban, *Legal Modernism* (Ann Arbor: University of Michigan Press, 1994), 335.

216. Smith, ed., *The American Road to Nuremberg*, 35. According to international legal theorists Oppenheim and Lauderpacht, traditional war crimes consisted of: violations of the recognized rules of war, hostilities committed by individuals who are not members of armed forces, espionage, treason, and marauding acts. According to critics, the Allies had no precedent or positive statute to justify trying statesmen and industrialists. (Nuremberg defense attorney Otto Kranzbühler in Wilbourn Benton, ed., *Nuremberg: German Views of the War Trials* [Dallas: Southern Methodist University Press, 1955], 111).

217. Smith, ed., *The American Road to Nuremberg*, 34. The notion that Germans could not be punished for crimes against German Jews highlighted the obsolescence of the laws of war. The bombing of cities was not a war crime; neither the United States nor Germany signed 1925 Geneva accords. There was a sense that executions and court-martials would not reach the root of the problem: "the Bernays plan sought to solve the need to purge German society by means other than the Morgenthau Plan" (55). These acts would not go unpunished under the Bernays plan: "Therefore, such technicalities as the question whether the extermination of fellow Germans by Nazi Germans was unlawful, or whether this could be a 'war crime' if it was perpetrated before there was a state of war, would be unimportant, if you recognize as the basic crime the Nazi conspiracy" (33).

218. Smith, ed., *The American Road to Nuremberg*, 35. "Trial of the German War Criminals by Col. Murray Bernays," September 15, 1944, in Smith, ed., *The American Road to Nuremberg*, 33.

219. Smith, ed., *The American Road to Nuremberg*, 36.

220. Smith, ed., *The American Road to Nuremberg*, 36.

221. Hans Ehard, "The Nuremberg Trial Against the Major War Criminals and International Law," *The American Journal of International Law* 43 (1949): 225. Ehard commented on the concept of conspiracy in Continental law: "the concept is not one familiar to continental law. It has developed in Anglo-Saxon customary law" (227).

222. Hans Ehard, "The Nuremberg Trial Against the Major War Criminals and International Law," *The American Journal of International Law* 43 (1949): 225. See also Tusa, *The Nuremberg Trial*, 57; Taylor, *The Anatomy of the Nuremberg Trials*, 36–37. Telford Taylor described the plan's major deviation as "the Bernays additions."

223. "Memo for the President from the Secretaries of State, War and Navy," November 11, 1944, in Smith, ed., *The American Road to Nuremberg*, 43. The Secretary of War attempted to combine the Bernays Plan with his own pet project (33–35). During the war, several of the smaller, weaker Allied nations resurrected the idea of criminalizing "aggressive war." Stimson seized the opportunity to deem aggression the Nazi's "supreme crime" (33–35). Otto Kirchheimer, *Political Justice: The Use of Legal Procedure for Political Ends* (Princeton: Princeton University Press, 1961), viii, 19, 51. "By utilizing the devices of justice, politics contracts some

ill-defined and spurious obligations. Circumstantial and contradictory, the link-
age of politics and justice is characterized by both promise and blasphemy" (9).
Henry Stimson diary entry, January 19, 1945, in Smith, ed., *The American Road to
Nuremberg*, 130.

224. Smith, ed., *The American Road to Nuremberg*, 76–77.

225. "Attorney General's Memo on the Punishment of Criminals," January 5, 1945, in
Smith, ed., *The American Road to Nuremberg*, 91. See also Weschler's critique of the
aggression charge, 84–90.

226. James Weingartner, *Crossroads of Death: The Story of the Malmedy Massacre and
Trial* (Berkeley: University of California Press, 1979), 10. Also see Michael Reynolds, *The Devil's Adjutant: Jochen Peiper, Panzer Leader* (New York: Sarpedon,
1995); Lothar Greil, *Oberst der Waffen SS Joachim Peiper und der Malmedy Process*
(Munchen: Schild-Verlag, 1977) and Leo Kessler, *SS Peiper* (London: Leo Cooper,
1986).

227. Weingartner, *Crossroads of Death*, 10.

228. Weingartner, *Crossroads of Death*, 65.

229. Tusa, *The Nuremberg Trial*, 30. There is a consensus among Nuremberg historians
that the Malmedy Massacre marked a turning point in the debate over America's
war crimes policy: "America, thanks to geography, had been insulated against the
horrors of the War. Only in December 1944 did the American public have its first
direct experience of Nazi brutality."

230. Weingartner, *Crossroads of Death*, 12.

231. Smith, ed., *The American Road to Nuremberg*, 89. "Memo from Assistant Attorney General Herbert Weschler to Attorney General Francis Biddle," December 29,
1944, in Smith, ed., *The American Road to Nuremberg*, 84–90.

232. "Presidential Memo for the Secretary of State," January 3, 1945, in Smith, ed., *The
American Road to Nuremberg*, 92. By 1945, a once civil discourse among various
government agencies had turned into a no-holds-barred battle for control of war
crimes policy. After having his well-considered criticism unceremoniously brushed
aside, Major General John Weir called on Harvard Law School Dean Edmund
Morgan to assess the conspiracy and aggressive war charges. "Questions posed by
Major General John Weir to Edmund Morgan, January 12, 1945," in Smith, ed.,
The American Road to Nuremberg, 107. Morgan found the conspiracy charge "so
highly questionable and so novel to international law that it should be entertained
only in the most necessitous circumstances. . . . The conspiracy theory is too thin a
veneer to hide the real purpose, namely, the creation of a hereto unknown international offense by individuals, *ex post facto*."

233. Stimson wrote in his diary, "I told him [FDR] of my own view of the importance
as a matter of record of having a state trial with records" ("Diary Entry of Henry L.
Stimson," January 19, 1945, in Smith, ed., *The American Road to Nuremberg*, 130).

234. "Diary Entry of Henry L. Stimson," January 19, 1945, in Smith, ed., *The American
Road to Nuremberg*, 130. The Secretaries of State, War, and Treasury prepared another memo for the President to take to Yalta, in the hope that the Big Three would
commit to joint proceedings against the Axis leaders. But the issue never made

the agenda; the Third Reich was collapsing nearly as fast as the tripartite alliance and questions about the fate of the Axis leaders were eclipsed by larger issues— namely, the fate of Europe (Smith, ed., *The American Road to Nuremberg*, 52–53). Tusa, *The Nuremberg Trial*, 18, 19, 66–67. Ironically, this was a reverse of the situation after World War I, when the Americans were clinging to the conservative position as part of a larger effort to thwart the war crimes prosecutions sought by the British, the French, and the Belgians. An American delegation traveled to London in early April 1945, to confer with the British about war crimes policy. British foreign secretary Lord Simon attempted to force them into accepting a more traditional plan with summary trials and executions for Hitler and his cronies ("The argument for summary process against Hitler and co., Prepared by Lord Simon," in Smith, ed., *The American Road to Nuremberg*, 155–157).

235. Tusa, *The Nuremberg Trial*, 66; Smith, ed., *The American Road to Nuremberg*, 139. Cutter and Rosenman hoped to redraft the proposal to make the proceedings appear more like a trial.

236. Tusa, *The Nuremberg Trial*, 66. See also Smith, ed., *The Road to Nuremberg*, 170–173.

237. Tusa, *The Nuremberg Trial*, 66.

238. Tusa, *The Nuremberg Trial*, 66.

239. Tusa, *The Nuremberg Trial*, 67. See also "Memo on Proposals for the Prosecution and Punishment of Certain War Criminals and other Offenders," April 25–30, 1945, in Smith, ed., *The American Road to Nuremberg*, 162–172.

240. Tusa, *The Nuremberg Trial*, 69. Daniel Patrick Moynihan, *On the Law of Nations*, 144.

241. Tusa, *The Nuremberg Trial*, 68. In 1941, Jackson had argued that war could no longer be considered a right of states and explicitly rejected the traditional rules of the European state system and argued that they had been replaced by new concepts: "It does not appear necessary to treat all wars as legal and just simply because we have no courts to try the accused" (Tusa, *The Nuremberg Trial*, 68). In 1941, in a speech before the American Bar Association, Jackson claimed: "The fundamental principles of the 19th century, according to which all warring parties must be handled equally, have been swept away by the League of Nations to the principal sanctions against aggressors, through the Kellogg-Briand Pact and the Argentina Declaration outlawing war. We must return to earlier and healthier conceptions."

242. Tusa, *The Nuremberg Trial*, 69.

243. Taylor describes Jackson's view of the court's legal basis: "Jackson not only invoked the Kellogg-Briand Pact but, more compellingly the history of the English common law, which developed not primarily by act of parliament but by 'decisions reached from time to time in adapting settled principles to new situations' " (*The Anatomy of the Nuremberg Trials*, 55).

244. Taylor, *The Anatomy of the Nuremberg Trials*, 55. In June 1945, when, according to Bradley Smith, "American idealistic fervor was burning at white heat," Taylor candidly admitted that many of these decisions were political and recognized the necessity of acknowledging this basic fact. He maintained that the *ex post facto* ar-

gument was "Not, I believe, a bothersome question if we keep in mind that this is a *political* decision to declare and apply a principle of international law." See also "An Approach to the Preparation of the Prosecution of Axis Criminality by Telford Taylor, early June 1945," in Bradley F. Smith, ed., *The American Road to Nuremberg: The Documentary Record 1944–1945* (Stanford: Hoover Institution Press, 1982), 209. During the pretrial period Taylor wrote a memo arguing that a trial for the German leaders would "give meaning to the war. To validate the casualties we have caused."

3. THE AMERICAN WAR CRIMES PROGRAM

1.   Conrad Crane, *Bombs, Cities, and Civilians* (Lawrence: University of Kansas Press, 1993), 1, 143.

2.   Crane, *Bombs, Cities, and Civilians*, 143. See Geoffrey Best, *War and Law Since 1945* (Oxford: Clarendon, 1994), 51 on total war and the role of civilians: "the civilian's probable participation in the workings of an economy perhaps totally mobilized for national struggle made it difficult to distinguish him as clearly as the principle of non-combatant immunity required."

3.   Otto Kirchheimer, *Political Justice: The Use of Legal Procedure for Political Ends* (Princeton: Princeton University Press, 1961), 336–337. The philosophers (Kirchheimer and Arendt) tend to be more dismissive of *tu quoque* charges than the lawyers. Kirchheimer finds this argument extremely weak: "In a wider sense, the *tu quoque* argument could be leveled against any type of terrestrial justice. Only the archangel descending on judgment day would be exempt from the reproach that blame and praise have not been distributed according to everyone's due desert" (337).

4.   Ann and John Tusa, *The Nuremberg Trial* (New York: Atheneum, 1984), 72. The British Foreign Office and the U.S. State Department made similar arguments. George Kennan was another important official who criticized Soviet participation in any trial.

5.   Allen Paul, *Katyn: The Untold Story of Stalin's Polish Massacre* (New York: Scribners, 1991), 58. See also Ronald Hingley, *The Russian Secret Police* (New York: Simon and Schuster, 1970), 168–171. On the NKVD under Beria and the first mobile killing squads see Lennard Gerson, *The Secret Police in Lenin's Russia* (Philadelphia: Temple University Press, 1976). Both Alan Bullock (*Hitler and Stalin* [New York: Knopf, 1992]) and Robert Conquest claim that between thirteen million and fifteen million died during collectivization (*The Great Terror: A Reassessment* [New York: Oxford University Press, 1990], 277). Walter Lacquer has described Stalin's actions as "without precedence in peacetime in modern history" (*Stalin* [London: Undwin and Hyman, 1990], 125).

6.   Paul, *Katyn*, 72. According to Troutbeck: "Surely the Russians had 'entered into a common plan or enterprise aimed at domination over other nations' which involved 'atrocities, persecutions and deportations' on a colossal scale. 'Is not the Soviet government not employed today in the very same thing in Poland, the Baltic States, the Balkan States, Turkey and Persia? (Someone added in the margin: And

what about Finland?') . . . There have been two criminal enterprises this century—by Germans and Russians. To set up one lot of conspirators as judges of the other robs the whole procedure of the basis of morality.'" For more on Stalin's massacre of Soviet nationals see Lacquer, *Stalin* and Robert Conquest, *The Harvest of Sorrow* (New York: Oxford University Press, 1986). For a comparison to Hitler see Bullock, *Hitler and Stalin.* See also Peter Baldwin, *Reworking the Past: Hitler, the Holocaust, and the Historians' Debate* (Boston: Beacon, 1991), 14 and Sven Lindqvist, *Exterminate All the Brutes,* trans. Joan Tate (New York: New Press, 1996). Lindqvist offers a novel argument about the *Historikerstreit:* "All German historians participating in this debate seem to look in the same direction. None looks to the west. But Hitler did. What Hitler wished to create when he sought *Lebensraum* in the east was a continental equivalent of the British Empire. It was in the British and other western European peoples that he found the models, of which the extermination of the Jews is, in Nolte's words, 'a distorted copy'" (10).

7. Bullock, *Hitler and Stalin,* 497.

8. Paul, *Katyn,* 111, x, 58. The Cheka perfected what the Germans later called *Nackenschuss,* or a shot in the nape of the neck. By the 1930s it had become the standard method used by the NKVD to kill Stalin's purge victims and others.

9. Between August 9 and August 13, 1941, Roosevelt and Churchill met in Newfoundland to outline their war aims. The eight-point Atlantic Charter was a vague restatement of Wilsonian goals like collective security and national self-determination. Richard Lukas, *The Forgotten Holocaust* (Lexington: University of Kentucky Press, 1986), 232. It was difficult for the Allies to denounce Stalin; they had gone to great lengths to reinvent him. In 1943, Stalin was named *Time* magazine's man of the year. Paul, *Katyn,* xi. Thomas Paterson, J. Garry Clifford, and Kenneth Hagan, eds., *American Foreign Policy: A History—1900 to Present* (Lexington: D. C. Heath, 1988), 2:372–375.

10. Lukas, *The Forgotten Holocaust,* 232.

11. Lukas, *The Forgotten Holocaust,* x.

12. Robert Abzug, *Inside the Vicious Heart* (New York: Oxford University Press, 1985), 30.

13. Abzug, *Inside the Vicious Heart,* 52.

14. Abzug, *Inside the Vicious Heart,* 90.

15. Abzug, *Inside the Vicious Heart,* 90.

16. Abzug, *Inside the Vicious Heart,* 94.

17. Abzug, *Inside the Vicious Heart,* 93.

18. Paul Fussell, *Doing Battle: The Making of a Skeptic* (Boston: Little, Brown, 1996), 291.

19. Fussell, *Doing Battle,* 291.

20. Fussell, *Doing Battle,* 291.

21. Telford Taylor, *The Anatomy of the Nuremberg Trials: A Personal Memoir* (New York: Knopf, 1992).

22. Taylor, *The Anatomy of the Nuremberg Trials,* 63.

23. Tusa, *The Nuremberg Trial,* 76–77.

24. Tusa, *The Nuremberg Trial,* 75.

25. Tusa, *The Nuremberg Trial*, 77.

26. Tusa, *The Nuremberg Trial*, 78. The Tusas described the Soviet judge's action as "so untypical . . . one wonders if he had been ordered by Moscow to trail a coat."

27. Tusa, *The Nuremberg Trial*, 78. "An Approach to the Preparation of the Prosecution of Axis Criminality" in Bradley F. Smith, ed., *The American Road to Nuremberg: The Documentary Record 1944–1945* (Stanford: Hoover Institution Press, 1982), 211.

28. Taylor, *The Anatomy of the Nuremberg Trials*, 62–63.

29. Taylor, *The Anatomy of the Nuremberg Trials*, 61.

30. Taylor, *The Anatomy of the Nuremberg Trials*, 63. "In all probability Jackson was making a 'show of force,' and in fact he had a lot of force to show" (62–63).

31. Taylor, *The Anatomy of the Nuremberg Trials*, 81, 67. Tusa, *The Nuremberg Trial*, 76–77. Gros rejected the notion that "The prosecutor could come out of the blue with evidences which were completely unknown until the moment of the trial, opening a Pandora's box of unhappy surprises" (77).

32. Taylor, *The Anatomy of the Nuremberg Trials*, 67. In *Aggression and World Order: A Critique of United Nations Theories on Aggression* (Berkeley: University of California Press, 1958), Julius Stone considered the comparison between international and domestic to be erroneous: "But in international society no means exist even of collective redress of the gravest wrongs, whether judicial or private, legal or moral, much less of collective adjustment of law to minimum standards of justice. In such a society, this single notion of 'aggression' is being asked to perform within the monstrously wide ambit of all inter-State relations, most of the major tasks of criminal and constitutional law, not to speak of much of the law of property, torts and procedure" (130).

33. Taylor, *The Anatomy of the Nuremberg Trials*, 66.

34. Taylor, *The Anatomy of the Nuremberg Trials*, 66.

35. Taylor, *The Anatomy of the Nuremberg Trials*, 67. See also Tusa, *The Nuremberg Trial*, 73. Jackson argued that "the idea of separate trials for each nation . . . might be the easiest and most satisfactory way of reconciling it."

36. Taylor, *The Anatomy of the Nuremberg Trials*, 70. Dean believed the source of friction was William Donovan, who "clearly does not like the Russians much." Dean believed the Americans were trying "to magnify the differences between their views" and those of the Russians.

37. Taylor, *The Anatomy of the Nuremberg Trials*, 70; Tusa, *The Nuremberg Trial*, 103; Robert Conot, *Justice at Nuremberg* (New York: Carroll and Graf, 1983), 482–485. B. F Smith also agreed that by the end of the London Conference, Justice Jackson hoped to exclude the Soviets from the proceedings.

38. Taylor, *The Anatomy of the Nuremberg Trials*, 68.

39. Taylor, *The Anatomy of the Nuremberg Trials*, 70–71. Article VII reads: "The Three Governments have taken note of the discussions which have been proceeding in recent weeks in London . . . with a view to reaching agreement on the methods of trial of those major war criminals." Whitney Harris, *Tyranny on Trial* {Dallas: Southern Methodist University Press, 1954), 21.

40. Tusa, *The Nuremberg Trial*, 79–80.

41. Jay Baird, ed., *From Nuremberg to My Lai* (Lexington, Ky.: D. C. Heath, 1972), 3–8. This very interesting collection includes both the London Agreement and the Charter.

42. David Luban, *Legal Modernism* (Ann Arbor: University of Michigan Press, 1994), 335*n*.

43. Luban, *Legal Modernism*, 335*n*.

44. Taylor, *The Anatomy of the Nuremberg Trials*, 648.

45. Taylor, *The Anatomy of the Nuremberg Trials*, 648.

46. Jörg Friedrich, "Nuremberg and the Germans," in Belinda Cooper, ed., *War Crimes: The Legacy of Nuremberg* (New York: TV Books, 1999), 87. Historian John Teschke makes a similar point in *Hitler's Legacy: West Germany Confronts the Aftermath of the Third Reich* (New York: Peter Lang, 1999): "After the treatment the Soviet Union had received at the hands of Nazi armies, the Russian soldiers exercised all of the traditional perquisites of conquerors as a way of settling a few scores" (15).

47. Friedrich, "Nuremberg and the Germans," 87.

48. Friedrich, "Nuremberg and the Germans," 87.

49. David Irving, *Nuremberg: The Last Battle* (London: Focal Point, 1999), 161. See also Aleksandr Solzhenitsyn, *The Gulag Archipelago* (New York: Harper & Row, 1978) and Conquest, *The Great Terror*.

50. For more on purges, see Andrei Vyshinksky, "The Treason Case Summed Up," Red Flag, 1938, in The Nuremberg Trial and International Law, ed. George Ginsburg and V. N. Kudriartsev (Leiden: Martinus Nijhoff Publishers, 1990), 23.

51. Irving, *Nuremberg*, 161.

52. Irving, *Nuremberg*, 161–162.

53. Tusa, *The Nuremberg Trial*, 86.

54. Bradley F. Smith, *Reaching Judgment at Nuremberg* (New York: Basic, 1977), 303.

55. Wilbourn Benton, ed., *Nuremberg: German Views of the War Trials* (Dallas: Southern Methodist University Press, 1953), 228–230.

56. Benton, ed., *Nuremberg*, 228–230.

57. Otto Kranzbühler in *Nuremberg: A Courtroom Drama*, a film produced by Michael Kloft for Chronos Films. It first aired in Germany and France in November 1995 on Arte Television.

58. International Military Tribunal, *Trial of the Major War Criminals Before the International Military Tribunal* (Washington, D.C.: U.S. Government Printing Office, 1949), 2:99. John Alan Appleman, *Military Tribunals and International Crimes* (Westport, Conn.: Greenwood, 1971), 15. See also IMT, *Trial of the Major War Criminals*, 14:462–463. The German attorneys were quick to recognize the revolutionary implications of the Nuremberg trials. Defense counsel Carl Haensel wrote: "The Nuremberg Tribunals place us anew before the problems of whether positivism really represents the final conclusion of wisdom and coronation of jurisprudence, or whether we have entered a new cultural period and thus, also a new period to be comprehended in legal history, in which . . . an argument emerges which is not based solely on positive norms and their interpretation according to the opinion of the lawmaker" (Benton, ed., *Nuremberg*, 123). The revolutionary

implications of Nuremberg were conceded by German attorney Otto Kranzbühler: "In a revolution one will always have to accept violence and injustice. . . . Its worth or worthlessness is determined by what it contains for the future" (107). See also Werner Maser, *Nuremberg Trial: A Nation on Trial* (New York: Scribner, 1979), 287.

59. IMT, *Trial of the Major War Criminals*, 2:99.
60. IMT, *Trial of the Major War Criminals*, 2:101.
61. IMT, *Trial of the Major War Criminals*, 2:101.
62. IMT, *Trial of the Major War Criminals*, 2:102.
63. Otto Kranzbühler in *Nuremberg: A Courtroom Drama*.
64. Howard Levie, *Terrorism in War: The Law of War Crimes* (Dobbs Ferry, N.Y.: Oceana, 1993), 55n66.
65. Gustav Gilbert, *Nuremberg Diary* (New York: Farrar, Straus & Giroux, 1947), 45–46.
66. IMT, *Trial of the Major War Criminals*, 3:99.
67. IMT, *Trial of the Major War Criminals*, 3:144.
68. Gilbert, *Nuremberg Diary*, 66.
69. Telford Taylor in Kloft, *Nuremberg: A Courtroom Drama*. Taylor, *The Anatomy of the Nuremberg Trials*, 247–248.
70. Telford Taylor in Kloft, *Nuremberg: A Courtroom Drama*.
71. Telford Taylor in Kloft, *Nuremberg: A Courtroom Drama*.
72. IMT, *Trial of the Major War Criminals*, 4:478–479.
73. IMT, *Trial of the Major War Criminals*, 4:485.
74. Michael Marrus, ed., *The Nuremberg War Crimes Trial 1945–1946* (New York: Bedford, 1997), 165.
75. Gilbert, *Nuremberg Diary*, 102–103.
76. Marrus, ed., *The Nuremberg War Crimes Trial 1945–1946*, 92.
77. IMT, *Trial of the Major War Criminals*, 7:169.
78. IMT, *Trial of the Major War Criminals*, 7:170.
79. IMT, *Trial of the Major War Criminals*, 7:190
80. IMT, *Trial of the Major War Criminals*, 7:190. 679,000 million was the number offered by the Soviets.
81. IMT, *Trial of the Major War Criminals*, 8:302.
82. IMT, *Trial of the Major War Criminals*, 8:307.
83. IMT, *Trial of the Major War Criminals*, 8:308.
84. Gilbert, *Nuremberg Diary*, 161–163.
85. Marrus, ed., *The Nuremberg War Crimes Trial 1945–1946*, 180.
86. Marrus, ed., *The Nuremberg War Crimes Trial 1945–1946*, 181.
87. Marrus, ed., *The Nuremberg War Crimes Trial 1945–1946*, 182.
88. Marrus, ed., *The Nuremberg War Crimes Trial 1945–1946*, 98. See also Conot, *Justice at Nuremberg*, 337. According to Goering, the practices of contemporary total war had made the old laws obsolete.
89. Marrus, ed., *The Nuremberg War Crimes Trial 1945–1946*, 98.
90. Marrus, ed., *The Nuremberg War Crimes Trial 1945–1946*, 98. IMT, *Trial of the Major War Criminals*, 9:311, 364.

91. IMT, *Trial of the Major War Criminals*, 9:272–273.

92. IMT, *Trial of the Major War Criminals*, 9:274–275. See also Baird, *From Nuremberg to My Lai*, 57.

93. IMT, *Trial of the Major War Criminals*, 9:274–275.

94. IMT, *Trial of the Major War Criminals*, 9:49.

95. IMT, *Trial of the Major War Criminals*, 9:507.

96. IMT, *Trial of the Major War Criminals*, 9:508.

97. IMT, *Trial of the Major War Criminals*, 9:509–510.

98. Conot, *Justice at Nuremberg*, 412.

99. Kranzbühler interview in Kloft, *Nuremberg: A Courtroom Drama.*

100. Conot, *Justice at Nuremberg*, 417.

101. Conot, *Justice at Nuremberg*, 417.

102. IMT, *Trial of the Major War Criminals*, 11:400.

103. IMT, *Trial of the Major War Criminals*, 11:398.

104. Conot, *Justice at Nuremberg*, 452.

105. Paul, *Katyn*, 229.

106. Friedrich, "Nuremberg and the Germans," 87.

107. IMT, *Trial of the Major War Criminals*, 10:313.

108. IMT, *Trial of the Major War Criminals*, 14:283.

109. IMT, *Trial of the Major War Criminals*, 14:284–285.

110. Conot, *Justice at Nuremberg*, 420; Taylor, *Anatomy of the Nuremberg Trials*, 417.

111. For a more complete refutation of Speer's claims see Matthias Schmidt, *Albert Speer: The End of a Myth*, trans. Joachim Neugroschel (London: Harrap Limited, 1985). See also Gitta Sereny, *Albert Speer: His Battle with Truth* (New York: Knopf, 1995) and Dan van der Vat, *The Good Nazi: The Life and Times of Albert Speer* (New York: Houghton Mifflin, 1997).

112. Smith, *Reaching Judgment at Nuremberg*, 218–219.

113. Smith, *Reaching Judgment at Nuremberg*, 171.

114. Gerald Reitlinger, *The SS: Alibi of a Nation* (New York: Viking, 1957), 266.

115. Marrus, ed., *The Nuremberg War Crimes Trial 1945–1946*, 98.

116. Marrus, ed., *The Nuremberg War Crimes Trial 1945–1946*, 98.

117. Gilbert, *Nuremberg Diary*, 103.

118. Taylor, *The Anatomy of the Nuremberg Trials*, 228.

119. Gilbert, *Nuremberg Diary*, 45–46.

120. Smith, *Reaching Judgment at Nuremberg*, 304–305. Smith considers the court's conservative opinion their greatest achievement: "By advancing a conservative and cautious interpretation of the law of the London Charter, the Court sharply limited the utility of such concepts as 'aggressive war' and 'crimes against humanity' in any future victors' trials. Of even greater importance was the Tribunal's achievement in virtually eliminating the collective guilt features by emasculating the conspiracy-common plan charge and the system for prosecuting members of organizations."

121. Smith, *Reaching Judgment at Nuremberg*, 305.

122. Smith, *Reaching Judgment at Nuremberg*, 304. David Luban, *Legal Modernism* (Ann Arbor: University of Michigan Press, 1994), 350.

123. Levie, *Terrorism in War*, 417n31.

124. Kranzbühler in Kloft, *Nuremberg: A Courtroom Drama*.

125. Levie, *Terrorism in War*, 57.

126. Irving, *Nuremberg: The Last Battle*, 182. Hermann Goering was unrepentant and self-aggrandizing until the end. "I have therefore chosen the manner of death of the Great Hannibal." See also Ben Swearington, *The Mystery of Hermann Goering's Suicide* (New York: Harcourt Brace Jovanovich, 1985).

127. Friedrich, "Nuremberg and the Germans," 87.

128. Tusa, *The Nuremberg Trial*, 465. According to the Tusas, the Soviet judges were ordered to dissent: "He [Nikitchenko] confessed to Biddle that he had consulted Moscow about his problems and received orders to dissent—to object to the acquittals, state that Hess should have been hanged and insist that declarations of criminality should have been made against the Reich Cabinet, General Staff and High Command" (465–466). Otto Kranzbühler stated: "The presence of the Russians was a shame by itself. The whole case of aggressive war, the real undisputable aggressive war was the Polish war. They had instigated it. If you apply the *tu quoque* principle there should be no sentences whatsoever" (interview with the author).

129. Friedrich, "Nuremberg and the Germans," 88. Quincy Wright made a very important point about the Nuremberg debates that is still relevant today: "the favorable or unfavorable character of comments upon events related to the theory of international law often depend less upon events related to the theory of international law assumed by the commentator." William Bosch, *Nuremberg: American Attitudes Towards the Major German War Crimes Trials* (Chapel Hill: University of North Carolina Press, 1970), 41.

130. Howard Levie raises important questions about using trials for "reeducation" in *Terrorism in War:* "How much the trials themselves had to do with this transformation from deadly enemies to close friends and partners can only be a matter of conjecture" (8). Best, *War and Law Since 1945,* comments that "The second lesson is that not much effect is to be expected from the prospect of trial and punishment, which the aftermath of the Second World War suddenly made loom so large" (63). See also Robert Wolfe, ed., *Americans as Proconsuls: United States Military Government in Germany and Japan, 1944–1952* (Washington, D.C.: U.S. Government Printing Office, 1978), 246.

131. Although he praises the court's final decision, Bradley F. Smith charges the Americans with gross hypocrisy. "So the Allies lost the moral triumph over Nazism with a double-edged quid pro quo of saturation bombing and a trial" (*Reaching Judgment at Nuremberg* 305). These criticisms aside, Smith concludes that the proceedings were unique and a departure from the tradition of primitive political justice: "As it was, the Allied governments and the prosecutors prevented an anarchic bloodbath, though had they been able to work their will, Nuremberg might well have been a trial pro forma. The top leaders would have been quickly condemned and the declarations of criminality against the six organizations would have been confirmed, establishing a procedure whereby hundreds of thousands of people might have been punished. . . . The Nuremberg court performed its real service by remedying the most dangerous defects of the Allied war crimes policy" (305). The

Tusas argue that the cooperation of the IMT was impressive, despite the Soviet dissent. According to Smith, "Repeatedly, the judges emphasized to each other the vital importance of compromise in order to avoid the unpleasant appearance that would result if a judge wrote a public dissenting opinion. . . . The Court's actions on organizations goaded the Moscow government, though, and shamefacedly, Nikitchenko had to inform the other judges that the Soviet members would write dissenting opinions and make them public, after all" (169).

132. Friedrich, "Nuremberg and the Germans," 88. "At the conclusion of the trial of the major defendants in October 1946, OMGUS surveys indicated that 55 percent of the German population found the guilty verdicts to be just, 21 percent thought them too mild, and only nine percent found them to be harsh. Overall, 78 percent regarded the proceedings as fair." Jeffrey Herf, *Divided Memory: The Nazi Past in the Two Germanys* (Cambridge: Harvard University Press, 1997), 206.

133. The Tokyo Charter had not prohibited attacks against the court's legal legitimacy. Like the German lawyers at Nuremberg, "prominent Japanese lawyers, Takayanagi Kenzo and Kiyose Ichiro . . . questioned the very legitimacy of the tribunal" (John Dower, *Embracing Defeat: Japan in the Wake of World War II* [New York: Norton, 1999], 462). For an overview of American war crimes policy in the Far East see Philip Piccigallo, *The Japanese on Trial* (Austin: University of Texas Press, 1979), 49–68; Appleman, *Military Tribunals and International Crimes*, 237–267. For critical views of Far Eastern policy see Richard Minear, *Victors' Justice: The Tokyo War Crimes Trial* (Princeton: Princeton University Press, 1972); Richard Lael, *The Yamashita Precedent* (Wilmington, Del.: Scholarly Resources, 1982). Lael offers the most comprehensive examination of the Yamashita case and the novel doctrine of command responsibility. Yamashita's lawyer, Frank Reel, wrote a book entitled *The Case of General Yamashita* (Chicago: University of Chicago Press, 1949); Dower's book provides excellent analysis of U.S. policy in postwar Japan. The Tokyo Charter was a series of laws modeled after the London Agreement by an executive decree of General Douglas MacArthur.

134. William Manchester, *American Caesar: Douglas MacArthur* (Boston: Little, Brown, 1978), 484.

135. Dower, *Embracing Defeat*, 461.

136. Judith Shklar, *Legalism: Law, Morals and Political Trials* (Cambridge: Harvard University Press, 1964), 184. Keenan claimed the aggressive war charges were valid on the grounds of "the Christian-Judaic absolutes of good and evil" (184). The American prosecutor overlooked the fact that the natural law was totally foreign to the Japanese. Shklar observes: "Natural law . . . was a Western notion, meaningless to the men being tried and their fellow citizens. In any case, it cannot serve as the enforceable law of the world community because there is no world community. To enforce the 'common good' internationally is impossible, because no one, certainly not one set of nations, can be the custodian of that good" (186).

137. Nisuki Ando, Chihiro Hosoya, Richard Minear, and Yasuaki Onuma, eds., *The Tokyo War Crimes Trial: An International Symposium* (Tokyo: Kodansha, 1986), 17. Röling described Webb as "Quarrelsome at times, he embarrassed some of the judges with his court behavior" (19).

138. Appleman, *Military Tribunals and International Crimes,* 197. "The attitude of the president of the Tribunal throughout toward defense counsel was one not consistent with standards commonly observed in courts of the United States" (197).

139. Levie, *Terrorism in War,* 386.

140. Levie, *Terrorism in War,* 39. See also Piccigallo, *The Japanese on Trial,* 14. The indictment in the IMTFE was hopelessly complicated. There were twenty different conspiracy counts that stretched back nearly eighteen years. For more on the IMTFE indictment, see Levie, *Terrorism in War,* 389–390.

141. Minear, *Victors' Justice,* 67.

142. Levie, *Terrorism in War,* 46.

143. Piccigallo, *The Japanese on Trial,* 21–23.

144. Piccigallo, *The Japanese on Trial,* 21–23. See also Minear, *Victors' Justice,* 50–53.

145. Piccigallo, *The Japanese on Trial,* 23. See also diplomatic historian Waldo Heinrichs on U.S.–Japanese relations and the events leading up to Pearl Harbor in *Threshold of War: Franklin D. Roosevelt and American Entry Into World War II* (New York: Oxford University Press, 1988).

146. Kurt Tauber, *Beyond Eagle and Swastika: German Nationalism Since 1945* (Middletown, Conn.: Wesleyan University Press, 1967), 1:26. Tauber writes: "The difficulty with these agreements was that there was no vivid understanding of the tacit assumptions underlying them. The agreements clearly meant that Germans had to be punished. But was it merely, negatively, to prevent a recurrence of so tragic a chapter in Western history: or was it rather, positively, to effect *inner* changes, to re-educate the Germans to the ways of peaceful neighborliness and democratic tolerance?"

147. Levie, *Terrorism in War,* 133.

148. Levie, *Terrorism in War,* 179–180.

149. Lael, *The Yamashita Precedent,* 79–95. For a less temperate view see Manchester, *American Caesar,* 486.

150. Lael, *The Yamashita Precedent,* 79–95.

151. Lawrence Taylor, *A Trial of Generals: Homma, Yamashita, MacArthur* (South Bend, Ind.: Icarus, 1981), 163.

152. Manchester, *American Caesar,* 487. George Marshall warned MacArthur and his staff "that there was no precedent here for charging a Field Commander with the negligence of duty in controlling his troops" (487). See also Levie, *Terrorism in War,* 157.

153. Reel, *The Case of General Yamashita,* 27. See also Levie, *Terrorism in War* for a significantly less sympathetic account.

154. Reel, *The Case of General Yamashita,* 157.

155. Taylor, *A Trial of Generals,* 137. General MacArthur considered the rules of evidence "obstructionist." Article 13 of his "Special Proclamation" stated: "The Tribunal shall not be bound by technical rules of evidence. It shall adopt and apply to the greatest possible extent expeditious and non-technical procedure, and shall admit any evidence which it deems to have probative value" (137).

156. Taylor, *A Trial of Generals,* 137.

157. Manchester, *American Caesar,* 487.

158. Reel, *The Case of General Yamashita*, 142.

159. Piccigallo, *The Japanese on Trial*, 53–54. See also Taylor, *A Trial of Generals*, 168.

160. Lael, *The Yamashita Precedent*, 105.

161. Taylor, *A Trial of Generals*, 162–163.

162. Reel, *The Case of General Yamashita*, 173.

163. Manchester, *American Caesar*, 488. MacArthur's commission was closer to military custom than either of the international tribunals, or as the prosecution described it, "retail justice for wholesale slaughter" (101).

164. Manchester, *American Caesar*, 488.

165. Howard Levie describes the professional military's continuing reluctance to reject the doctrine of superior orders in *Terrorism in War*. Levie has taught the laws of war to officers at the U.S. Naval War College; according to Levie, "it would be a liberal estimate to say that half a dozen have supported the idea of denying the validity of the defense of superior orders" (521). General Lucius Clay made a similar point in his oral history at Columbia University: "I've spent most of my life as a soldier, and I could not honestly tell you today, in my own mind, when I could make a distinction between refusing to obey an order because I decided it was not a legal order and, or obeying it because I was a soldier" (568).

166. Manchester, *American Caesar*, 488. Manchester traces MacArthur's idea of war back to more chivalrous times: "In his view, therefore, these two Japanese commanders had betrayed, not just Dai Nippon, nor even Manila's violated Filipinos, but MacArthur's own profession" (488). See also Piccigallo, *The Japanese on Trial*, 53–54; Taylor, *Trial of the Generals*, 168.

167. MacArthur was ordered by the Secretary of War to issue a stay of execution while the Supreme Court reviewed the case.

168. Lael, *The Yamashita Precedent*, 105. According to Chief Justice Stone, the Quirin decision "demonstrated that Congress by passing the articles of war, had recognized and sanctioned the use of military tribunals to try war criminals." Stone went on to claim that the military tribunals were "not courts whose rulings and judgments are subject to review by this court." This limited the Supreme Court to two questions: "Did the government have the right to detain Yamashita for trial? Did the military tribunals have lawful authority in this instance to try to condemn him?" Although Stone privately opposed the war crimes proceedings, he was an advocate of judicial restraint and feared that meddling in the Yamashita case might lead to "unnecessary and unwise judicial interference with the other branches of government" (105). He was bolstered by Justice Frankfurter. For more on Stone's philosophy see Alpheus Mason, *Harlan Fiske Stone: Pillar of the Law* (New York: Viking, 1956) and C. Herman Pritchett, *The Roosevelt Court: A Study in Judicial Politics and Values, 1937–1947* (New York: Macmillan, 1948).

169. Lael, *The Yamashita Precedent*, 105. Lael claims, "Murphy's jabs at the military may have been influenced to some small degree by his dislike for MacArthur. When Murphy became high commissioner for the Philippines in the 1930s, he and MacArthur frequently clashed" (130). For more on Murphy see J. Woodford Howard Jr., *Mr. Justice Murphy: A Political Biography* (Princeton: Princeton University Press, 1968).

170. Lael, *The Yamashita Precedent,* 105. Both dissenters were outraged by the military commission's inability "to demonstrate that Yamashita had committed or ordered the commission of war crimes." Rutledge pointed out: "It is not in our tradition for anyone to be charged with crime which is defined after his conduct . . . has taken place. . . . Mass guilt we do not impute to individuals, perhaps in any case but certainly in none where the person is not charged or shown actively to have participated in or knowingly to have failed in taking action to prevent the wrongs done by others, having both the duty and power to do so" (105).

171. Nisuki Ando et al., eds., *The Tokyo War Crimes Trial,* 17. Manchester, *American Caesar,* 487. For a differing view on the Yamashita case see Gary Solis, "Yamashita Had It Coming," *Proceedings of "Accounting for Atrocities: Prosecuting War Crimes Fifty Years After Nuremberg," October 5–6, 1998* (Annandale-on-Hudson, N.Y: Bard College Publications, 2000), 37–49. Dower, *Embracing Defeat,* 516; Levie, *Terrorism in War,* 164.

172. Robert Edgerton, *Warriors of the Rising Sun* (New York: Norton, 1997), 14. See also John Dower, *War Without Mercy* (New York: Pantheon, 1986); Yuki Tanaka, *Hidden Horrors: Japanese War Crimes in World War II* (Boulder, Colo.: Westview, 1996); Iris Chang, *The Rape of Nanking* (New York: Basic, 1997); for a prisoner's account see Gavan Daws, *Prisoners of the Japanese* (New York: Morrow, 1994).

173. Chang, *The Rape of Nanking,* 4–5. Chang estimates the numbers killed in Nanking in the late months of 1937 and into early 1938 ranging between 260,000 and 350,000. This was more civilians than Britain (61,000), France (108,000), and the Netherlands (242,000) lost during the entire war. See also Howard French, "Japanese Call '37 Massacre a War Myth, Stirring Storm," *New York Times,* January 23, 2000. Sheldon Harris, *Factories of Death: Japanese Biological Warfare 1932–45 and the American Cover-Up* (London: Routledge, 1994), 149, 205. Piccigallo, *The Japanese on Trial,* 16; Dower, *Embracing Defeat,* 465; Hal Gold, *Unit 731: Testimony* (Tokyo: Yen Books, 1996), 96.

    According to Hal Gold, the men of Unit 731 did their best to destroy their facilities and were able to return to Japan before the Russians could capture them (92–93). "The Japanese hoped to use their knowledge as a tool for gaining freedom from prosecution as war criminals" (95–96).

    General MacArthur granted permission to offer the men of Unit 731 a deal— if they surrendered all of their research data, they would be immune from war crimes prosecution.

    According to Awaya Kentaro, professor of history at Rikyyo University, morality proved to be no match for postwar strategy: "At the time of the Tokyo trial, the Soviet Union vigorously demanded the investigation of Ishii [commander] and his staff. GHQ did not respond to these demands. It is said that Ishii and others escaped prosecution by turning over to the United States the data on their experiments and their use of germ and chemical warfare in the field" (Minear, *Victor's Justice,* 85–86). Years after the trial, Judge Röling charged: "The American military authorities wanted to avail themselves of the results of the experiments, criminally obtained in Japan, and at the same time prevent them from falling into the hands of the Soviet Union" (4).

174. James Weingartner, *Crossroads of Death: The Story of the Malmedy Massacre and Trial* (Los Angeles: University of California Press, 1979), 75.

175. Army Command War Crimes Branch, Cases Tried, General Administration Files, RG 338. National Archives Modern Military Branch, Suitland, Maryland.

176. Army Command War Crimes Branch, Cases Tried, General Administration Files, RG 338.

177. Weingartner, *Crossroads of Death*, 118.

178. Weingartner, *Crossroads of Death*, 104. According to one of Peiper's men, the commander said: "We will fight in the same manner as we did in Russia in the action which will follow" (84). The commander's next statement supports the contention that the rules of war only applied in the West: "The certain rules which have applied in the West until now will be omitted" (84). Telford Taylor and many others also make the point that the Wehrmacht fought a more restrained war in the West and disregarded the laws of war in the East (interview by author, 1993).

179. Weingartner, *Crossroads of Death*, 89. These were Pringel's orders to Peiper.

180. Weingartner, *Crossroads of Death*, 95–96.

181. Weingartner, *Crossroads of Death*, 98. In regard to evidence, the court was very much like MacArthur's military commission: "no evidence no matter how tenuous was to be excluded if in the opinion of the bench, it had a bearing on the case. The bench was also free to exclude any evidence it considered to be irrelevant" (98).

182. Senate Subcommittee of the Committee on Armed Services, *Investigation of Army Action with Respect to Trial of Persons Responsible for the Massacre of American Soldiers, the Battle of the Bulge, near Malmedy, Belgium, December, 1944* (Washington, D.C.: U.S. Government Printing Office, 1945), 1012.

183. Ibid.

184. Weingartner, *Crossroads of Death*, 116.

185. Weingartner, *Crossroads of Death*, 116.

186. Weingartner, *Crossroads of Death*, 116.

187. Weingartner, *Crossroads of Death*, 133. A number of the American military men respected and sympathized with Peiper. McCowan claimed, "I have met few men who impressed me in as short a space of time as the German officer" (127).

188. Weingartner, *Crossroads of Death*, 116.

189. Weingartner, *Crossroads of Death*, 130.

190. Weingartner, *Crossroads of Death*, 137.

191. Weingartner, *Crossroads of Death*, 185–187.

192. Weingartner, *Crossroads of Death*, 187.

4. A SHIFT IN PRIORITIES

1. John Mendelson, "War Crimes Trials and Clemency in Japan and Germany," in Robert Wolfe, ed., *Americans as Proconsuls: United States Military Government in Germany and Japan, 1944–1952* (Carbondale: Southern Illinois University Press, 1984), 261. The most comprehensive monograph on America's war crimes policy is Frank M. Buscher's *The U.S. War Crimes Trial Program in Germany, 1946–1955* (Westport, Conn.: Greenwood, 1989) (see 31). Carl Anthony, "Reeducation for De-

mocracy," in Wolfe, ed., *Americans as Proconsuls*, 262. Even Friedrich Meinecke wrote of the need for German reeducation: "So far as the victors try to eradicate National Socialist influences and thereby provide the atmosphere for Christian Occidental sound morals, we must not only recognize that they are fundamentally right but must ourselves help them and try to prevent them only from schematic exaggerations and mistakes" (*The German Catastrophe* [Boston: Beacon, 1950], 104).

2. Buscher, *The U.S. War Crimes Trial Program*, 8–9. For a more comprehensive account of the trial's objectives, see Bradley E Smith, *The Road to Nuremberg* (New York: Basic, 1981).

3. John McCloy, "From Military Government to Serf-Government," in Wolfe, ed., *Americans as Proconsuls*. The Assistant Secretary of War described JCS 1067 as "rather Draconian . . . not as bad as the Morgenthau Plan—but it was pretty negative" (119). John Montgomery called the reeducation program an "artificial revolution" because it was not a German initiative. Buscher convincingly argues that the German objection to the program had roots stretching back to the war guilt clause in the Treaty of Versailles: "The historian Hajo Holborn was sent to Germany in 1947, and reported that some Germans he encountered—according to Holborn, predominantly simple and non-intellectual people—were ashamed of their country's wartime deeds. Almost everyone rejected the concept of collective guilt" (109).

4. Howard Levie, *Terrorism in War: The Law of War Crimes* (Dobbs Ferry, N.Y.: Oceana, 1993), 126.

5. Elmer Plischke, "Denazification in Germany," in Wolfe, ed., *Americans as Proconsuls*, 199. According to Kurt Tauber, "Most serious of all, the very excesses of denazification procedure not only unjustly discredited the entire idea in the eyes of a large segment of the population but also created a climate of opinion which the Nazis could use for their own purposes" (*Beyond Eagle and Swastika: German Nationalism Since 1945* [Middletown, Conn.: Wesleyan University Press, 1967], 245).

6. Plischke, "Denazification in Germany," 216–217.

7. Jörg Friedrich, "Nuremberg and the Germans," in Belinda Cooper, ed., *War Crimes: The Legacy of Nuremberg* (New York: TV Books, 1999), 90. Friedrich describes denazification as "a form of political purge" with "no basis in international law."

8. Hans Schmitt, ed., *U.S. Occupation of Europe After World War II* (Lawrence: Regents Press of Kansas, 1978), 93. Thomas H. Etzold and John Lewis Gaddis, eds., *Containment: Documents on American Policy and Strategy, 1945–1950* (New York: Columbia University Press, 1979).

9. This was a residual effect of the Morgenthau Plan, but the perception was based more on fantasy than fact. However, there were enough Jewish war crimes officials (prosecutors, interrogators, translators, etc.) to provide a germ of truth. There is no evidence to support the contention that these individuals were vindictive in accordance with American policy. If anything, as Peter Grose points out, U.S. policy was moving in a different direction: "As Major General Stephen J. Chamberlin, director of army intelligence in Washington, informed Eisenhower, 'valuable intelli-

gence on Russia and Russian dominated countries can be developed more rapidly by this method than other.' In the less formal language of an American staff officer in Frankfurt, speaking to journalist John Gunther, 'Are we dealing with our former enemies, or our future allies? We have not yet decided whether we want to win the last war or the next one" (Peter Grose, *Operation Rollback* [New York: Houghton Mifflin, 2000], 25).

10. Schmitt, *U.S. Occupation of Europe*, 35.

11. Columbia University Oral History Project, Benjamin Buttenweiser, 1:28, 2:201. The former Assistant High Commissioner stressed, "our primary goal was to get Germany 'on its feet' as soon as possible" (31). Due to the American mishandling of denazification, "Many ... seemingly unjustly treated by a badly floundering administration of the law, withdrew in sullen resentment, a ready audience for the irresponsible demagogy of unreconstructed Nazi leaders" (Tauber, *Beyond Eagle and Swastika*, 36). See Etzold and Gaddis, eds., *Containment*, 118–119. The Policy Planning Staff made the observation in the February 24, 1948 "Review of Current Trends."

12. Louis Snyder, *The Roots of German Nationalism* (Bloomington: Indiana University Press, 1978), 175. Although Snyder is referring to the German reaction to the Treaty of Versailles, this background knowledge is key to understanding the post–World War II nationalists' attitudes toward war crimes. "The old Germany was suffering on the cross while the terrible punishment of Bolshevism hovered over the world as the Divine vengeance for the Victors. Here was the added feature of the myth— the initial suggestion that the Allies never understood that Germany was the vital bulwark against Bolshevik expansionism" (175).

13. Robert Jackson, letter to President Harry Truman, 4 December 1945. From Telford Taylor, *Final Report to the Secretary of the Army on the Nuernberg War Crimes Trials Under Control Council Law No. 10* (Washington, D.C.: United States Government Printing Office, 1949), 262–263.

14. Lucius Clay, *Decision in Germany* (New York: Doubleday 1950), 251.

15. Jean Smith, ed., *The Papers of General Lucius Clay* (Bloomington: Indiana University Press, 1974), 658. For more on Clay and clemency see Columbia University Oral History Project, Lucius Clay.

16. Jean Smith, *Lucius D. Clay: An American Life* (New York: Holt, 1990), 308. Clay stood firmly behind the trials and impressed Telford Taylor: "He would listen and decide quickly and firmly. I liked him. I thought he was a fine commanding officer and I had very high regard for him" (251).

17. Telford Taylor, "An Approach to the preparation of the prosecution of Axis Criminality," early June 1945, in Bradley F. Smith, ed., *The American Road to Nuremberg: The Documentary Record 1944–1945* (Stanford: Hoover Institution Press, 1982), 209. Smith praises Taylor's contribution: "Jackson and his staff had also raised the level of legal draughtsmanship, and the new executive agreement was more tightly and precisely composed than any of its predecessors. In addition, among the new faces brought in by the justice were such men as Colonel Telford Taylor, who, although they did not play a part in this drafting, would soon leave their mark by asking tough, direct questions" (142).

18. Many military men were offended by the preponderance of high-ranking, Harvard-educated lawyers at Nuremberg. Tom Bower observes that "control of the operation was firmly—too firmly some said afterwards—in the hands of a Harvard law school mafia. . . . They diligently tried to covert a group of undistinguished and conservative American judges to a radical theory: that educated, respected and otherwise normal businessmen could be guilty of murder" (*Blind Eye to Murder: Britain, America and the Purging of Nazi Germany—A Pledge Betrayed* [London: Andre Deutsch, 1981], 256).

19. Robert Kempner, interview by author, tape recording, Locarno, Switzerland, 23 February 1988.

20. Robert Kempner, interview by author, tape recording, Locarno, Switzerland, 23 February 1988. Otto Kranzbühler described Robert Kempner to this author: "He was a divided personality, he really felt as a German, he loved Germany. He was full of hate for Hitler and those who did not allow him to love his country. I had a very good relationship with the opposite points of view. He asked me to defend Hitler's adjunct . . . in a denazification trial. [He] was one of Kempner's proteges and he wanted him to come free—typical Kempner, some people he really helped." See Bower, *Blind Eye to Murder,* 278–279.

21. Bower, *Blind Eye to Murder,* 278–279. Some in the prosecution staff (Taylor and Sprecher) worked for New Deal agencies. Former Indiana Congressman Charles LaFollette served as a prosecutor in the Justice case. One can safely assume that the vast majority of the prosecutors were sympathetic to the prosecution's broadened conception of international law.

22. Taylor, *Final Report to the Secretary of the Army on the Nuernberg War Crimes Trials,* 164.

23. Clay, *Decision in Germany,* 251.

24. Ann and John Tusa, *The Nuremberg Trial* (New York: Atheneum, 1984), 69.

25. Joseph Borkin, *The Crime and Punishment of I. G. Farben* (New York: Free Press, 1978), 139.

26. Robert Conot, *Justice at Nuremberg* (New York: Carroll and Graf, 1983), 517. See George E. Kennan, *Memoirs 1925–1950* (Boston: Atlantic Monthly, 1967), 260. Philip Piccigallo observes in *The Japanese on Trial: Allied War Crimes Operations in the East, 1945–1951* (Austin: University of Texas Press, 1979): "United States authorities, in accordance with Kennan's advice, recognized the need to stabilize Japan, politically and economically, and to 'win' that nation to its side in the Cold War" (46).

27. Kennan, *Memoirs 1925–1950,* 260. Gaddis describes the impact of the Long Telegram: "This 8,000-word telegram from George Kennan probably did more than any other single document to influence the evolution of early postwar United States foreign policy. The 'long telegram' was both an analysis of Soviet behavior and a prescription for American action. In it, Kennan advanced the now famous argument that Soviet hostility sprang from nothing the West had done, but from the need Russian leaders felt for a hostile outside world as a means of justifying their own autocratic rule" (50).

28. Kennan, *Memoirs 1925–1950,* 260.

29. Kennan, *Memoirs 1925–1950,* 260.

30. Kennan, *Memoirs 1925–1950*, 260.

31. Kennan, *Memoirs 1925–1950*, 260.

32. Kennan, *Memoirs 1925–1950*, 260.

33. Christopher Simpson, *The Splendid Blond Beast: Money, Law, and Genocide in the Twentieth Century* (New York: Grove, 1993), 98.

34. Kennan, *Memoirs 1925–1950*, 260.

35. Christopher Simpson, *Blowback: America's Recruitment of Nazis and Its Effects on the Cold War* (New York: Weidenfield and Nicolson, 1988), 41. For a self-serving but highly entertaining firsthand account see Reinhard Gehlen, *The Service* (New York: World Publishing, 1972). The best study in English is Mary Ellen Reese's *General Reinhard Gehlen* (Fairfax, Va.: George Mason University Press, 1990), 8–9. Gehlen and the captured Germans were interrogated by U.S. Captain John Bokor: "Not only did he know where the precious archives were buried, but he had also maintained the embryo of an underground espionage operation that could put the records to use against the Soviet Union" (*General Reinhard Gehlen* 41). Bokor kept the details of Gehlen's offer and managed to get his top generals off the Allied war criminal lists in violation of the Yalta accords, which required the United States to hand over Germans involved in the eastern front.

36. Simpson, *Blowback*, 42. See also Reese, *General Reinhard Gehlen*, 32. The OSS was tipped off about the existence of the microfilm and was soon jockeying for control of the spymaster and his records. According to Simpson, "Gehlen and seven of his senior officers were transferred to the camp [Camp King], where they were constituted as a 'historical study group,' supposedly working on a report on the German general staff. Gehlen's precious cache of records was located and shipped to the interrogation center under such secrecy that not even the CIC's chain of command was informed" (*Blowback* 53).

37. Simpson, *Blowback*, 42. The American espionage chief commented on the lack of information: "Even the most elementary facts were unavailable—on roads and bridges, on the location and production of factories, on city plans and airfields." Rositzke credits Gehlen with playing a "primary role" in providing the Americans with this basic information. See also Reese, *General Reinhard Gehlen*, 142.

38. Reese, *General Reinhard Gehlen*, 69. "Americans did not know the degree of Soviet preparedness, a lack which played into Reinhard Gehlen's hands." Reese places the absorption of the Nazi intelligence operation (*Fremde Heere Ost*) into context: "As the Soviets provoked more hostile incidents . . . and as the Americans began to appreciate how little they understood Soviet intentions and capabilities, Gehlen's confidence began to revive. And with good reason, information about the new adversary was at a premium, and compared with many former Nazis being used by Army Intelligence, Gehlen looked benign as well as smart."

39. Smith, ed., *The Papers of General Lucius Clay*, 252. At the time the Military Governor supported the war crimes trials: "In 1947, I urged the Department of the Army to permit the Foreign Ministry, Military Command and Krupp cases to be brought to trial before the program was discontinued, and to find additional judges for the requisite courts. This was approved with the understanding that no further cases would be considered. I was unable to meet my commitment of July 1948 for com-

pletion because defense counsel had to be given as much time as it desired to prepare its evidence."

40. "It was difficult to recruit top level judges, the Nuremberg Trials were not front-page stuff after the first trial." The trials were not held one at a time; several were conducted simultaneously. Drexel Sprecher, interview by author, tape recording, Chevy Chase, Maryland, 29 May 1987.

41. Taylor, *Final Report to the Secretary of the Army on the Nuernberg War Crimes Trials*, 118.

42. Taylor, *Final Report to the Secretary of the Army on the Nuernberg War Crimes Trials*, 164

43. Articles 4 through 20 of the 1907 Hague Conventions specifically prohibit far less extreme types of POW mistreatment.

44. Taylor, *Final Report to the Secretary of the Army on the Nuernberg War Crimes Trials*, 164. Adam Roberts and Richard Guelff, eds., *Documents on the Laws of War* (New York: Oxford University Press, 1989), 48–49. Article 4 of the 1907 Hague Agreement's Annex to the Convention states: "Prisoners of war are in the power of the hostile Government, but not of the individuals or corps who capture them. They must be humanely treated." Article 6 is more specific: "The State may utilize the labor of prisoners of war according to their rank and aptitude, officers excepted. The tasks shall not be excessive and shall have no connection with the operations of the war."

45. Walter Beals, *The First German War Crimes Trial* (Chapel Hill: Documentary Publications, 1985), 141–185.

46. John Alan Appleman, *Military Tribunals and International Crimes* (Indianapolis: Bobbs-Merrill, 1954), 146.

47. Taylor, *Final Report to the Secretary of the Army on the Nuernberg War Crimes Trials*, 177. For the scientific standards see Appleman, *Military Tribunals and International Crimes*, 147–148. See also Robert J. Lifton, *The Nazi Doctors* (New York: Basic, 1983) and Michael Kater, *Doctors Under Hitler* (Chapel Hill: University of North Carolina Press, 1989).

48. Taylor, *Final Report to the Secretary of the Army on the Nuernberg War Crimes Trials*, 118.

49. Appleman, *Military Tribunals and International Crimes*, 158 and Taylor, *Final Report to the Secretary of the Army on the Nuernberg War Crimes Trials*, 155. See also *U.S. Military Tribunal Nuremberg, Transcript, Case II, Milch*, 2258.

50. Appleman, *Military Tribunals and International Crimes* provides an extensive discussion of "the Nuremberg defense": "Defense counsel frequently brought out this testimony, in their arguments, that the individual defendants had no choice but to perform the acts charged against them. Particularly in a dictatorship . . . there was but one leader, the rest were followers. They raised the question, with reference to subordinates, of the legal defense of respondeat superior—or, let the master answer, rather than the servant; and, in the case of those in command, of the doctrine of Act of State—or, in other words, the act of the leader is the act of the sovereign, and the State should answer instead of the individual" (54).

51. Appleman, *Military Tribunals and International Crimes,* 147–148.

52. Taylor, *Final Report to the Secretary of the Army on the Nuernberg War Crimes Trials,* 118.

53. Taylor, *Final Report to the Secretary of the Army on the Nuernberg War Crimes Trials,* 175.

54. Taylor, *Final Report to the Secretary of the Army on the Nuernberg War Crimes Trials,* 176–177.

55. Levie, *Terrorism in War,* 301.

56. Appleman, *Military Tribunals and International Crimes,* 167. The quote is from Taylor's *Final Report to the Secretary of the Army on the Nuernberg War Crimes Trials,* 177.

57. None of the defendants was found guilty of aggression or conspiracy. The vast majority of the convictions were for "war crimes" or traditional violations of the codes of war and the broadened conception of "crimes against humanity." Roberts and Guelff, eds., *Documents on the Laws of War,* 48–49.

58. Ingo Müller, *Hitler's Justice,* trans. Deborah Lucas Schneider (Cambridge: Harvard University Press, 1991), 270–271. U.S. Government, *Trials of the German War Criminals Before the Nuernberg Military Tribunals Under Control Council No. 10,* Vols. 1–15 (Washington, D.C.: U.S. Government Printing Office, 1949), 966.

59. Taylor, *Final Report to the Secretary of the Army on the Nuernberg War Crimes Trials,* 169.

60. Appleman, *Military Tribunals and International Crimes,* 158.

61. American Nuremberg Trials, *Case 3—United States v. Josef Altstoetter et al.,* 1167.

62. Taylor, *Final Report to the Secretary of the Army on the Nuernberg War Crimes Trials,* 173.

63. Taylor, *Final Report to the Secretary of the Army on the Nuernberg War Crimes Trials,* 173.

64. *U.S. Military Tribunal Nuremberg, Transcript, Case III, Altstoetter* (Nuremberg: Secretariat for Military Tribunals, 1949), 10793–94.

65. *U.S. Military Tribunal Nuremberg, Transcript, Case III, Altstoetter,* 966.

66. Taylor, *Final Report to the Secretary of the Army on the Nuernberg War Crimes Trials,* 173–174.

67. Robert Maguire, letter to family, 21 October 1947, Constance Maguire Wilson Papers, Eureka, California (in possession of the author). Maguire provided his family with a running commentary on his experiences at Nuremberg. His letters begin in the fall of 1947 and end in December 1948. While he was writing the tribunal opinion, his wife, Ruth, continued the correspondence until their departure in the spring of 1949.

68. Robert Maguire, letter to family, 21 October 1947, Constance Maguire Wilson Papers.

69. Robert Jackson, quoted in Michael Luders, "The Strange Case of Ernst von Weizsaecker," M.A. thesis, Columbia University, 1988, 7.

70. Ibid.

71. U.S. Government, *Trials of the German War Criminals Before the Nuernberg Military Tribunals Under Control Council No. 10,* Vols. 1–15 (Washington, D.C.: U.S. Government Printing Office, 1949), 12:139. See also *The New York Times,* January 7, 1948, 10, col. 5.

72. Levie, *Terrorism in War,* 386. My student at Columbia University, Greg Lembrich, also pointed this fact out in his paper on the Ernst von Weizsäcker case

73. American Nuremberg Trials, *Case 11—United States v. Ernst von Weizsaecker,* 12:150.

74. William Seabury, *Wilhelmstrasse: A Study of German Diplomats Under the Nazi Regime* (Berkeley: University of California Press, 1954), 14. From Luders, "The Strange Case of Ernst von Weizsaecker," 32. Fritz Stern, *The Politics of Cultural Despair: A Study in the Rise of Germanic Ideology* (Berkeley: University of California Press, 1974). "Even before 1933, the National Socialists had made deep inroads into the ranks of the German elites. Hitler knew how to cultivate their vulnerabilities, how to reassure the elites that he was a German nationalist, the true redeemer" (165).

75. See Ian Buruma, *The Wages of Guilt: Memories of War in Germany and Japan* (New York: Penguin, 1994), 175.

76. American Nuremberg Trials, *Case 11—United States v. Ernst von Weizsaecker,* 12:151.

77. American Nuremberg Trials, *Case 11—United States v. Ernst von Weizsaecker,* 12:151, 156–157.

78. American Nuremberg Trials, *Case 11—United States v. Ernst von Weizsaecker,* 12:151, 157, 160.

79. American Nuremberg Trials, *Case 11—United States v. Ernst von Weizsaecker,* 12:151, 221.

80. American Nuremberg Trials, *Case 11—United States v. Ernst von Weizsaecker,* 12:151, 150, 154, 158–160. Ambassador Karl Ritter and Ministerial Dirigent Otto von Erdmannsdorf also organized the actions of pro-Nazi groups.

81. American Nuremberg Trials, *Case 11—United States v. Ernst von Weizsaecker,* 12:151, 140–141. The prosecution argued that "Members of the Reich Chancellory were responsible for informing the Fuehrer and Reich Chancellor about current questions of policy and prepare directives" (141). The Tusas describe Hans Lammers's performance in the IMT: "His very appearance might have weighed against his evidence, but then under cross-examination the authoritative, contemptuous bureaucrat gave way. He was so desperate to save himself that he shoveled blame onto Hitler and Bormann—all the time failing to notice or even not caring that every word backed up prosecution charges of criminal policies" (*The Nuremberg Trial* 312).

82. American Nuremberg Trials, *Case 11—United States v. Ernst von Weizsaecker,* 12:151, 199. Other headlines included "firing on ethnic germans by rural police."

83. American Nuremberg Trials, *Case 11—United States v. Ernst von Weizsaecker,* 12:151, 200, 202. *U.S. Military Tribunal Nuremberg, Transcript, Case XI, Weizsaecker,* 28244.

84. American Nuremberg Trials, *Case 11—United States v. Ernst von Weizsaecker,* 12:151, 193–194. Richard Walter Darre's National Socialist zealotry attracted Hitler in 1930.

Darré described the German peasantry as "the Life Spring of the Nordic Race" (194).

85. American Nuremberg Trials, *Case 11—United States v. Ernst von Weizsaecker*, 12:151, 194, 205. Other longtime National Socialists were State Secretary to the Reich Ministry of Interior Wilhelm Stuckart and Presidential Chancellor Otto Meissner. Stuckart was responsible for the civil administration of Germany's conquered territories (205).

86. *U.S. Military Tribunal Nuremberg, Transcript, Case XI, Weizsaecker*, 28222, 142, 172, 179. Paul Koerner met Hermann Goering in 1926; four years later he went to work in the Offices of the Four-Year Plan, where he also met and aided Heinrich Himmler. In 1936, when the Office of the Four-Year Plan took control of the German economy, Koerner was named State Secretary for the Four-Year Plan

87. *U.S. Military Tribunal Nuremberg, Transcript, Case XI, Weizsaecker*, 28222, 169. See also Tusa, *The Nuremberg Trial,* 272. "Koerner, once State Secretary in the Prussian Ministry, also pressed the line that everyone had seen, heard and spoken no evil, even arguing that since Germany had built up agricultural production in countries she occupied, she had a right to take a little of the 'surplus.' As Dean said in a cable to the Foreign Office that evening, both Koerner and Brauchitsch had 'made a very bad impression' and were too obviously lying."

88. *U.S. Military Tribunal Nuremberg, Transcript, Case XI, Weizsaecker*, 28222. David Kaiser describes the Four-Year Plan in *Politics and War* (Cambridge: Harvard University Press, 1990). "The Four-Year Plan concentrated upon expanding heavy industrial capacity and developing synthetic substitutes for two critical imported raw materials, oil and rubber. To achieve these goals, Goering rapidly increased state ownership of the economy and reserved the Maximum possible foreign exchange for imports of raw materials" (373). The economic mobilization was so successful in restructuring the German economy to withstand the pressures of war that Plenipotentiary of the War Economy Walter Funk was moved to comment on October 14, 1939, "It is known that the German war potential has been strengthened very considerably by the conquest of Poland. We owe it mainly to the Four-Year Plan, that we could enter the war economically so strong and well prepared." Defendants Paul Pleiger and Hans Kehrl served as industrial and economic experts under Koerner.

89. *U.S. Military Tribunal Nuremberg, Transcript, Case XI, Weizsaecker*, 28222, 187. The bankers were involved in the intimate details of concentration camp construction and liquidation of confiscated property like gold and glasses. Defendant Rasche played such a prominent role in the rearmament that he earned himself a jingle: "Who marches behind the leading tank? It is Dr. Rasche of the Dresdner Bank."

90. *U.S. Military Tribunal Nuremberg, Transcript, Case XI, Weizsaecker*, 28222, 176, 208–210. Schwerin von Krosigk was designated a political heir in Hitler's will. He was Minister of Finance until the fall of the Reich; he was in charge of collecting a one-billion-RM loan and storing concentration camp loot.

91. *U.S. Military Tribunal Nuremberg, Transcript, Case XI, Weizsaecker*, 28222, 192.

92. *U.S. Military Tribunal Nuremberg, Transcript, Case XI, Weizsaecker*, 28291–92., 12:176–177, 193. Puhl attempted to shift the onus of guilt to Funk when he testi-

fied before the IMT (Conot, *Justice at Nuremberg*, 406). His performance on the stand led Conot to conclude: "It was evident that Funk, Puhl, and Thorns were all lying about the extent of their knowledge—though at the beginning they had not been fully aware of the manner in which the SS had acquired their booty" (404–408). For more on Puhl laundering gold and other valuables for the Nazis, see Tom Bower, *Nazi Gold* (New York: HarperCollins, 1997).

93. *U.S. Military Tribunal Nuremberg, Transcript, Case XI, Weizsaecker*, 28378. Chief of Prisoner of War Affairs Gottlob Berger faced a mountain of damning evidence, like the fact that he proposed the "Heu Aktion" project to Alfried Rosenberg. This was the code name for a plan to enslave 50,000 10- to 14-year-olds. Berger was also involved in the formation and activities of the Dirlewanger Brigade.

94. Gerald Reitlinger, *The SS: Alibi of a Nation 1922–1945* (New York: Viking, 1957), 171. In 1935, Dirlewanger was sentenced to two years' imprisonment for "offenses on a minor." According to Reitlinger, "When he was released, Berger used his influence to get poor old Oskar into the Condor Legion, who were serving in Spain under General Franco. In 1939, when Dirlewanger had to return to Germany, Berger, as head of the SS Staff Office, got him reinstated as a colonel of the general SS Reserve" (172). For more on Dirlewanger see French MacLean, *The Cruel Hunters* (Atglen, Pa: Schiffer Military History, 1998).

95. Reitlinger, *The SS: Alibi of a Nation 1922–1945*, 174n4. At Nuremberg, Berger and others tried to maintain that killing units like the Dirlewanger regiment were not part of the SS. Reitlinger rejects this contention: "The text of Himmler's second Posen speech was only discovered in 1953, and it casts a dubious light on the testimony, given years previously at Nuremberg, by Gottlob Berger. . . . Both fought hard to maintain that the Dirlewanger regiment was not part of the SS at all" (172).

96. *U.S. Military Tribunal Nuremberg, Transcript, Case XI, Weizsaecker*, 218–220. Walter Schellenberg was an SS general and also a close friend and confidant of Heinrich Himmler. For more on Schellenberg, see Richard Breitman, *Official Secrets* (New York: Hill and Wang, 1998), 227, 255.

97. Reitlinger, *The SS: Alibi of a Nation 1922–1945*, 351, 353.

98. Robert Kempner, interview by author, tape recording, Locarno, Switzerland, 23 February 1988.

99. The *New York Times* described her testimony in the Ministries case: "On his return at 5 a.m. the Czech was a broken man, pale and exhausted, the witness said. He informed her that he capitulated after Hitler had ranted and shouted for hours and Goering had assured him as an alternative to a signing of the proffered papers he would leave immediately and order the destruction of Prague by the Luftwaffe to demonstrate its efficiency to the Western powers" (*New York Times*, 13 January 1948, 9, col. 1). Kathleen McLaughlin described the significance of this testimony: "Her testimony implicated especially the No. 1 defendant, Baron Ernst von Weizsaecker, and Otto Meissner on the trial of Nazi diplomats and officials" (9).

100. Robert Maguire, letter to family 25 January 1948, Constance Maguire Wilson Papers, 1.

101. This became the crux of von Weizsäcker's defense against the charges of crimes against peace.

102. Walter LaFeber, *America, Russia, and the Cold War* (New York: Knopf, 1985), 71–72.

103. LaFeber, *America, Russia, and the Cold War*, 72.

104. Jean Smith, "The View from USFET: General Clay's Interpretation of Soviet Intentions in Germany, 1945–1948," in Schmitt, ed., *The U.S. Occupation of Europe*, 73.

105. Ibid.

106. Clay, letter to General Eisenhower, 28 July 1947, in Smith, ed., *The Papers of General Lucius Clay*, 1:389–390.

107. Clay, letter to General Eisenhower, 28 July 1947, in Smith, ed., *The Papers of General Lucius Clay*, 1:390.

108. Simpson, *Blowback,* 54. Heinz Hohne of *Der Spiegel* claimed that during the first few years of the Cold War "seventy percent of all the U.S. government's information on Soviet forces came from the Gehlen organization" (54).

109. Simpson, *Blowback,* 65. This comment echoes John Kenneth Galbraith, who once observed that the Cold War produced an American James Bondism "based on the thesis that Communist disrespect for international law and accepted standards of behavior could only be countered by an even more sanguinary immorality on the part of the United States" (Galbraith, "The Sub-Imperial Style of American Foreign Policy," *Esquire 77* [1972]: 79–84).

110. Smith, *Lucius D. Clay,* 75. "In February, while Congress debated the Marshall Plan for European recovery, Czechoslovakia receded further behind the Iron Curtain as the non-Communist members of government were ousted. Doomsayers in Washington believed their prediction fulfilled, although as George Kennan has noted, such a move changed very little and should have been anticipated. On the heels of events in Prague, Lt. Gen. S.J. Chamberlin, Director of Army Intelligence, visited Clay in Berlin. He impressed upon Clay the pitiful unreadiness of U.S. armed forces, the fact that military appropriations were pending before Congress, and the need to galvanize public support for substantial rearmament" (75).

111. Smith, *Lucius D. Clay,* 75–76. "In fairness to Clay, it must be recognized that he did not envision how the cable would be used or what its effects would be. His intent was to assist the Army before Congress; it was not to create war hysteria in the country. In fact, Clay was appalled when its contents were leaked to the *Saturday Evening Post.* 'The revelation of such a cablegram,' he advised Bradley, 'is not helpful and in fact discloses the viewpoint of a responsible commander out of context with many parallel reports'" (Smith, ed., *The Papers of General Lucius Clay*, 2:961–962).

112. Smith, *Lucius D. Clay,* 76.

113. Michael Howard, "Governor General of Germany," *Times Literary Supplement,* 29 August 1975.

114. Etzold and Gaddis, eds., *Containment,* 120.

115. Taylor, *Final Report to the Secretary of the Army on the Nuernberg War Crimes Trials,* 202–203.

116. Taylor, *Final Report to the Secretary of the Army on the Nuernberg War Crimes Trials,* 203.

117. *Trials of War Criminals before Nuernberg Military Tribunals Under Control Council No. 10* (Washington, D.C.: U.S. Government Printing Office, 1949).

118. *Trials of War Criminals before Nuernberg Military Tribunals Under Control Council No. 10,* 789.

119. Taylor, *Final Report to the Secretary of the Army on the Nuernberg War Crimes Trials,* 203. Transcripts, case 7, 10, 446.

120. Taylor, *Final Report to the Secretary of the Army on the Nuernberg War Crimes Trials,* 204. General Taylor's description of the judgment leaves open the possibility of legitimate legal differences: "One can easily understand these protests, but, in the writer's view, they have tended to obscure the admirable workmanship of the judgment. Furthermore, these were much mooted questions, with highly political overtones, and it is hard to criticize the court's conservative determination to apply international law, 'as we find it,' not 'as we would have it.' In the long run, this may well promote the revision of international law along more enlightened lines, which is far more important than the decision with respect to these particular defendants" (207).

121. *U.S. Military Tribunal Nuremberg, Transcript, Case VII, List* (Nuremberg: Secretariat for Military Tribunals, 1949), 10441. The first paragraph read: "In no other way can an army guard and protect itself from the gadfly tactics of such armed resistance. And, on the other hand, members of such resistance forces must accept the increased risks involved in this mode of fighting. Such forces are technically lawful belligerents and are not entitled to protection as prisoners when captured."

122. *U.S. Military Tribunal Nuremberg, Transcript, Case VII, List* (Nuremberg: Secretariat for Military Tribunals, 1949), 10441.

123. Appleman, *Military Tribunals and International Crimes,* 192; Transcripts, case 7, 10441–2.

124. *U.S. Military Tribunal Nuremberg, Transcript, Case VII, List,* 10446.

125. *U.S. Military Tribunal Nuremberg, Transcript, Case VII, List,* 10446. See also Roberts and Guelff, eds., *Documents on the Laws of War,* 48–49.

126. Appleman, *Military Tribunals and International Crimes,* 186.

127. *U.S. Military Tribunal Nuremberg, Transcript, Case VII, List,* 10542. Charles Wennerstrum's comments appeared in the conservative *Chicago Tribune* on February 23, 1948. Telford Taylor's rebuttal was printed the same day in a *New York Times* article entitled, "Prosecutor Scores War-Crimes Judge." Tom Schwartz describes the role assumed by the *Chicago Tribune* in the Nuremberg debates: "The conservative Chicago Tribune, with the remarks of Judge Charles Wennerstrum ... made itself the mouthpiece of the critics of the Nuremberg trials" (*"Die Begnadigung deutscher Kriegsverbrecher—John J. McCloy und die Häftlinge von Landsberg"* in *Vierteljahrshefte für Zeitgeschichte* 38 [July 1990]: 382).

128. Buscher, *The U.S. War Crimes Trial Program,* 188. "Nazi Trial Judge Rips 'Injustice,'" *Chicago Tribune,* February 23, 1948.

129. Buscher charges in *The U.S. War Crimes Trial Program* that Hal Foust's transmissions were intercepted by the army in violation of U.S. wiretapping laws (35). Taylor described how he received Wennerstrum's comments before they were printed in the United States: "There was a place in Frankfurt where most of the American newspapers had their headquarters where the members of the press hung up what

was going out." Telford Taylor, interview by author, tape recording, New York City, 24 February 1993.

130. Schwartz, "*Die Begnadigung deutscher Kreigsverbrecher*," 380. Translation by the author and Martin Splichal.

131. Telford Taylor, letter to Charles Wennerstrum, 21 February 1948, reprinted in Appleman, *Military Tribunals and International Crimes*, 190–191. "It has come to my attention that yesterday, a few hours before your departure from Nürnberg, you gave an interview to a representative of the *Chicago Tribune*, in the course of which you made a deliberate, malicious, and totally unfounded attack on the integrity of the very trials in which you yourself were a presiding judge. It is clear from the nature of your remarks that you were not speaking on behalf of your Tribunal or in your official capacity, but were volunteering purely personal views. Since your remarks are subversive of the interests and policies of the United States, they must not go unanswered" (190). When Wennerstrum returned to the United States on February 24, 1948, he was met by the press with a copy of Taylor's comments. The judge stood behind his prior statements. *The New York Times* reported: "Questioned as to his original criticism of persons 'with personal ambitions,' he said they applied 'to the prosecutors and their superior'" (February 25, 1948, 10, col. 3). The other two judges from the Hostage case were unwilling to side with their colleague, according to the same article: "They refused to enter the controversy. Both associate judges, however, asserted that they were satisfied with the outcome."

132. Appleman, *Military Tribunals and International Crimes*, 191. The Chief Counsel pointed out the weakness of Wennerstrum's *ad hominem* attack: "Instead of making any constructive moves while you were here, you have chosen to give out a baseless, malicious attack during the last hours of your eight-month stay and then leave town rather than confront those whom you have so outrageously slandered."

133. *Congressional Record*, December 16, 1948, 11468.

134. As Buscher notes in *The U.S. War Crimes Trial Program*, American criticism provided a pretext for German critics.

135. Buscher, *The U.S. War Crimes Trial Program*, 35–36.

136. Robert Maguire, letter to Constance Maguire Wilson, 24 February 1948 (in possession of the author).

137. Maguire was somewhat pessimistic about the revolutionary impact of the Nuremberg trials: "The more one looks into the history of peoples, particularly those of Russia and the East, the less enthusiastic he is likely to be; they have in the past and they are now, bogged down in the age old jealousies, ideology, racial, religious, and political that have been the eternal causes of war, and the people of each country refuse to examine their own mirrors to see where they have been wrong, but insist on the errors and shortcomings of their neighbors." (Robert Maguire, letter to Constance Maguire Wilson, 24 February 1948, 2).

138. Robert Maguire, letter to Constance Maguire Wilson, 24 February 1948. The conservative Republican remained unconvinced by the anti-Soviet siren song and wrote in late March 1948, "I don't think Russia wants war, nor do I believe that for a sizable number of years, she could wage war, but that short of going to war she will do everything she can to get everything she can."

139. American Nuremberg Trials, *Case 11—United States v. Ernst von Weizsaecker,* 13:97.

140. James Brand, letter to Robert Maguire, 12 May 1948, Betty Maguire Frankus Papers, 1.

141. James Brand, letter to Robert Maguire, 12 May 1948, Betty Maguire Frankus Papers, 1.

142. Walter Rockler, interview by author, tape recording, Washington, D.C., 18 April 1987. Robert Maguire, letter to family, 14 April 1948, Constance Maguire Wilson Papers, 2.

143. American Nuremberg Trials, *Case 9—United States v. Otto Ohlendorf,* 531. The evidence in the Einsatzgruppen case was specific and highly incriminating. The majority of it consisted of the group's reports from the Soviet Union.

144. Appleman, *Military Tribunals and International Crimes,* 202.

145. Appleman, *Military Tribunals and International Crimes,* 202. See Christopher Browning, *Ordinary Men* (New York: HarperCollins, 1998).

146. Appleman, *Military Tribunals and International Crimes,* 202. On the stand Ohlendorf testified, "I was the leader in Einsatzgruppen D in the southern sector, and in the course of the year . . . it liquidated approximately 90,000 men, women and children. The majority of those liquidated were Jews, but there were among them some communist functionaries" (International Military Tribunal, *Trial of the Major War Criminals* [Nuremberg: IMT, 1947], 4:206).

147. American Nuremberg Trials, *Case 9—United States v. Otto Ohlendorf,* 569, 530–531; Appleman, *Military Tribunals and International Crimes,* 202.

148. See Appleman, *Military Tribunals and International Crimes,* 202–203, for a summary of Taylor's closing statement.

149. Taylor, *Final Report to the Secretary of the Army on the Nuernberg War Crimes Trials,* 183.

150. Taylor, *Final Report to the Secretary of the Army on the Nuernberg War Crimes Trials,* 181.

151. Taylor, *Final Report to the Secretary of the Army on the Nuernberg War Crimes Trials,* 184.

152. Levie, *Terrorism in War,* 376.

153. Levie, *Terrorism in War,* 376.

154. *Interrogation Report of Carl Schmitt, Nuremberg Office of U.S. Chief Counsel for War Crimes, Evidence Division,* transcript No. 1842. Reprinted in *Telos* 72 (Summer 1987). Although Schmitt offered no substantive comments on Ernst von Weizsäcker, his initial reaction is telling when compared to his responses about other important Nazis like Hans Lammers. Schmitt seemed genuinely surprised by von Weizsäcker's inclusion and the activities in which the diplomat was involved.

155. Richard von Weizsäcker, *From Weimar to the Wall,* trans. Ruth Hein (New York: Broadway, 1999), 48.

156. *Case Eleven—Ernst von Weizsaecker,* XII: 237–238.

157. Robert Louis Stevenson, *The Strange Case of Dr. Jekyll and Mr. Hyde,* from Luders, "The Strange Case of Ernst von Weizsaecker," 111.

158. Von Weizsäcker, *From Weimar to the Wall*, 48. According to German diplomatic historian Klemens von Klemperer, "Weizsäcker no doubt pursued what Hans Ruthfels called a *Sonderpolitik* designed to protect the integrity of the Foreign Service and especially to counteract the aggressive plans of the Foreign Minister, von Ribbentrop, and thus prevent the great war" (Klemens von Klemperer, *German Resistance Against Hitler* [Oxford: Clarendon, 1992], 102).

159. Von Weizsäcker, *From Weimar to the Wall*, 90.

160. "1). A resister is someone with a political philosophy, which, whatever it may be, is clearly and honestly opposed to the philosophy and ideology of Nazism. 2). Resistance requires active intent to remove Nazism from power and influence by revolutionary action or active participation in, incitement to, or preparation for such action. This would usually, if not necessarily, include political planning or preparation of a policy which is to replace the removed one. 3). Active prevention and/or sabotage of such measures and propaganda which made Nazism what it is" (Luders, "The Strange Case of Ernst von Weizsaecker," 63–64). In the cases that preceded it, "Unlike in the case of Weizsaecker, in which political resistance played a decisive part in his defense, it had merely been stated as a mitigating circumstance that both defendants had occasionally advocated the tempering of certain measures. The key distinction was that in the IMT cases none of the defendants nor their witnesses considered their actions to constitute political resistance" (68*n*29).

161. Von Weizsäcker, *From Weimar to the Wall*, 95. Von Weizsäcker claimed that the British foreign office "ordered these men to keep silent."

162. *Trials of War Criminals before Nuernberg Military Tribunals Under Control Council No. 10*, XII:152–153.

163. *Trials of War Criminals before Nuernberg Military Tribunals Under Control Council No. 10*, XII:154–156.

164. *U.S. Military Tribunal Nuremberg, Transcript, Case XI, Weizsaecker*, 28328; Kaiser, *Politics and War*, 432–433.

165. John Cornwell, *Hitler's Pope: The Secret History of Pius XII* (New York: Viking, 1999), 300. See also Guenter Lewy, *The Catholic Church and Nazi Germany* (New York: Da Capo, 1964), 300–302.

166. Cornwell, *Hitler's Pope*, 311. According to Cornwell, "The letter indicates the subtle double game that Weizsäcker had played throughout the deportation episode. It was Weizsäcker who helped stop the further arrests of Jews by raising the threat of papal protests that Pacelli had no intention of making. Now that no further arrests were to come, he could speak complacently of the Pope's willingness to remain silent. But what of the thousands who had died?" (312). Ian Buruma on von Weizsäcker's role in the Vatican: "Since 1943, he had served as ambassador to the Vatican—a rather crucial posting, since the Germans wanted to make sure the Pope kept silent about the Final Solution. Whether or not it was due to Weizsaecker's diplomatic skills, the Pope did not disappoint them" (Buruma, *The Wages of Guilt*, 142). See also Michael Phayer, *The Catholic Church and the Holocaust* (Bloomington: Indiana University Press, 2000).

167. *Trials of War Criminals before Nuernberg Military Tribunals Under Control Council No. 10*, XII:148.

168. *Trials of War Criminals before Nuernberg Military Tribunals Under Control Council No. 10*, XII:152.

169. *Trials of War Criminals before Nuernberg Military Tribunals Under Control Council No. 10*, XII:148–153.

170. *U.S. Military Tribunal Nuremberg, Transcript, Case XI, Weizsaecker*, 28331. Parts of Hassell's diary were introduced as rebuttal evidence by the prosecution (NG 5759, Exhibit C-288, Doc. Bk. 204A); from Luders, "The Strange Case of Ernst von Weizsaecker." For more on the resistance see Hans Gisevius, *To the Bitter End* (Boston: Houghton Mifflin, 1947); Peter Hoffman, *The History of the German Resistance, 1933–1945* (Cambridge: MIT Press, 1979); Allen Dulles, *Germany's Underground* (New York: Macmillan, 1947).

171. *U.S. Military Tribunal Nuremberg, Transcript, Case XI, Weizsaecker*, 8538.

172. LaFeber, *America, Russia and the Cold War*, 71–72.

173. William Caming, conversation with author, 7 July 1987. William Caming, interviews by author, tape recording, Summit, New Jersey, 9 October 1987, fall 1989. Similar sentiments were expressed to the author by Telford Taylor, Drexel Sprecher, Robert Kempner, and Walter Rockler in interviews and conversations. The Italians were in the midst of an election campaign and the Communist Party was running strong. George Kennan and other high-level policy makers were greatly alarmed by the prospect of the Italian Communist Party gaining control of the government through a popular election. The list of men involved in the anti-Communist effort in Italy reads like a Cold War all-star team roster. It includes George Kennan, Allen Dulles, James Angleton, Frank Wisner, and William Colby. The Americans worked with the Vatican on behalf of Christian Democrat candidates. Their aid included various types of agitprop, specifically designed to highlight "American munificence and communist atrocities, both real and manufactured." See Simpson, *Blowback*, 90–91. For more on the CIA's role in the Italian election see William Corson, *The Armies of Ignorance* (New York: Dial/James Wade, 1977); see also Wilson Miscamble, *George F. Kennan and the Making of American Foreign Policy* (Princeton: Princeton University Press, 1992).

174. Friedrich, "Nuremberg and the Germans," 92.

175. *Defense Brief—Lammers-Meissner-Cross Closing*, X1B11:4, 42.

176. *Defense Brief—Lammers-Meissner-Cross Closing*, X1B11:67.

177. American Nuremberg Trials, *Case 11—United States v. Ernst von Weizsaecker*, 12:257.

178. American Nuremberg Trials, *Case 11—United States v. Ernst von Weizsaecker*, 12:358. Edmund Veesenmayer's attorney made a similar argument: "His work there was guided only by the thought of helping his comrades who were fighting desperately against the overwhelming power of the Red Army . . . this man moved along a lonely ridge between life and death in his work, day by day, year by year, motivated by his love for Germany, and moved by the thought of achieving a better European order" (300). *Green Series* vol. XII, 358–359.

179. American Nuremberg Trials, *Case 11—United States v. Ernst von Weizsaecker*, 12:358.

180. *U.S. Military Tribunal Nuremberg, Transcript, Case XI, Weizsaecker,* 28432. In a speech at a 1935 Nazi Party rally, Dietrich described his view of the press under a modern dictatorship: "The liberalistic age boasted of the Press as a Seventh Power. . . . In National Socialist Germany that kind of press was eliminated with lightning speed by the arm of the law! A fate which it deserved a thousand fold, overtook it on the first day of the revolution. . . . In National Socialist Germany, enemies of the state and the people are not tolerated in the press; they are exterminated" (28432).

181. The IMT set the precedent followed by the tribunals in the Flick, Farben, and Krupp cases. The majority of the American courts bowed to the IMT's conservative precedents.

182. Schacht was found innocent under Counts 1 and 2 and acquitted. Appleman, *Military Tribunals and International Crimes,* 171–172.

183. *U.S. Military Tribunal Nuremberg, Transcript, Case X, Krupp* (Nuremberg: Secretariat for Military Tribunals, 1949), 13435–37.

184. Taylor, *Final Report to the Secretary of the Army on the Nuernberg War Crimes Trials,* 197.

185. Taylor, *Final Report to the Secretary of the Army on the Nuernberg War Crimes Trials,* 319.

186. Taylor, *Final Report to the Secretary of the Army on the Nuernberg War Crimes Trials,* 319.

187. Borkin, *The Crime and Punishment of I. G. Farben,* 142.

188. Borkin, *The Crime and Punishment of I. G. Farben,* 144.

189. Borkin, *The Crime and Punishment of I. G. Farben,* 134.

190. Borkin, *The Crime and Punishment of I. G. Farben,* 148.

191. Borkin, *The Crime and Punishment of I. G. Farben,* 149.

192. Borkin, *The Crime and Punishment of I. G. Farben,* 149.

193. Borkin, *The Crime and Punishment of I. G. Farben,* 149.

194. Borkin, *The Crime and Punishment of I. G. Farben,* 150.

195. Borkin, *The Crime and Punishment of I. G. Farben,* 151.

196. Borkin, *The Crime and Punishment of I. G. Farben,* 154. See Josiah DuBois, *The Devil's Chemists: 24 Conspirators of the International Farben Cartel Who Manufacture Wars* (Boston: Beacon, 1952) for his account of the trial.

197. Borkin, *The Crime and Punishment of I. G. Farben,* 151. Appleman, *Military Tribunals and International Crimes,* 181. Judge Hebert agreed: "bowing to such weighty precedents as the acquittal by the International Military Tribunal of Schacht and Speer on the charges of Crimes Against Peace; of the acquittal by Military Tribunal III of the leading officials of the Krupp firm on similar charges . . . I do not agree with the majority's conclusion that the evidence presented in this case falls so far short of sufficiency as the Tribunal's opinion would seem to indicate. The issues of fact are truly so close as to cause genuine concern as to whether or not justice has actually been done because of the enormous and indispensable role these defendants were shown to have played in the building of the war machine which made Hitler's aggressions possible" (181).

198. Borkin, *The Crime and Punishment of I. G. Farben*, 151.

199. Borkin, *The Crime and Punishment of I. G. Farben*, 155.

200. Levie, *Terrorism in War*, 480.

201. Appleman, *Military Tribunals and International Crimes*, 211.

202. Taylor, *Final Report to the Secretary of the Army on the Nuernberg War Crimes Trials*, 193. The Krupp Works' use of slave labor violated a number of the convention's articles.

203. *U.S. Military Tribunal Nuremberg, Transcript, Case X, Krupp*, 12380–81.

204. *U.S. Military Tribunal Nuremberg, Transcript, Case X, Krupp*, 13451–52.

205. Appleman, *Military Tribunals and International Crimes*, 180–181.

206. Taylor, *Final Report to the Secretary of the Army on the Nuernberg War Crimes Trials*, 193. Appleman, *Military Tribunals and International Crimes*, 177–178. The most severe sentences were two eight-year terms. Eleven of the twenty-three defendants were acquitted or released for time served. The weekly *Christ und Welt* featured a picture of Curtis Shake, presiding judge at the Farben trial, with the following caption: "The president of the U.S. Military Tribunal in the Nuremberg I. G. Farben trial, who excelled by his just conduct of the proceedings, by his absolute objectivity and disregard for all vindictive sentiments, as well as by his endeavor to understand the nature of German conditions between 1933 and 1945." Appleman, *Military Tribunals and International Crimes*, 181mb.

207. Robert Maguire, letter to Katie Maguire, 27 July 1948 (in possession of the author).

208. *U.S. Military Tribunal Nuremberg, Transcript, Case XI, Weizsaecker*, 28087. The Ministries case transcript was 28,085 pages long, and this does not include the 9,067 pages of documentary exhibits.

209. John Dower, *Embracing Defeat: Japan in the Wake of World War II* (New York: Norton, 1999), 453; Piccigallo, *The Japanese on Trial*, 46.

210. Richard H. Minear, *Victor's Justice: The Tokyo War Crimes Trial* (Princeton: Princeton University Press, 1971), 72. The trial lasted 31 months, from May 3, 1946 through November 1948. Seven were sentenced to death, 16 to life, one to 20 years, and one to 7 years. There were no acquittals. Five died in prison, while the remaining 12 prisoners were paroled between 1954 and 1956. "In 1958, the last ten were granted clemency following discussions with the former victorious powers" (Dower, *Embracing Defeat*, 450). In Khabarovsk, 12 former members of Japan's infamous Unit 731 were put on trial; all pled guilty and confessed (Dower, *Embracing Defeat*, 449). See Yuki Tanaka, *Hidden Horrors: Japanese War Crimes in World War II* (Boulder, Colo.: Westview, 1996), 2 and Dower, *Embracing Defeat*, 450. From 1945 to 1951, Allied military commissions in the Far East sentenced 920 to death and 3,000 to various prison terms (vi). U.S. trials in the Pacific were held in the Philippines (215); China (75); Pacific Islands (123); and Yokohama (996) (Piccigallo, *The Japanese on Trial*, 74).

211. Judith Shklar, *Legalism: Laws, Morals, and Political Trials* (Cambridge: Harvard University Press, 1964), 185–186. Shklar points out the weakness of natural law as a basis for the charge of aggressive war: "Many observers have noted that natural law is capable of too many interpretations in any concrete situation to provide an

objective and impersonal basis for international criminal trials. At Tokyo there was a telling illustration of this point. Justice Bernard based his dissent on natural law too, but in his view it rendered the charge of waging aggressive war illegitimate. In short, the very charge which Mr. Keenan's natural law supported, Justice Bernard's natural law rejected" (185). In his dissenting opinion, the French justice wrote that the defendants were only "accomplices," and the "principal author . . . escaped all prosecution" (Dower, *Embracing Defeat*, 460).

212. "The Emperor's authority was required for war. If he did not want war he should have withheld his authority" (Dower, *Embracing Defeat*, 460). See also Piccigallo, *The Japanese on Trial*, 29. For more on Hirohito's wartime role and nonindictment, see Herbert Bix, *Hirohito and the Making of Modern Japan* (New York: Harper Collins, 2000).

213. Piccigallo, *The Japanese on Trial*, 30.

214. Levie, *Terrorism in War*, 390.

215. R. John Pritchard and Sonia Magbanua Zaide, eds., *The Tokyo War Crimes Trials* (New York: Garland, 1981), 21:1226. Pal wrote: "For reasons given in the foregoing pages, I would hold that each and every one of the accused must be found not guilty of each and every one of the charges in the indictment and should be acquitted of all those charges. . . . I believe that this is really an appeal to the political power of the victor nations with a pretense of legal justice. It only amounts to piecing up want of legality with matter of convenience" (1226).

216. David Luban, *Legal Modernism* (Ann Arbor: University of Michigan Press, 1994), 340–341. Levie wrote that Judge Pal "went to Tokyo prepared to strike a blow for Asia's freedom from European colonization" (*Terrorism in War* 152).

217. Pritchard and Zaide, eds., *The Tokyo War Crimes Trials*, 279; Dower, *Embracing Defeat*, 473.

218. Luban, *Legal Modernism*, 341.

219. Piccigallo, *The Japanese on Trial*, 31.

220. Pritchard and Zaide, eds., *The Tokyo War Crimes Trials*, 1091. Dower, *Embracing Defeat*, 473.

221. Shklar, *Legalism*, 186–187.

222. Pritchard and Zaide, eds., *The Tokyo War Crimes Trials*, 279; Dower, *Embracing Defeat*, 460.

223. Robert Maguire, letter to Katie Maguire, 27 July 1948, 1. Maguire knew his trial would be the last to finish in the summer of 1948 when he wrote his mother: "Our case moves along but not very rapidly to my disgust and disappointment but there is little we can do about it" (2).

224. Ruth Maguire, letter to Katie Maguire, 13 January 1949. Now it was clear Powers would not concur with the majority opinion, and this added several months to the Maguires' stay. "If he had known that he would have to stay as long as this he said he would not have come. However, when it's all over, I think he will be glad to have had the experience over here—in spite of the grueling last months" (1).

225. *Stars and Stripes*, April 12, 1949.

226. American Nuremberg Trials, *Case 11—United States v. Ernst von Weizsaecker*, 14:316.

227. *U.S. Military Tribunal Nuremberg, Transcript, Case XI, Weizsaecker,* 28092–93.

228. *U.S. Military Tribunal Nuremberg, Transcript, Case XI, Weizsaecker,* 28093.

229. *U.S. Military Tribunal Nuremberg, Transcript, Case XI, Weizsaecker,* 28093.

230. *U.S. Military Tribunal Nuremberg, Transcript, Case XI, Weizsaecker,* 28096–97. Jack Raymond of *The New York Times* observed this in an article entitled "Five High Nazis Guilty of Helping Hitler to Violate Peace": "The court rejected the defense claim that the Soviet-German treaty disclosed that the Soviet Union was just as guilty as Germany of waging aggressive war" (*New York Times,* April 12, 1949, 1, col. 1).

231. *U.S. Military Tribunal Nuremberg, Transcript, Case XI, Weizsaecker,* 28097. *The New York Times* reported the convictions for crimes against peace: "The conviction on the aggressive war count was the first in the twelve trials conducted by the United States since the International Military Court at Nuremberg convicted Hermann Goering and other makers of Nazi high policy" (Raymond, "Five High Nazis Guilty," 1).

232. *U.S. Military Tribunal Nuremberg, Transcript, Case XI, Weizsaecker,* 28121. Jack Raymond described the court's reasoning: "Although the court conceded Weizsaecker 'continuously discouraged Ribbentrop's penchant for aggressive war,' a 'radically different' attitude was attributed to him after the Munich pact. 'The reason for this we think is obvious,' the court declared. 'Before Munich he feared that France and England would take up arms in defense of Czechoslovakia and that if it did so, Germany would suffer defeat. After Munich he felt danger to Germany had vanished and he looked with complaisance if not approval on the future fate of Czechoslovakia'" (Raymond, "Five High Nazis Guilty," 1).

233. *U.S. Military Tribunal Nuremberg, Transcript, Case XI, Weizsaecker,* 28121.

234. *U.S. Military Tribunal Nuremberg, Transcript, Case XI, Weizsaecker,* 28121.

235. *U.S. Military Tribunal Nuremberg, Transcript, Case XI, Weizsaecker,* 28140.

236. *U.S. Military Tribunal Nuremberg, Transcript, Case XI, Weizsaecker,* 28122.

237. *U.S. Military Tribunal Nuremberg, Transcript, Case XI, Weizsaecker,* 28293.

238. *U.S. Military Tribunal Nuremberg, Transcript, Case XI, Weizsaecker,* 28292.

239. *U.S. Military Tribunal Nuremberg, Transcript, Case XI, Weizsaecker,* 28096–97.

240. Powers rejected the charges on the grounds that these acts were not traditional war crimes because they were not committed by combatants or (in the cases of Austria and Czechoslovakia) during wartime.

241. *U.S. Military Tribunal Nuremberg, Transcript, Case XI, Weizsaecker,* 28116.

242. American Nuremberg Trials, *Case 11—United States v. Ernst von Weizsaecker,* 14:877.

243. American Nuremberg Trials, *Case 11—United States v. Ernst von Weizsaecker,* 14:872. The standard by which Judge Powers measured individual guilt favored the defendants; he wrote, "to establish personal guilt it must appear that the individual defendant must have performed some act which has a causal connection with the crimes charged, and must have performed it with the intention of committing a crime." See Levie, *Terrorism in War,* 95.

244. American Nuremberg Trials, *Case 11—United States v. Ernst von Weizsaecker,* 14:890.

245. Appleman, *Military Tribunals and International Crimes*, 222–223.

246. *U.S. Military Tribunal Nuremberg, Transcript, Case XI, Weizsaecker*, 28285.

247. *U.S. Military Tribunal Nuremberg, Transcript, Case XI, Weizsaecker*, 28285.

248. American Nuremberg Trials, *Case 11—United States v. Ernst von Weizsaecker*, 12:219–220.

249. "Report of the Advisory Board on Clemency for War Criminals to the U.S. High Commission for Germany Advisory Clemency Report," RG 59, Box 5 (Clemency Board on German War Criminals), 13, NA.

250. Ibid..

251. Appleman, *Military Tribunals and International Crimes*, 223.

252. Levie, *Terrorism in War*, 478n36.

253. American Nuremberg Trials, *Case 11—United States v. Ernst von Weizsaecker*, 14:931. According to Judge Powers's conservative reading of the laws of war: "To be guilty—I repeat—the defendant must have participated in the initiation of a war of aggression. In order to do that, he must have committed some act intended to have some effect in bringing about a war, knowing it would become a war of aggression. That evidence is conspicuous by its absence here" (894). Jack Raymond analyzed the Powers dissent in an article entitled "Nuremberg Judge Dissents on Guilt" (*The New York Times*, April 14, 1949, 8, col. 1): "Most of the court's verdicts were immediately condemned by one of its members, Judge Leon W Powers. He said in a dissenting opinion that his two colleagues were endorsing a 'strange doctrine' of attributing guilt to those who merely had knowledge of a crime. . . . Judge Powers' contention that 'guilt is personal and individual and must be based on personal acts of an individual charged,' was in direct contradiction to the majority view that those who did the planning and administrative work of the crimes were 'equally guilty' with concentration camp commanders and other implementers of the crimes."

254. American Nuremberg Trials, *Case 11—United States v. Ernst von Weizsaecker*, 14:930.

255. American Nuremberg Trials, *Case 11—United States v. Ernst von Weizsaecker*, 14:931.

256. American Nuremberg Trials, *Case 11—United States v. Ernst von Weizsaecker*, 14:866–871.

257. William Caming, paper delivered at University of South Carolina College, September 11, 1998, 13; American Nuremberg Trials, *Case 11—United States v. Ernst von Weizsaecker*, 14:947. "Ernst Von Weizsaecker, Gustav Adolf Steenracht von Moyland, Wilhelm Keppler, Wilhelm Stuckart, Richard Walter Darré, Otto Dietrich, Gottlob Berger, Walter Schellenberg, Lutz Scherin von Krosigk, Emil Puhl, Paul Koerner, Paul Pleiger, and Hans Kehrl presented to and filed with the Tribunal a motion to set aside the decision and the judgment of conviction 'on the grounds that said decision and judgment is contrary to the facts, contrary to law, and against the weight of the evidence; on the ground that this Court has no jurisdiction to hear and determine the alleged charges, and on the further ground that the facts alleged and the facts found do not constitute an offense against the law of nations or against the laws of the sovereign power of the United States,' and on

the ground 'that the rulings made are not in conformity with the principles of the due process of law, and the Constitution and laws of the United States, the international law, and the rules of law generally applicable to the trial of criminal cases" (14:946 – 947).

258. *Stars and Stripes,* April 15, 1949, 1.
259. *Stars and Stripes,* April 15, 1949, 1.
260. Wilbourn Benton, ed., *Nuremberg: German Views of the War Trials* (Dallas: Southern Methodist University Press, 1953), 197.

5. NUREMBERG: A COLD WAR CONFLICT OF INTEREST

1. Robert Maguire, letter to Kathy Bomke, 29 April 1959, 2 (in possession of the author).

2. Robert Maguire, letter to Kathy Bomke, 29 April 1959, 2 (in possession of the author). While praising the fairness of the Nuremberg trials, von Knieriem made a very important observation: "No one who occupies himself with the legal problems of the Nuremberg trials can avoid a consideration of the laws of warfare. But what has happened to these rules of law during the last decades? Have they not perhaps disappeared? Each modern war has been more radical and more horrible than the preceding one; each war has swept away a part of the international law of warfare" (Wilbourn Benton, ed., *Nuremberg: German Views of the War Trials* [Dallas: Southern Methodist University Press, 1953], xxi).

3. Richard von Weizsäcker, *From Weimar to the Wall,* trans. Ruth Hein (New York: Broadway Books, 1999), 90, 95. "Since then, the extensive literature on the contemporary history of both Germany and the rest of the world has left little serious doubt about the appropriateness of the charges against my father."

4. Klemens von Klemperer, *German Resistance Against Hitler* (Oxford: Clarendon, 1992), 26. Klemperer describes it as "social refusal" rather than resistance. German historian Marion Thielenhaus examines the period 1938 – 41 and portrays Ernst von Weizsäcker as an "ultranationalist" trying to keep the German Foreign Office from being absorbed by the National Socialists and to prevent a larger war from breaking out. Richard von Weizsäcker's book does not mention the role that Ernst von Weizsäcker played in the deportation of European Jews, or the fact that the State Secretary regularly reviewed the reports of the *Einsatzgruppen.*

   A review of Thielenhaus's study of a group of German diplomats, *Zwischen Anpassung und Widerstand: Deutsche Diplomaten, 1938–1941* (Paderborn: Ferdinand Schöningh, 1985) by Gerhard Weinberg (*Journal of Modern History* 9 [Sept. 1987]: 638) raises many of the same questions as the tribunal majority in the Ministries case: "If she had extended her scope to include at least minimal reference to von Weizsäcker's regular review of the reports of the murder squads (Einsatzgruppen), his role in the extraction of Jews from all over Europe for dispatch to the killing centers, his rejection out of hand of the Swedish government's offer to accept the Norwegian Jews to prevent their being murdered, and his postwar admiring comment on one of the leaders of the murder squads, she might have seen more clearly a side of the central figure in the book that is entirely blocked out by the tunnel vision of this monograph."

5. Jörg Friedrich, "Nuremberg and the Germans," in Belinda Cooper, ed., *War Crimes: The Legacy of Nuremberg* (New York: TV Books, 1999), 92. *U.S. Military Tribunal Nuremberg, Transcript, Case XI, Weizsaecker* (Nuremberg: Secretariat for Military Tribunals, 1949), 28122; see also 28328.

6. John Cornwell, *Hitler's Pope: The Secret History of Pius XII* (New York: Viking, 1999), 310.

7. David Oshinsky, *A Conspiracy So Immense: The World of Joe McCarthy* (New York: Free Press, 1983), 74.

8. *Malmedy Massacre Investigation: Investigation of Army Action with Respect to Trial of Persons Responsible for the Massacre of American Soldiers, Battle of the Bulge, near Malmedy, Belgium, December, 1944* (Washington, D.C.: U.S. Government Printing Office, 1949), 352.

9. Ibid. McCarthy bore into one witness with his most famous statement during the hearings: "I assume that you and I would agree that an innocent man will scream about as loudly as a guilty man if you are kicking him in the testicles, and an innocent man will perhaps sign the same confession that a guilty man will if you kick him long and hard enough" (Oshinsky, *A Conspiracy So Immense*, 50).

10. Oshinsky, *A Conspiracy So Immense*, 80.

11. Frank M. Buscher describes how the Malmedy investigations played into the hands of the German propagandists: "The Board of Review report would undoubtedly have been of great value to the German anti-war crimes propaganda. But the bishops did not really need such confidential information to criticize the operation. Fortunately for them, there were the Malmedy hearings in the spring and fall of 1949, which lent themselves to this purpose. The German Protestant bishops became downright theatrical during this phase of the Malmedy controversy" (*The U.S. War Crimes Trial Program in Germany, 1946–1955* [Westport, Conn.: Greenwood, 1989], 100).

12. Alfred Seidl offered this characterization during the Ministries case. Martin Hillenbrand, "The United States and Germany," in Wolfram Handrider, ed., *West German Foreign Policy 1949–1979* (Boulder: Westview, 1990), 74–75. See also Buscher, *The U.S. War Crimes Trial Program*, 37, 93–95. Buscher writes, "The clemency program of the American war crimes operation can be divided into two parts. During the first phase from 1946 to January 1951 . . . American officials thought that the early clemency programs should serve another purpose. Since U.S. authorities in Germany viewed the war crimes program as an important part in their effort to reform and reeducate the German people, the post-trial treatment of war criminals, in addition to the trials themselves, became a vital part of this educational device. The United States intended to use the proceedings against war criminals to demonstrate to the Germans the horrendous crimes Nazism had inflicted on its victims" (69).

13. Buscher, *The U.S. War Crimes Trial Program*, 37.

14. American Nuremberg Trials, *Case 11—United States v. Ernst von Weizsaecker*, 14:952; "The defendants von Weizsaecker and Woermann insist that our judgment

against them on count five is based upon the false hypothesis that at the time they had knowledge of the extermination program established at Auschwitz. Such is not the fact. We were and are convinced beyond reasonable doubt that both were aware that the deportation of Jews from occupied countries to Germany and the East meant their ultimate death. No one can read the record concerning the Dutch Jews and have any question as to the facts." The tribunal majority reaffirmed their rejection of the defense argument that the German diplomats thought that Auschwitz was merely a labor camp: "In an attempt to persuade us that these concentration camps, including Auschwitz, were merely labor camps and not murder factories until after 1942, the defense has offered much testimony. An analysis reveals that great care was exercised not to state that prior to that time Jews were merely labored and were not murdered, but to emphasize that the mass murder program had not been instituted until after 1942, when convoys of Jews were driven into the gas chambers immediately on arrival at the camps" (957–958).

15. American Nuremberg Trials, *Case 11—United States v. Ernst von Weizsaecker*, 14:960; William Caming, "The Nuremberg Prosecutors Reflect on the Triumph of Justice and Morality," September 26, 1997; paper delivered at the University of South Carolina, 1998, 14.

16. Theo Kordt, letter to Lord Halifax, 13 December 1949, RG 59, Box 16 (War Crimes 1949, 1950, October 16, 1952–December 31, 1952), NA. Kordt strongly supported von Weizsäcker's claim that he had accepted the job of State Secretary in 1938 in order to prevent war: "My friends and I felt that he was making a personal sacrifice with a view to preserve the peace and bring about the restitution of legal and decent government in Germany." He ended on an emotional note: "All those who gave their lives, most of them personal friends of mine, considered Weizsacker as their example and their spiritual leader."

17. Friedrich, "Nuremberg and the Germans," 92. See Kurt Tauber, *Beyond Eagle and Swastika: German Nationalism Since 1945*, 2 vols. (Middletown, Conn.: Wesleyan University Press, 1967), 40: "Apart from the program of de-nazification, the Allied policy which aroused the most intense public controversy . . . and which most affected the development of radical nationalism was undoubtedly the trial and conviction of the top Nazi leaders before the International Military Tribunal at Nuremberg. . . . Without a doubt, the vast majority of Germans were disabused of certain illusions, some of them deeply rooted, about the Nazi regime." Tauber makes an important point about the irrationality of this debate: "Horrendous and overwhelming as the evidence against the Nazi leaders was, or perhaps *because* it was so horrendous and overwhelming, there was a widespread inclination to discount it as propaganda. It must be appreciated that the Germans had been surfeited with the Big Lie for twelve long years. They had, on the whole, developed a certain skeptical immunity to it. When the Allies, in apparent ignorance of that fact, began their publicity campaign for the trials, nationalists and bitter opponents of the occupation regimes quickly exploited this widespread suspicion to cast doubt on the entire procedure" (40).

18. Ann and John Tusa, *The Nuremberg Trial* (New York: Atheneum, 1984), 66–67; Thomas Alan Schwartz, *America's Germany: John J. McCloy and the Federal Repub-*

lic of Germany (Cambridge: Harvard University Press, 1991), 42–43. See also Mc-
Cloy obituary, *The New York Times,* March 12, 1989.

19. Buscher, *The U.S. War Crimes Trial Program,* 56. See also Walter LaFeber, *America,
Russia, and the Cold War* (New York: Knopf, 1985), 71–72.

20. Thomas Schwartz, "From Occupation to Alliance: John J. McCloy and the Allied
High Commission in the Federal Republic of Germany, 1949–1952" (Ph.D. diss.,
Harvard University, 1985), 137; LaFeber, *America, Russia, and the Cold War,* 73. East
Germany held war crimes trials of its own. "In 1964 the East Germans noted that
of a total of 12,807 convictions related to the Nazi era, 11,274 took place between
1948 and 1950. In 1950 alone the Waldheim trials led to 4,092 convictions, including 49 executions, 160 life sentences, and 2,914 sentences longer than ten years. The
Waldheim trials took place from April to June 1950. Trumpeted as an example of
East German determination to confront the Nazi past, the trials instead did more
to undermine East German claims to upholding the rule of law. Many cases were
decided on the basis of past membership in organizations such as the Nazi Party,
the SS, or the Wehrmacht, rather than demonstration of individual responsibility for crimes." Jeffrey Herf, *Divided Memory: The Nazi Past in the Two Germanys*
(Cambridge: Harvard University Press, 1997), 73.

21. Schwartz, "From Occupation to Alliance," 306. Paul Nitze, George Kennan,
H. Freeman Matthews, and Averell Harriman all urged Secretary of State Dean
Acheson to rearm Germany. Tom Bower, *Blind Eye to Murder: Britain, America and
the Purging of Nazi Germany—A Pledge Betrayed* (London: Andre Deutsch, 1981)
states that the German influence increased "in direct proportion to the rising tension in Europe." German scorn for the trials initially stemmed from the Allies' "association with Stalin's Russia." Their hurt feelings of national honor could not be
ignored "after the murder of Masaryk and the communist coup in February 1948"
(253). David Kaiser describes the unprecedented political aims of both Cold War
protagonists in *Politics and War* (Cambridge: Harvard University Press, 1990), 423.
Schwartz, "From Occupation to Alliance," 305. There is considerable fluctuation
in the estimates of Soviet military strength. Schwartz's numbers make the differ-
entiation between battle-ready divisions (27) and reserve divisions (75). Stephen E.
Ambrose claims in *The Rise to Globalism* (New York: Penguin, 1980) that the ratio of Soviet superiority in ground forces was ten to one. Schwartz, "From Occupation to Alliance," 265. Adenauer stated in an interview with an American newspaper that the United States would have to assume the burden of defending West
Germany.

22. See Schwartz, "From Occupation to Alliance," 266–267 for more on Adenauer
and rearmament. For more on the rise of Konrad Adenauer see Richard Hiscocks,
The Adenauer Era (New York: Lippincott, 1966). In the first elections of the West
German *Bundestag* in 1949, the Christian Democratic Union took a majority of
seats and Adenauer was elected Chancellor by one vote. See "Judge Advocate General to the Assistant Secretary of War, November 22, 1944," in Bradley F. Smith,
The American Road to Nuremberg: The Documentary Record 1944–1945 (Stanford:
Hoover Institution Press, 1982). Cramer's suggestions are interesting given the final
fate of the German war criminals and the more recent efforts to revise the history

of the Third Reich: "I feel quite strongly that the world cannot afford to dispose of the war guilt question by compelling the vanquished nations to make an admission under duress, as it did in article 231 of the Versailles Treaty in 1919. There must be convincing proof of guilt, which should be preserved in such form that the record of trial can be widely distributed" (58).

23. On April 1, 1950, Landsberg Prison held 663 war criminals convicted by American courts (Buscher, *The U.S. War Crimes Trial Program*, appendix B).

24. For a detailed, case-by-case analysis of the verdicts and sentences see Telford Taylor, *Final Report to the Secretary of the Army on the Nuernberg War Crimes Trials* (Washington, D.C.: U.S. Government Printing Office, 1949) and John Alan Appleman, *Military Tribunals and International Crimes* (Westport, Conn.: Greenwood, 1971). See also Jean Smith, ed., *The Papers of General Lucius Clay* (Bloomington: Indiana University Press, 1974), 962. Contrary to the claims of the High Commissioner, General Clay had ordered his legal staff (Alvin Rockwell, Judge Madden, and Colonel Raymond) to review all of the death sentences in an effort to see if any grounds existed for commutation. After the staff issued their report, Clay reviewed each case and upheld all but one death sentence. McCloy's premise for creating a clemency board was that no review had been provided. There were a number of death sentences in the Medical case (7), the Pohl case (3), and the Einsatzgruppen case (13). Howard Levie, *Terrorism in War: The Law of War Crimes* (Dobbs Ferry, N.Y.: Oceana, 1993), 135–136.

25. Buscher, *The U.S. War Crimes Trial Program,* 107. "The veterans and refugee groups clearly equated the . . . war criminals with regular POWs" (106–107).

26. Because the IMT was in the hands of the four powers and the Germans were incarcerated in Spandau Prison, their sentences were not easily manipulable because modification required a consensus. The Russians were not as forgiving in the cases of major war criminals.

27. The High Commissioner made this point most strenuously in his letter to Eleanor Roosevelt and maintained it until his death.

28. Office of the U.S. High Commissioner for Germany, *Landsberg: A Documentary Report* (Frankfurt: U.S. Army, 1951), 18. This report was the first official pronouncement of the High Commissioner's decisions regarding clemency for the German war criminals. It was included in the February 1951 issue of the High Commissioner's "Information Bulletin." McCloy decided to review the sentences of the now "controversial" American war crimes program and offered this justification for his action: "It is a fundamental principle of American justice that accused persons shall be given every opportunity to maintain their innocence." General Clay intended to execute those on Landsberg's death row. He did not want to pass the burden to his successor. Langer's Senate resolution forced the Military Governor to await the findings of the Baldwin committee (a Senate investigation) before proceeding (Smith, ed., *The Papers of General Lucius Clay*, 1012).

29. Friedrich, "Nuremberg and the Germans," 93. According to Buscher, the German clergy's disapproving statements about American war crimes policy "clearly showed that U.S. efforts to use the trials to reeducate the Germans were in serious trouble. American officials, convinced that National Socialism had resulted from

Germany's authoritarian and militaristic past, hoped that the war crimes program would underscore the need to democratize German society. In contrast, the Germans interpreted war crimes trials as an attempt to prove their collective guilt. Wurm and Dibelius's attitudes confirmed that the Germans viewed themselves as victims of arbitrary and cruel occupation policies, and not as a people ready and willing to assume responsibility for the Holocaust and other Nazi atrocities" (Buscher, *The U.S. War Crimes Trial Program,* 101–102).

30. High Commissioner's press release, 11 January 1950, RG 59, Box 16 (War Crimes 1949, 1950, October 16, 1952–December 31, 1952), NA.

31. John Raymond warned, "Any presentation of new evidence by the defendants without the prosecution being represented would be *ex parte* and open to criticism." John Raymond, letter to Colonel Byroade, 2 February 1950, RG 59, Box 16 (War Crimes 1949, 1950, 1952), NA.

32. Smith, ed., *The Papers of General Lucius Clay,* 305. "In terms of procedure, the Nuremberg trials were much easier to follow; it was much easier to determine whether justice had been done. In Dachau, I had some doubt."

33. John Hohenberg, "Stalling Baffles U.S. Prosecutor," *New York Post,* February 2, 1950.

34. John Hohenberg, *New York Post,* February 3, 1950.

35. Dean Acheson, confidential cable to HICOG, RG 59, Box 16 (War Crimes 1949, 1950, October 16, 1952–December 31, 1952). Dean Acheson, letter to John McCloy, 5 February 1950, RG 466, U.S. High Commission for Germany, Security-Segregated General Records 1949–1952, Box 28, 321.6, War Criminals File, NA. The same day, State Department legal advisor John Raymond discussed the review board with the State Department's Henry Byroade and warned against appointing anyone to the board "who had personal convictions against the Nuremberg trial concept." Raymond cautioned, "We must also watch the religious aspect." They agreed that "a detailed study of fact, or law is not contemplated," and that the review of the war crimes trials should take "sixty days at a maximum" (John Raymond, memo of conversation, 2 February 1950, RG 59, Box 16 [War Crimes 1949, 1590, 1952], NA).

36. Office of the U.S. High Commissioner for Germany, *Landsberg: A Documentary Report,* 3.

37. Office of the U.S. High Commissioner for Germany, *Landsberg: A Documentary Report,* 3. It is interesting to note that Moran was trained in social work and was an outspoken advocate of parole as "an instrument of rehabilitation."

38. Schwartz, "From Occupation to Alliance," 286.

39. Political theorist Robert Jervis has written that in international politics the preconceptions and expectations of the observer are often as important as the empirical facts. "The perceiver's expectations and needs strongly influence what he will see. Subtle messages are easily missed; when they are not, they are usually assimilated to the perceiver's pre-existing beliefs." Robert Jervis, *The Logic of Images in International Relations* (New York: Columbia University Press, 1989), xix. Robert Leckie, *The War in Korea* (New York: Random House, 1963), 20–21. Walter LaFeber, "NATO and the Korean War: A Context," *Diplomatic History* 3 (Spring

1986): 461. LaFeber considers this an example of American preconceptions being confirmed.

Robert Jervis attaches importance to the Korean War in "The Impact of the Korean War on the Cold War," *The Journal of Conflict Resolution* 24, no. 4 (Dec. 1980): "the Korean War shaped the course of the Cold War by both resolving the incoherence which characterized U.S. foreign and defense efforts in the period 1946–1950 and establishing important new lines of policy" (563). Theodore White most famously described what the Korean War brought for Germany: "quick, complete and unconditional profit" (*Fire in the Ashes* [New York: William Sloan Associates, 1953], 157). William Manchester, *The Arms of Krupp* (New York: Bantam, 1968), 751. For a differing point of view on the impact of the Cold War and the war criminals, see Jeffrey Herf, *Divided Memory*.

40. Robert Divine, *Since 1945: Politics and Diplomacy in Recent American History* (New York: Knopf, 1985), 35.

41. Schwartz, "From Occupation to Alliance," 306. Thomas H. Etzold and John Lewis Gaddis, eds., *Containment: Documents on American Policy and Strategy, 1945–1950* (New York: Columbia University Press, 1978), 383–384. Gaddis argues that the new American strategic doctrine, outlined in "NSC-68 constitutes the most elaborate effort made by United States officials during the early Cold War years to integrate political, economic and military considerations into a comprehensive statement of national security policy. . . . NSC-68 can be viewed as a 'call to arms' to stave off that prospect by significantly upgrading Western defense capabilities" (383–384; for text of NSC-68 see 385–442). For more on NSC-68 see Paul Hammond, "NSC-68: Prologue to Rearmament," in Warner Schilling, Paul Hammond, and Glenn Snyder, eds., *Strategy, Politics and Defense Budgets* (New York: Columbia University Press, 1962), 267–378.

42. Walter Isaacson and Evan Thomas, *The Wise Men* (New York: Simon and Schuster, 1986), 513. This is one of McCloy's most famous statements as High Commissioner. Many have accused him of engaging in convenient hyperbole. As early as February he told a West German audience, "there will be no German army or air force." Drew Middleton, "McCloy Warns the Germans Against a Revival of Nazism," *The New York Times*, February 7, 1950.

43. Manchester, *The Arms of Krupp*, 753. The official decision to rearm Germany came on September 11, 1950, in NSC-82. It initially called for a European defense force with Soviet participation.

44. Hiscocks, *The Adenauer Era*, 220.

45. Hiscocks, *The Adenauer Era*, 220.

46. Buscher, *The U.S. War Crimes Trial Program*, 44.

47. *U.S. Military Tribunal Nuremberg, Transcript, Case XI, Weizsaecker*, 28087.

48. Manchester, *The Arms of Krupp*, 756.

49. John Raymond, confidential memo to Robert Bowie, 11 September 1950, RG 59, Box 18 (War Crimes Clemency 1950–1955). Fredrick Moran reflected on his experience in Germany in a letter to Conrad Snow in October 1950: "I reduced the material to a minimum, but the human beings in Landsberg are still in my mind. I can't forget the 'Generals' who are sick old men, existing in a world which

has discarded the values by which they formerly lived. These men are the only people at Landsberg towards whom I wish we had been more generous in our recommendations."

50. Robert Bowie, letter to John Raymond, 11 September 1950, RG 59, Box 18 (War Crimes Clemency 1950–1955), NA.

51. Robert Bowie, letter to John Raymond, 11 September 1950, RG 59, Box 18 (War Crimes Clemency 1950–1955), NA.

52. Confidential memo of conversation with the President, 16 November 1950, RG 59, Box 29, NA.

53. William Langer with Senator McCurran, *Congressional Record,* December 18, 1950 (Washington, D.C.: U.S. Government Printing Office), 16707–9. When asked to "differentiate between the first Nuremberg trials and the latter Nuremberg trials," Langer replied, "The first Nuremberg trials were tried by Allied courts. . . . The other trials were conducted by American judges and American prosecutors according to American laws specifically enacted for that purpose."

54. Security for McCloy's family was increased, as kidnapping threats were made against his children (Columbia University Oral History Project, Benjamin Buttenweiser, 112). The High Commissioner received a secret letter in early January from Henry Byroade objecting to the tone of the clemency board's final report: "the tenor of the statement seems a little more apologetic than it need be or should be." Byroade believed that "a firm and positive statement will do more to counter the reaction in Germany which inevitably will be bad" (Secret letter from Henry Broade to John McCloy, 6 January 1951, RG 59, Box 18 [War Crimes Clemency, 1950–1955], NA).

55. Jack Raymond, "Bonn Legislators Press McCloy for Amnesty for War Criminals," *New York Times,* January 10, 1951. According to Arthur Krock of the *New York Times,* "Dr. Schmid and his colleagues pointed out the new political developments taking place in Western Germany, said many Germans felt such an amnesty would assuage demands for restoration of the honor of German soldiers." This January 12, 1951, cable from a liaison officer to High Commissioner McCloy described the mood of the Bundestag leaders: "During informal conversation January 11, Bundestag President Ehlers stated McCloy's interview regarding Landsberg executions made a strong and favorable impression on Parliamentary delegation. Germans were especially impressed with High Commissioner's sincere and honest desire to explore even the slightest bit of evidence in favor of condemned war criminals. . . . Only disappointment voiced by delegation after interview, according to Ehlers, centered around refusal of High Commissioner to accept German argument based Article 102 Basic Law (abolition of death penalty)" (Samuel Reber to McCloy, 12 January 1951, Misc. Administration File, RG 338, NA).

56. *The New York Times,* January 10, 1951.

57. *Der Spiegel* magazine (1/31/51) accused John McCloy of having "an almost pathological love for Germany."

58. *The New York Times,* January 10, 1951. See also Samuel Reber to John McCloy, 12 January 1951, Misc. Administration Files, RG 338, NA, Modern Military Branch, Suitland.

West German Deputy Minister of Justice Walter Strauss claimed that keeping men on death row for three years was a crime against humanity and presented a paragraph of the Ministries case majority opinion to McCloy: "To permit one sentenced to death to remain for months or even years, without knowledge of his reprieve and untolerable anxiety and mental stress of not knowing whether the next day would be his last day on earth, is a trait typical of the sadism of the Nazi regime, and if anything could be considered a crime against humanity, such a practice is" (Bower, *Blind Eye to Murder*, 368.).

59. Martin Lee, *The Beast Reawakens* (New York: Little, Brown), 69. See also *The New York Times*, "Defends War Criminals: Skorzeny Hitler Aide, Warns in Spain Against Executions," January 13, 1951. See also Rand C. Lewis, *A Nazi Legacy: Right-Wing Extremism in Postwar Germany* (New York: Praeger, 1991). Buscher describes the early resurgence of post–World War II German nationalism: "Nonetheless, German nationalism between 1946 and 1955 . . . differed from its aggressive predecessor during the Third Reich, although it bore some features which were reminiscent of the widespread post–World War I reaction to the Treaty of Versailles" (91).

60. Office of the U.S. High Commissioner for Germany, *Landsberg: A Documentary Report*, 55.

61. Buscher, *The U.S. War Crimes Trial Program*, 63.

62. Manchester, *The Arms of Krupp*, 756. Once again, McCloy's interpretation was not borne out by the facts. Krupp and his father wholeheartedly aided the Nazi rise. Manchester shows how McCloy repeats the arguments made by Krupp's defense team. Moreover, these arguments had been rejected by an extremely conservative American war crimes tribunal in 1948. On McCloy's letter to Eleanor Roosevelt, Manchester writes: "At times the explanations which went out over his signature bordered on sophistry; the confiscation decree had 'already been partially rescinded by General Clay' (Clay had merely pointed out that he couldn't enforce it outside the American zone), and in his reference to foreign workers he merely mentioned Krupp's 'use' of them, never Krupp's *treatment* of them, the hard rock upon which Telford Taylor had built his case" (766). Thomas Schwartz's most thorough analysis of the war crimes question is "*Die Begnadigung Deutscher Kriegsverbrecher. John J. McCloy und die Haftlinge von Landsberg*," in *Vierteljahrshefe für Zeitgeschichte* 38 (July 1990).

63. Appleman, *Military Tribunals and International Crimes*, 219.

64. Office of the U.S. High Commissioner for Germany, *Landsberg: A Documentary Report*, 55.

65. Manchester described the Krupp Works as "a hallowed institution of war" (*The Arms of Krupp*, 766).

66. *The New York Times*, February 2, 1951.

67. Buscher considered the reason to be that "The Germans did not think that their actions in the East were considerably different from what other powers had done in the countries they had occupied. This was coupled with a tendency to blame Germany's post-war problems, such as the loss of the Eastern territories and the economic hardships of the immediate post-war years, on an Allied conspiracy, instead of viewing them as one of the consequences of military defeat. In short, the

Germans viewed themselves as a victimized nation. Such an interpretation of the recent past was bound to affect the war crimes program. As early as 1946 there were indications that even the average German was at least indifferent, if not opposed, to American education attempts in that area" (91–92).

68. Office of the U.S. High Commissioner for Germany, *Landsberg: A Documentary Report*, 64.

69. Office of the U.S. High Commissioner for Germany, *Landsberg: A Documentary Report*, 64.

70. Office of the U.S. High Commissioner for Germany, *Landsberg: A Documentary Report*, 63–64.

71. Office of the U.S. High Commissioner for Germany, *Landsberg: A Documentary Report*, 64.

72. Office of the U.S. High Commissioner for Germany, *Landsberg: A Documentary Report*, 64.

73. Office of the U.S. High Commissioner for Germany, *Landsberg: A Documentary Report*, 3. Judge Gordon Simpson reaffirmed the findings of the Army court: "I am likewise convinced that Peiper was the motivating spirit of the terror spreading, killing-prisoner-of-war procedure of this spearhead. The record of the trial is detailed and voluminous. The evidence is compelling and has convinced everyone who has read it objectively that these criminals committed the acts as found by the court which tried them."

74. Office of the U.S. High Commissioner for Germany, *Landsberg: A Documentary Report*, 67.

75. Office of the U.S. High Commissioner for Germany, *Landsberg: A Documentary Report*, 65.

76. Tauber, *Beyond Eagle and Swastika*, 1:39. This book describes the important role of the German veteran groups in the early 1950s.

77. McCloy defended his role in the Japanese concentration camps similarly. In 1981, he testified before a congressional committee on Japanese internment. McCloy biographer Kai Bird describes the debacle: "When he tried to describe conditions in the internment camps as 'very pleasant,' the audience burst into spontaneous laughter" (*The Chairman: John J. McCloy, the Making of the American Establishment* [New York: Simon and Schuster, 1992], 659–660). Jacob Heilbrunn makes a simple, yet often overlooked point: "Certainly McCloy's lack of compassion for the Jews trapped in Auschwitz contrasts curiously with his solicitude for their prosecutors" ("The Real McCloy," *The New Republic* [October 16, 1992], 44). Heilbrunn's statement about McCloy's role in the deportation of Japanese Americans is telling. "The cunning with which McCloy carried out the internment of the issei and the nisei, first- and second-generation Japanese respectively, proved that he was a good student of Root's on flouting the Constitution and abdicating moral responsibility. . . . He came down on the Army's side. 'If it is a question of the safety of the country, [or] the Constitution of the United States,' he exclaimed, 'why the Constitution is just a scrap of paper to me'" (42). Many years after leaving Germany, McCloy best described the mindset of the American lawyer-statesmen: "I saw my public service in terms of getting things done. . . . I never considered myself a poli-

tician, but rather a lawyer, so the question I asked myself in the various jobs I had was 'What should we do to solve the problem at hand?' then I tried to solve the problem" (*New York Times* obituary, March 12, 1989).

78. Friedrich, "Nuremberg and the Germans," 98. "The distinction that they did make was purely theoretical, allowing them to argue that those who had been punished by no means deserved it. Thus the public called not for clemency and reintegration, but for amnesty and rehabilitation," Friedrich points out.

79. Buscher, *The U.S. War Crimes Trial Program,* 101.

80. Buscher, *The U.S. War Crimes Trial Program,* 118. Buscher describes the shortcomings of the American system: "However, this system was without a foundation due to the absence of a more general long-range punishment policy encompassing all aspects of the occupation. . . . A second important shortcoming was the lack of any planning for an appellate court" (22). Tom Schwartz places the lack of careful planning into the larger context of American foreign policy: "The historical memory of the Americans, as is well known, is very short, and just as the prohibition of fraternization with the German people was abandoned, the passionate anti-German posture did not last as long as the trials dragged on" (*"Die Begnadigung deutscher Kriegsverbrecher"* [translation by the author and Martin Splichal] 378). Buscher describes the role that sentence review played in the post-trial period: "Most importantly, these operations put in place a mechanism which made the political abuse of sentence reviews and clemency possible in the coming years. It is not surprising that the Allies and the Germans decided to rely on this method of sentence reduction after January 1951" (*The U.S. War Crimes Trial Program* 59). Bower, *Blind Eye to Murder,* 368. The most prominent German private interest group was the *Heidelberg Juristenkreis,* or Heidelberg circle of jurists. According to Frank Buscher, "The group maintained close ties with Adenauer and his government, and it carried enough political weight to arrange conferences with American occupation authorities. This allowed the Juristenkreis to work as a clearing house for information and to draw up policy proposals for the German government regarding possible solutions to the war criminals problem. As a result, this secretive organization credited itself with two major developments in the early 1950s: the Article 6 Allied-German mixed clemency commission in 1952 and the concept of the interim mixed boards in 1953" (*The U.S. War Crimes Trial Program* 101). The less respectable advocacy group was Ernst Achenbach's Preparatory Committee for a General Amnesty, also known as the Essen Amnesty Committee. Their argument was *"Nach totale kreig, totale Amnestie"*—the committee wanted all war criminals freed, regardless of their crimes (101).

81. Otto Kranzbühler, interview by author, tape recording, Tegensee, Germany, 16 August 1996.

82. Otto Kranzbühler, interview by author, tape recording, Tegensee, Germany, 16 August 1996.

83. Otto Kranzbühler, interview by author, tape recording, Tegensee, Germany, 16 August 1996.

84. Buscher, *The U.S. War Crimes Trial Program,* 105. American Consul General LaVerne Baldwin to State Department, Washington, 28 February 1952, RG 59, Box 29, NA.

85. An interesting report was issued by the Political and Public Affairs Section of the American Consulate General, August 20, 1951, and classified all the clemency appeals according to the interests of the petitioning parties. RG 466, Box 28, 321.6. See also Buscher, *The U.S. War Crimes Trial Program,* 91–92. A 1952 HICOG survey, "Current West German View on the War Crimes Issue," indicated that the powerful and educated were most aggressive in their rejection of the trials and imprisonment of the war criminals (HICOG Office of Public Affairs, Research Analysis Staff, 8 September 1952, RG 338, Box 469).

86. Princess Isemberg waged a one-woman battle to win freedom of the convicted German war criminals. She sent telegrams to President Truman, Secretary of State Acheson, and Mrs. McCloy (who was a distant cousin of Konrad Adenauer). According to *Der Spiegel,* the princess even dined with the McCloys and pleaded the case of the condemned for two and a half hours. According to one account, Mrs. McCloy sent the princess a check to aid the prisoners and wrote: "I too feel that we have to bridge our mutual problems, and I assure you, it was for Mr. McCloy and myself not only an honor but also a great joy to have you as our guest" (*Der Spiegel,* 31 January 1951; quoted in Haren Tetens, *The New Germany and the Old Nazis* [New York: Random House, 1961], 209). See also Princess Helene von Isemberg, telegram to General Handy, 11 September 1951, RG 338, NA.

   Much of the German historiography concurs: "Recent studies indicate that the West German elites provided the most resistance to Allied occupation policies and reform efforts. Wolfgang Benz described this phenomenon in his survey on Allied initiatives to reform the civil service" (92; see also Wolfgang Benz, "*Versuche zur Reform des öffentlichen Dienstes in Deutschland 1945–52: Deutsche Opposition gegen alliierte Initiativen,*" *Vierteljahrshafte für Zeitgeschichte* 29 [1981]: 216–245; Verena Botzenhart-Viehe, "The German Reaction to the American Occupation 1944–1947," Ph.D. diss., University of California-Santa Barbara, 1980). Botzenhart-Viehe also documents the role of German elites in "instigating the opposition to American reeducation efforts" (from Buscher, *The U.S. War Crimes Trial Program,* 115). Thomas Schwartz makes a similar point: "One of the main problems remained the extent to which a significant portion of the political, economic, ecclesiastical and economic elites of the new Federal Republic sympathized with the condemned war criminals. This solidarity undermined the attempt of the Americans" ("*Die Begnadigung deutscher Kriegsverbrecher*" 379).

87. Herman Guthard, letter to General Handy, 25 January 1951, Army Command War Crimes Branch, Misc. Admin. Files, RG 338, NA.

88. Buscher, *The U.S. War Crimes Trial Program,* 118.

89. Article 131 of the Federal Republic of Germany's Basic Law denied members of the Waffen SS their military pensions. Waffen SS veterans would later argue that they had been collectively branded with guilt by association.

90. Tauber, *Beyond Eagle and Swastika,* 346.

91. Tauber, *Beyond Eagle and Swastika,* 349. They stretched this interpretation, arguing that the Nuremberg ruling that the SS was a criminal organization was no longer binding. Former SS officer and veteran group organizer Harald Milde: "Men like Adenauer and Heuss shall not be mentioned in the same breath with a man

like Adolf Hitler. . . . There is perhaps only one chance and that is that we soldiers, we front-line soldiers of all nations join together before it is too late." Buscher describes the military's attitudes toward the issue of war crimes: "The former military men considered the release of the war criminals a prerequisite to a German contribution to the EDC. The veterans condemned the Allied war crimes trials, and particularly those involving Wehrmacht officers, as a direct attack on the honor of the German soldier. . . . The German response to the punishment of the war criminals strongly points to a continuity in German nationalism. The 1945 surrender evidently did not lead to a clean break and a completely new national identity, even though post-war German nationalism did not contain the militaristic and authoritarian features of its predecessor" (*The U.S. War Crimes Trial Program* 91–92).

92. Tauber, *Beyond Eagle and Swastika*, 349. "In addition, U.S. officials wanted Adenauer to win the September 1953 federal elections. But the war criminals problem had put the chancellor in the very awkward position of appearing to be more pro-Allied than pro-German" (148).

    The forty thousand-strong association of ex-soldiers called the *Schutz-Bund Ehemaliger Soldaten* stated in 1951 that the American decision not to grant a general amnesty proved that "the defamation of the German people in the spirit of Morgenthau continues" ("Bavarian Reactions to Decisions Concerning Landsberg War Criminals," 2 February 1951, RG 59, Box 18 [War Crimes Clemency 1950–1955], NA).

93. Tauber, *Beyond Eagle and Swastika*, 259.

94. Field Marshal Kesselring's letter was restrained in comparison to the more zealous nationalists, but he struck the same anti-Soviet chords: "However, I am sure, Sir, that you are as interested in the formation of first-class troops as I, the former German leader, am interested in seeing the German troop contingent formed. Our neighbor in the East whose disadvantages and advantages I know quite well, will easily find out whether or not the new German soldier will equal the one of 1940 to 1945. The Kremlin will draw its conclusions accordingly. . . . It is our duty as soldiers to abandon our usual reserve in order to tell the politicians very clearly that the direction taken in 1945 will result in severe damage and disadvantages to the soldiers of today and tomorrow—damage which will make the difference between victory and defeat in war" (Kesselring to Eddy, 31 December 1952, Army Command War Crimes Branch, Misc. Admin. Files, RG 338, NA).

95. Lee, *The Beast Reawakens*, 65.

96. "West German Reactions to the Landsberg Decisions," U.S. High Commission confidential report, 6 March 1951, RG 59, Box 5 (Clemency Board on German War Criminals), NA.

97. "Bavarian Reaction to Decision Concerning Landsberg War Criminals," 9 February 1951, RG 59, Box 18 (War Crimes Clemency 1950–1955), NA. Some of the motives people offered for America's clemency decisions: "1) The Americans have missed their chance to make good friends of the Germans. 2) Nuernberg has never been accepted by Germans, partic, in this case where the trial procedures were in many cases doubtful." "According to Bavarian leaders, the reactions of the man-

in-the-street do not seem as favorable as those registered by the press and public officials."

98. "Further Findings on West German Reactions to the Landsberg Decisions," State Department Office of Public Affairs, 30 March 1951, RG 59, Box 18 (War Crimes Clemency 1950–1955), NA.

99. *The New York Times* quoted Governor Dewey's description of Peck Panel member Fredrick Moran in his obituary: "a pioneer leader in parole." Leo Crespi, head American pollster, concluded, "Whatever the stimulus German Buergermeisters might offer for support in the Landsberg decisions, it seems clear that in the *interpretation* of these actions they are, by and large, propagating views varying from an alleged American retreat from Nuremberg to outright political expediency." Crespi reached the same conclusion after conducting another survey of eight hundred urban West Germans on March 30: "The public, for the most part, attributes the postponement of the execution of the death sentences pending the appeal of the U.S. Supreme Court to uncertainty, weakness, or ulterior purpose on the part of the U.S." ("Further Findings on West German Reactions to the Landsberg Decisions," State Department Office of Public Affairs, 30 March 1951, RG 59, Box 18 [War Crimes Clemency 1950–1955], NA).

100. "Germany's 'Dreyfus Affair': I Accuse! An open letter from General Oswald Pohl (in Landsberg Prison) to General Karl Wolff," RG 59, Box 29, NA; HICOG Bonn to State Department Washington, 24 May 1951, RG 59, Box 29, NA.

101. Buscher, *The U.S. War Crimes Trial Program*, 125–127.

102. John McCloy, letter to Eleanor Roosevelt, 12 March 1951, 2, Roosevelt Library, Hyde Park, New York.

103. John McCloy, letter to Eleanor Roosevelt, 12 March 1951, 2, Roosevelt Library, Hyde Park, New York, 2–3. As the years went by McCloy grew prickly about his more controversial legacies (the Landsberg decisions, the concentration camps in California, and the decision not to bomb the railways leading to Auschwitz). In the late 1970s he still clung to the position that there was "not a goddamn bit of truth" to the contention that international politics had motivated his decisions. When William Manchester presented the former High Commissioner with the case against him, he merely looked at the paper and replied, "That's ancient history" (Manchester, *The Arms of Krupp*, 770).

What further complicates the McCloy case is the number and prominence of his supporters. Benjamin Ferencz, the former Chief Counsel in the Einsatzgruppen case, defends the High Commissioner. In a letter to the author, Ferencz wrote: "As misguided as the commutations may have been, and as detrimental to the Nuremberg proceedings as they were, it is my own considered judgment that as far as McCloy is concerned, there were other motives that were decisive, and the rearmament consideration—if it existed at all—was rather a sub-conscious desire to get the past behind us and move on to a new Germany as part of a unified western alliance" (Benjamin Ferencz, letter to author, 23 February 1990). McCloy wrote Ferencz a most revealing letter in the spring of 1980: "At long last I acknowledge receipt of your book which I have read with great interest. It opened up a number of facts which were new to me. I am much impressed by the research that must have gone into it. If I had all the facts I now have, I might have reached a more just result. It was an ordeal that I would not care to repeat" (John McCloy, letter to Ben Ferencz, 10 April 1980 [courtesy of Benjamin Ferencz]). *The New York Times,* John McCloy obituary, March 12, 1989. Jacob Heilbrunn, "The Real McCloy," *The New Republic,* May 11, 1992, 40.

104. John McCloy, letter to Eleanor Roosevelt, 12 March 1951, Roosevelt Library, Hyde Park, NY, 2.

105. "In one case, in which the judgment was not rendered until a few months before General Clay's departure, he was unable to take action in the time remaining. This case and only this one case was not 'disposed of finally' at the time Mr. McCloy took office. . . . To my personal knowledge, this legal staff gave extensive and careful consideration to the records and judgments in the Nuremberg trials, and General Clay gave conscientious and perceptive personal attention to their recommendations before he took action" (*New York Herald Tribune,* March 29, 1951).

106. *New York Herald Tribune,* March 29, 1951. The *Information Bulletin* refused to print Telford Taylor's response to McCloy's Eleanor Roosevelt letter.

107. "Shawcross Condemns Leniency Granted to War Criminals," *New York Herald Tribune,* March 29, 1951. The U.S. embassy in London cabled a copy of the speech to Secretary of State Dean Acheson with the following message: "In this connection domestic polit import Shawcross speech shld not (rpt not) be overlooked" (State Department London to Secretary of State, 29 March 1951, RG 59, Box 18 [War Crimes Clemency 1950–1955], NA).

108. John McCloy, telegram to Dean Acheson, 30 March 1951, RG 59, Box 18 (War Crimes Clemency 1950–1955), NA.

109. *The New York Times,* May 25, 1951.

110. *The New York Times,* June 8, 1951.

111. American Vice Consul Ernest Ramsaur, confidential cable to State Department, 29 June 1951, RG 59, Box 29, NA.

112. American Vice Consul Ernest Ramsaur, confidential cable to State Department, 29 June 1951, RG 59, Box 29, NA.

113. American Vice Consul Ernest Ramsaur, confidential cable to State Department, 29 June 1951, RG 59, Box 29, NA. Friedrich, "Nuremberg and the Germans," 98.

6. THE RAPID LIQUIDATION OF THE WAR CRIMES PROBLEM

1. Frank M. Buscher, *The U.S. War Crimes Trial Program in Germany, 1946–1955* (New York: Greenwood, 1989), 132–133.

2. Buscher, *The U.S. War Crimes Trial Program,* 135.

3. State Department Bonn, secret cable to Secretary of State, 30 October 1951, RG 59, Box 29, NA. One State Department cable to Washington: "This solution wld require recognition by Gers of Nuremberg and similar judgments, which wld be difficult politically as Gers have heretofore consistently contested their validity." See also Jörg Friedrich, "Nuremberg and the Germans," in Belinda Cooper, ed., *War Crimes: The Legacy of Nuremberg* (New York: TV Books, 1999), 99. A cable to

Washington expressed the fear that once the German government took possession of the convicts, "they wld probably use their authority to effect release, extended parole or other differential treatment, thus negating effect of sentences."

4. U.S. Embassy London (Gifford), secret cable to Secretary of State, 21 December 1951, RG 59, Box 24 (War Crimes Clemency July 1952–December 1953), NA. One State Department cable reported: "Brit propose Gers should be given custody when contractual arrangements go into effect. Gers will be rquired to recognize validity of sentences." Once again, the Americans tried to rule questions about the Nuremberg trials' legal validity off limits: "Tribunal will have no (rpt no) power to question validity of sentences." It was clear that the British were softening on the war crimes question. British High Commissioner Ivonne Kirkpatrick reduced the parole requirements and immediately released twenty-five convicted war criminals from Werl Prison. Kirkpatrick proposed that the Germans should be given custody of the remaining war criminals once the contractual arrangements went into effect in 1952.

5. High Commissioner McCloy, secret cable to Secretary of State, 21 December 1951, RG 59, Box 29, NA.

6. High Commissioner McCloy, secret cable to Secretary of State, 21 December 1951, RG 59, Box 29, NA.

7. Buscher, *The U.S. War Crimes Trial Program*, 75.

8. Buscher, *The U.S. War Crimes Trial Program*, 135.

9. Kurt Tauber, *Beyond Eagle and Swastika: German Nationalism Since 1948* (Middletown, Conn.: Wesleyan University Press, 1967), 259.

10. Charles Thayer, secretary report to the State Department, 12 March 1952, RG 59, Box 29, NA.

11. Charles Thayer, secretary report to the State Department, 12 March 1952, RG 59, Box 29, NA.

12. Otto Kranzbühler, interview by author, tape recording, Tegernsee, Germany, August 1996. See also Friedrich, "Nuremberg and the Germans," 99.

13. Otto Kranzbühler, interview by author, tape recording, Tegernsee, Germany, August 1996.

14. Otto Kranzbühler, interview by author, tape recording, Tegernsee, Germany, August 1996.

15. Friedrich, "Nuremberg and the Germans," 102–105. The treaty articles related to war crimes are reprinted in Cooper, ed., *War Crimes*.

16. Otto Kranzbühler, interview by author, Tegernsee, Germany, August 1996; Buscher, *The U.S. War Crimes Trial Program*, 127. From Richard Hiscocks, *The Adenauer Era* (New York: Lippincott, 1966): "The Brussels Treaty of 1948 was to be extended to include the German Federal Republic and Italy and was to become known as the Western European Union; the Federal Republic was to become a member of NATO; and the Bonn agreements of May 1952, subject to certain minor alterations, were to come into force. These arrangements, known as the Paris treaties, were ratified in February 1955 by the Federal Republic and in March by France. They went into effect on May 5. The Western occupation of Germany came to an end; the Allied high commissioners became ambassadors; subejct only to the reserva-

tions agreed upon in May 1952, the Federal Republic attained full sovereignty; and it became a member of the Western alliance" (39).

17. Otto Kranzbühler, interview by author, tape recording, Tegernsee, Germany, August 1996.

18. "McCloy Confident on West Germany," *The New York Times,* July 17, 1952; see also Buscher, *The U.S. War Crimes Trial Program,* 141: "If you are asking if there is to be a jail delivery to get ratification through, the answer is no."

19. Admiral Gottfried Hansen to Matthew Ridgeway, 10 August 1952, RG 59, Box 29, NA. See also Adelbert Weinstein, "A Mortage of a Special Kind," *Frankfurt Allgemeine,* 18 August 1952.

20. Friedrich, "Nuremberg and the Germans," 97. Germany's old elites "had to be rehabilitated for reuse."

21. HICOG, Secret Report on War Criminals to State Department, 6 September 1952, RG 59, Box 29, NA. "Whether we like it or not, the German politicians and press are making the subject of the war criminals an important factor at this time." The report described the German critics' attacks on the validity of the original sentences: "To the extent that attacks bear analysis, develop along one or more or combinations of the following: (a) There were no crimes and therefore no legal basis for the trials."

   In a cable to Secretary of State Acheson, U.S. High Commissioner Walter Donnelly warned that the war criminal problem threatened "both the wholeheartedness of the Ger def effort and the Chancellor's chances of success at the polls in the early summer of 1953 unless problem has been both rapidly and finally solved after EDC comes into effect, and not (rpt not) so soon before the election as to look contrived."

22. State Department Office of Public Affairs August Flash Survey, 16 September 1952, RG 59, Box 29, NA. See also Buscher, *The U.S. War Crimes Trial Program,* 109.

23. Buscher, *The U.S. War Crimes Trial Program,* 144. See also State Department Bonn to Secretary of State, 17 September 1952, RG 59, Box 29, NA.

24. Buscher, *The U.S. War Crimes Trial Program,* 144.

25. Buscher, *The U.S. War Crimes Trial Program,* 143. See also appendix B.

26. Buscher, *The U.S. War Crimes Trial Program,* 80. In a secret letter to the High Commissioner, James Riddleberger, director of the State Department's Office of Political Affairs, also saw an interim parole board as "a good device" that "made things easier" for Germany and allowed the United States to maintain "all the basic elements of our position." He anticipated trouble from the German board members: "The fact that the Board will not be able to question the validity of the war crimes judgments will be a continuing objection to it in the German view." James Riddleberger, secret letter to Walter Donnelly, 13 October 1952, RG 59, Box 16 (War Crimes 1949, 1950, October 16, 1952–December 31, 1952), NA.

27. Christopher Simpson, *The Splendid Blond Beast: Money, Law, and Genocide in the Twentieth Century* (New York: Grove, 1993), 20–22.

28. Simpson, *The Splendid Blond Beast,* 25; Columbia Oral History Project, John McCloy, 21. "Dulles had very definite views about Germany," McCloy observed. "He'd

spent a good bit of time in Germany, had a number of German clients and he was deeply interested in it."

29. "Political Brief No. 5" described "Political Aspects of the War Crimes Question" (1 February 1953, RG 59, Box 17 [War Crimes 1953–1959], NA).

30. "Political Brief No. 5: Political Aspects of the War Criminal Question," 1 February 1953, RG 59, Box 17 (War Crimes 1953–1959), NA. On May 15, State Department legal advisor John Raymond warned the Department of Defense to limit the jurisdiction of any proposed parole board "to matters of parole (not clemency) and exclude any basis for attempt by German member to reopen cases or question original convictions. Similar precautions should be taken with respect provisions for parole supervision, in which we suppose Germans will also participate, so that we shall have nearest possible equivalent to explicit recognition by Germans of validity war crimes judgments" (John Raymond to the Department of Defense, 15 May 1953, RG 59, Box 18 [War Crimes Clemency 1950–1955], NA).

31. Preconference memo on the war criminals prepared by State Department legal advisor John Auchincloss, 31 March 1953, RG 59, Box 17 (War Crimes 1953–1959), NA

32. Preconference memo on the war criminals prepared by State Department legal advisor John Auchincloss, 31 March 1953, RG 59, Box 17 (War Crimes 1953–1959), NA

33. Preconference memo on the war criminals prepared by State Department legal advisor John Auchincloss, 31 March 1953, RG 59, Box 17 (War Crimes 1953–1959), NA

34. "U.S.-German Political Talks, April 8, 1953: Minutes—Second General Meeting," RG 59, Box 18 (War Crimes Clemency 1950–1955), NA.

35. The minutes of the talks are also in *The Foreign Relations of the United States: Germany and Austria 1952–1954* (Washington, D.C.: U.S. Government Printing Office, 1983), 434. Townsend Hoopes, *The Devil and John Foster Dulles* (Boston: Little, Brown, 1973), 67. Dulles was a consummate strategic legalist whose Wall Street firm had strong ties with German industrialists.

36. *The Foreign Relations of the United States: Germany and Austria 1952–1954,* 434, 442–443.

37. *The New York Times,* July 14, 1953.

38. "U.S.–German Political Talks, April 8, 1953: Minutes—First General Meeting," RG 59, Box 18 (War Crimes Clemency 1950–1955), NA. In a secret memo to the U.S. Secretary of State, High Commissioner James Conant wrote: "Chancellor attaches great importance to some accomplishment as regards war criminals for political reasons" (James Conant to Secretary of State, 1 April 1953, RG 59, Box 18 [War Crimes Clemency 1950–1955], NA).

39. John Foster Dulles to U.S. High Commission in Bonn, 25 June 1953, RG 59, Box 17 (War Crimes 1953–1959), NA. On June 26, Dulles sent a secret cable, drafted by John Auchincloss, to the U.S. embassy. It warned, "Board's terms of reference must be carefully defined so as to limit its jurisdiction to matters of parole (not clemency) and exclude any basis for attempt by German member to reopen cases or question original convictions." German participation on the parole board was as close as the Americans were going to get to an explicit recognition of the validity of the war crimes judgments. According to the memo, "Such recognition has

been and presumably still is politically impossible for Germans to give" (Memo on war criminal paroles written by John Auchincloss and John Raymond for Secretary of State John Foster Dulles, 26 June 1953, RG 59, Box 17 [War Crimes 1953–1959], NA).

40. Buscher, *The U.S. War Crimes Trial Program,* 81–82.

41. Colonel Howard Levie (JAG Chief of Internal Affairs) to Brigadier General George Gardes, 5 March 1956, Army Command War Crimes Branch, Misc. Admin. Files, RG 338, NA. See also Buscher, *The U.S. War Crimes Trial Program,* 81–84.

42. Levie to Gardes, 5 March 1956. See also RG 59, Box 17, War Crimes: 1953–1959, "Briefing for Secretary's Press Conference December 6, 1955."

43. Levie to Gardes, 5 March 1956.

44. Levie to Gardes, 5 March 1956. The mandate was very explicit: "The Board is authorized, without questioning the validity of the convictions and sentences, to make recommendations to the competent U.S. authorities for the termination or reduction of sentences or for the parole of persons convicted by the War Crimes Tribunals."

45. Levie to Gardes, 5 March 1956.

46. Michael Balfour, *West Germany: A Contemporary History* (London: Croom Helm, 1982), 190. By 1952, Chancellor Adenauer publicly vowed to wage an all-out effort to free the German war criminals. Alan Cowell, "Germany Defends Pensions for SS Veterans," *The New York Times,* May 9, 1999: "More than half a century after World War II, the German authorities have acknowledged that war disability pensions are still being paid to members of Waffen-SS units and even to war criminals."

47. From T. H. Tetens, *The New Germany and the Old Nazis* (New York: Random House, 1961), 65–66.

48. Tetens, *The New Germany and the Old Nazis,* 67.

49. Dr. Friedrich Middelhauve to Thomas Handy, RG 466, 321.6, NA.

50. Paul Gernert, U.S. Parole Officer to the High Commissioner, 23 April 1954, Army Command War Crimes Branch, Misc. Admin. Files, RG 338, NA. "No problems have been reported, and the German press has been cooperative in avoiding any publicity concerning parolees or their release." Frank Buscher considers the action of the IMPAC board a sell-out of American war crimes policy: "Although IMPAC did not release all war criminals from American custody, it sufficiently reduced the problem so that German rearmament and sovereignty were no longer in jeopardy. The United States had sold out its war crimes program—so had the British and French. Thus, the trial operation, which was to punish the perpetrators and, at the same time, teach the Germans the virtues of democracy by demonstrating the evils of Nazism, simply fell by the wayside" (*The U.S. War Crimes Trial Program* 85).

51. John Dower, *Embracing Defeat: Japan in the Wake of World War II* (New York: Norton, 1999), 514, 453; State Department legal advisor John Auchincloss to Geoffrey Lewis at the U.S. embassy in Bonn, 28 January 1954, RG 59, Box 16 (War Crimes 1949, 1950, October 16, 1952–December 31, 1952), NA.

52. Dower, *Embracing Defeat,* 514, 453; State Department legal advisor John Auchincloss to Geoffrey Lewis at the U.S. embassy in Bonn, 28 January 1954, RG 59, Box 16 (War Crimes 1949, 1950, October 16, 1952–December 31, 1952), NA.

53. Dower, *Embracing Defeat,* 514, 453; State Department legal advisor John Auchin-
     closs to Geoffrey Lewis at the U.S. embassy in Bonn, 28 January 1954, RG 59, Box 16
     (War Crimes 1949, 1950, October 16, 1952–December 31, 1952), NA.

54. Dower, *Embracing Defeat,* 514, 453; State Department legal advisor John Auchin-
     closs to Geoffrey Lewis at the U.S. embassy in Bonn, 28 January 1954, RG 59, Box 16
     (War Crimes 1949, 1950, October 16, 1952–December 31, 1952), NA.
     The State Department officers drafted a preconference memo arguing
     strongly against a political solution in Asia because of the dramatic repercussions it
     would have in Germany. "The Germans have never accepted the principles of the
     war crimes trials and do not believe in the guilt of those still in confinement. Be-
     cause of the similarity of the two situations, it is apparent that an amnesty in Ja-
     pan would inevitably lead to an amnesty in Germany, and EUR should emphasize
     strongly that an amnesty ought not be granted in Japan" (Drafted by John Auchin-
     closs for Cecil Lyon to James Bonbright, State Department, 16 February 1954,
     RG 59, Box 17 [War Crimes 1953–1959], NA).

55. "Memorandum of Conversation: General Amnesty for Japanese War Criminals,
     February 16, 1954," RG 59, Box 18 (War Crimes Clemency 1950–1955), NA. The
     participants in this meeting included State Department Far East heads Ambassa-
     dor John Allison and Walter Robertson. State Department legal advisor John Ray-
     mond, former Peck Panel member Conrad Snow, and Cecil Lyon represented the
     State Department's German interests.

56. "Memorandum of Conversation: General Amnesty for Japanese War Criminals,
     February 16, 1954," RG 59, Box 18 (War Crimes Clemency 1950–1955), NA. Alli-
     son conceded that an amnesty would cause problems in Germany and asked "if it
     would be possible to take some action less than amnesty with respect to Japanese
     war criminals." Conrad Snow pointed out that those still in prison had been con-
     victed of "particularly heinous crimes" and would not be eligible for parole until
     1960 or 1961. He offered a solution, noting "that it would be possible for the Board
     to change the 'ground rules' so as to make lifers eligible for parole after serving 10
     instead of 15 years."

57. Secretary of State John Foster Dulles to Ambassador Allison, 26 May 1954, RG 59,
     Box 18 (War Crimes Clemency 1950–1955), NA. "In view of serious nature crimes
     committed by remaining war criminals and fact 145 out of 293 have life sentences
     and 30 have sentences of over 30 years, impossible release any sizeable bloc per
     your recommendation."

58. Buscher, *The U.S. War Crimes Trial Program,* 149–151. A good summary of the
     death of the EDC Treaty.

59. *The New York Times,* August 30, 1954. FDP leader Eric Mende stated that as a for-
     mer German officer, he personally could not support ratification and rearmament
     until German military leaders like Field Marshal Eric von Manstein were released
     from Allied prisons. The Paris Treaties, incorporating Articles 6 and 7 of the Bonn
     Agreements, would outline the new Allied–German plan. Western leaders signed
     the conventions in Paris in October 1954.
     Admiral Heye, a deputy in the CDU Party, believed that the "unresolved issue
     of war criminals would deter many individuals with a strong sense of honor and

duty from volunteering for the new armed forces." Although the admiral was willing to admit that "many of the remaining prisoners had committed criminal acts and deserved punishment," he rejected their trials' legal validity. Van Merkatz also attacked the war crimes trials "in a very emotional manner." He stated that "many of the trials had not been conducted in accordance with established legal procedure . . . and maintained that the whole sorry episode of war criminals should be concluded by an amnesty for those remaining." The State Department noted that this was the first time in recent months German politicians had raised the question of a war crimes amnesty for war criminals (State Department Bonn Memorandum: "Conversation with Von Meratz and Heye," 18 January 1955, RG 59, Box 18, NA).

60. Richard Hagan, secret letter to John Raymond, 4 March 1955, RG 59, Box 18, NA.

61. *The New York Times,* July 26, 1953.

62. Buscher, *The U.S. War Crimes Trial Program,* 153.

63. Secretary of State, cable to State Department Bonn, 25 July 1955, RG 59, Box 19 (War Crimes Clemency January 1956–1959), NA.

64. Colonel Howard Levie to Brigadier General George Gardes, 5 March 1956, 2, Army Command War Crimes Branch, Misc. Admin. Files, RG 338, NA.

65. Colonel Howard Levie to Brigadier General George Gardes, 5 March 1956, 2, Army Command War Crimes Branch, Misc. Admin. Files, RG 338, NA.

66. See Stephen Ambrose, *Citizen Soldiers* (New York: Touchstone, 1997), 224–225, for more on Bastogne.

67. Knox Lamb, U.S. Embassy Bonn to State Department, 3 August 1955, RG 59, Box 16 (War Crimes 1949, 1950, October 16, 1952–December 31, 1952), NA.

68. American Embassy Bonn to State Department Washington, 3 August 1955, RG 59, Box 17, NA.

69. American Embassy Bonn to State Department Washington, 3 August 1955, RG 59, Box 17, NA.

70. State Department Bonn to State Department Washington, 16 September 1955, Box 18 (War Crimes Clemency 1950–1955), RG 59, NA.

71. For more on Dietrich, see Gerald Reitlinger, *The SS: Alibi of a Nation 1922–1945* (New York: Viking, 1957), 56–57.

72. Ambassador Conant to Secretary of State, 4 November 1955, RG 59, Box 18 (War Crimes Clemency 1950–1955), NA.

73. Veterans of Foreign Wars Commander Joseph Lombardo to Secretary of Defense Charles Wilson, 8 November 1955, RG 59, Box 18 (War Crimes Clemency 1950–1955), NA. "It is the thought of this office that the reasons of the American member of the Mixed Board for voting favorably on the release of the Hitlerite Killer should be investigated and his resignation immediately forthcoming to wipe out the dishonor to the memory of our murdered comrades at Malmedy."

74. Veterans of Foreign Wars Commander Joseph Lombardo to Secretary of Defense Charles Wilson, 8 November 1955, RG 59, Box 18 (War Crimes Clemency 1950–1955), NA.

75. Ambassador Conant to Secretary of State, 30 November 1955, RG 59, Box 18 (War Crimes Clemency 1950–1955), NA. Conant sensed an impending blowback: "A

failure to bring this fact out clearly in previous statements from Washington as well as failure to emphasize nature of parole and unfortunate first statement tending to place the blame on the Army has seriously embarrassed U.S. member of Mixed Board and thus embarrassed U.S. Government in its relation to the French, British as well as the Federal Republic."

76. "Briefing for Secretary's Press Conference," 6 December 1955, RG 59, Box 17 (War Crimes 1953–1959), NA.

77. John Raymond, secret memo to Ambassador Conant, 27 December 1955, RG 59, Box 17 (War Crimes 1953–1959), NA. On December 30, Merchant wrote Conant, "We were unaware that the Peiper case was already up for consideration and the leaks of the possibility of Peiper's release have now intensified the controversy greatly." Merchant conceded that the Dietrich release had gone very badly from a public relations point of view—"Looking back, it seems clear that we have not put our best foot forward on the subject"—and warned that the Peiper parole would probably be opposed by the army: "While our relations with the people most directly concerned with the problem at the legal and public information level is good, I should be frank to say that there are people at the higher levels in the Pentagon who are not very sympathetic with the program, which may eventually be a source of difficulty." Merchant informed Ambassador Conant that during an upcoming trip to Washington, they should meet to discuss the ongoing war crimes problem. He also requested that the conversation be held behind closed doors—off the record. Conant would also meet with the leaders of American veteran groups in an effort to quiet them down (Livingston Merchant to Ambassador Conant, 30 December 1955, RG 59, Box 17 [War Crimes 1953–1959], NA).

78. Papal Nuncio Archbishop Fargo to Secretary of State Dulles, 6 January 1956, RG 59, Box 19 (War Crimes Clemency January 1956–1959), NA.

79. The British hoped to avoid another fiasco like the Sepp Dietrich parole: "Her Majesty's Government wish to do everything possible to assist the Board in meeting public criticism, but they do not believe that the inner workings of the Board, which is an independent body, should be revealed" (British Embassy Washington to State Department, 1 January 1956, Box 19 [War Crimes Clemency January 1956–1959], RG 59, NA).

80. British Embassy Washington to State Department, 1 January 1956, Box 19 (War Crimes Clemency January 1956–1959), RG 59, NA. "It would be contrary to long-established precedent in the United Kingdom to publish the reasons on which the recommending majority bases advice to the executive authority on the exercise of clemency."

81. John Auchincloss to Max Meron, 3 February 1956, RG 59, Box 19 (War Crimes Clemency January 1956–1959), NA.

82. State Department general counsel Knox Lamb to State Department, 13 February 1956, RG 59, Box 19 (War Crimes Clemency January 1956–1959), NA. When the three West German members of the Mixed Board got word of his removal, they proposed protesting to Conant. "The said members expressed the feeling that the action in transferring Mr. Plitt had been taken because . . . he had voted to transfer Dietrich from prison to parole status and that Plitt's removal was a reflection

on the entire membership of the Board." The Germans were calmed by the British board member, who advised them that any such protest would be "improper" without consulting their respective governments.

83.   State Department legal advisor John Raymond to assistant legal advisor John Auchincloss, 8 March 1956, RG 59, Box 19 (War Crimes Clemency January 1956–1959), NA. See also "258 Germans under American Law in the Sovereign Federal Republic" in *Der Stern*, March 17, 1956. In a letter to John Auchincloss about their official position, John Raymond considered how to handle the public inquiries: "We cannot possibly tell others it is none of their business to ask such questions nor can we refer them to the Board for an answer. Perhaps we should even stress the fact that if such information is not forthcoming and if further decisions are rendered which cannot be explained and which have a violent reaction in this country, it may jeopardize the whole program."

84.   Robert Upton to John Raymond, 29 March 1956, RG 59, Box 19 (War Crimes Clemency January 1956–1959), NA. Senator Upton requested some instructions from the State Department on these questions. Legal advisor John Raymond appears to have been startled by the news that Peiper would soon be released. In a letter to John Auchincloss, Raymond wrote, "The attached letter from Senator Upton gives me much concern. Apparently Peiper may be released any day" (State Department legal advisor John Raymond to assistant legal advisor John Auchincloss, 11 April 1956, RG 59, Box 16 [War Crimes 1949, 1950, October 16, 1952–December 31, 1952], NA).

To further complicate matters, the U.S. Army had already expressed deep misgivings about Joachim Peiper's parole. Army Assistant Judge Advocate General, Major General Claude Mickelwait, took grave exception not only to Peiper's release but also to Edwin Plitt's statements about the army's conduct in the Dachau trials. Mickelwait charged that both Plitt and the Mixed Board had exceeded the scope of their legal mandate. Finally, the Assistant Judge Advocate General leveled his most serious charge—that the Mixed Board had acted like an appellate or review court. "Mr. Plitt is not only admitting that the Interim Mixed Board illegally constituted itself as an appellate court, but also arrogating to the board an unwarranted conscience, while clearly implying lack of competence and justice on the part of the trial courts." He pointed out that this was "a favorite tactic of those who have found it expedient to attack the German war crimes program." Although the State Department vigorously denied the army's charges, they were preparing for the fallout over Peiper's imminent release (Major General Claude Mickelwait to State Department legal advisor John Raymond, 12 April 1956, RG 59, Box 19 [War Crimes Clemency January 1956–1959], NA).

85.   Senator Robert Upton to State Department legal advisor John Raymond, 29 March 1956, RG 59, Box 19 (War Crimes Clemency January 1956–1959), NA.

86.   Senator Robert Upton to State Department legal advisor John Raymond, 29 March 1956, RG 59, Box 19 (War Crimes Clemency January 1956–1959), NA. Upton cited the opinion of Army General Thomas Handy: "My review of the case leads to the same general conclusions. In my opinion Col. Peiper must be held primarily responsible for the violations of the laws and customs of warfare committed by his

combat group." The new American Mixed Board member also objected to Peiper's parole plan to work in the sales department of Porsche: "Because of the widespread and intense feeling for and against Col. Peiper, it is inadvisable that he be employed in a position where he may be in contact with the general public including foreign customers of the Porsche Co."

87. Robert Upton to John Raymond, 8 May 1956, RG 59, Box 19 (War Crimes Clemency January 1956–1959), NA.

88. Numbers from Colonel Howard Levie to General George Gardes, 25 January 1956, Parole Report, Army Command War Crimes Branch, Misc. Admin. Files, RG 338, NA.

89. Elim O'Shaughnessy, State Department Bonn, to Secretary of State, 9 June 1956, RG 59, Box 19 (War Crimes Clemency January 1956–1959), NA. The German diplomat "mentioned the shock felt German Circles when Plitt removed; thought Plitt's government should have supported him; said removal under pressure home politics had seriously undermined confidence in independence of Board."

90. "Chancellor Adenauer Visit, Washington: German War Criminals Held by the United States," 8 June 1956, RG 59, Box 19 (War Crimes Clemency January 1956–1959), NA.

91. Robert Upton to John Raymond, 11 June 1956, RG 59, Box 19 (War Crimes Clemency January 1956–1959), NA.

92. Robert Upton to John Raymond, 11 June 1956, RG 59, Box 19 (War Crimes Clemency January 1956–1959), NA.

93. Robert Upton to John Raymond, 11 June 1956, RG 59, Box 19 (War Crimes Clemency January 1956–1959), NA.

94. "Memorandum of Conversation: The Mixed Board," 26 June 1956, RG 59, Box 19 (War Crimes Clemency January 1956–1959), NA. The participants in this meeting were Robert Upton, John Raymond, and Robert Creel from the State Department's German section.

   The former Mixed Board member saw the program as "one of gradual parole for prisoners, and gradual clemency for those on parole." He "thought it was important for his successor to understand a situation that has developed and which will certainly be a problem with which he will be confronted." Raymond admitted that both the IMPAC Board and the Mixed Board were following a flawed parole procedure: "Apparently the Interim Board and the present Board prior to the arrival of Senator Upton proceeded on the theory either that the nature of the offense had no bearing on parole or that it had a bearing merely as reflecting the character of the prisoner and his ability to readjust in society." Senator Upton regretfully informed the State Department that he was "unable to convert any of the members of the Board to this point of view, but he believes it is absolutely sound and should be held by the U.S. member."

95. "Memorandum of Conversation: Public Information in German War Crimes Cases," 31 July 1956, RG 59, Box 19 (War Crimes Clemency January 1956–1959), NA. The participants in this meeting were John Raymond, John Auchincloss, Spencer Phenix, Mr. Kearney, and Mr. Lampson. Senator Upton told his replacement why he left Germany "with feelings of regret" and chose not to continue as a

member of the Mixed Board (Robert Upton to John Raymond, 7 September 1956, RG 59, Box 19 [War Crimes Clemency January 1956–1959], NA).

96. Spencer Phenix to John Raymond, 8 February 1957, RG 59, Box 19 (War Crimes Clemency January 1956–1959), NA. There was a cover letter and memos A and B.

97. Spencer Phenix to John Raymond, 8 February 1957, RG 59, Box 19 (War Crimes Clemency January 1956–1959), NA. There was a cover letter and memos A and B.

98. Spencer Phenix to John Raymond, 8 February 1957, RG 59, Box 19 (War Crimes Clemency January 1956–1959), NA. There was a cover letter and memos A and B.

99. Spencer Phenix to John Raymond, 8 February 1957, RG 59, Box 19 (War Crimes Clemency January 1956–1959), NA. There was a cover letter and memos A and B.

100. Spencer Phenix to John Raymond, 8 February 1957, RG 59, Box 19 (War Crimes Clemency January 1956–1959), NA. There was a cover letter and memos A and B.

101. John Raymond's handwritten comment was clipped to the Phenix cover letter, 14 March 1957, RG 59, Box 19 (War Crimes Clemency January 1956–1959), NA.

102. Spencer Phenix, secret letter to John Raymond, 21 July 1957, RG 59, Box 19 (War Crimes Clemency January 1956–1959), NA.

103. Spencer Phenix to John Raymond, 17 April 1957, RG 59, Box 19 (War Crimes Clemency January 1956–1959), NA.

104. Spencer Phenix to John Raymond, 17 April 1957, RG 59, Box 19 (War Crimes Clemency January 1956–1959), NA. "They agreed that the Board, as a Board, and particularly I myself as the U.S. member, had shouldered a considerable responsibility however, but we are all hopeful that no controversial publicity will develop. . . . In this controversial area I dislike to quote anyone, but I can safely say that I found no opposition to the action taken by the Board. . . . I think the Board's action was something of a relief since being unanimous it has the result of confronting them with recommendations which, under the terms of the Bonn Convention, are binding on the Commander-in-Chief, thereby relieving him of all responsibility."

105. Spencer Phenix to John Raymond, 17 April 1957, RG 59, Box 19 (War Crimes Clemency January 1956–1959), NA.

106. Spencer Phenix to John Raymond, 2 July 1957, RG 59, Box 19 (War Crimes Clemency January 1956–1959), NA.

107. Ambassador Bruce, secret cable to Secretary of State, 14 December 1957, RG 59, Box 19 (War Crimes Clemency January 1956–1959), NA. In December 1957, President Eisenhower abolished the Japanese war crimes parole and clemency board and transferred authority to the U.S. ambassador in Tokyo and a "responsible nonpolitical Japanese Board to review application for parole of prisoners now in confinement." According to a secret State Department cable, a similar offer had been made to the West German government: "Chapter 1, Article 6, paras 4 and 5 Settlement Convention contemplate transfer of custody of war criminals to German authorities and US is prepared to make immediate transfer if Germans will accept custody. . . . If Germans wish, we would be prepared to raise with other signatories Bonn Conventions possibility amending Settlement Convention by abolishing Mixed Board and replacing it with a German Board along the lines proposed for Japanese." However, once again, the validity question posed a stumbling block: "US cannot agree to any course of action which would bring into question valid-

ity of trials of war criminals or sentences imposed on them" (Ambassador Bruce, secret cable to Secretary of State, 14 December 1957, RG 59, Box 19 [War Crimes Clemency January 1956–1959], NA). The State Department in Bonn responded with a secret cable to the Secretary of State. The ambassador did not believe that the action in Japan would have much of an impact on the situation in Germany.

108. See Office of the U.S. High Commissioner for Germany, *Landsberg: A Documentary Report* (Frankfurt: U.S. Army, 1951) for a breakdown of the individual cases. RG 59, Box 19 (War Crimes Clemency January 1956–1959), NA.

109. American Nuremberg Trials, *Case 9—United States v. Otto Ohlendorf*, vol. 4, 542, 562, 569.

110. Spencer Phenix to John Raymond, 30 April 1956, RG 59, Box 19 (War Crimes Clemency January 1956–1959), NA.

111. Ambassador Bruce to Secretary of State, 6 May 1958, RG 59, Box 19 (War Crimes Clemency January 1956–1959) and John Raymond to Spencer Phenix, 7 May 1958, RG 59, Box 19 (War Crimes Clemency January 1956–1959), NA.

112. Robert Wolfe, ed., *Americans as Proconsuls: United States Military Government in Germany and Japan, 1944–1952* (Washington, D.C.: U.S. Government Printing Office, 1978), 238. See also Dower, *Embracing Defeat*, 514.

113. Spencer Phenix to John Raymond, 13 May 1958, RG 59, Box 19 (War Crimes Clemency January 1956–1959), NA.

114. John Raymond to Spencer Phenix, 23 June 1958, RG 59, Box 19 (War Crimes Clemency January 1956–1959), NA.

CONCLUSION

1. "Inactive Inmates—201 Files to Be Retired," Cases Tried—Misc. Administration Files: Correspondence and Reports—U.S. Parole Supervisor (Misc. Files), RG 338, NA.

2. Frank Buscher, *The U.S. War Crimes Program in Germany, 1946–1955* (Westport, Conn.: Greenwood, 1989), 153.

3. Jörg Friedrich, "Nuremberg and the Germans," in Belinda Cooper, ed., *War Crimes: The Legacy of Nuremberg* (New York: TV Books, 1999), 93.

4. Jeffrey Herf, *Divided Memory: The Nazi Past in the Two Germanys* (Cambridge: Harvard University Press, 1997), 206.

5. Ibid., 296. According to Raul Hilberg, between 1958 and 1977, the West German government formally charged 816 and sentenced 118 to life; 398 were sentenced to prison terms, but there were no convictions in 3,000 cases. For more on the West German post–1958 trials, see Raul Hilberg, *The Destruction of the European Jews* (New York: Holmes and Meier, 1985), 1086–1088; see also Adalbert Rückerl, *The Investigation of Nazi Crimes: 1945–1978* (Hamden, Conn.: Archon, 1980).

6. Interview with author, Locarno, Switzerland, 17 January 1990.

7. Nayan Chanda, *Brother Enemy: The War After the War* (New York: Harcourt, Brace, Jovanovich, 1986), 377..

8. *Die Angkar*, produced and directed by Heynowsky and Scheuman Studios, 1981. Sary was interviewed by an East German camera crew in 1981.

9. There are many interpretations of the Melian dialogue found in Thucydides' *The History of the Peloponnesian War*. Michael Walzer considered the "dialogue between the Athenian generals Cleomedes and Tisias and magistrates of the island state of Melos . . . one of the high points of Thucydides' *History* and the climax of his realism. . . . His spokesmen are two Athenian generals, who demand a parley and then speak as generals have rarely done in military history. Let us have no fine words about justice, they say. . . . We will instead talk about what is feasible and what is necessary" (Michael Walzer, *Just and Unjust Wars* [New York: Basic, 1977], 5).

   The powerful Athenians attempt to coerce the isolated Melians into accepting a deal: "Instead we recommend that you should try to get what it is possible for you to get, taking into consideration what we both really do think; since you know as well as we do that, when these matters are discussed by practical people, the standard of justice depends on the equality of power to compel and that in fact the strong do what they have the power to do and the weak accept what they have to accept" (Thucydides, *History of the Pelopennesian War* [New York: Penguin, 1972], 401–402). The Melians refuse to submit, so the Athenians build a wall around the city of Melos. After a few skirmishes, more Athenian forces arrive and "siege operations were carried on vigorously" (408). The story grows tragic: "The Melians surrendered unconditionally to the Athenians, who put to death all the men of military age whom they took, and sold the women and children as slaves. Melos itself they took over for themselves, sending out later a colony of 500 men" (408).

10. Daniel Patrick Moynihan, *On the Law of Nations* (Cambridge: Harvard University Press, 1990), 1.

11. Michael Ignatieff, *Warrior's Honor* (New York: Holt, 1997), 6.

12. For more on the UN and U.S. responses to Rwanda, see *Report of the Independent Inquiry Into the Actions of the United Nations During the 1994 Genocide in Rwanda*, UN document, December 15, 1999..

13. Michael Ignatieff, *Virtual War* (New York: Holt, 2000), 118. George Kennan, *Around the Cragged Hill* (New York: Norton, 1993), 206

14. Barbara Crossette, "Helms, in Visit to U.N., Offers Harsh Message," *The New York Times*, January 21, 2000, 1.

15. Telford Taylor, *Nuremberg and Vietnam: An American Tragedy* (New York: Bantam, 1971), 207. See also Peter Maguire, "War Criminals Have Little to Fear," *New York Newsday*, January 22, 1999.

16. Eugene Davidson, *The Nuremberg Fallacy* (New York: Macmillan, 1973), 9. To Kurt Vonnegut, World War II veteran and survivor of the Dresden firebombing, neither war nor law was the problem—rather, it was man.

17. Sven Lindqvist, *Exterminate All the Brutes*, trans. Joan Tate (New York: New Press, 1996), 2.

POSTSCRIPT: THE NEW AMERICAN PARADIGM

1. Testimony of Cofer Black to the Joint Congressional Intelligence Committee, September 26, 2002; http://www.fas.org/irp/congress/2002_hr/092602black.html.

2. Jameel Jaffer and Amrit Singh, *Administration of Torture* (New York: Columbia University Press, 2007), A1–5. "But under this New Paradigm, the President gave terror suspects neither the rights of criminal defendants nor the rights of prisoners of war," wrote Jane Mayer in her groundbreaking book, *The Dark Side: The Inside Story of How the War on Terror Turned Into a War on American Ideals* (New York: Doubleday, 2008), 51–52.

3. Bush also announced that the United States could use military force preemptively against terrorist organizations or the states that harbor or support them. Mayer, *The Dark Side*, 64–65. According to one of John Yoo's 2001 memos, "These decisions, under our Constitution, are for the President alone to make."

4. Alfred McCoy, *A Question of Torture* (New York: Metropolitan Books, 2006). "War means killing people," the architect of the new American paradigm, John Yoo, explained in a 2007 interview. "If we are entitled to kill people, we must be entitled to injure them."

5. Jaffer and Singh, *Administration of Torture*, A1–5.

6. McCoy, *A Question of Torture*, 112; Scott Shane, "Soviet-Style 'Torture' Becomes 'Interrogation,'" *The New York Times*, June 3, 2007. "When you say something down the chain of command like, 'The Geneva Conventions don't apply,' that sets the stage for the kind of chaos we have seen," said retired Judge Advocate General Rear Admiral John Hutson.

7. Mayer, *The Dark Side*, 240–41.

8. Deputy Secretary for Defense Intelligence, Lieutenant William Boykin called the War on Terror a "holy war against Satan." According to Boykin, "Our spiritual enemy will only be defeated if we come against them in the name of Jesus." Richard Leiby, "Christian Soldier," *Washington Post*, November 6, 2003.

9. "Was the USA unleashing pent-up rage, seeking vengeance for every military engagement it had lost or terrorist act that it had suffered?" asked former Guantanamo Bay prisoner Mossam Begg. "Well, almost. The common denominator was Islam." David Horowitz, "Jimmy Carter: Jew-Hater, Genocide-Enabler, Liar," *Front Page Magazine*, December 14, 2006; Moazzam Begg and Victoria Brittain, *Enemy Combatant: My Imprisonment at Guantanamo Bay, Bagram, and Kandahar* (New York: New Press, 2007), 111.

10. Max Boot, *The Savage Wars of Peace* (New York: Basic Books, 2002), 352.

11. David Frumm and Richard Perle, *An End to Evil* (New York: Random House, 2003), 9. Disney/ABC radio host Paul Harvey did his best to stiffen the American spine and in the process demonstrated the insidious effects of "torture's perverse pathology" in one 2005 radio address: "we didn't come this far because we're made of sugar candy. Once upon a time, we elbowed our way onto and into this continent by giving smallpox-infected blankets to Native Americans. Yes, that was biological warfare! And we used every other weapon we could get our hands on to grab this land from whomever. And we grew prosperous. And, yes, we greased the skids with the sweat of slaves" (*Paul Harvey Show*, ABC Radio, June 23, 2005). According to a Gallup poll, by 2005, more than one in four Americans approved of the use of nuclear weapons in the War on Terror. Another survey found that a majority of American high school students believed that newspapers "should not be allowed to

publish without government approval," and even more shocking, one in five said that "Americans should be prohibited from expressing unpopular opinions."

12. Helen Thomas, *Media Matters* interview, May 12, 2006; http://vodpod.com/watch/97344-helen-thomas-on-the-medias-failure.

13. Ron Steel blasted Ignatieff in a *New York Times* review of Ignatieff's book *The Lesser Evil*: "In concocting a formula for a little evil lite to combat the true evildoers, Michael Ignatieff has not provided, as his subtitle states, a code of 'political ethics in an age of terror' but rather an elegantly packaged manual of national self-justification." Alfred McCoy was also extremely critical of Ignatieff. He described the American press and public's "willful blindness" and "studied avoidance" of American conduct in the War on Terror. The human rights advocate turned Canadian politician did a one-eighty after the Abu Ghraib debacle and subsequently wrote an embarrassingly feeble *mea culpa* in which he blamed his lapse of judgment on too many years as a hothouse academic at Harvard. "The Lesser Evil," *The New York Times*, July 25, 2004.

14. McCoy, *A Question of Torture*, 128. Major General Jack Rives, Air Force Judge Advocate General, argued that the more extreme interrogation techniques not only put "the interrogators and chain of command at risk of criminal accusations abroad," they also damaged the military's "culture and self image."

15. David Hackworth, "Fry the big fish, too," February 1, 2005, www.worldnetdaily.com.

16. Colin Powell, Memo to the Counsel to the President, January 26, 2002.

17. Robert Baer, "Why KSM's Confession Rings False," *Time*, March 15, 2007; Katherine Shrader, "Officials: Mohammed Exaggerated Claims," *AP*, March 15, 2007; Josh Meyer, "Detainee Says He Confessed to Stop Torture," *Los Angeles Times*, March 31, 2007.

18. Meng Try Ea, *The Chain of Terror* (Phnom Penh: The Documentation Center of Cambodia, 2002), 2: "Upper echelon wanted answers, and wanted them now. I soon left, ashamed at being unable to perform my duty."

19. News.findlaw.com/hdocs/docs/iraq/tagubarpt.html.

20. Robert Jervis, *The Logic of Impressions in International Relations* (New York: Columbia University Press, 1989). "Unlike Nuremberg, which led with the trials of the top leadership of the Third Reich and only gradually worked its way down to the bottom of that evil ladder," wrote Col. David Hackworth, "our leaders are, so far, successfully ducking any responsibility for the crimes perpetrated on their watch."

21. Sworn statement taken at Baghdad Airport Confinement Facility, June 6, 2003. Another U.S. soldier wrote in a sworn statement: "X choked him until he passed out X stated that X was beating him because Y is a Muslim and X is a Christian."

22. Jane Mayer, "The Experiment," *The New Yorker*, July 11 and 18, 2005.

23. Hackworth, "Fry the big fish, too."

24. www.cbsnews.com/htdocs/pdf/FBI_gitmo_detainees.pdf.

25. Ibid.

26. James Rosen, "Saddam Trial at Uncertain Juncture," *McClatchy Newspapers*, February 13, 2006.

27. "Annan Backs UN Guantanamo Demand," *BBC,* February 17, 2006; "Guantanamo Inmates Can Be Held in Perpetuity," *Reuters,* June 15, 2005; "I think if you combine excessive arrogance and excessive ignorance, you wind up 78 months later where we are in this process," said former Gitmo prosecutor Colonel Morris Davis, who resigned in protest. Josh White, "Prosecutor Alleges, Pentagon Played Politics," *Washington Post,* October 20, 2007

28. White, "Prosecutor Alleges, Pentagon Played Politics"; Carol Williams, "Defender Says Advisor Exerts Illegal Sway," *Los Angeles Times,* March 28, 2008; William Glaberson, "An Unlikely antagonist in the Detainees' Corner," *New York Times,* June 19, 2008.

29. "Guantanamo Bay Prosecutor Steps Down," *BBC,* September 25, 2008; Mike Melia, "Former Gitmo Prosecutor Blasts Tribunals," *AP,* September 26, 2008; Deputy Prison Camp Commander Brigadier General Gregory Zanetti called Hartmann's conduct "abusive, bullying, and unprofessional." Lieutenant Colonel Darrel Vandeveld resigned rather than prosecute a case against an Afghan teenager accused of throwing a grenade at U.S. soldiers. Vandeveld said that he could no longer serve due to the "slipshod" evidentiary procedures.

30. Carol Williams, "Detainee's Plea Deal Angers Some Legal Experts," *Los Angeles Times,* April 1, 2007; "Hicks Case Points up Problems Facing US 'Terror' Tribunals," *AFP,* April 1, 2007; "Guantanamo Follies," *The New York Times,* editorial, April 6, 2007.

31. "Trial Would Have Done Stalin Proud—Lawyer," *Sydney Morning Herald,* April 1, 2007.

32. "U.S. Diplomats to Use Nuremberg Defense," *The Australian,* February 14, 2008; Matthew Lee, "U.S Likens Death Penalty War Court to Nuremberg," *AP,* February 12, 2008.

33. Dan Ephron, "Fair, Open, Just, Honest: A Chat with the Adviser to the Gitmo Military Commissions," *Newsweek,* June 2, 2008.

34. Frank M. Buscher, *The U.S. War Crimes Program in Germany, 1946–1955* (Westport, Conn.: Greenwood, 1989), appendix A.

35. Martha Neil, "Nuremberg Attorney: Gitmo Trials Unfair," *ABA Journal,* June 11, 2007. To King, the United States "has always stood for fairness. We were the ones who started war crimes tribunals and we're the architects. I don't think we should turn our back on that architecture."

36. www.hamdanvrumsfeld.com/.

37. Hal Bernton and Sara Jean Green, "Ressam Judge Decries U.S. Tactics," *The Seattle Times,* July 28, 2005.

38. Mayer, *The Dark Side,* 228.

39. http://www.roberthjackson.org/Man/theman2–7-8–1/.

GLOSSARY

AUCHINCLOSS, JOHN Office of German Political Affairs, 1951–June 1953; thereafter
 International Relations Officer, Office of German Affairs, 1952–54
BONBRIGHT, JAMES Counselor of the U.S. Embassy in Paris; Deputy Assistant Sec-
 retary of State for European Affairs, 1951
BOWIE, ROBERT Chief of the Office of the General Counsel, HICOG, 1951–May
 1953; thereafter Director of the Policy Planning Staff
BYROADE, COLONEL HENRY Director of the Bureau of German Affairs, 1949–
 April 1952
CC10 Control Council Law Ten
CDU Christlich-Demokratische Union (Christian Democratic Union)
CLAY, GENERAL LUCIUS U.S. Military Governor, 1947–49
CONANT, JAMES B. U.S. High Commissioner, January 1953–May 1955
DDR Deutsche Demokratische Union (German Democratic Republic)
DEAN, PATRICK Head of the German Political Department, British Foreign Office
DONNELLY, WALTER U.S. High Commissioner, July 1952–January 1953
DP Deutsche Partei (German Party)
EBERT, FRIEDRICH Member of the Politburo of the German Socialist Unity Party
EDC European Defense Community
EDF European Defense Force
EHARD, HANS Minister President of Bavaria
ELBRICK, BURKE Deputy Assistant U.S. Secretary of State, 1955–58
EUCOM European Command, United States Army
FDP Freie Demokratische Partei (Free Democratic Party)

FRANÇOIS-PONCET, ANDRÉ French High Commissioner

GDR German Democratic Republic

HANDY, GENERAL THOMAS Commander in Chief, EUCOM after 1949

HICOG U.S. High Commission for Germany

HICOM U.S. High Commissioner for Germany

ICC International Criminal Court

IMPAC Interim Parole and Clemency Board, 1953–55 (U.S. zone)

IMT International Military Tribunal

IMTFE International Military Tribunal Far East

JAG Judge Advocate General

JCS Joint Chiefs of Staff

KENNAN, GEORGE Director, Policy Planning Staff; Chairman of the Steering of the NSC Subcommittee on the German Question, 1949

KIRKPATRICK, IVONNE British High Commissioner

LANDSBERG PRISON U.S. prison for convicted war criminals

LEWIS, GEOFFREY Assistant to Assistant U.S. Secretary of State for Occupied Areas, 1948; Deputy Director, Bureau of German Affairs, 1951–53; Acting Director, Office of German Affairs, 1952–54

LYON, CECIL Special Assistant to the U.S. Commander in Berlin; Director, Berlin HICOG, 1951; Director, Office of German Affairs from 1954

MATHEWS, H. FREEMAN Director, Office of European Affairs, Department of State, December 1944–July 1947; Deputy Under-Secretary of State, 1950–1953

MCCLOY, JOHN J. Assistant Secretary of War, 1941–1945; U.S. High Commissioner, June 1949–July 1952

MCNARNEY, GENERAL JOSEPH U.S. Military Governor, 1945–47

MICKELWAIT, COLONEL C. B. EUCOM Theatre Judge Advocate

MERCHANT, LIVINGSTON Deputy Assistant Secretary of State for Far Eastern Affairs until November 1951; Special Assistant for Mutual Security Affairs; Assistant Secretary of State for European Affairs, 1953–56

MORRIS, BREWSTER Secretary, Office of the U.S. Political Advisor for German Affairs from 1952; Officer in Charge of German Political Affairs, Office of German Affairs, November 1953–June 1954

NATO North Atlantic Treaty Organization

NSC National Security Council

OMGUS Office of United States Military Government

RAYMOND, JOHN Assistant Legal Advisor for German Affairs, 1952–54

REBER, SAM Director of Political Affairs, HICOG Office of Political Affairs until July 1953

REINSTEIN, JACQUES Special Assistant to Assistant U.S. Secretary of State, Economic Affairs, 1948; Special Assistant to Assistant U.S. Secretary of State for European Affairs until August 1955; thereafter Director, Office of German Affairs

RIDDLEBERGER, JAMES Chief, Division of Central European Affairs, State Department, January 1944–July 1947; Counselor of Mission, Office of the U.S. Political Advisor for German Affairs from October 1947; Counselor of the Mission of the U.S. Political Advisor for Germany at Berlin, 1948; Director of the Office of Political Affairs, Office of Military Government for Germany, OMGUS; Political Advisor to USHC, 1949; Director of Political Affairs, Office of Political Affairs; Director of Bureau of European Affairs, May 1952–July 1953

ROYALL, KENNETH   Under-Secretary of War, 1945–47; Secretary of War, July–September 1947; Secretary of Army from September 1947

SNOW, CONRAD   Acting Assistant Legal Advisor for Far Eastern Affairs

SCAP   Supreme Commander Asia-Pacific U.S.

SHAEF   Supreme Headquarters, Allied Expeditionary Force (1944–45)

SPD   Sozialdemokratische Partei Deutschlands (Social Democratic Party of Germany)

USAREUR   U.S. Army, Europe

VOORHEES, TRACY   Special assistant to U.S. Secretary of War

VOPOS   Volkspolizei

WAHL, EDUARD   CDU member of the Bundestag and member of the Heidelberg Juristenkreis

WERL   British prison for war criminals

WITTLICH   French prison for war criminals

BIBLIOGRAPHY

PRIMARY SOURCES

NATIONAL ARCHIVES MODERN MILITARY BRANCH, SUITLAND, MARYLAND
Record Group (RG) 338 General Administration Files RG 446

NATIONAL ARCHIVES, COLLEGE PARK, MARYLAND
RG 59
    Box 5: Clemency Board on German War Criminals
    Box 16: War Crimes 1949, 1950, October 16, 1952–December 31, 1952
    Box 17: War Crimes 1953–1959
    Box 18: War Crimes Clemency 1950–1955
    Box 19: War Crimes Clemency January 1956–1959
    Box 24: War Crimes Clemency July 1952–December 1953
    Box 29

COLUMBIA UNIVERSITY ORAL HISTORY PROJECT, NEW YORK
Benjamin Buttenweiser
Lucius Clay
John Foster Dulles
John McCloy

FRANKLIN D. ROOSEVELT LIBRARY, HYDE PARK, NEW YORK
Papers of Eleanor Roosevelt

Unpublished Nuremberg Trial Records

Case No. 111, Document Books. Nos. 58A, 58B, 59, 60A, 90A, 90B, 91, 120, 203, 204, 204A. Nürnberg: Secretariat for Military Tribunals, 1949.

Defense Briefs: Lammers and Meissner, Cross/Closing, XIB. Nürnberg: Secretariat for Military Tribunals, 1949.

Prosecution Briefs: Individual 1–2, Lammers and Stuckart. Nürnberg: Secretariat for Military Tribunals, 1949.

U.S. Military Tribunal Nuremberg, Transcript, Case XI, Weizsaecker, 1–28085. Nürnberg: Secretariat for Military Tribunals, 1949.

Official Documents

Belgium and Germany: Texts and Documents. Ed. Henri Davignon. Brussels: Belgian Government Publication, 1921.

Committee on Alleged German Outrages. *Report on Alleged German Outrages.* Reprint, New York: Macmillan, 1964.

The Foreign Relations of the United States: Paris Peace Conference 1919. Washington, D.C.: U.S. Government Printing Office, 1945, vols. I–IV.

The Foreign Relations of the United States: The Conference at Quebec, 1944. Washington, D.C.: U.S. Government Printing Office, 1972, 124–125.

The Foreign Relations of the United States: 1945. Vol. 3. Washington, D.C.: U.S. Government Printing Office, 1968.

The Foreign Relations of the United States: European Security and the German Question 1951. Vol. 3. Washington, D.C.: U.S. Government Printing Office.

The Foreign Relations of the United States: Germany and Austria 1952–1954. Vol. 7. Washington, D.C.: U.S. Government Printing Office, 1983.

German Imperial Foreign Office. *The Belgian People's War: A Violation of International Law.* New York: Press of John C. Rankin, 1915.

U.S. Chief of Counsel. *Nazi Conspiracy and Aggression: Opinion and Judgment.* Washington, D.C.: U.S. Government Printing Office, 1947.

High Commission Reports

Documents on Germany Under Occupation 1945–1954. London: Oxford University Press, 1955.

Office of the U.S. High Commissioner for Germany. *Landsberg: A Documentary Report.* Frankfurt: U.S. Army, 1951.

——. *Report on Germany, September 21,1949–July 31,1952.* Cologne: Greven and Bechtold, 1952.

Published Trial Records

U.S. Government. *Trials of the German War Criminals Before the Nuernberg Military Tribunals Under Control Council No. 10.* Vols 1–15. Washington, D.C.: U.S. Government Printing Office, 1949.

    Case 1. *The United States v. Karl Brandt et al.* (the Medical case)

    Case 2. *The United States v. Erhard Milch* (the Milch case)

    Case 3. *The United States v. Josef Alstoetter et al.* (the Justice case)

Case 4. *The United States v. Oswald Pohl et al.* (the Pohl case)

Case 5. *The United States v. Fredrich Flick et al.* (the Flick case)

Case 6. *The United States v. Carl Krauch et al.* (the Farben case)

Case 7. *The United States v. Wilhelm List et al.* (the Hostage case)

Case 8. *The United States v. Ulrich Greifelt et al.* (the RuSHA case)

Case 9. *The United States v. Otto Ohlendorf et al.* (the Einsatzgruppen case)

Case 10. *The United States v. Alfried Krupp von Bohlen und Halbach et al.* (the Krupp case)

Case 11. *The United States v. Ernst von Weizsaecker et al.* (the Ministries case)

Case 12. *The United States v. Wilhelm von Leeb et al.* (the High Command case)

Jackson, Robert. *The Nürnberg Case as Presented by Robert H. Jackson, Chief of Counsel for the United States, Together with Other Documents.* New York: Knopf, 1946.

Malmedy Massacre Investigation: Hearings Before a Subcommittee of the Committee on Armed Services, United States Senate, Eighty-First Congress, First Session Pursuant to Senate Resolution 42. Washington, D.C.: U.S. Government Printing Office, 1949.

Taylor, Telford. *Final Report to the Secretary of the Army on the Nuernberg War Crimes Trials.* Washington, D.C.: U.S. Government Printing Office, 1949.

Trials of the Major War Criminals Before the International Military Tribunal, Nuernberg, Germany: 14 November 1945–1 October 1946. 42 vols. Nürnberg: International Military Tribunal, 1947–1949.

Trials of War Criminals Before the Nuremberg Military Tribunals Under Control Council Law No. 10. 15 vols. Nürnberg: International Military Tribunal, 1953.

DISSERTATIONS AND UNPUBLISHED MATERIALS

Botzenhart-Viehe, Verena. "The German Reaction to the American Occupation, 1944–1947." Ph.D. diss., University of California–Santa Barbara, 1980.

Clark, Harry H. "The Laws of War, Prisoner of War Policy, and United States Practices." Ph.D. diss., The Catholic University of America, 1987.

Luders, Michael. "The Strange Case of Ernst von Weizsaecker." Masters thesis, Columbia University, 1988.

Schwartz, Thomas. "From Occupation to Alliance: John J. McCloy and the Allied High Commission in the Federal Republic of Germany, 1949–1952." Ph.D. diss., Harvard University, 1985.

NEWSPAPERS AND PERIODICALS

Stars and Stripes 1946–1949

The New York Times

Chicago Tribune

New York Herald Tribune 1946–1949

Paris Herald Tribune 1946–1949

Newsweek 1946–1949

Time 1945–1949

Der Spiegel 1981

Abenend Post 1952

LETTERS

Brand, James. Letter to Robert Maguire, 17 February 1948. Betty Frankus Maguire Papers, Portland, Oregon.

Caming, William. Letters to author, 24 June 1987, 14 October 1987, 5 February 1990, 14 September 1998.

Ferencz, Ben. Letter to author, 23 February 1990.

Kempner, Dr. Robert. Letters to author, 5 November 1987, 12 October 1988, 17 January 1990.

Koblitz, Robert. Letter to author, 20 May 1996.

Kranzbühler, Otto. Letter to author, 11 July 1996.

Maguire, Robert. Letters to friends and family from Europe, September 1947–May 1949. In possession of the author.

Olson, Ron. Letter to author, 5 June 1990.

Preston, William. Letter to author, 1 September 1990.

Schwartz, Thomas. Letter to author, 8 July 1990.

Shonfeld, Peter (for Richard von Weizsäcker). Letter to author, 12 April 1989.

Sprecher, Drexel. Letters to author, 27 December 1987, 20 February 1992, 9 June 1994.

Taylor, Telford. Letter to author, 13 May 1988.

Willand, John. Letter to author, 20 January 1995.

INTERVIEWS

Brand, Thomas. Interview by author. Tape recording. Portland, Oregon, 2 December 1993.

Caming, William. Interviews by author. Tape recording. Summit, New Jersey, 9 October 1987 and 20 September 1990.

Frankus, Betty. Interviews by author. Tape recording. Portland, Oregon, 20 March 1987 and 16 August 1987.

Friedrich, Jörg. Interviews by author. Tape recording. Berlin, Germany, 21 September 1995 and 16 August 1996.

Hampsten, Alfred. Interview by author. Tape recording. Portland, Oregon, 19 March 1987.

Kempner, Dr. Robert. Interview by author. Tape recording. Locarno, Switzerland, 23 February 1988.

Kester, Randolph. Interview by author. Tape recording. Portland, Oregon, 19 March 1987.

Koenig, Werner. Conversations with author. Trancas, California, 10 July 1987 and 20 August 1993.

Kranzbülhler, Otto. Interview by author. Tape recording. Tegernsee, Germany, 15 August 1996.

Kremen, Hattie. Interview by author. Tape recording. Salem, Oregon, 15 August 1987.

Maguire, Robert Jr. Interviews by author. Tape recording. Carpenteria, California, 27 March 1987 and 13 September 1987.

Olson, Ron. Conversations with author. Los Angeles, California, 1988–1991.

Primeaux, Bob (Standing Rock Sioux Tribe official elder). Conversations with author. Summer 1999.

Rockler, Walter. Interview by author. Tape recording. Washington, D.C., 18 April 1987.

Rockwell, Alwyn. Interview by author. Tape recording. San Francisco, California, 21 July 1988.

Sprecher, Drexel. Interviews by author. Tape recording. Chevy Chase, Maryland, 29 May 1987 and 11 October 1990.

Taylor, Telford. Interviews by author. Tape recording. New York City, 8 April 1987, 21 October 1988, 8 March 1989, and spring 1993.

Wilson, Constance Maguire. Interviews by author. Denver, Colorado, 30 March 1987 and 12 September 1987.

Wilson, Joseph. Conversations with author. Jalama, California, 12 September 1987.

SECONDARY SOURCES

BOOKS

Abzug, Robert. *Inside the Vicious Heart.* New York: Oxford University Press, 1985.

Adenauer, Konrad. *Memoirs.* Chicago: H. Regnery, 1966.

Ambrose, Stephen E. *Eisenhower and Berlin, 1945: The Decision to Halt at the Elbe.* New York: Norton, 1967.

——. *Citizen Soldiers.* New York: Touchstone, 1977.

——. *Rise to Globalism.* New York: Penguin, 1980.

Ambrosius, Lloyd. *Wilsonian Statecraft.* Wilmington, Del.: Scholarly Resources, 1991.

Anderson, Gary and Alan Woolworth, eds. *Through Dakota Eyes: Narrative Accounts of the Indian War of 1862.* St. Paul: Minnesota Historical Society Press, 1988.

Ando, Nisuki, Hosoya Chihiro, Richard H. Minear, and Onuma Yasuaki, eds. *The Tokyo War Crimes Trial: An International Symposium.* Tokyo: Kodansha, 1986.

Appleman, John Alan. *Military Tribunals and International Crimes.* Indianapolis: Bobbs-Merrill, 1954.

Arendt, Hannah. *Eichmann in Jerusalem: A Report on the Banality of Evil.* New York: Penguin, 1977.

Bailey, Thomas Andrew. *The Man in the Street: The Impact of American Public Opinion on Foreign Policy.* New York: Macmillan, 1948.

Baird, Jay, ed. *From Nuremberg to My Lai.* Lexington: D. C. Heath, 1974.

Baldwin, Peter, ed. *Reworking the Past: Hitler, the Holocaust and the Historians' Debate.* Boston: Beacon, 1990.

Balfour, Michael. *West Germany: A Contemporary History.* London: Croom Helm, 1982.

Beals, Walter. *The First German War Crimes Trial.* Chapel Hill: Documentary Publications, 1985.

Benton, Wilbourn, ed. *Nuremberg: German Views of the War Trials.* Dallas: Southern Methodist University Press, 1953.

Bernstein, Victor. *Final Judgment: The Story of Nuremberg.* New York: Boni and Gaer, 1947.

Best, Geoffrey. *War and Law Since 1945.* Oxford: Clarendon, 1994.

Bird, Kai. *The Chairman: John J. McCloy, the Making of the American Establishment.* New York: Simon and Schuster, 1992.

Black, Jeremy. *The Rise of the European Powers 1679–1793.* London: Edward Arnold, 1990.

Blum, John Morton. *From the Morgenthau Diaries.* 3 vols. Boston: Houghton Mifflin, 1967.

Borkin, Joseph. *The Crime and Punishment of I. G. Farben.* New York: Free Press, 1979.

Bosch, William. *Judgment on Nuremberg.* Chapel Hill: University of North Carolina Press, 1970.

Botting, Douglas. *From the Ruins of the Reich: Germany 1945–1949.* New York: Crown, 1985.

Bower, Tom. *Blind Eye to Murder: Britain, America and the Purging of Nazi Germany— A Pledge Betrayed.* London: Andre Deutsch, 1981.

Boyd, Robert. *How the Indians Fought by a Survivor of the Battle of Birch Cooley.* Minneapolis: Pamphlets in American History, c. 1930.

Brackman, Arnold. *The Other Nuremberg: The Untold Story of the Tokyo War Crimes Trials.* New York: Morrow, 1987.

Brodie, Bernard and Fawn Brodie. *From Crossbow to H-Bomb.* Bloomington: Indiana University Press, 1973.

Brogan, Hugh. *The Pelican History of the United States of America.* London: Pelican, 1987.

Brown, Dee. *Bury My Heart at Wounded Knee.* New York: Holt, 1970.

Browning, Christopher. *Ordinary Men.* New York: HarperCollins, 1998.

Bryant, Charles and Abel Murch. *A History of the Great Massacre by the Sioux Indians in Minnesota.* Millwood, N.Y.: Kraus Reprint, 1973.

Bullock, Alan. *Hitler, a Study in Tyranny.* New York: Macmillan, 1967.

——. *Hitler and Stalin.* New York: Knopf, 1992.

Buruma, Ian. *The Wages of Guilt: Memories of War in Germany and Japan.* New York: Penguin, 1994.

Buscher, Frank M. *The U.S. War Crimes Trial Program in Germany, 1946–1955.* Westport, Conn.: Greenwood, 1989.

Calleo, D. *The German Problem Record.* New York: Cambridge University Press, 1978.

Caridi, Ronald. *The Korean War and American Politics: The Republican Party as a Case Study.* Philadelphia: University of Pennsylvania Press, 1968.

Carley, Kenneth. *The Sioux Uprising of 1862.* Minneapolis: Minnesota State Historical Society, 1961.

Cesarani, David. *Justice Delayed.* London: William Heineman, 1992.

Chambers, John Whiteclay, ed. *The Eagle and the Dove: The American Peace Movement and United States Foreign Policy 1900–1922.* Syracuse, N.Y.: Syracuse University Press, 1991.

Chanda, Nayan. *Brother Enemy: The War After the War.* New York: Harcourt Brace Jovanovich, 1986.

Chang, Iris. *The Rape of Nanking.* New York: Basic, 1997.

Choate, Joseph. *The Two Hague Conferences.* 1913; reprint, New York: Kraus Reprint, 1969.

Clausewitz, Karl von. *War, Politics, and Power: Selections from* On War, *and* I Believe and Profess. Trans. Edward M. Collins. Washington, D.C.: Regnery Gateway, 1962.

Clay, Lucius. *Decision in Germany.* New York: Doubleday, 1950.

——. *The Papers of General L. D. Clay 1945–1949.* Bloomington: Indiana University Press, 1978.

Cole, Hugh. *The Ardennes: Battle of the Bulge.* Washington, D.C.: U.S. Government Printing Office, 1965.

Cookridge, E. H. *Gehlen: Spy of the Century.* New York: Random House, 1971.

Conant, James Bryant. *Germany and Freedom, A Personal Appraisal.* Cambridge: Harvard University Press, 1958.

Conot, Robert. *Justice at Nuremberg.* New York: Carroll and Graf, 1983.

Conquest, Robert. *The Great Terror: A Reassessment.* New York: Oxford University Press, 1990.

Cooper, Belinda, ed. *War Crimes: The Legacy of Nuremberg.* New York: TV Books, 1999.

Corbett, Percy Elwood. *The Individual and World Society.* Princeton: Princeton University Press, 1953.

Cornwell, John. *The Study of International Law.* Garden City, N.Y.: Doubleday, 1955.

——. *Hitler's Pope: The Secret History of Pius XII.* New York: Viking, 1999.

Corson, William. *The Armies of Ignorance.* New York: Dial/James Wade, 1977.

Cox, General Jacob. *Sherman's Battle for Atlanta.* New York: Da Capo Reprint, 1994.

Craig, Gordon. *Germany 1866–1945.* Oxford: Oxford University Press, 1980.

Crane, Conrad. *Bombs, Cities, and Civilians.* Lawrence: University of Kansas Press, 1993.

Dastrup, Boyd. *Crusade in Nürnberg: Military Occupation.* Westport, Conn.: Greenwood, 1986.

Davidson, Eugene. *The Death and Life of Germany: An Account of U.S. Occupation.* New York: Knopf, 1959.

——. *The Trial of the Germans.* New York: Macmillan, 1966.

Davignon, Henri. *Belgium and Germany: Text and Documents.* London: T. Nelson and Sons, 1915.

Davis, Calvin DeHormond. *The United States and the Second Hague Convention.* Durham: Duke University Press, 1975.

Daws, Gavan. *Prisoners of the Japanese.* New York: Morrow, 1994.

De Landa, Manuel. *War in the Age of Intelligent Machines.* New York: Swerve Editions, 1991.

Delbrück, Hans. *The Dawn of Modern Warfare.* Lincoln: University of Nebraska Press, 1961.

Deloria, Vine Jr. and Clifford Lytle. *American Indians, American Justice.* Austin: University of Texas Press, 1983.

Dettremond, Calvin. *The United States and the Second Hague Peace Conference.* Durham: Duke University Press, 1975.

De Zayas, Alfred M. *The Wehrmacht War Crimes Bureau, 1939–1945.* Lincoln: University of Nebraska Press, 1979.

Dickinson, Edwin. *Law and Peace.* Philadelphia: University of Pennsylvania Press, 1951.

Divine, Robert. *Since 1945: Politics and Diplomacy in Recent American History.* New York: Knopf, 1985.

Dower, John. *War Without Mercy.* New York: Pantheon, 1986.

——. *Embracing Defeat: Japan in the Wake of World War II*. New York: Norton, 1999.

Drinnon, Richard. *Facing West: The Metaphysics of Indian-Hating and Empire-Building*. Norman: University of Oklahoma Press, 1980.

Dulles, Allen. *Germany's Underground*. New York: Macmillan, 1947.

Edgerton, Robert. *Warriors of the Rising Sun*. New York: Norton, 1997.

Eisenhower, Dwight D. *Crusade in Europe*. New York: Doubleday, 1948.

Elliott, Charles Burke. *The Philippines: To the End of the Military Regime*. Indianapolis: Bobbs-Merrill, 1917.

Ellis, Richard. *General Pope and U.S. Indian Policy*. Albuquerque: University of New Mexico Press, 1970.

Elshtain, Jean Bethke, ed. *Just War Theory*. New York: New York University Press, 1992.

Etzold, Thomas H. and John Lewis Gaddis, eds. *Containment: Documents on American Policy and Strategy, 1945–1950*. New York: Columbia University Press, 1978.

Ferencz, Benjamin. *Less Than Slaves*. Cambridge: Harvard University Press, 1979.

——. *Enforcing International Law: A Way to World Peace*. New York: Oceana, 1983.

Ferguson, Niall. *The Pity of War*. New York: Basic, 1998.

Ferrell, Robert. *Peace in Their Time: The Origins of the Kellogg-Briand Pact*. New York: Yale University Press, 1952.

Fleming, Gerald. *Hitler and the Final Solution*. Berkeley: University of California Press, 1982.

Foucault, Michel. *Discipline and Punish*. New York: Vintage, 1979.

Foner, Eric. *Reconstruction: America's Unfinished Revolution 1863–1877*. New York: Harper and Row, 1988.

Friedman, Leon, ed. *The Laws of War*, vol. 1. New York: Random House, 1972.

Friedmann, Wolfgang. *The Changing Structure of International Law*. New York: Columbia University Press, 1964.

Friedrich, Carl Joachim. *The Philosophy of Law in Historical Perspective*. Chicago: University of Chicago Press, 1958.

Friedrich, Jörg. *Die kalte Amnestie*. Frankfurt: Fischer, 1984.

Friedrich, Jörg and Jörg Wallenberg. *Licht in den Schatten der Vergangenheit*. Frankfurt/Main: Ullstein, 1987.

Fritzsche, Hans. *The Sword in the Scales*. Trans. Diana Pyke and Heinrich Freenkel. London: Wingate, 1953.

Fuller, J. F. C. *The Conduct of War 1789–1961*. New York: Da Capo, 1961.

——. *Decisive Battles of the U.SA*. New York: Da Capo Reprint, 1993.

Fussell, Paul. *The Great War and Modern Memory*. New York: Oxford University Press, 1975.

——. *Doing Battle: The Making of a Skeptic*. Boston: Little, Brown, 1996.

Fyfe, Sir David Maxwell, ed. *UN War Crimes Commission, The Belsen Trial*. New York: Howard Fertig, 1983.

Gaddis, John. *The United States and the Origins of the Cold War, 1941–1947*. New York: Columbia University Press, 1972.

Gatske, Hans. *Germany and the United States: A Special Relationship?* Cambridge: Harvard University Press, 1980.

Gehlen, Reinhard. *The Service: The Memoirs of General Reinhard Gehlen.* Trans. David Irving. New York: World, 1972.

Genovese, Eugene. *Roll, Jordan, Roll: The World the Slaves Made.* New York: Vintage, 1976.

German Imperial Foreign Office. *The Belgian People's War: A Violation of International Law.* New York: Press of John C. Rankin, 1915.

Germany Reichsgericht. *German War Trials: Report of Proceedings Before the Supreme Court.* London: H. M. Stationary Office, 1921.

Gerson, Leonard. *The Secret Police in Lenin's Russia.* Philadelphia: Temple University Press, 1976.

Gilbert, Gustav. *Nuremberg Diary.* New York: Farrar, Straus & Giroux, 1947.

Gilbert, Martin. *Auschwitz and the Allies.* New York: Holt, 1981.

Gimbel, John. *The American Occupation of Germany: Politics and the Military, 1945–1949.* Palo Alto: Stanford University Press, 1968.

Gisevius, Hans. *To the Bitter End.* Boston: Houghton Mifflin, 1947.

Glueck, Sheldon. *The Nuernberg Trial and Aggressive War.* New York: Knopf, 1946.

Goebbels, Josef. *The Goebbels Diaries.* New York: Eagle, 1948.

Gold, Hal. *Unit 731: Testimony.* Tokyo: Yen Books, 1996.

Gorlitz, Walter, ed. *The Kaiser and His Court: Note Books and Letters of Admiral Georg Alexander von Muller, Chief of Naval Cabinet 1914–1918.* London: MacDonald, 1961.

Graebner, Norman A., ed. *The National Security: Its Theory and Practice, 1945–1960.* New York: Oxford University Press, 1986.

Graff, Henry, ed. *American Imperialism: The Philippine Insurrection.* Boston: Little, Brown, 1969.

Gray, Edwyn. *The U-Boat War.* London: Leo Cooper, 1973.

Greenspan, Morris. *The Modern Law of Land Warfare.* Berkeley: University of California Press, 1959.

Greenfell, Russell. *Unconditional Hatred: German War Guilt and the Future of Europe.* New York: Devin Adair, 1953.

Greil, Lothar. *Oberst der Waffen SS Joachim Peiper und der Malmedy Process.* München: Schild-Verlag, 1977.

Griffith, Robert, ed. *Ike's Letters to a Friend 1941–1958.* Lawrence: University of Kansas Press, 1984.

Grotius, Hugh. *De Jure Belli Ac Pacis Libri Tres, The Classics of International Law.* Trans. Francis W. Kelsey. Ed. James Brown Scott. Oxford: Clarendon, 1925.

Hagedorn, Hermann. *Roosevelt in the Badlands.* Boston: Houghton Mifflin, 1921.

Halle, Louis. *Dream and Reality: Aspects of American Foreign Policy.* New York: Harper, 1958.

Handrider, Wolfram, ed. *West German Foreign Policy 1949–1979.* Boulder: Westview, 1990.

Harbutt, Eraser. *The Iron Curtain.* New York: Oxford University Press, 1986.

Harris, Sheldon. *Factories of Death: Japanese Biological Warfare 1932–45 and the American Cover-Up.* London: Routledge, 1994.

Harris, Whitney. *Tyranny on Trial: The Evidence of Nuernberg.* Dallas: Southern Methodist University Press, 1954.

Hart, B. H. Liddell. *Strategy.* New York: Penguin, 1991.

Hartigan, Richard, ed. *Lieber's Code and the Laws of War.* Chicago: Precedent, 1983.

Hartle, Anthony. *Moral Issues in Military Decision Making.* Lawrence: University of Kansas Press, 1989.

Hastings, Max. *Bomber Command: The Myths and Reality of the Strategic Bombing Offensive 1939–45.* New York: The Dial Press/James Wade, 1979.

Hays, Robert. *A Race at Bay.* Carbondale: Southern Illinois University Press, 1997.

Heckscher, August. *Woodrow Wilson.* New York: Scribners, 1992.

Heinrichs, Waldo. *Threshold of War: Franklin D. Roosevelt and American Entry into World War II.* New York: Oxford University Press, 1988.

Henkin, Louis. *How Nations Behave: Law and Foreign Policy.* New York: Columbia University Press, 1968.

Herf, Jeffrey. *Divided Memory: The Nazi Past in the Two Germanys.* Cambridge: Harvard University Press, 1997.

Heydecker, Joe J. and Johannes Leeb. *The Nuernberg Trial: A History of Nazi Germany as Revealed Through the Testimony at Nuernberg.* Ed. R. A. Downey. Cleveland: World, 1952.

Hill, Alfred. *The History of Company E of the Sixth Minnesota Regiment of Volunteer Infantry.* St. Paul: Pioneer, 1899.

Hillgruber, Andreas. *Germany and the Two World Wars.* Trans. William C. Kirby. Cambridge: Harvard University Press, 1981.

Hingley, Ronald. *The Russian Secret Police.* New York: Simon and Schuster, 1970.

Hiscocks, Richard. *The Adenauer Era.* New York: Lippincott, 1966.

Hitchcock, Henry. *Marching with Sherman.* New Haven: Yale University Press, 1927.

Hitler, Adolf. *Mein Kampf.* Trans. Ralph Manheim. Boston: Houghton Mifflin, 1971.

Hobsbawm, E. J. *Nations and Nationalism Since 1780: Programme, Myth, Reality.* Cambridge: Cambridge University Press, 1990.

Hodgson, Godfrey. *The Life and Wars of Henry Stimson.* New York: Knopf, 1990.

Hodos, George H. *Show Trials: Stalinist Purges in Eastern Europe 1948–1954.* New York: Praeger, 1987.

Hoedeman, Paul. *Hitler or Hippocrates: Medical Experiments and Euthanasia in the Third Reich.* Sussex: Book Guild, 1991.

Hoffmann, Peter. *The History of the German Resistance, 1933–1945.* Cambridge: MIT Press, 1979.

Holmes, Richard. *Acts of War: The Behavior of Men in Battle.* New York: Free Press, 1985.

Hoopes, Townsend. *The Devil and John Foster Dulles.* Boston: Little, Brown, 1973.

Hovannisan, Richard, ed. *The Armenian Genocide In Perspective.* New Brunswick: Rutgers University Press, 1986.

Howard, Michael. *War in European History.* New York: Oxford University Press, 1976.

———. *Restraints on War.* New York: Oxford University Press, 1979.

Howard, Michael, George Andreopoulos, and Mark Shulman. *The Laws of War.* New Haven: Yale University Press, 1994.

Hoyt, Edwin. *Three Military Leaders: Togo, Yamamoto, Yamashita.* Tokyo: Kodansha, 1993.

Hull, William. *The Two Hague Conferences and Their Contribution to International Law.* Boston: Ginn, 1908.

Hyde, Harlow A. *Scraps of Paper: The Disarmament Treaties Between the World Wars.* Lincoln: Media Publishing, 1988.

Iggers, Georg. *The German Theory of History.* Middletown: Wesleyan University Press, 1968.

——. *Leopold von Ranke and the Shaping of the Historical Discipline.* Syracuse: Syracuse University Press, 1990.

Ignatieff, Michael. *Warrior's Honor.* New York: Holt, 1997.

Irving, David. *The Last Battle.* London: Focal Point, 1999.

Isaacson, Walter and Evan Thomas. *The Wise Men.* New York: Simon and Schuster, 1986.

Jervis, Robert. *The Logic of Images in International Relations.* New York: Columbia University Press, 1989.

Jessup, Phillip. *Elihu Root.* Hamden, Conn.: Archon, 1964.

Kaiser, David. *Politics and War.* Cambridge: Harvard University Press, 1990.

Kaplan, Fred. *The Wizards of Armageddon.* New York: Touchstone, 1983.

Kaplan, Morton and Nicholas de B. Katzenbach. *The Political Foundations of International Law.* New York: Wiley, 1961.

Kater, Michael. *Doctors Under Hitler.* Chapel Hill: University of North Carolina Press, 1989.

Keegan, John. *The Face of Battle.* New York: Penguin, 1976.

——. *Fields of Battle: The Wars for North America.* New York: Knopf, 1996.

——. *The First World War.* New York: Knopf, 1998.

Keen, Maurice. *Nobles, Knights, and Men-at-Arms in the Middle Ages.* Ohio: Hambaldon, 1996.

Kelsen, Hans. *Law and Peace in International Relations.* Cambridge: Harvard University Press, 1942.

——. *Peace Through Law.* Chapel Hill: University of North Carolina Press, 1944.

——. *General Theory of Law and State.* Cambridge: Harvard University Press, 1949.

——. *Principles of International Law.* New York: Rhinehart, 1959.

Kempner, Robert M. W. *Ein Advokat für die Humanität.* Osnabrück: Universität Osnabrück, 1986.

Kennan, George F. *American Diplomacy, 1900–50.* Chicago: University of Chicago Press, 1953.

——. *Realities of American Foreign Policy.* Princeton: Princeton University Press, 1954.

——. *Memoirs 1925–1950.* Boston: Atlantic Monthly, 1967.

——. *Around the Cragged Hill: A Personal and Political Philosophy.* New York: Norton, 1993.

Kennedy, John Fitzgerald. *Profiles in Courage.* New York: Harper, 1961.

Kennedy, Paul. *The Rise of German-Anglo Antagonism, 1860–1914.* Boston: Allen and Unwin, 1980.

Keohane, Robert O., ed. *Neorealism and Its Critics.* New York: Columbia University Press, 1986.

Kerruish, Valerie. *Jurisprudence as Ideology.* New York: Routledge, 1991.

Kessler, Leo. *S.S. Peiper: The Life and Death of S.S. Colonel Jochen Peiper.* London: Leo Cooper, 1986.

Kirakosyan, Jon. *The Armenian Genocide.* Madison: Sphinx, 1992.

Kirchheimer, Otto. *Political Justice: The Use of Legal Procedure for Political Ends.* Princeton: Princeton University Press, 1961.

Kitchen, Martin. *Europe Between Wars.* London: Longman, 1988.

Klee, Ernst, ed. *The Good Old Days: The Holocaust as Seen by Its Perpetrators and Bystanders.* Trans. Deborah Burnstone. New York: Free Press, 1988.

Klemperer, Klemens von. *German Resistance Against Hitler.* Oxford: Clarendon, 1992.

Kneeshaw, Stephen J. *In Pursuit of Peace: The American Reaction to the Kellogg-Briand Pact, 1928–1929.* New York: Garland, 1991.

Knieriem, August von. *The Nuernberg Trials.* Trans. Elizabeth Schmitt. Chicago: Regnery, 1959.

Koch, H. W. *In the Name of the Volk: Political Justice in Hitler's Germany.* New York: St. Martin's, 1989.

Kochavi, Arieh. *Prelude to Nuremberg: Allied War Crimes Policy and the Question of Punishment.* Chapel Hill: University of North Carolina Press, 1998.

Koselleck, Reinhard. *Critique in Crisis.* New York: Berg, 1988.

Kreiger, Wolfgang. *General Lucius D. Clay.* Stuttgart: Klett-Cotta, 1987.

Lacquer, Walter. *Stalin.* London: Unwin and Hyman, 1990.

Lael, Richard. *The Yamashita Precedent.* Wilmington, Del.: Scholarly Resources, 1982.

LaFeber, Walter. *America, Russia, and the Cold War.* New York: Knopf, 1985.

Lansing, Robert. *War Memoirs of Robert Lansing, Secretary of State.* Indianapolis: Bobbs-Merrill, 1935.

——. *The Peace Negotiations: A Personal Narrative.* Port Washington, N.Y.: Kennikat, 1969.

Leckie, Robert. *The War in Korea.* New York: Random House, 1963.

Lee, Martin. *The Beast Reawakens.* New York: Little, Brown, 1997.

Leopold, Richard. *Elihu Root and the Conservative Tradition.* Boston: Little, Brown, 1954.

Lepore, Jill. *The Name of War: King Philip's War and the Origins of American Identity.* New York: Knopf, 1998.

Levie, Howard. *Terrorism in War: The Law of War Crimes.* Dobbs Ferry, N.Y.: Oceana, 1993.

Lewis, John. *Uncertain Judgment: A Bibliography of War Crimes Trials.* Santa Barbara: ABC-Clio, 1979.

Lewis, Rand C. *A Nazi Legacy: Right-Wing Extremism in Postwar Germany.* New York: Praeger, 1991.

Lifton, Robert J. *The Nazi Doctors.* New York: Basic, 1983.

Lindqvist, Sven. *Exterminate All the Brutes.* Trans. Joan Tate. New York: New Press, 1996.

Linn, Brian McAllister. *The U.S. Army and Counterinsurgency in the Philippines War, 1899–1902.* Chapel Hill: University of North Carolina Press, 1989.

Longstreet, Stephen. *Indian Wars of the Great Plains.* New York: Indian Head, 1970.

Lorenz, Konrad. *On Aggression.* Trans. Marjorie Kerr Wilson. New York: Bantam, 1966.

Luban, David. *Legal Modernism.* Ann Arbor: University of Michigan Press, 1994.

Lukas, Richard. *The Forgotten Holocaust.* Lexington: University of Kentucky Press, 1986.

MacLean, E. L. *The Cruel Hunters.* Atglen, Pa.: Schiffer Military History, 1998.

Mahan, Alfred Thayer. *Armaments and Arbitration: The Place of Force in the International Relations of States.* New York: Harper and Bros., 1912.

Maier, Charles S. *The Unmasterable Past: History, Holocaust, and German National Identity.* Cambridge: Harvard University Press, 1988.

Manchester, William. *The Arms of Krupp 1587–1968.* New York: Bantam, 1968.

——. *American Caesar: Douglas MacArthur 1880–1964.* Boston: Little, Brown, 1978.

Mann, Abby. *Judgment at Nuernberg.* New York: New American Library, 1961.

Mann, Michael. *States, War and Capitalism.* Oxford: Basil Blackwell, 1991.

Manstein, Erich von. *Lost Victories.* Novato, Calif.: Presidio, 1994.

Marks, Sally. *The Illusion of Peace.* New York: St. Martin's, 1976.

Marrus, Michael. *The Holocaust in History.* New York: Penguin, 1987.

——, ed. *The Nuremberg War Crimes Trial 1945–1946.* New York: Bedford, 1997.

Maser, Werner. *Nuremberg Trial: A Nation on Trial.* New York: Scribners, 1979.

Mason, Alpheus. *Harlan Fiske Stone: Pillar of the Law.* New York: Viking, 1956.

Mayer, Arno. *Wilson v. Lenin: The Political Origins of the New Diplomacy.* Cleveland: World, 1964.

McDougall, Walter. *Promised Land, Crusader State.* Boston: Houghton Mifflin, 1997.

McGeehan, Robert. *The German Rearmament Question: American Diplomacy After World War II.* Urbana: University of Illinois Press, 1971.

McNeill, William H. *The Pursuit of Power: Technology, Armed Force, and Society Since a.d. 1000. Chicago: University of Chicago Press, 1982.*

McPherson, James. *Battle Cry of Freedom.* New York: Ballantine, 1989.

Meinecke, Friedrich. *The German Catastrophe: Reflections and Recollections.* Boston: Beacon, 1950.

——. *Machiavellism: The Doctrine of Raison d'Etat and Its Place in Modern History.* Boulder: Westview, 1984.

Mendelson, John. *The Use of Seized Records in the United States Proceedings at Nürnberg.* New York: Garland, 1988.

Merrit, Richard. *Public Opinion in Occupied Germany: The OMGUS Surveys 1945–1949.* Urbana: University of Illinois Press, 1970.

——. *Democracy Imposed: U.S. Occupation Policy and the German Public, 1945–1949.* New Haven: Yale University Press, 1995.

Middleton, Drew. *The Struggle for Germany.* Indianapolis: Bobbs-Merrill, 1949.

Miller, Stuart Creighton. *Benevolent Assimilation: The American Conquest of the Philippines, 1899–1903.* New Haven: Yale University Press, 1982.

Minear, Richard H. *Victor's Justice: The Tokyo War Crimes Trial.* Princeton: Princeton University Press, 1971.

Miscamble, Wilson. *George F. Kennan and the Making of American Foreign Policy, 1947–1950*. Princeton: Princeton University Press, 1992.

Montgomery, John. *Forced to be Free: The Artificial Revolution in Germany and Japan*. Chicago: University of Chicago Press, 1957.

Morgan, Edmund. *American Slavery, American Freedom*. New York: Norton, 1975.

Morgenthau, Hans. *Scientific Man vs. Power Politics*. Chicago: University of Chicago Press, 1946.

——. *In Defense of National Interest: A Critical Examination*. New York: Knopf, 1951.

——. *Politics Among the Nations: The Struggle for Power and Peace*. New York: Knopf, 1961.

Morgenthau, Hans Jr. *Morgenthau Diaries Vols. I–II*. New York: Da Capo, 1974.

Morse, Arthur D. *While Six Million Died: A Chronicle of American Apathy*. Woodstock, N.Y.: Overlook, 1983.

Moynihan, Daniel Patrick. *On the Law of Nations*. Cambridge: Harvard University Press, 1990.

Müller, Ingo. *Hitler's Justice: The Courts of the Third Reich*. Trans. Deborah Lucas Schneider. Cambridge: Harvard University Press, 1991.

Mullins, Claud. *The Leipzig Trials*. London: H. F. G. Witherby 1921.

Murphy, Robert. *A Diplomat Among Warriors*. New York: Doubleday 1964.

Murray, Williamson. *Luftwaffe*. Baltimore: The Nautical and Aviation Publishing Company of America, 1985.

Musicant, Ivan. *Empire by Default: The Spanish-American War and the Dawn of the American Century*. New York: Holt, 1998.

Myers, Frank. *Soldiering in the Dakota Among the Indians 1863–1865*. Huron, Dakota: Huronite Press, 1888.

National Council of the National Front of Democratic Germany. *White Book on the American and British Policy Intervention in West Germany and the Revival of German Imperialism*. 1951.

Neave, Airey. *On Trial at Nuremberg*. Boston: Little, Brown, 1978.

Nelson, Walter. *Germany Rearmed*. New York: Simon and Schuster, 1972.

Neumann, Inge. *European War Crimes Trials: A Bibliography*. New York: Carnegie Endowment for International Peace, 1951.

Neumann, Sigmund. *Germany: Promise and Perils*. New York: Foreign Policy Association, 1950.

New York Constitutional Convention 1938. *Proceedings of the Constitutional Convention of the State of New York Commemorative of the Life and Public Service of Elihu Root*. Albany: J. B. Lyon, 1938.

Nobleman, Eli. *American Military Courts in Germany: With Special Reference to Historic Practice and Their Role in the Democratization of the German People*. Fort Gordon, Ga.: U.S. Army, Civil Affairs School, 1961.

Noltke, Ernst. *The Three Faces of Fascism*. New York: Holt, Rinehart, and Winston, 1966.

Nyiri, Nicolas. *The United Nations' Search for a Definition of Aggression*. New York: Peter Lang, 1989.

Olsen, Marvin E. and Martin Marger, eds. *Power in Modern Societies*. San Francisco: Westview, 1993.

Orwell, George. *A Collection of Essays*. New York: Harcourt Brace Jovanovich, 1946.

Oshinsky, David. *A Conspiracy So Immense*. New York: Free Press, 1983.

O'Toole, G. J. A. *The Spanish War*. New York: Norton, 1984.

Pagden, Anthony and Jeremy Lawrance, eds. *Francisco DeVitoria: Political Writings*. Cambridge: Cambridge University Press, 1991.

Page, James Madison. *The True Story of Andersonville*. New York: Neale Publications, 1908.

Parish, Peter. *Slavery: History and Historians*. New York: Harper and Row, 1989.

Passelecq, Fernand. *Truth and Travesty: An Analytical Study of the Belgian Government to the German White Book*. London: Sir Joseph Causton and Sons, 1916.

Paterson, Thomas, J. Garry Clifford, and Kenneth Hagan, eds. *American Foreign Policy: A History—1900 to Present*. Vol. 2. Lexington: D. C. Heath, 1988.

Paul, Allen. *Katyn: The Untold Story of Stalin's Polish Massacre*. New York: Scribners, 1991.

Piccigallo, Philip. *The Japanese on Trial: Allied War Crimes Operations in the East, 1945–1951*. Austin: University of Texas Press, 1979.

Plischke, Elemer. *The Allied High Commission for Germany*. Bad Godesberg: HICOG, 1953.

Pound, Roscoe. *Interpretations of Legal History*. New York: Macmillan, 1923.

Pridley, Russell. *Charles E. Flandrau and the Defense of New Ulm*. New Ulm, Minn.: Brown County Historical Society, 1962.

Pritchard, R. John and Sonia Magbanua Zaide, eds. *The Tokyo War Crimes Trial*. New York: Garland, 1981.

Pritchett, C. Herman. *The Roosevelt Court: A Study in Judicial Politics and Values, 1937–1947*. New York: Macmillan, 1948.

Rabb, Theodore. *The Thirty Years War: Problems of Motive, Extent and Effect*. Washington, D.C.: University Press of America, 1981.

Ramsey, Paul. *The Just War: Force and Political Responsibility*. Savage, Md.: Littlefield Adams, 1983.

Rappaport, Armin. *Henry Stimson and Japan*. Chicago: University of Chicago Press, 1963.

Reel, Frank. *The Case of General Yamashita*. Chicago: University of Chicago Press, 1949.

Reese, Mary Ellen. *General Reinhard Gehlen: The CIA Connection*. Fairfax, Va: George Mason University Press, 1990.

Reitlinger, Gerald. *The SS: Alibi of a Nation 1922–1945*. New York: Viking, 1957.

Reynolds, Michael. *The Devil's Adjutant: Jochen Peiper, Panzer Leader*. New York: Sarpedon, 1995.

Riley-Smith, Jonathan. *The Crusades: A Short History*. New Haven: Yale University Press, 1987.

Roberts, Adam and Richard Guelff, eds. *Documents on the Laws of War*. New York: Oxford University Press, 1989.

Robertson, Richard. *The Development of RAF Strategic Bombing Doctrine, 1919–1939*. Westport, Conn.: Praeger, 1995.

Rodnick, David. *Post-War Germans.* New Haven: Yale University Press, 1948.

Röling, B. V. A. and Antonio Cassese. *The Tokyo Trial and Beyond.* Cambridge: Polity, 1993.

Root, Elihu. *Addresses on International Subjects.* Cambridge: Harvard University Press, 1916.

——. *Miscellaneous Addresses.* Cambridge: Harvard University Press, 1917.

——. *Men and Policies.* Cambridge: Harvard University Press, 1925.

——. *Elihu Root, President of the Century Club Association, 1918–1927.* New York: The Century Club, 1937.

——. *The Military and Colonial Policy of the United States.* New York: AMS Press, 1970.

Ropp, Theodore. *War in the Modern World.* New York: Collier, 1962.

Royster, Charles. *The Destructive War: William Tecumseh Sherman, Stonewall Jackson, and the Americans.* New York: Knopf, 1991.

Rückerl, Adalbert. *The Investigation of Nazi Crimes, 1945–1978.* Hamden, Conn.: Archon, 1980.

Satterlee, Marion. "A Description of the MASSACRE BY SIOUX INDIANS. In Renville County, Minnesota, August 18–19." Minneapolis: Fisher Paper Co., 1916.

Scheingold, Stuart A. *The Politics of Law and Order: Street Crime and Public Policy.* New York: Longman, 1984.

Schellenberg, Walter. *The Labyrinth.* New York: Harper, 1956.

Schilling, Werner, Paul Hammond, and Glenn Snyder, eds. *Strategy, Politics and Defense Budgets.* New York: Columbia University Press, 1962.

Schlesinger, Arthur Jr. *The Cycles of American History.* Boston: Houghton Mifflin, 1986.

Schmidt, Matthias. *Albert Speer: The End of a Myth.* Trans. Joachim Neugroschel. London: Harrap, 1985.

Schmitt, Carl. *The Concept of the Political.* New Brunswick: Rutgers University Press, 1976.

Schmitt, Hans, ed. *U.S. Occupation of Europe After World War II.* Lawrence: Regents Press of Kansas, 1978.

Scott, James Brown. *The Hague Peace Conferences of 1899 and 1907.* New York: Garland Library of War and Peace, 1972.

Schwabe, Karl. *World War, Revolution, Germany and Peacemaking.* Chapel Hill: University of North Carolina Press, 1985.

Schwartz, Karl. *World War, Revolution, Germany and Peacemaking 1918–19.* Chapel Hill: University of North Carolina Press, 1985.

Schwartz, Thomas Alan. *America's Germany: John J. McCloy and the Federal Republic of Germany.* Cambridge: Harvard University Press, 1991.

Schwarz, Hans Peter. *Die Ära Adenauer: Gründerjahre der Republik.* Stuttgart: Deutsche Verlags-Anstalt; Wiesbaden: Brockhaus, 1983.

Seabury, William. *Wilhelmstrasse: A Study of German Diplomats Under the Nazi Regime.* Berkeley: University of California Press, 1954.

Sereny, Gitta. *Into That Darkness: An Examination of Conscience.* New York: Vintage, 1983.

——. *Albert Speer: His Battle with Truth.* New York: Knopf, 1995.

Settel, Arthur. *This Is Germany.* New York: Sloane, 1950.

Sherman, William T. *Personal Memoirs of William Tecumseh Sherman*. Vol. 2. New York: Library of America, 1990.

Shirer, William L. *The Rise and Fall of the Third Reich: A History of Nazi Germany*. New York: Fawcett Crest, 1950.

Shklar, Judith N. *Legalism: Laws, Morals, and Political Trials*. Cambridge: Harvard University Press, 1964.

Simpson, Christopher. *Blowback: America's Recruitment of Nazis and Its Effects on the Cold War*. New York: Weidenfield and Nicolson, 1988.

———. *The Splendid Blond Beast: Money, Law, and Genocide in the Twentieth Century*. New York: Grove, 1993.

Smith, Bradley F. *Reaching Judgment at Nuremberg*. New York: Basic, 1977.

———. *The Road to Nuremberg*. New York: Basic, 1981.

———. *The American Road to Nuremberg: The Documentary Record 1944–1945*. Stanford: Hoover Institution Press, 1982.

Smith, Glenn. *Langer of North Dakota: A Study in Isolationism*. New York: Garland, 1978.

Smith, Jean Edward. *Lucius D. Clay: An American Life*. New York: Holt, 1990.

Smith, Jean, ed. *The Papers of General Lucius Clay*. Bloomington: Indiana University Press, 1974.

Snyder, Glenn. *Strategy, Politics and Defense Budgets*. New York: Columbia University Press, 1962.

Snyder, Louis. *The Roots of German Nationalism*. Bloomington: Indiana University Press, 1978.

Solzhenitsyn, Aleksandr. *The Gulag Archipelago*. New York: Harper and Row, 1985.

Spector, Ronald. *Eagle Against the Sun: The American War with Japan*. New York: Vintage, 1985.

Speer, Albert. *Inside the Third Reich: Memoirs*. Trans. Richard and Clara Winston. New York: Collier, 1970.

———. *Spandau: The Secret Diaries*. Trans. Richard and Clara Winston. New York: Macmillan, 1976.

Sprecher, Drexel. *Inside the Nuremberg Trial*. New York: University Press of America, 1999.

Stein, Harold, ed. *American Civil-Military Decisions*. Birmingham: University of Alabama Press, 1963.

Stephanson, Anders. *Kennan and the Art of Foreign Policy*. Cambridge: Harvard University Press, 1989.

———. *Manifest Destiny: American Expansionism and the Empire of Right*. New York: Hill and Wang, 1995.

Stern, Fritz. *The Politics of Cultural Despair: A Study in the Rise of Germanic Ideology*. Berkeley: University of California Press, 1974.

———. *Dreams and Delusions: The Drama of German History*. New York: Vintage, 1989.

Stimson, Henry and McGeorge Bundy. *On Active Service in Peace and War*. New York: Harper, 1947.

Stone, Julius. *Aggression and World Order: A Critique of United Nations Theories on Aggression*. Berkeley: University of California Press, 1958.

———. *Legal Controls of International Conflict*. New York: Rhinehart, 1959.

Swearingen, Ben. *The Mystery of Hermann Goering's Suicide*. New York: Harcourt Brace Jovanovich, 1985.

Taft, Robert. *A Foreign Policy for Americans*. Garden City, N.Y.: Doubleday 1951.

Tanaka, Yuki. *Hidden Horrors: Japanese War Crimes in World War II*. Boulder: Westview, 1996.

Tauber, Kurt. *Beyond Eagle and Swastika: German Nationalism Since 1945*. 2 vols. Middle-town: Wesleyan University Press, 1967.

Taylor, A. J. P. *The Origins of the Second World War*. New York: Atheneum, 1961.

Taylor, Lawrence. *A Trial of Generals: Homma, Yamashita, MacArthur*. South Bend, Ind.: Icarus, 1981.

Taylor, Telford. *Nuremberg and Vietnam*. New York: Bantam, 1971.

———. *The Anatomy of the Nuremberg Trials: A Personal Memoir*. New York: Knopf, 1992.

Teschke, John. *Hitler's Legacy: West Germany Confronts the Aftermath of the Third Reich*. New York: Peter Lang, 1999.

Tetens, T. H. *The New Germany and the Old Nazis*. New York: Random House, 1961.

Thomas, Ann and A. J. Thomas. *The Concept of Aggression*. Dallas: Southern Methodist University Press, 1972.

Thucydides. *History of the Peloponnesian War*. New York: Penguin, 1972.

Trachtenberg, Marc. *History and Strategy*. Princeton: Princeton University Press, 1991.

Trumpner, Ulrich. *Germany and the Ottoman Empire*. Princeton: Princeton University Press, 1968.

Turner, Henry Ashby Jr. *German Big Business and the Rise of Hitler*. New York: Oxford University Press, 1985.

———. *The Two Germanies Since 1945*. New Haven: Yale University Press, 1987.

Tusa, Ann and John Tusa. *The Nuremberg Trial*. New York: Atheneum, 1984.

Thomas, A. J. *The Concept of Aggression*. Dallas: Southern Methodist University Press, 1972.

Thomas, Evan and Walter Isaacson. *The Wise Men*. New York: Simon and Schuster, 1986.

Utley, Freda. *The High Cost of Vengeance*. Chicago: Regnery, 1949.

Van Creveld, Martin. *The Transformation of War*. New York: Free Press, 1991.

Veale, F. J. P. *Advance to Barbarism: How the Reversion to Barbarism in Warfare and War-Trials Menaces Our Future*. Appleton, Wis.: C. C. Nolan, 1953.

Vetter, Charles. *Sherman: Merchant of Terror*. Gretna, La.: Pelican, 1992.

Vidal-Naquet, Pierre. *Assassins of Memory: Essays on the Denial of the Holocaust*. Trans. Jeffrey Mehlman. New York: Columbia University Press, 1992.

Vitoria, Francisco de. *Political Writings*. Cambridge: Cambridge University Press, 1991.

Wallace, Anthony. *Jefferson and the Indians: The Tragic Fate of the First Americans*. Cambridge: Bell Knapp, 1999.

Waltz, Kenneth N. *Man, the State and War: A Theoretical Analysis*. New York: Columbia University Press, 1954.

Walzer, Michael. *Just and Unjust Wars*. New York: Basic, 1977.

Ward, Geoffrey. *The Civil War*. New York: Knopf, 1990.

Weingartner, James. *Crossroads of Death: The Story of the Malmedy Massacre and Trial*. Los Angeles: University of California Press, 1979.

Weitz, John. *Hitler's Diplomat: The Life and Times of Joachim von Ribbentrop.* New York: Ticknor and Fields, 1992.

Weizsäcker, Richard von. *From Weimar to the Wall.* Trans. Ruth Hein. New York: Broadway, 1999.

Wellman, Paul. *The Indian Wars of the West.* New York: Indian Head, 1992.

Welsh, Herbert. *The Other Man's Country.* Philadelphia: Lippincott, 1900.

West, Rebecca. *A Train of Powder.* New York: Viking, 1955.

White, Theodore H. *Fire in the Ashes: Europe in Mid-Century.* New York: William Sloane Associates, 1953.

———. *In Search of History: A Personal Adventure.* New York: Harper and Row, 1978.

Whiting, Charles. *Massacre at Malmedy.* New York: Stein and Day, 1971.

Williams, Emilio. *A Way of Life and Death: Three Centuries of Prussian-German Militarism.* Nashville: Vanderbilt University Press, 1986.

Willis, James. *A Prologue to Nuremberg.* Westport, Conn.: Greenwood, 1982.

Wilson, Robert Renbert. *The International Law Standard in Treaties of the United States.* Cambridge: Harvard University Press, 1953.

Wittner, Lawrence. *Cold War America.* New York: Praeger, 1974.

Woetzel, Robert. *The Nuernberg Trials in International Law.* London: Stevens, 1960.

Wolfe, Robert, ed. *Americans as Proconsuls: United States Military Government in Germany and Japan, 1944–1952.* Carbondale: Southern Illinois University Press, 1984.

Wolff, Leon. *Little Brown Brother.* London: Longmans, 1961.

Wright, Quincy. *Problems of Stability and Progress in International Relations.* Berkeley: University of California Press, 1954.

———. *The Study of International Relations.* New York: Appleton-Century-Crofts, 1955.

———. *The Role of International Law in the Elimination of War.* Manchester: Manchester University Press, 1961.

———. *A Study of War.* Chicago: University of Chicago Press, 1969.

Wyman, David S. *The Abandonment of the Jews: America and the Holocaust, 1941–1945.* New York: Pantheon, 1984.

Zink, Harold. *The U.S. Military Government in Germany.* New York: Macmillan, 1947.

———. *The United States in Germany, 1944–55.* Princeton, N.J.: Van Nostrand, 1957.

Articles

Alderman, Sidney. "Background and High Lights of the Nuremberg Trial." *I.C.C. Practitioners' Journal* 14 (Nov. 1946): 99–113.

Benz, Wolfgang. "*Versuche zur Reform des öffentlichen Dienstes in Deutschland 1945–1952: Deutsche Opposition gegen alliierte Initiation.*" *Vierteljahrshafte für Zeitgeschichte* 29 (1981): 216–245.

Bernays, Murray. "Legal Basis of the Nuremberg Trials." *Survey Graphics* 35 (Jan. 1946): 390–391.

———. "Letters of Fortune: The Nuremberg Novelty." *Fortune* 33 (Feb. 1946): 10–11.

Biddle, Francis. "Report from Francis Biddle to President Truman." *Department of State Bulletin* 15 (Nov. 24, 1946): 956–957.

———. "The Nuremberg Trial." *Virginia Law Review* 33 (Nov. 1947): 679–696.

——. "Nuremberg: The Fall of the Supermen." *American Heritage* 13 (Aug. 1962): 65–76.

Borchard, Edwin. "International Law and International Organization." *American Federation of International Law* 41 (Jan. 1947): 106–108.

Brand, James. "Crimes Against Humanity and the Nürnberg Trials." *Oregon Law Review* 28 (Feb. 1949).

Briggs, Herbert. "New Dimensions in International Law." *American Political Science Review* 46 (Sept. 1952): 677–698.

Caravajal, Doreen. "History's Shadow Foils Nanking Chronicle." *Los Angeles Times,* May 20, 1999.

Chomsky, Carol. "The United States-Dakota War Trials: A Study in Military Injustice." *Stanford Law Review* 43, no. 1 (Nov. 1990).

Doman, Nicholas. "The Political Consequences of the Nuremberg Trial." *Annals of the American Academy* 246 (July 1946): 81–90.

——. "The Nuremberg Trials Revisited." *American Bar Association Journal* 47 (Mar. 1961): 260–264.

Dorn, Walter. "*Die Debatte über die amerikanischen Besatzungspolitik für Deutschland 1944–5.*" *Vierteljahrshefte für Zeitgeschichte* 20 (1972): 39–62.

Dulles, John Foster. "International Law and Individuals, A Comment on Enforcing Peace." *American Bar Association Journal* 35 (Dec. 8, 1945): 1–3, 7.

Ehard, Hans. "The Nuremberg Trial Against the Major War Criminals and International Law." *The American Journal of International Law* 43 (1949).

Elbe, Joachim Von. "The Evolution of the Concept of the Just War in International Law." *The American Journal of International Law* 33 (Oct. 1934): 665–688.

Emmet, Christopher. "Verdict on Nuremberg." *Commonweal* 45 (Nov. 22, 1946): 138–141.

Eulau, Heinz. "The Nuremberg War-Crime Trials, Revolution in International Law." *New Republic* 113 (Nov. 12, 1945): 625–628.

Falk, Richard. "The Fallen Eagles." *Time* 46 (Dec. 3, 1945): 28–30.

——. "The Realities of International Law." *World Politics* (Jan. 1962): 353–363.

Ferencz, Benjamin. "The Nuremberg Procedure and the Rights of the Accused." *Journal of Criminal Law and Criminology* 39 (July–Aug. 1948): 144–151.

Finch, George. "The Nuremberg Trial and International Law." *The American Journal of International Law* 41 (Jan. 1947): 20–37.

——. "The Progressive Development of International Law." *The American Journal of International Law* 41 (July 1947): 611–616.

Freeman, Alwyn. "War Crimes by Enemy Nationals Administering Justice in Occupied Territories." *The American Journal of International Law* 41 (July 1947).

Gault, P. F. "Prosecution of War Criminals." *Journal of Criminal Law and Criminology* 36 (Sept.–Oct. 1946): 180–183.

Genet (Janet Flanner). "Letter from Nuremberg." *The New Yorker* 21 (Mar. 23, 1946): 78–84.

——. "Letter from Nuremberg." *The New Yorker* (Mar. 30, 1946): 78–84.

Gimbel, John. "The American Reparations Stop in Germany. An Essay on the Political Uses of History." *Historian* 37 (1974/75): 276–296.

Glueck, Sheldon. "The Nuremberg Trial and Aggressive War." *Harvard Law Review* 59 (Feb. 1946): 396–456.

Gross, Leo. "The Peace of Westphalia, 1648–1948." *The American Journal of International Law* 42 (1948).

Harris, Whitney. Review of *Nuremberg Trials,* by August von Knieriem. *The American Journal of International Law* 54 (April 1960): 443–444.

Hauser, Ernst. "The Backstage Battle at Nuremberg." *Saturday Evening Post* 218 (Jan. 19, 1946): 18, 19, 137.

Heilbrunn, Jacob. "The Real McCloy." *The New Republic* (Oct. 16, 1992).

Hirsh, Felix. "Lessons of Nuremberg." *Current History* 11 (Oct. 1946): 312–318.

Hobbs, Malcolm. "Nuernberg's Indecent Burial." *Nation* 169 (Dec. 3, 1949): 634–635.

Hoffman, Stanley. "International Systems and International Law." *World Politics* 14 (Oct. 1961): 205–237.

———. "The Delusion of World Order." *The New York Review of Books* 7 (1992).

Hoover, Glenn. "The Outlook for 'War Guilt' Trials." *Political Science Quarterly* 59 (Mar. 1944): 40–48.

Howard, Michael. "Governor General of Germany." *Times Literary Supplement,* 29 August 1975.

Hubert, Cecil. "Nuremberg—Justice or Vengeance?" *Military Government Journal* 1 (Mar. 1944): 11–14.

Hula, Erich. "Punishment for War Criminals." *Social Research* 13 (Mar. 1945): 1–23.

———. "The Revival of the Idea of Punitive War." *Thought* 82 (Sept. 1946): 405–434.

Hull, Cordell. "Indictment of War Criminals." *American Bar Association Journal* 31 (Dec. 1945): 645–646, 673.

———. "Indefensibles' Defense." *Time* 47 (Mar. 18, 1946): 29.

———. International Military Tribunal. "Judgment and Sentences." *The American Journal of International Law* 41 (Jan. 1947): 172–333.

Jackson, Robert. "Final Report to the President from Supreme Court Justice Jackson." *Department of State Bulletin* 13 (Oct. 27, 1946): 771–776.

———. "The Nuremberg Trial, Civilization's Chief Salvage from World War II." *Vital Speeches* 13 (Dec. 1, 1946): 114–117.

———. "Nuremberg in Retrospect, Legal Answer to International Lawlessness." *American Bar Association Journal* 25 (Oct. 1949): 814–815, 881–881.

Jackson, William. "Germany's Dance of Death." *Saturday Review of Literature* 30 (May 10, 1947): 15, 34.

Jaffe, Sidney. "Natural Law and the Nuremberg Trial." *Nebraska Law Review* 26 (Nov. 1946): 90–95.

Jervis, Robert. "The Impact of the Korean War on the Cold War." *Journal of Conflict Resolution* 24 (Dec. 1980): 563–592.

Jessup, Phillip. "The Crime of Aggression and the Future of International Law." *Political Science Quarterly* 62 (Mar. 1947): 1–10.

Karsten, Thomas and James Mathias. "The Judgment at Nuremberg." *New Republic* 115 (Oct. 21, 1946): 512.

Kennan, George F. "The Balkan Crisis, 1913 and 1993." *The New York Review of Books* 60 (13) (July 15, 1993).

Kunz, Josef. "The Swing of the Pendulum: From Overestimation to Underestimation of International Law." *American Journal of International Law* 44 (Jan. 1950): 135–140.

——. "Bellum Justum et Bellum Legale." *American Journal of International Law* 45 (July 1951): 528–534.

LaFeber, Walter. "NATO and the Korean War: A Context." *Diplomatic History* 3 (Spring 1986): 461–477.

Leonhardt, Hans. "The Nuremberg Trial, A Legal Analysis." *Review of Politics* 11 (Oct. 1949): 449–460.

Leventhal, Harold, Sam Harris, John M. Woolsley Jr., and Warren Farr. "The Nuremberg Verdict." *Harvard Law Review* 60 (July 1947): 857–907.

Levin, Bernhard. "Bertrand Russell: Prosecutor, Judge and Jury." *New York Times Magazine* (Feb. 19, 1967): 24, 55, 57, 60, 62, 67, 68.

Lippmann, Walter. "The Meaning of the Nuremberg Trial." *Ladies Home Journal* 63 (June 1946): 32, 188–190.

Maguire, Robert. "The Unknown Art of Making Peace: Are We Sowing the Seeds of World War III?" *American Bar Association Journal* 35 (Nov. 1949): 905–909, 972–973.

McDougal, Myres. "The Role of Law in World Politics." *Mississippi Law Journal* 20 (May 1949): 253–283.

Morgenthau, Hans, Eric Hula, and Moorhouse E. X. Millar. "Views on Nuremberg: A Symposium." *America* 76 (Dec. 7, 1946): 266–268.

Neumann, Franz. "The War Crimes Trials." *World Politics* 2 (Oct. 1949): 137–147.

Piccone, Paul and G. L. Ulman. "American Imperialism and International Law." *Telos* 72 (Summer 1987).

Schick, Franz. "The Nuernberg Trial and the International Law of the Future." *The American Journal of International Law* 41 (Oct. 1947): 770–894.

Schuster, George. "Hanging at Nuernberg: The Truth Was Not Allowed to Emerge." *Commonweal* 45 (Nov. 15, 1946): 110–113.

Schwartz, Thomas. "*Die Begnadigung deutscher Kriegsverbrecher. John J. McCloy und die Haftlinge von Landsberg.*" *Vierteljahrshefte für Zeitgeschichte* 38 (July 1990): 382.

Schwarzenberger, Georg. "Settling the Issue of War Guilt, Conclusive Verdict Against Nazis." *United States News* 21 (Oct. 11, 1946): 24–25.

Solis, Gary. "Yamashita Had It Coming." *Proceedings of "Accounting for Atrocities: Prosecuting War Crimes Fifty Years After Nuremberg," October 5–6, 1998.* Annandale-on-Hudson, N.Y.: Bard College Publications, 2000, 37–49.

Stimson, Henry. "The Nuernberg Trial, Landmark in Law." *Foreign Affairs* 15 (Jan. 1947): 179–189.

Storey, Robert. "Nuernberg Trials." *Tennessee Law Review* 19 (Dec. 1946): 517–525.

Taft, Robert. "Equal Justice Under Law." *Vital Speeches* 13 (Nov. 1, 1946): 44–48.

——. "The Republican Party." *Fortune* 39 (April 1949): 108–118.

Taylor, Telford. "Nuremberg War Crimes Trials: An Appraisal." *Academy of Political Science* 23 (May 1949): 239–254.

Thompson, Dorothy. "Germany Must Be Salvaged." *American Mercury* 56 (June 1943): 647–662.

——. "Trial by Victory." *Time* 48 (Aug. 5, 1948): 31.

——. "The Trial Begins." *Newsweek* 69 (May 2, 1967): 64.

Tucker, Robert. "Brave New World Order." *The New Republic* (Feb. 24, 1992): 26.

Vambery, Rustem. "Criminals and War Crimes." *Nation* 160 (May 19, 1945): 567–568.

——. "Law and Legalism." *Nation* 61 (Dec. 1, 1945): 573–575.

——. "The Law of the Tribunal." *Nation* 163 (Oct. 12, 1946): 400–401.

Walkinshaw, Robert. "The Nuremberg and Tokyo Trials, Another Step Towards International Justice." *American Bar Association Journal* 35 (April 1949): 299–302, 362–363.

Walsh, Moira. "Crime and Punishment." *America* 106 (Jan. 20, 1962): 542–544.

Weinberg, Gerhard. Book review. *Journal of Modern History* 9 (Sept. 1987): 638.

West, Rebecca. "Reporter at Large." *The New Yorker* 22 (Sept. 7, 1946): 34–47.

——. "The Birch Leaves Fall." *The New Yorker* 22 (Oct. 26, 1946): 93–105.

——. "Will Nuernberg Stop New Aggressors?" *Saturday Evening Post* 219 (Nov. 2, 1946): 164.

Williams, Walter. "United States Indian Policy and the Debate Over Philippine Annexation: Implications for the Origins of American Imperialism." *The Journal of American History* 66 (Mar. 1980): 810–831.

Winner, Percy. "The Atom at Nuernberg." *Commonweal* 43 (Mar. 22, 1946): 566–569.

Wright, Quincy. "Outlawry of War and the Law of War." *The American Journal of International Law* 39 (April 1945): 257–285.

——. "War Criminals." *The American Journal of International Law* 39 (April 1945): 257–285.

——. "The Crime of 'War Mongering.'" *The American Journal of International Law* 40 (April 1946): 398–406.

——. "Due Process and International Law." *The American Journal of International Law* 40 (April 1946): 128–136.

——. "The Nuernberg Trial." *The Annals of the American Academy* 246 (July 1946): 72–80.

——. "International Law and Guilt by Association." *The American Journal of International Law* 42 (Jan. 1947): 38–72.

——. "The Law of the Nuernberg Trial." *The American Journal of International Law* 42 (Jan. 1947): 38–72.

INDEX